PROFESSIONAL SPORTS FRANCHISE RELOCATION: ANTITRUST IMPLICATIONS

HEARING

BEFORE THE

COMMITTEE ON THE JUDICIARY
HOUSE OF REPRESENTATIVES

ONE HUNDRED FOURTH CONGRESS

SECOND SESSION

FEBRUARY 6, 1996

Serial No. 57

Printed for the use of the Committee on the Judiciary

U.S. GOVERNMENT PRINTING OFFICE
WASHINGTON : 1996

23–463 CC

For sale by the U.S. Government Printing Office
Superintendent of Documents, Congressional Sales Office, Washington, DC 20402
ISBN 0-16-052708-2

COMMITTEE ON THE JUDICIARY

HENRY J. HYDE, Illinois, *Chairman*

CARLOS J. MOORHEAD, California
F. JAMES SENSENBRENNER, JR., Wisconsin
BILL McCOLLUM, Florida
GEORGE W. GEKAS, Pennsylvania
HOWARD COBLE, North Carolina
LAMAR SMITH, Texas
STEVEN SCHIFF, New Mexico
ELTON GALLEGLY, California
CHARLES T. CANADY, Florida
BOB INGLIS, South Carolina
BOB GOODLATTE, Virginia
STEPHEN E. BUYER, Indiana
MARTIN R. HOKE, Ohio
SONNY BONO, California
FRED HEINEMAN, North Carolina
ED BRYANT, Tennessee
STEVE CHABOT, Ohio
MICHAEL PATRICK FLANAGAN, Illinois
BOB BARR, Georgia

JOHN CONYERS, JR., Michigan
PATRICIA SCHROEDER, Colorado
BARNEY FRANK, Massachusetts
CHARLES E. SCHUMER, New York
HOWARD L. BERMAN, California
RICK BOUCHER, Virginia
JOHN BRYANT, Texas
JACK REED, Rhode Island
JERROLD NADLER, New York
ROBERT C. SCOTT, Virginia
MELVIN L. WATT, North Carolina
XAVIER BECERRA, California
JOSÉ E. SERRANO, New York
ZOE LOFGREN, California
SHEILA JACKSON LEE, Texas

ALAN F. COFFEY, JR., *General Counsel/Staff Director*
JULIAN EPSTEIN, *Minority Staff Director*

(II)

CONTENTS

HEARING DATE

	Page
February 6, 1996	1

OPENING STATEMENT

Hyde, Hon. Henry J., a Representative in Congress from the State of Illinois, and chairman, Committee on the Judiciary 1

WITNESSES

Chillura, Joe, Jr., county commissioner, Hillsborough County, FL	48
Flanagan, Hon. Michael Patrick, a Representative in Congress from the State of Illinois	24
Glenn, Hon. John, a Senator in Congress from the State of Ohio	27
Hoke, Hon. Martin R., a Representative in Congress from the State of Ohio	16
Keller, Bruce, Esq., Debevoise & Plimpton, on behalf of the International Trademark Association	112
Lanier, Bob, mayor, city of Houston, TX	33
Locke, Gary, county executive, King County, WA	56
Roberts, Prof. Gary R., Tulane Law School	120
Stokes, Hon. Louis, a Representative in Congress from the State of Ohio	31
Tagliabue, Paul, commissioner, National Football League, accompanied by Jerry Richardson, owner, Carolina Panthers, Charlotte, NC	79
Thompson, John "Big Dawg"	53
Zimbalist, Prof. Andrew, Smith College	148

LETTERS, STATEMENTS, ETC., SUBMITTED FOR THE HEARING

Chillura, Joe, Jr., county commissioner, Hillsborough County, FL: Prepared statement	50
Flanagan, Hon. Michael Patrick, a Representative in Congress from the State of Illinois: Prepared statement	26
Glenn, Hon. John, a Senator in Congress from the State of Ohio: Prepared statement	29
Hoke, Hon. Martin R., a Representative in Congress from the State of Ohio: Prepared statement	20
Hyde, Hon. Henry J., a Representative in Congress from the State of Illinois, and chairman, Committee on the Judicary: Opening statement	2
Jackson Lee, Hon. Sheila, a Representative in Congress from the State of Texas: Prepared statement	8
Keller, Bruce, Esq., Debevoise & Plimpton, on behalf of the International Trademark Association: Prepared statement	114
Lanier, Bob, mayor, city of Houston, TX: Prepared statement	35
Locke, Gary, county executive, King County, WA: Prepared statement	58
Roberts, Prof. Gary R., Tulane Law School: Prepared statement	122
Tagliabue, Paul, commissioner, National Football League: Prepared statement	82
Thompson, John "Big Dawg": Prepared statement	55
Zimbalist, Prof. Andrew, Smith College: Prepared statement	149

APPENDIX

Material submitted for the hearing	163

PROFESSIONAL SPORTS FRANCHISE RELOCATION: ANTITRUST IMPLICATIONS

TUESDAY, FEBRUARY 6, 1996

House of Representatives,
Committee on the Judiciary,
Washington, DC.

The committee met, pursuant to notice, at 9:35 a.m., in room 2141, Rayburn House Office Building, Hon. Henry J. Hyde (chairman of the committee) presiding.

Present: Representatives Henry J. Hyde, Carlos J. Moorhead, F. James Sensenbrenner, Jr., Bill McCollum, George W. Gekas, Lamar Smith, Charles T. Canady, Martin R. Hoke, Sonny Bono, Steve Chabot, Michael Patrick Flanagan, John Conyers, Jr., Patricia Schroeder, Robert C. Scott, Zoe Lofgren, and Sheila Jackson Lee.

Also present: Alan F. Coffey, Jr., general counsel/staff director; Joseph Gibson, counsel; Dan Freeman, parliamentarian; Nicole Robilotto, assistant counsel; and Perry Apelbaum, minority counsel.

OPENING STATEMENT OF CHAIRMAN HYDE

Mr. HYDE. The committee will come to order. Today the House Judiciary Committee turns its focus to professional sports and, in particular, professional football.

Even the most casual sports fan knows the National Football League has recently been confronted with a difficult and confusing situation because so many of its teams are seeking to relocate to other cities. Last year the Raiders moved back to Oakland after having spent 13 years in their temporary home in Los Angeles. Also last year the Los Angeles Rams, a franchise located in that city since 1946, moved to St. Louis.

Now, of course, the Cleveland Browns are seeking to move to Baltimore and the Seattle Seahawks have announced their intention to move to Los Angeles, and the Houston Oilers are expected to seek league approval for a move to Nashville, TN. A number of other NFL franchises, including the Tampa Bay Buccaneers, the Cincinnati Bengals, and the Phoenix Cardinals, are also rumored to be considering other locations for their teams.

In my hometown of Chicago, the Bears have expressed dissatisfaction with Soldier Field and are exploring other options. The Bears have played football in Chicago since 1922 when the Decatur Staleys chose to relocate. The Bears, the "Monsters of the Midway," are a team with a glorious history. Legendary players such as Red Grange, Bronco Nagurski, Sid Luckman, and more recently Gayle Sayers, Dick Butkus, and Walter Payton have all worn the Bear uniform. In 1933, the Bears won the first NFL championship playoff game, and subsequently they won NFL championships in 1940, 1941, 1943, 1946, and 1963, as well as the Super Bowl in 1986. To me, the Bears are a part of the fabric of the city of Chicago and the State of Illinois.

I also remember another Chicago football team called the Cardinals, but that team flew away to become the St. Louis Cardinals in 1960, and later on that migratory bird went to the Southwest and became known as the Arizona Cardinals. Now rumor has it those same Cardinals are looking longingly at a possible fourth home in Los Angeles, but the Seattle Seahawks hope to land there first. One could say that the migratory habits of these particular birds boggle the minds of sports fans as well as ornithologists.

With no fewer than 8 out of the NFL's 30 franchises either having moved or considering moving in a period of less than 2 years, there is an obvious air of uncertainty. This instability is disruptive to the league itself, to the cities involved, the players, and the fans. Without question, fan loyalty is severely tested, and one cannot fault public criticism about sports becoming too much of a business.

There is no question but that professional football is a business and a big business at that. The gross revenues of the NFL teams far exceed $2 billion annually and the average player's salary is $714,000 a year. With the lucrative television contracts, luxury box revenues, tax advantages, big salaries and player free agency, these days you have to have an M.B.A. or a law degree to be an informed sports fan. But a football team can also be an emotional matter. It involves tradition, personal memories, nostalgia, community pride. It is one way a citizen identifies with his or her community.

Still, many ask why should Congress get involved in the internal workings of a private business? What is the compelling public interest here? Well, this committee's jurisdiction over the Federal antitrust laws gives us a legal perspective from which to consider and review this situation. All professional sports leagues have rules governing franchise relocation, and such rules have been subject to antitrust court challenges in the past.

Our committee also has jurisdiction over the Federal trademark law, and one of the bills pending before us on this subject raises certain trademark issues. I am not certain that legislation is necessary or justified in this case, but I do intend to listen carefully to the testimony we will receive today. I am not unmindful that many cities, counties and States have a strong interest in the outcome of this debate. I look forward to hearing from a number of interested parties and experts today as the Judiciary Committee continues to consider this matter.

[The opening statement of Mr. Hyde follows:]

OPENING STATEMENT OF HON. HENRY J. HYDE, A REPRESENTATIVE IN CONGRESS FROM THE STATE OF ILLINOIS, AND CHAIRMAN, COMMITTEE ON THE JUDICIARY

Today, the House Judiciary Committee turns its focus to professional sports and, in particular, to professional football.

Even the most casual sports fan knows the National Football League has recently been confronted with a difficult and confusing situation, because so many of its teams are seeking to relocate to other cities. Last year, the Raiders moved back to Oakland after having spent 13 years in their temporary home in Los Angeles. Also last year, the Los Angeles Rams—a franchise located in that city since 1946—moved to St. Louis. Now, of course, the Cleveland Browns are seeking to move to Baltimore, the Seattle Seahawks have announced their intention to move to Los Angeles, and the Houston Oilers are expected to seek League approval for a move to Nashville, Tennessee. A number of other NFL franchises including the Tampa Bay Buccaneers, the Cincinnati Bengals, and the Phoenix Cardinals are also rumored to be considering other locations for their teams.

In my own hometown of Chicago, the Bears have expressed dissatisfaction with Soldier Field and are exploring other options. The Bears have played football in Chicago since 1922, when the "Decatur Staleys" chose to relocate. The Bears—the "Monsters of the Midway"—are a team with a glorious history. Legendary players such as Red Grange, Bronko Nagurski, Sid Luckman and, more recently, Gayle Sayers, Dick Butkus, and Walter Payton have all worn the Bear uniform. In 1933, the Bears won the first NFL championship playoff game and subsequently, they won NFL championships in 1940, 1941, 1943, 1946, and 1963, as well as the Super Bowl in 1986. To me, the Bears are part of the fabric of the City of Chicago and the State of Illinois.

I also remember another Chicago football team called the "Cardinals"—but that team flew away to become the "St. Louis Cardinals" in 1960. Later on, that transient bird went to the Southwest and became known as the "Arizona Cardinals." Now, rumor has it that those same Cardinals are looking longingly at a possible fourth home in Los Angeles, but the Seattle Seahawks hope to land there first. One could say that the migratory habits of these particular birds, boggles the minds of sports fans as well as ornithologists.

With no fewer than eight out of the NFL's 30 franchises either moved or considering moving—in a period of less than two years—there is an obvious air of uncertainty. This instability is disruptive to the League itself, to the cities involved, the players and the fans. Without question, fan loyalty is severely tested and one can't fault public criticism about sports becoming too much of a business.

There is no question but that professional football is a business and a big business at that—the gross revenues of the NFL teams far exceed $2 billion annually and the average player's salary is $714,000 a year. With the lucrative television contracts, luxury box revenue, tax advantages, big salaries and player free agency—these days you have to have an MBA or a law degree to be a sports fan.

But a football team can also be an emotional matter. It involves tradition, personal memories, nostalgia, and community pride—it is one way a citizen identifies with his or her community. Still, many ask why should Congress get involved with the internal workings of a private business. What is the compelling public interest here?

Well, this Committee's jurisdiction over the federal antitrust laws gives us a legal perspective from which to consider and review this situation. All professional sports leagues have rules governing franchise relocation and such rules have been subject to antitrust court challenges in the past. Our Committee also has jurisdiction over the federal trademark law and one of the bills pending before us on this subject raises certain trademark issues.

I am not certain that legislation is necessary or justified in this case. But I do intend to listen carefully to the testimony we will receive today. I am not unmindful that many cities, counties and states have a strong interest in the outcome of this debate. I look forward to hearing from a number of interested parties and experts today as the Judiciary Committee continues to consider the matter.

Mr. HYDE. At this point, I will recognize the committee's ranking minority member from Michigan, the Honorable John Conyers, for an opening statement.

Mr. CONYERS. Good morning, and thank you, Mr. Chairman. I concur with your comments and on calling this hearing, and remind the Members of my continuing interest in moving legislation repealing yet another sports antitrust exemption, baseball, an institution which is also in very critical shape as we meet.

It becomes increasingly difficult to understand why baseball is entitled to a nonstatutory antitrust exemption based on a 1922 Supreme Court decision which has long been repudiated, and at the same time when no other professional sport is entitled to the same treatment. So, that is why I have legislation which would repeal the exemption baseball enjoys with respect to labor matters, and that too is within the jurisdiction of this distinguished committee.

As for the specific issues before us today, I hope the Members will forgive me if I am just a bit skeptical of the proposition that giving a monopoly comprised of 30 of the wealthiest individuals in America an exemption from our antitrust laws is an answer to our franchise relocation problems. The real issue is not how we can protect a monopoly from antitrust liability. The answer to that is simple: Abandon your monopoly status and do not discourage competition.

The real issue is how can we protect our cities from blackmail by vagabond sport franchises playing the cities and their taxpayers against each other. This is a problem we face in all professional sports. Even baseball, which boasts of its franchise stability courtesy of its nonstatutory exemption, frequently uses the threat of relocation to negotiate lucrative stadium deals at taxpayer expense.

Before this hearing is over, I am hoping someone will explain why we are being told that the price of keeping your city's football or baseball team is a new stadium with boxes for the wealthy paid for by taxes of the workers. If a stadium is safe and clean and people pay good money to fill its seats, as they have done in Cleveland in the last 50 years, why is that not enough? Why do we even need to talk about Cleveland imposing new taxes to entice Mr. Modell or the NFL to keep a team there?

Unfortunately, I have seen precious little indication that the NFL or other sports leagues are willing to do anything to respond to the problem. Instead, the leagues have created a chronic shortage of franchises, adopted revenue sharing rules which practically force owners to press for lucrative new stadiums, and promulgated relocation rules which stacked the decks against the cities. So before the NFL asks for legislative relief, I urge them to take some good-faith gestures to respond to problems of owners and the way they treat cities, which I believe are very much of the NFL's own making.

I will try to keep as open a mind as this statement will allow me to for the rest of the day. Thank you, Mr. Chairman.

Mr. HYDE. Thank you, Mr. Conyers. The gentleman from California, Mr. Carlos Moorhead.

Mr. MOORHEAD. Thank you, Mr. Chairman. I am pleased that we are taking this opportunity to examine the antitrust and other implications of relocating professional sports teams. As we have seen recently in Cleveland and Baltimore, this is an issue that strikes a nerve in many of the loyal fans and profoundly affects local governments, businesses and entire communities.

I can certainly sympathize with the gentlemen from Ohio. As a native of southern California, I have witnessed a great deal of team shifting. Within the last few years I have seen the exodus of two Los Angeles professional football teams, the Rams and the Raiders, and now there is talk of another team coming to town.

Today we will hear about a variety of proposals to discourage the relocation of established sports teams, including provisions that affect the trademark law. As the chairman of the Subcommittee on Courts and Intellectual Property, I advise that any changes to trademark law be very carefully deliberated.

After years of careful study, we completely overhauled the Federal trademark law in 1988. This was the first comprehensive revision of the Lanham Act since it was first enacted in 1946. These changes, which took effect in 1989, modernized trademark law and struck an important balance in protecting intellectual property and promoting commerce.

With this background in mind, I look forward to a thorough hearing process in examining all the issues involved with this very important topic.

Mr. HYDE. Thank you.

The gentleman from Virginia, Mr. Scott.

Mr. SCOTT. Thank you, Mr. Chairman. Some of what I had intended to say has already been said, and the question is: What is the congressional interest in these hearings?

Obviously, there is a significant fan interest, the excitement and the traditions that the teams have, but there is also a lot of public money involved. Public money is often involved in building stadiums, building roads to the stadium, and other services and costs involved in the traffic and services. Teams also have a significant economic impact. When a team leaves an area, it results in significant unemployment and economic disruption.

One of the issues that I would like to pursue is the issue of public ownership of some of the teams. I understand that is not possible right now. There are exceptions, and that would cure many of the problems because if a team were locally owned, the chances of it leaving would be much more remote.

As is not the case with I think just about everybody else here, my area does not have a professional team either coming or going in the foreseeable future, but we are trying. And if we do make the public investment in a team, I would certainly hope that it would not pick up and leave shortly after that investment were made.

Thank you, Mr. Chairman.

Mr. HYDE. Thank you, Mr. Scott. Before I ask Mr. Sensenbrenner for an opening statement, I have here the statement of Congressman Norm Dicks of the State of Washington, and I ask unanimous consent that this statement be made a part of the record. Without objection, so ordered.

[See appendix, page 163.]

Mr. HYDE. The gentleman from Wisconsin, Mr. Sensenbrenner.

Mr. SENSENBRENNER. Thank you very much. I had not planned on making an opening statement until I heard the gentleman from Michigan, Mr. Conyers, bring the subject of the baseball antitrust exemption into the debate on this legislation.

The antitrust exemption is an entirely different issue with different factors coming up from what we are here today to listen to, and that is the proclivity of some teams, particularly in the National Football League, to take flight and to leave for greener pastures or what they perceive to be greener pastures.

Let me say that this is not a problem in baseball. And where there has been the urge to move teams, most recently in Pittsburgh, baseball has been able to take care of that to protect the franchises in the city where they are.

And I am confident that baseball, unlike football, is sensitive to the fact that community spirit is necessary to have a successful team, and yes, even a profitable team. I remember back in the bad old days when the Milwaukee Braves left for Atlanta. The last 2 years they played in Milwaukee, they played to an empty stadium, and that hurt the then owners in the pocketbook pretty severely. I think the owners got the lesson as a result of that, and that is why we don't see the problems in baseball that we are seeing in football today.

I would like to say there is one community-owned team in the NFL. It is the Green Bay Packers, and not only are we in Wisconsin proud of how the Packers have done on the field this year, but we are also proud of the fact that because the Packers are community-owned, the problems that exist relative to stadium building and stadium expansion have not existed in Green Bay.

Lambeau Field in Green Bay has been expanded. Nobody has complained about it. Tax money has been used to expand the stadium which is owned by the city of Green Bay, because the people in Green Bay know that the Packers are an asset and, more importantly, that their tax money is not being used to line the pockets of somebody who is in to make a profit rather than to simply provide a good football team and quality entertainment for the people in the community of Green Bay.

Before signing off, however, I have to take exception to my chairman talking about the glorious Chicago Bears. How glorious were they in the two games they played with the Packers this year?

Mr. HYDE. You guys cheated.

Mr. SENSENBRENNER. I yield back my time.

Mr. HYDE. The Honorable Sheila Jackson Lee.

Ms. JACKSON LEE. Mr. Chairman, I come from a town that has an emerging glorious team. But, in any event, I am appreciative of the chairman having this hearing today. This is an important issue to millions of sports fans and to residents who live in cities where pro football franchises are located.

I represent the 18th Congressional District of Texas, which includes a significant part of the city of Houston. As many of you know, our city's professional football team, the Houston Oilers, has reached an agreement with local officials of the city of Nashville to move the team to Nashville, TN. As you can imagine, many Houstonians are disturbed about the proposed move of the Houston Oilers and wonder whether there is anything that could have been done on a governmental level to encourage the team to remain in Houston. Many efforts were tried.

The citizens of Houston are not alone. Last year the Los Angeles Raiders moved to Oakland, CA, and the Los Angeles Rams moved to St. Louis at a very high cost. The Cleveland Browns have entered into an agreement to move the team to Baltimore. Under this agreement, the State of Maryland would build a stadium for the Cleveland Browns for $200 million and the Browns would not have to pay any rent. Listening to the local television commentary, many are commenting on what will we do for our children in education and streets and roads?

There are reports that the Seattle Seahawks are considering moving to Los Angeles. Some news reports suggest that the Seattle Seahawks are asking for $150 million in improvements. Media reports also indicate that the professional teams in Tampa Bay, Arizona, and Cincinnati may consider relocating if they do not get better facilities.

The question is, when will it all end? It will not end unless we change the status quo. Those relocation decisions and preliminary discussions by other teams have created a crisis of confidence in the National Football League by sports fans and city officials throughout the country, and have generated a virtual bidding war among various cities to secure a professional league franchise at a time when city resources and county resources and State resources are being stretched.

The issue of sports franchise relocation is a controversial issue and an emotional issue. I recognize that a professional sports team is a business and certainly welcome those who have invested in this business. The owners should have the option to move their teams to other cities if the financial condition of the business dictates such a move. This is America.

Nevertheless, the taxpayers of such cities as Houston have invested millions of dollars in securing and maintaining their professional teams along with emotional commitment, along with the excitement that these teams bring to the community and, yes, the charitable efforts that many of them have participated in.

In Houston, city and county taxpayers have invested $100 million since 1987 in remodeling the Astrodome and implementing other improvements to keep the Oilers in Houston. We really want our team. Certainly, the presence of our professional teams has strengthened Houston's economy and helped our city to attract businesses and residents, and many of our citizens are employed by these franchises and get their living.

Our sports teams have helped to create jobs, fostered the development of new businesses, and helped create a sense of pride in the community. There is nothing more exciting than to see that playoff or to watch your team win a very close game.

This hearing today will help us to determine whether legislation is necessary to ensure that sports franchise relocation is done in an orderly and equitable fashion. Congressman Stokes and Congressman Hoke have introduced bills on this issue, and I will certainly discuss the merits of their proposals. I am pleased to report that I have cosponsored both bills. I believe that it is necessary for Congress to help clarify the procedures surrounding this contentious issue. This is a compelling issue. Both bills provide for a narrow antitrust exemption for professional leagues that utilize specific relocation criteria in determining whether to approve a relocation request.

Additionally, the bills require that owners give advanced notice to cities of their intent to relocate their team. The bills, however, contain some different approaches on certain issues. Most of the professional leagues have already formulated a list of criteria including factors such as fan loyalty. Our cities have that. Community support, our cities have that and the adequacy of current facilities and the existence of a bona fide offer to purchase the team. Such leagues, however, have been concerned that, if they rejected an owner's request to move his team, the owner would more likely prevail in a lawsuit on the basis of antitrust law. By providing this narrow antitrust exemption, the National Football League, for example, would be able to make decisions on sports franchise relocation on an objective basis without such fear.

I recognize the Congress has traditionally been hesitant to grant antitrust exemption. These two bills, however, should receive careful consideration. The notice provision in the bills would require owners to give 180-day notice prior to moving a team. This provision would enable local governments to make a realistic offer and a concerted offer and an offer based on community effort to keep the team in their cities, just simply being fair.

I look forward to working with my colleagues on the Judiciary Committee and in the House to find a reasonable compromise on this important issue so that local governments and sports leagues owners can negotiate their differences and maybe even work together on a more level and even playing field.

I yield back the balance of my time, Mr. Chairman.

[The prepared statement of Ms. Jackson Lee follows:]

PREPARED STATEMENT OF HON. SHEILA JACKSON LEE, A REPRESENTATIVE IN CONGRESS FROM THE STATE OF TEXAS

MR. CHAIRMAN, I THANK YOU FOR CONVENING THIS HEARING TODAY ON THE SUBJECT OF SPORTS FRANCHISE RELOCATION. THIS IS AN IMPORTANT ISSUE TO MILLIONS OF SPORTS FANS AND TO RESIDENTS WHO LIVE IN CITIES WHERE PRO FOOTBALL FRANCHISES ARE LOCATED.

I REPRESENT THE 18TH CONGRESSIONAL DISTRICT OF TEXAS, WHICH INCLUDES A SIGNIFICANT PART OF THE CITY OF HOUSTON. AS MANY OF YOU KNOW, OUR CITY'S PROFESSIONAL FOOTBALL TEAM, THE HOUSTON OILERS, HAS REACHED AN AGREEMENT WITH LOCAL OFFICIALS OF NASHVILLE TO MOVE THE TEAM TO NASHVILLE, TENNESSEE.

AS YOU CAN IMAGINE, MANY HOUSTONIANS ARE VERY DISAPPOINTED ABOUT THE PROPOSED MOVE OF THE HOUSTON OILERS AND WONDER WHETHER THERE IS ANYTHING THAT THEY COULD HAVE DONE OR GOVERNMENTAL OFFICIALS COULD HAVE DONE TO ENCOURAGE THE TEAM TO REMAIN IN HOUSTON. THE CITIZENS OF HOUSTON ARE NOT ALONE. LAST YEAR, THE LOS ANGELES RAIDERS MOVED TO OAKLAND, CALIFORNIA AND THE LOS ANGELES RAMS MOVED TO ST. LOUIS. THE CLEVELAND BROWNS HAVE

PAGE 2

ENTERED INTO AN AGREEMENT TO MOVE THE TEAM TO BALTIMORE. UNDER THIS AGREEMENT, THE STATE OF MARYLAND WOULD BUILD A STADIUM FOR THE CLEVELAND BROWNS FOR $200 MILLION AND THE CLEVELAND BROWNS WOULD NOT HAVE TO PAY RENT. THERE ARE REPORTS THAT THE SEATTLE SEAHAWKS ARE CONSIDERING MOVING TO THE LOS ANGELES AREA. SOME NEWS REPORTS SUGGEST THAT THE SEATTLE SEAHAWKS ARE ASKING FOR $150 MILLION IN IMPROVEMENTS. MEDIA REPORTS ALSO INDICATE THAT THE PROFESSIONAL TEAMS IN TAMPA BAY, ARIZONA AND CINCINNATI MAY CONSIDER RELOCATING IF THEY DO NOT GET BETTER FACILITIES. THE QUESTION IS WHEN WILL IT ALL END. IT WILL NOT END UNLESS WE CHANGE THE STATUS QUO.

THOSE RELOCATION DECISIONS AND PRELIMINARY DISCUSSIONS BY OTHER TEAMS HAVE CREATED A CRISIS OF CONFIDENCE IN THE NATIONAL FOOTBALL LEAGUE BY SPORTS FANS AND CITY OFFICIALS THROUGHOUT THE COUNTRY AND HAS GENERATED A VIRTUAL BIDDING WAR AMONG VARIOUS CITIES TO SECURE A PROFESSIONAL LEAGUE FRANCHISE.

THE ISSUE OF SPORTS FRANCHISE RELOCATION IS A CONTROVERSIAL ISSUE AND AN EMOTIONAL ISSUE. I RECOGNIZE THAT A PROFESSIONAL SPORTS TEAM IS A BUSINESS AND THE OWNERS SHOULD HAVE THE OPTION TO MOVE THEIR TEAMS TO OTHER CITIES IF THE FINANCIAL CONDITION OF THE BUSINESS DICTATES SUCH MOVE. NEVERTHELESS, THE TAXPAYERS OF CITIES SUCH AS HOUSTON HAVE INVESTED MILLIONS OF DOLLARS IN SECURING AND MAINTAINING THEIR PROFESSIONAL TEAMS.

PAGE 3

IN HOUSTON, CITY AND COUNTY TAXPAYERS HAVE INVESTED $100 MILLION SINCE 1987 IN REMODELING THE HOUSTON ASTRODOME AND IMPLEMENTING OTHER IMPROVEMENTS TO KEEP THE HOUSTON OILERS IN HOUSTON. CERTAINLY, THE PRESENCE OF OUR PROFESSIONAL TEAMS HAVE STRENGTHENED HOUSTON'S ECONOMY AND HELPED OUR CITY TO ATTRACT BUSINESSES AND RESIDENTS. OUR SPORTS TEAMS HAVE HELPED TO CREATE JOBS, FOSTER THE DEVELOPMENT OF NEW BUSINESSES AND HELPED CREATE A SENSE OF PRIDE WITHIN THE COMMUNITY.

THIS HEARING TODAY WILL HELP TO US DETERMINE WHETHER LEGISLATION IS NECESSARY TO ENSURE THAT SPORTS FRANCHISE RELOCATION IS DONE IN AN ORDERLY AND EQUITABLE FASHION. CONGRESSMAN STOKES AND CONGRESSMAN HOKE HAVE INTRODUCED BILLS ON THIS ISSUE AND WE WILL CERTAINLY DISCUSS THE MERITS OF THEIR PROPOSALS. I AM PLEASED TO REPORT THAT I HAVE CO-SPONSORED BOTH BILLS. I BELIEVE THAT IT IS NECESSARY FOR CONGRESS TO HELP CLARIFY THE PROCEDURES SURROUNDING THIS CONTENTIOUS ISSUE. BOTH BILLS PROVIDE FOR A NARROW ANTITRUST EXEMPTION FOR PROFESSIONAL LEAGUES THAT UTILIZE SPECIFIC RELOCATION CRITERIA IN DETERMINING WHETHER TO APPROVE A RELOCATION REQUEST. ADDITIONALLY, THE BILLS REQUIRE THAT OWNERS GIVE ADVANCE NOTICE TO CITIES OF THEIR INTENT TO RELOCATE THEIR TEAMS. THE BILLS, HOWEVER, CONTAIN SOME DIFFERENT APPROACHES ON CERTAIN ISSUES.

PAGE 4

MOST OF THE PROFESSIONAL LEAGUES HAVE ALREADY FORMULATED A LIST OF CRITERIA. THIS CRITERIA, IN MOST CASES, INCLUDES FACTORS SUCH AS FAN LOYALTY, COMMUNITY SUPPORT, THE ADEQUACY OF CURRENT FACILITIES AND THE EXISTENCE OF A BONA FIDE OFFER TO PURCHASE THE TEAM. SUCH LEAGUES, HOWEVER, HAVE BEEN CONCERNED THAT IF THEY REJECTED AN OWNER'S REQUEST TO MOVE HIS TEAM, THE OWNER WOULD MOST LIKELY PREVAIL IN A LAWSUIT ON THE BASIS OF ANTITRUST LAW. BY PROVIDING THIS NARROW ANTITRUST EXEMPTION, THE NATIONAL FOOTBALL LEAGUE, FOR EXAMPLE, WOULD BE ABLE TO MAKE DECISIONS ON SPORTS FRANCHISE RELOCATION ON AN OBJECTIVE BASIS WITHOUT SUCH FEAR. I RECOGNIZE THAT CONGRESS HAS TRADITIONALLY BEEN HESITANT TO GRANT ANTITRUST EXEMPTIONS. THESE TWO BILLS, HOWEVER, SHOULD RECEIVE CAREFUL CONSIDERATION.

THE NOTICE PROVISION WITHIN THE BILLS WOULD REQUIRE OWNERS TO GIVE LOCAL GOVERNMENTS A 180-DAY NOTICE PRIOR TO MOVING A TEAM. THIS PROVISION WOULD ENABLE LOCAL GOVERNMENTS TO MAKE AN OFFER TO KEEP THE TEAM IN THEIR CITIES.

I LOOK FORWARD TO WORKING WITH MY COLLEAGUES ON JUDICIARY COMMITTEE AND IN THE HOUSE TO FIND A REASONABLE COMPROMISE ON THIS IMPORTANT ISSUE SO THAT LOCAL GOVERNMENTS AND SPORTS LEAGUE OWNERS CAN NEGOTIATE THEIR DIFFERENCES ON A MORE LEVEL PLAYING FIELD.

Mr. HYDE. The gentleman from Pennsylvania, Mr. Gekas.

Mr. GEKAS. I thank the Chair. Unlike many of the members of the committee, I come to this hearing with a closed mind. And don't anyone say, "as usual." But it is closed because I have a prejudice to start with against having the Congress interfere in the private business that is entailed in this relocation or any other that we have witnessed over the several recent years.

I still have not figured out the odyssey of the Raiders, to whom reference has been made, or the Rams and now the Seahawks, the Browns, which are the crux of this particular hearing; but in each one I felt that the Congress should and did, as it turned out, lay back and allow the free enterprise system within certain confines to take its course.

The one thing that will partially open my mind, if it can be opened, will be the testimony of my colleagues at the table who have a strong interest in this particular situation and have information and background that will perhaps help creak open my little mind.

But whether or not we should interfere, we did not interfere in the baseball strike that occurred a few years back. There is a difference. There is no question about it. But I started off then with that same closed mind. Fortunately, I feel for the American people, the Congress did not get involved in that baseball strike.

There is another caveat to my closed mind. If the Steelers or the Eagles ever contemplated such a move, I would be the first to be down at that witness table.

In any event, I yield back the balance of my time.

Mr. HYDE. The gentleman's candor is refreshing.

The gentlewoman from California, Ms. Lofgren.

Ms. LOFGREN. Thank you, Mr. Chairman.

I represent San Jose, CA, in the Congress, and San Jose does not have a Major League baseball team. San Jose doesn't have a football team, and so I am not here in order to prevent our team from going. We do have a hockey team that has not yet ended up at the top of the win-loss column. However, it has ended up at the top of the profitability column because San Jose fans are pretty enthusiastic. It is a big family town.

I am here to listen today with a quasi-open mind because I want to know how this legislation might impact the situation of local governments, which I see are often held up by professional sports franchises for funds that really are necessary for other essential needs. When I think of our country where only 3 percent of the classrooms have a connection to the Internet in them; where a recent analysis has indicated that a majority of the schools in the United States are substandard; and then I see the amount of funds going into sports arenas and stadiums, it makes me wonder what role this legislation before us today could have in preventing the holdup of local governments when local resources are so essential for very basic needs of our citizens.

I said I have a quasi-open mind. I must confess I have a bias or at least a skepticism about antitrust exemptions for anyone. However, I hope to learn a lot today from the witnesses, and I thank the chairman for holding the hearing.

Mr. HYDE. I thank the gentlewoman. The gentleman from Ohio, Mr. Chabot.

Mr. CHABOT. Thank you. During today's hearings, we will not spend very much time discussing the issues that have made professional football so important to generations of Americans. We will not find time to marvel at Jeff Blake's recent Pro Bowl performance, or reminisce about Kenny Anderson leading the Bengals to the Super Bowl, or talk about Boomer Esiason's MVP season or the defensive heroics of Tim Krumerie or Reggie Williams. I doubt that we will have the opportunity to debate what player was the National Football League's greatest running back. I am sure Mr. Hoke would argue that it was Jim Brown, while you, Mr. Chairman, might counter with Walter Payton. Of course, we all know it was the Cincinnati Bengals' Icky Woods.

At one time these were the sorts of issues that football fans in Cincinnati, and across the country, talked about. These were the types of memories that make professional football special. But today, these hearings will highlight the evolution of football from heroic gridiron competition to big business where the dollar ultimately governs most decisions.

Sadly, the fans are in danger of being left behind. Instead of learning the difference between a field goal and an extra point, today's young football fan grows up learning the intricacies of sky boxes and team movements. Listen to any local radio sports talk program and you will quickly learn that local concerns center on free agency and franchise relocation.

Not too long ago, speculation about moving a team with a history of the Cleveland Browns would have been immediately dismissed. More recently, however, loyal communities and fans have learned that franchise relocation can happen anywhere at any time.

The last 12 months in the NFL provide several troubling examples. The St. Louis Rams? The Baltimore Browns? The Nashville Oilers? The Los Angeles Seahawks? And what about the Oakland-Los Angeles-Oakland Raiders?

Some teams, it seems, will jump ship and leave the support of communities when multimillion-dollar promises of new high-tech stadiums are waved under their noses. These cut-and-run practices undermine fan loyalty and in the long run may prove extremely damaging to the NFL.

Recent moves have raised concerns in many Major League cities, including my hometown of Cincinnati. But so long as there is any other city out there seeking a pro team, every owner in the league can use that leverage to press his or her city for further public subsidies. That state of affairs is unsettling and disruptive to fan loyalty. It is not a good thing that fans in Cincinnati, who have supported the Bengals in good years and in bad, are being given cause to worry. The Bengals belong in Cincinnati, period.

The league says it understands the problem and wants the unquestioned power to say enough is enough. I, for one, hope that the league truly does appreciate the advantages of stability, tradition, and hometown loyalty.

No one, I think, wants the Federal Government in the business of running professional football. We don't want the same folks that pay $500 for a toilet seat setting the price of hot dogs, and I don't think we want some Hazel O'Leary type making up the schedule, or the playoff formula to be drafted by the same guys who brought us the Tax Code. The Federal Government shouldn't take over the sport, and I don't think we should be in the business of determining how many teams a professional league should have.

But the NFL argues, with some reason, that Federal intrusion is already contributing to the flurry of team movements. The league contends that fear of the Federal antitrust laws prevents the league from clamping down on team relocation. Although some antitrust lawyers say that the league is misreading the case law, certainly the law is far from clear and the costs of litigation are high. I personally favor providing a limited antitrust exemption that will, beyond question, permit the league to ensure geographic stability among its franchises.

While we can debate whether the league would do all it could to prevent promiscuous relocation, we shouldn't have to worry that the Federal Government itself is actually spurring such activity. I applaud the efforts of our colleagues who will testify here today, Mr. Hoke, Mr. Flanagan, Mr. Stokes, and Senator Glenn, to address these issues forthrightly.

I look forward to these hearings, and I think they are well timed. On the eve of the NFL league meeting, let us use this platform to send a strong message that we believe communities shouldn't be held hostage by the very teams in which they have invested significant public resources. I hope that we can hear today a strong statement from league officials that, if they are given the antitrust assurances that they purport to seek, they in turn will act responsibly to ensure stability.

Thank you, Mr. Chairman, for your concern with this important topic and for these hearings.

Mr. HYDE. The gentleman from Florida, Mr. Canady.

Mr. CANADY. Mr. Chairman, I want to congratulate you on holding this important hearing. You have assembled an impressive list of witnesses, and I look forward to hearing from each of them.

I particularly want to recognize Joe Chillura, the county commissioner from Hillsborough County, FL, who will be testifying later today. I represent part of Hillsborough County and many Tampa Bay Buccaneers fans who are concerned about the fate of their team. I have met personally with Mr. Chillura and others from Tampa Bay on this issue, and I know that the committee will benefit from Mr. Chillura's insight on this subject.

Professional sports franchise relocation has become the most important issue in the business of sports. Millions upon millions of dollars are bid and spent in the effort to move teams between cities. Caught in the middle of this high stakes game are the communities and the fans, those who have invested their time, their money and their emotion in support of their teams. We are here today because the law also plays an important role in this process.

Major League Baseball enjoys a general exemption from antitrust laws while the National Football League benefits from more limited exemptions. It is entirely appropriate that this committee examine the relationship between major league sport and the antitrust laws. While the NFL's policies on franchise relocation have been previously tested in Federal court, changes in league policy and the unique facts associated with each proposed franchise move demand that we take another look at this issue.

The two pieces of legislation we are examining today introduced by Congressman Hoke and Congressman Stokes seek to establish at least some degree of community control over local professional sports franchises in the major leagues.

Antitrust, trademark, contract, and labor law are all implicated by these proposals. Each of these proposals deserve careful consideration by this committee and the full Congress. In recent years, it has become increasingly clear that the law does not provide adequate protection for the legitimate interests of the fans and the communities without which professional sports would not exist. It is time that Congress act to address this important issue. I believe that the legislation before us today provides a very good starting point for our consideration.

Thank you, Mr. Chairman, for holding this hearing, and my thanks to each of the witnesses who are with us today.

Mr. HYDE. Thank you, Mr. Canady. The gentlewoman from Colorado, Mrs. Schroeder.

Mrs. SCHROEDER. Thank you, Mr. Chairman. I apologize for being a little late. In the interest of getting on with it, I am going to yield back the time.

Mr. HYDE. Thank you, Mrs. Schroeder. The gentleman from Florida, Mr. McCollum.

Mr. MCCOLLUM. Thank you, Mr. Chairman. I, too, look forward to hearing the witnesses today.

Being from Florida, I am very aware of the problems that may or may not exist in franchises, whether they be baseball or football, and the antitrust laws. Consequently, that is a particularly important thing for me, and I will not take more time of the committee with an opening statement. I look forward to the witnesses.

Mr. HYDE. I thank the gentleman.

Our first panel this morning is made up of distinguished Members of Congress. We have two members of the House Judiciary Committee who have taken a strong interest in this issue, Congressman Martin Hoke from Ohio, and Congressman Michael Patrick Flanagan from Illinois.

Congressman Hoke, who represents the people of the city of Cleveland, is the principal sponsor of H.R. 2740, the Fan Freedom and Community Protection Act of 1995. As we all know, the Cleveland Browns have recently announced they are leaving for the city of Baltimore.

Congressman Flanagan, who represents a district in the great city of Chicago, has, as I have been, actively following this issue as the Chicago Bears move closer to a decision about where they will be playing next season. We are also very pleased to have Congressman Louis Stokes with us. Congressman Stokes also represents the Cleveland area. He has introduced H.R. 2699, the Fans' Rights Act of 1995.

The Senate sponsor of similar legislation is also with us this morning, the distinguished Senator, John Glenn, from the State of Ohio, who has introduced the Fans' Rights Act of 1995 in the Senate, S. 1439. All of these Members have been active in this area, and we look forward to hearing their views on this issue.

Because we have a large number of witnesses, I would ask that the Members would refrain from directing questions to this panel. That way, the hearing will move along to the remaining panels, thank you.

Congressman Hoke.

STATEMENT OF HON. MARTIN R. HOKE, A REPRESENTATIVE IN CONGRESS FROM THE STATE OF OHIO

Mr. HOKE. Thank you very much, Mr. Chairman and members of the committee. I am grateful to participate today in an examination of the state of professional sports in America and Congress' role in their development and regulation, and also to discuss my proposed legislative solution to the growing problem of sports team relocations.

Before I begin my testimony, I particularly want to express my gratitude to Chairman Hyde for agreeing to hold this hearing. He and the entire Judiciary staff have been most generous in granting my requests and have worked very hard to arrange for all perspectives to be given a fair voice. I am very appreciative of your efforts. Thank you very much.

Mr. Chairman, this weekend American taxpayers and sports fans were unfortunately once again treated to the bizarre and disturbing image of a professional football team stealing away in the dead of night, abandoning the city which supported it through thick and thin, to flee to the financial embraces of a new city's tax coffers in a very ugly and now all-too-familiar greedy pursuit of bigger taxpayer-funded subsidies. When asked why, the owner's only explanation is that he is pursuing a "childhood dream."

Mr. Chairman, pro sports team relocations have reached epidemic proportions, especially in football, where the Raiders have moved from Oakland to Los Angeles and back, the Rams from L.A. to Anaheim to St. Louis, the Cardinals from St. Louis to Phoenix, the Colts to Indianapolis from Baltimore. And of course we should not forget Cleveland, and Houston, and now the latest—72 hours ago—the Seahawks to Los Angeles.

If you mapped out all the recent NFL moves, it would look a lot like one of Secretary O'Leary's trade missions. In fact, right now no fewer than 14 NFL teams are considered to be in play or seeking some sort of taxpayer-funded public subsidy or a better deal elsewhere. As more teams relocate, there will be increased pressure on Congress to take action to protect fans, communities and taxpayers.

Houston Mayor Bob Lanier, who bravely refused to bend to demands for $150 million for a new stadium to keep the Oilers from moving to Nashville—isn't Nashville Oilers not an oxymoron?—summed up best by asking, "How can you tax the average working guy to build luxury suites for rich people so they can support rich owners who pay rich players to play in a stadium where the average guy can no longer afford the ticket price? How many things have to be wrong with this picture before we do something about it?"

In the past 3 years, American cities have spent billions of dollars building or renovating stadiums for pro sports teams. Much of this money is being provided by taxpayers. For instance, in Cleveland there is on the table a $175 million stadium renovation plan that is funded entirely by taxpayers. About 90 percent of the L.A. Coliseum's $100 million renovation and Jacksonville's $160 million stadium renovation are being financed with Federal money.

The Disney Corp., part owner of the California Angels, has demanded that the city of Anaheim make over 100 million dollars' worth of improvements to the stadium and infrastructure, or the Angels are out of there. The State of Maryland is going to provide $73 million for projects related to the Redskins' soon-to-be-built stadium in Prince George's County, on top of the $200 million to build a new stadium for Art Modell.

Owners are getting away with these kinds of demands for two reasons: first, the financial stability that they have gained from the hugely lucrative broadcasting agreements which are made possible by a congressionally conferred antitrust exemption. Second, they are congressionally and judicially granted monopoly powers to limit the number of franchises that are available.

You are going to hear the NFL argue that what is going on here is no different than what automobile manufacturers do when they want to build a new plant. They shop around, they consider offers from different States, and then they cut the best deal for their company. But there is a big difference between an auto plant and a pro sports team. Auto manufacturers do not have a congressionally conferred limited antitrust exemption that allows them to operate as a cartel. Pro sports leagues do. As long as the leagues can control the number of franchises, they will continue to be able to pressure State and local governments to make more and more concessions. The only way to stop this form of legalized extortion is for Congress to act.

Mr. Chairman, at this point it is natural to ask by what right should Congress get involved in the business of professional sports, particularly a Congress which is a fierce champion of free markets and free enterprise? The short answer is the Sports Broadcasting Act of 1961, which at the request of the four major leagues—the NFL, the NBA, the NHL, and Major League Baseball—granted a limited antitrust exemption, allowing them to pool their separate broadcasting rights for sale to a single purchaser.

In the case of the National Football League, the antitrust exemption makes it possible for the league to divide among the owners over $1.2 billion in network television revenue, amounting to about $39 million per team for the 1995–1996 season. And that was before they sold a single ticket or one cup of beer, or local radio broadcasts, or parking, or a warmup jacket, or stadium advertising.

When you consider their self-imposed salary cap is $37 million, it is pretty obvious that this antitrust exemption has provided the financial foundation for every team in the league, which is fine. It is exactly what it was intended to do. But what was not intended was for the National Football League to take that economic power and use it as a bludgeon to beat even more money and greater benefits from cities, taxpayers and fans.

Here is what then-NFL Commissioner Pete Rozelle had to say about that act in testimony before the Congress: "The economic survival of every member club of the NFL fundamentally depends upon the operations, conduct, and decisions of the entire league.

Congress recognized this in enacting the 1961 sports television legislation, and Congress properly looks to the leagues for responsible conduct in the administration of their nationwide business affairs."
In 1966, Congress also passed legislation allowing the NFL and the old American Football League to merge. In justifying that merger before Congress, Mr. Rozelle testified again, "Professional football operations will be preserved in the 23 cities and 25 stadiums where such operations are being conducted presently. This alone is a matter of considerable public interest to local economies, stadium authorities, and consumers. Without the plan, franchise moves and/or franchise failures will occur as a matter of course within the next few years."

The uncontestable wisdom and implicit promise of that statement deserves closer examination in light of current events. It clearly was the NFL's point of view in 1966 that rapid franchise movement was a bad thing for cities and for fans. It was then, and it is now. The fact is, despite statements from the NFL and other sports leagues to the contrary, we have seen anything but responsible conduct from pro sports leagues. Because the leagues owe their very existence to a congressionally conferred antitrust exemption, Congress is not only justified in acting but has an obligation to exercise its authority to protect cities, fans, and taxpayers from exploitation.

The Fan Freedom and Community Protection Act was introduced to respond to this situation. It demands responsibility from pro sports leagues, and it strikes a much-needed balance between the interests of fans, owners, cities and taxpayers by giving for the first time ever negotiating leverage to cities.

It has four basic components. First, the bill codifies existing case law which permits leagues to enforce their own rules regarding the relocation of teams. This provision instructs the leagues to consider certain factors in determining whether a league should be allowed to relocate, including fan support, condition of the stadium, and good-faith efforts by the host community.

Unfortunately, many mistakenly believe that this provision alone will solve the problem, which is what the leagues, especially the NFL, want you to believe. But as the *National Basketball Association* v. *San Diego Clippers* case—which was the ninth circuit, the same circuit that decided Raiders I and Raiders II—better known as the *Clippers* case, makes clear, the fact is that the leagues already have this authority as a matter of existing case law. Consider this quote from the *Clippers* case: "A careful analysis of Raiders I makes it clear that franchise movement restrictions are not invalid as a matter of law." This is the same court that decided Raiders I. What could be clearer than that?

Indeed, an influential 1987 article in the National Law Journal put it correctly: "Raiders I was commonly viewed as holding that sports leagues would be unable to control franchise relocations unless they acted in accordance with a detailed set of expressed criteria able to withstand antitrust scrutiny and embodied in the applicable league rules."

The *Clippers* opinion rejected this perception. It is now certain that a professional sports league paying close attention to the discussion in the *Raiders* and *Clippers* cases can control team relocations in the appropriate circumstances. More to the point, codifying antitrust case law in this case doesn't compel leagues to enforce their rules; it merely confirms that they can.

The problem is not that leagues cannot restrict team movement, it is that they refuse to. They refuse to because it is clearly against the economic self-interest of the owners to do so. Each owner knows that he or she will someday want to be that week's Alonzo Mourning winner of the owner's form of free agency. The decision to prevent a move is still left where it always has been: with the owners. Yet owners of professional football teams have developed what Chicago Mayor Richard Daley has rightly called an "entrepreneurial culture" in which it is common practice to play one city off another for a better deal.

I submit that it is wishful thinking that we can solve this problem if we only give owners more power to do the right thing. Why would they unilaterally give up the negotiating tactic that has led to increased profits and higher team value? It would be like asking professional athletes to voluntarily give up free agency.

Mr. Chairman, I wonder if I could ask for unanimous consent for another 3 minutes just to finish this testimony?

Mr. HYDE. I am reluctant to do that because we have many witnesses today, and we are trying to do this in 1 day. I will give the gentleman another minute. Can you wind it up?

Mr. HOKE. Thank you, Mr. Chairman. I am going to close with this. I wish I had time to explain all the provisions of the bill. What I am going to do is shift gears and close with this.

Many Americans, especially parents, moms and dads who are trying to teach their children the value of education and hard work and faith and loyalty and fairness, many Americans, and I am one of them, have this growing and unsettling sense that as a nation we are trashing our culture and destroying the best that we have to offer our children because of a misprioritization of values. I believe the situation in pro sports is a clear reflection of that on many levels, first at the dollars and cents level.

Extremely scarce local taxpayer dollars are being spent on stadiums and not being spent on education, the arts, schools, roads, bridges, parks and neighborhoods. This is not play money; it is real money in very tight economies where budgets must be balanced in a zero-sum game.

What message does that send to our children about what we value, what is important to us and should be important to them? Is it any wonder that one can go into any city school in a depressed neighborhood, and the answer to the question "What do you want to be when you grow up?" is a bright, hopeful youngster saying, "A professional ball player." When was the last time you heard them say, "a doctor, a teacher, a firefighter or a minister?"

And what about the owners? What kind of behavior are we rewarding for them? Betrayal, disloyalty, secrecy, arrogance, greed, and selfishness. Why should the Congress sanction this? We are trying to preserve the future of a nation built on hard work and sacrifice and a passionate commitment to families and faith, and fundamental virtues like loyalty, honesty and fairness.

This Congress has the profound opportunity to both fix this limited problem in the area of sports and at the same time set an example of reordering our priorities in order to fix our much larger problems.

Thank you very much for your indulgence and for your time, Mr. Chairman.

[The prepared statement of Mr. Hoke follows:]

PREPARED STATEMENT OF HON. MARTIN R. HOKE, A REPRESENTATIVE IN CONGRESS FROM THE STATE OF OHIO

Thank you, Mr. Chairman, and Members of the committee. I am grateful to participate today in an examination of the state of professional sports in America, and Congress' role in their development and regulation; and to discuss my proposed legislative solution to the growing problem of sports team relocations—H.R. 2740, the Fan Freedom and Community Protection Act.

Before I begin my testimony I particularly want to express my gratitude to Chairman Hyde for agreeing to hold this hearing. He and the entire Judiciary staff have been most generous in granting my request to hold these hearings, and have worked very hard to arrange for all perspectives to be given a fair voice, and I am very appreciative of their efforts.

Mr. Chairman, this weekend American taxpayers and sports fans were unfortunately once again treated to the bizarre and disturbing image of a professional football team stealing away in the dead of night—abandoning a city which had supported it through thick and thin—to flee to the financial embraces of a new city's tax coffers in a very ugly and now all too familiar greedy pursuit of bigger taxpayer-funded subsidies. When asked why, the owner's only explanation is that he is pursuing a childhood dream.

Mr. Chairman, pro sports team relocations have reached epidemic proportions—especially in pro football where the Raiders have moved from Oakland to Los Angeles and back, the Rams from LA to Anaheim to St. Louis, the Cardinals from St. Louis to Phoenix, the Colts to Indianapolis from Baltimore. And let's not forget Cleveland, a Houston, and now the latest—72 hours ago of the Seattle Seahawks to Los Angeles.

If you mapped out all the recent NFL moves, it would look a lot like one of Hazel O'Leary's trade missions.

In fact, right now, no fewer than 14 NFL teams are considered to be "in play." or seeking some form of taxpayer-funded public subsidy or a better deal elsewhere. And as more teams relocate there will be increased pressure on Congress to take action to protect fans, communities, and taxpayers.

Houston Mayor Bob Lanier, who bravely refused to bend to demands for $150 million for a new stadium to keep the Oilers from moving to Nashville, (isn't Nashville Oilers an oxymoron?) summed up the problem best by asking: "How can you tax the average working guy to build luxury suites for rich people, so they can support rich owners, who pay rich players to play in a stadium where the average guy can no longer afford the ticket price?"

How many things have to be wrong with this picture before we do something about it?

In the past three years, American cities have spent over $1 billion building or renovating stadiums and arenas for pro sports teams. Much of this money is being provided by taxpayers. For instance:

the City of Cleveland has on the table a $175 million stadium renovation plan that is funded entirely by taxpayers;

about 90 percent of the Los Angeles Coliseum's $100 million renovation and Jacksonville's $160 stadium million renovation are being financed with federal money;

the Disney Corporation, part owner of the California Angels, have demanded that the City of Anaheim make over $100 million worth of stadium and infrastructure improvements or the Angels are out of there; and

the State of Maryland will provide $73 million for projects related to the Redskins' soon-to-be-built stadium in Prince Georges County, on top of the $200 million to build a new stadium for Art Modell.

Owners are getting away with making these kinds of demands for two reasons: First, the financial stability they've gained from hugely lucrative broadcasting agreements made possible by a Congressionally-conferred antitrust exemption; and second, their Congressionally and judicially granted monopoly powers to limit the number of franchises available. Now you will hear the NFL argue that what is going on here is no different than what automobile manufacturers do when they want to build a new plant—they shop around, consider offers from different states, and then cut the best deal for their company. But there is a big difference between an auto plant and a pro sports team. Auto manufacturers don't have a congressionally-conferred limited antitrust exemption that allows them to operate as a cartel. Pro sports leagues do. And as long as the leagues can control the number of franchises they will continue to be able to pressure state and local governments to make more and more concessions. The only way to stop this form of legalized extortion is for Congress to act.

Mr. Chairman, at this point it is perfectly natural to ask, "By what right should Congress should get involved in the business of professional sports. particularly a Congress which is a fierce champion of free markets and free enterprise?" The short answer is the Sports Broadcasting Act of 1961, which granted the four major sports leagues—football, basketball, baseball, and hockey—a limited antitrust exemption allowing them to pool their separate broadcasting rights for sale to a single purchaser.

In the case of the National Football League, the antitrust exemption makes it possible for the league to divide among the owners over $1.2 billion in network television revenue amounting to about $39 million per team for the 1995–96 season. And that is before they sold a single ticket or cup of beer or local radio broadcast. or parking, or warm-up jacket, or stadium advertising. When you consider that their self-imposed salary cap is $37 million, it's pretty obvious that this broadcast antitrust exemption has provided the financial foundation for every team in the league—which is fine and is exactly what it was intended to do. What wasn't intended was for the NFL to take that economic power and use it as a bludgeon to beat even more money and greater benefits from cities, taxpayers, and fans.

Here is what then-NFL Commissioner Pete Rozelle had to say about that Act in testimony before Congress in 1982:

"The economic survival of every member club of the NFL fundamentally depends upon the operations, conduct, and decisions of the entire league. Congress recognized this in enacting the 1961 sports television legislation . . . and Congress properly looks to the leagues for responsible conduct in the administration of their nationwide business affairs."

In 1966, Congress also passed legislation allowing the NFL and the old American Football League (AFL) to merge. In justifying the merger before Congress, Rozelle testified, "Professional football operations will be preserved in the 23 cities and 25 stadiums where such operations are presently being conducted. This alone is a matter of considerable public interest—to local economies, stadium authorities, and consumers. Without the plan, franchise moves and/or franchise failures will occur as a matter of course within the next few years."

The uncontestable wisdom and implicit promise of that statement deserves closer examination in light of current events. It clearly was the NFL's point of view in 1966 that rapid franchise movement is a bad thing for cities and fans. It was then and it is now.

The fact is, despite statements from the NFL and other sports leagues to the contrary, we have seen anything but responsible conduct from pro sports leagues. And because the leagues owe their very existence to a congressionally-conferred antitrust exemption, Congress is not only justified in acting, but has an obligation to exercise its authority to protect cities, fans, and taxpayers from exploitation.

The Fan Freedom and Community Protection Act was introduced to respond to this situation. It demands responsibility from pro sports leagues and strikes a much-needed balance between the interests of fans, owners, cities, and taxpayers by giving for the first time ever negotiating leverage to cities. It has four basic components.

First, the bill codifies existing case law, which permits leagues to enforce their own rules regarding the relocation of teams. This provision instructs the leagues to consider certain factors in determining whether a team should be allowed to relocate, including: fan support, condition of stadium, and good faith efforts by the host community.

Unfortunately, many mistakenly believe that this provision alone will solve the problem, which is what the leagues, especially the NFL, want you to believe. But, as the *National Basketball Association* v. *San Diego Clippers Basketball Club* case (9th Cir. 1987), better known as *Clippers*, makes clear, the fact is that the leagues already have this authority as a matter of existing case law. Consider this quote from the *Clippers* case: ". . . a careful analysis of *Raiders I* makes it clear that franchise movement restrictions are not invalid as a matter of law." What could be clearer than that?

Indeed, an influential 1987 article in the *National Law Journal* put it correctly. "*Raiders I* was commonly viewed as holding that sports leagues would be unable to control franchise relocations unless they acted in accordance with a detailed set of express criteria, able to withstand antitrust scrutiny and embodied in the applicable league rules. The *Clippers* opinion rejected this perception . . . it is now certain that a professional sports league paying close attention to the discussion in the *Raiders* and *Clippers* cases can control team relocations in the appropriate circumstances."

More to the point. codifying antitrust case law in this way doesn't compel leagues to enforce their rules, it merely confirms that they can. The problem is not that leagues can't restrict team movement—it is that they refuse to—and they refuse to because it is clearly against the owners' economic self-interest to do so. Each owner knows that he or she will want to be that week's Alonzo Mourning winner of the owners' form of free agency. The decision to prevent a move is still left right where it has always been—with the owners.

Yet owners of professional football teams have developed what Chicago Mayor Richard M. Daley has rightly called an "entrepreneurial culture in which it is common practice to play one city off another for a better deal." This negotiating technique—it's not really a negotiating technique, but legalized extortion—has proven to be very effective in increasing profits and the value of franchises. For example, according to the publication *Financial World*, it is estimated that the move to Baltimore will increase the value of Art Modell's team $60 million, from $160 to $220 million, a 37.5 percent increase.

I submit that it is wishful thinking that we can solve this problem if we only give owners more power to do the right thing. Why would they unilaterally give up the negotiating tactic that has led to increased profits and higher team values? It would be like asking professional athletes to voluntarily give up free agency.

The second major component of H.R. 2740 is a provision requiring that a pro sports team owner who wants to skip town with a team must give local officials and other league members six months notice. This will give cities an opportunity to present counter proposals or take other steps to retain their team. In some cases in which a team has announced the intention to move, cities would like to act in concert with their state legislatures to make a counterproposal. But as you know, many state legislatures only meet at certain times of the year. Therefore, cities can find themselves held hostage to the legislative calendar and not even get the option to counter. This provision has strong support among mayors across the country.

The third component is critical. It states that once a team has been located in a community for at least ten years, the team name, logo, and colors stay with the city. In other words, owners who decide to move can't take the team's name with them. The league itself would retain the name, logo, and colors, but could only use them in the city that made them famous. The bottom line—no Nashville Oilers; no Baltimore Browns. This is the only bill that lets communities keep the name of their team. Now we come to the heart of the bill, the silver bullet if you will; the provision that sets this bill apart from the others and empowers elected officials with the tools they need to protect those they represent.

The bill provides that if a team does in fact relocate, then the league must grant the abandoned city an expansion team if the city finds a qualified investor. If such an investor is found, the league will have one year to provide a new, expansion franchise. If the league refuses, it loses the antitrust exemption granted by the 1961 Sports Broadcasting Act for a year, and pays a fine equal to three times the last franchise fee. Let me explain what this would mean for communities with pro sports teams.

First, it gives them real leverage in negotiating with team owners who threaten to leave unless their exorbitant demands are met, because if an owner leaves, the communities control a replacement expansion franchise. In other words, the implied threat of "my way or the highway" becomes very hollow when a city can respond, "Fine, please leave—we've already been contacted by three investment groups who want to own your replacement."

Pressure on the owner to negotiate reasonably and in good faith will come most persuasively not from his or her own conscience, but from the other owners, because they have a direct personal self interest in restraining expansion, with the resulting dilution of their slice of the broadcast revenue pie.

Second, suppose a community does lose a franchise. Under this bill, instead of being pressed to steal a team from another city, or made to compete in a bidding war with other cities to win an expansion franchise—which we know from experience can cost taxpayers hundreds of millions of dollars—the community would, in essence, have control over a pro sports franchise provided it can identify investors who believe the market will support a pro team.

This would allow cities to entertain offers from various investors and strike the best possible deal for their fans and taxpayers. One option might even be broad public ownership, as in Green Bay, which has been a model franchise.

At the same time, H.R. 2740 does not force the leagues to put teams in communities that can't support them, because the market tests for new investors are substantial. First, the investor must pay the league 85 percent of its last expansion franchise fee ($140 million in the case of the NFL) and second, the new owner must capitalize the team in an amount sufficient to be financially viable. The fact is, if a community has not supported a team in the past it will be very difficult to locate investors willing to take a seven hundred million dollar flyer. Maybe in the days when franchises cost less than $10 million, but not at these prices.

In short, this provision puts cities and fans back in the driver's seat, or at least levels the playing field with the owners. A few moments of reflection will make you realize just how dramatically this bill changes the balance of power between cities and owners. And it is the only bill in Congress that provides a market tested mechanism to restore a team to a city if an owner decides to skip town.

H.R. 2740 already has the support of several major league cities, such as Anaheim, Houston, and Hillsborough County, where the Tampa Bay Buccaneers play. It also has the support of fans groups from across the country, which are listed in the information packets I have provided.

At 44, the bill also has far more cosponsors than any other bill in the House. And as you can see from the cosponsor list attached, this is a bipartisan effort and has attracted support from all regions of the country.

Mr. Chairman, with the passage of the Fan Freedom and Community Protection Act, cities will no longer be held hostage or pitted against one another in a poisonous bidding war that works only to the advantage of owners. It rewards fan loyalty. It protects taxpayers. It gives cities a fighting chance at the bargaining table. And it will restore some degree of stability—and respectability—to the leagues that is sorely missing.

Mr. Chairman, I would like to close by shifting gears a little. Many Americans, especially parents—moms and dads who are trying to teach their children the value of education, and hard work, and faith and loyalty and fairness—many Americans (and I am one of them) have this growing and unsettling sense that as a nation we are trashing our culture and destroying the best we have to offer our children because of a mis-prioritization of values. I believe the situation in pro sports today is a clear reflection of that on many levels. First, at the dollar and cents level. Extremely scarce local taxpayer dollars are being spent on stadiums and not being spent on education, the arts, roads, bridges, parks and neighborhoods. This isn't play money—it is real money in very tight situations where budgets must be balanced in a zero sum game. What message does that send to our children about what we value—what is important to us and should be important to them? Is it any wonder that one can go into any city school in a depressed neighborhood and the answer to the question, "What do you want to be when you grow up?" is a bright hopeful youngster saying, "A professional ball player." When was the last time you heard "a doctor, a teacher, a firefighter or a minister?"

And what about the owners? What kind of behavior are we rewarding for them? Betrayal, disloyalty, secrecy, arrogance, greed and selfishness. Why should the Congress sanction this? We are trying to preserve the future of a nation built on hard work and sacrifice, and a passionate commitment to families, and faith in God, and some fundamental virtues like loyalty and honesty and fairness. This Congress has a profound opportunity to fix this overall problem—and at the same time set an example of recording our priorities in order to fix our much larger problems. Thank you for your time.

COSPONSORS OF "FAN FREEDOM AND COMMUNITY PROTECTION ACT OF 1995"

44 COSPONSORS OF H.R. 2740 AS OF FEBRUARY 6, 1996

Spencer Bachus (R–AL), Ken Bensten (D–TX), Peter Blute (R–MA), Helen Chenoweth (R–ID), Frank Cremeans (R–OH), Barbara Cubin (R–WY), Tom DeLay (R–TX), Bob Dornan (R–CA), John J. Duncan, Jr. (R–TN), Michael Patrick Flanagan (R–IL), Sam Gibbons (D–FL), Wayne Gilchrest (R–MD), Gene Green (D–TX), Gil Gutknecht (R–MN), Alcee Hastings (D–FL), David L. Hobson (R–OH), Martin R. Hoke (R–OH), Sheila Jackson Lee (D–TX), Walter B. Jones, Jr. (R–NC), Sue W. Kelly (R–NY), Peter T. King (R–NY), Jack Kingston (R–GA), Scott Klug (R–WI), Steven LaTourette (R–OH), William O. Lipinski (D–IL), Marty Meehan (D–MA), Carrie Meek (D–FL), Jack Metcalf (R–WA), Dan Miller (R–FL), Susan Molinari (R–NY), Robert Ney (R–OH), Major R. Owens (D–NY), Michael Oxley (R–OH), Collin C. Peterson (D–MN), Rob Portman (R–OH), Deborah Pryce (R–OH), Jack Quinn (R–NY), Joe Scarborough (R–FL), John Shadegg (R–AZ), Linda Smith (R–WA), Steve Stockman (R-TX), Bob Stump (R-AZ), James A. Traficant, Jr. (D-OH), and C.W. Bill Young (R-FL).

Mr. HYDE. I thank the gentleman, and I regret that I didn't have the light on when the gentleman started.

We do have many witnesses, and so I would ask that you hit the core of your statement. The rest will be put in the record. As far as Mr. Flanagan and Mr. Hoke are concerned, as members of this committee they will be able to move up here and elicit further information from their questioning. So the gentleman from Chicago, Mr. Flanagan.

STATEMENT OF HON. MICHAEL PATRICK FLANAGAN, A REPRESENTATIVE IN CONGRESS FROM THE STATE OF ILLINOIS

Mr. FLANAGAN. Thank you, Mr. Chairman. I want to thank you, as Mr. Hoke did, for giving us all the opportunity to testify today. This is important legislation.

I would like to go right to Mr. Gekas of Pennsylvania and try and open your mind right away before we go any further. I have my crowbar with me today, so we will give it an effort.

Mr. Hoke has explained, the long and the short of this is that the National Football League, in the instance we are talking about, operates with congressional largesse, operates because we permitted it years ago to operate under an antitrust exemption.

It does what it does because we let it do what it does. It makes billions of dollars annually and divides that money amongst the teams, whereas, before, you had feudal empires and fiefdoms in large media markets making unbelievable sums of money in large important cities like Chicago, and vastly smaller tiny villages like Green Bay.

The long and the short of it is that, if Congress permits them to make this money with an antitrust exemption that no other business enjoys, but under the implicit promise of nonmovement of teams, of stability in the league and of continued vitality in the communities in which they started and, since we don't have that happening, what is the rationale for continuing the antitrust exemption?

Now, Mr. Hoke and I will both argue that there is an excellent rationale for continuing the exemption. The proper solution is to not permit the teams to continue to make vacuous promises that claim they will have stability for the communities and then let them loot the community's taxpayers for stadiums or whatever else they can achieve but to compound it in legislation and say, to continue this exemption, we are going to now have a penalty if you move. And the penalties are enumerated in the bill and none of them are too severe, not the least of which is that the name remains behind if you feel a need to move; not least of which is that Mayor Daley of Chicago has an excellent suggestion, which I will be offering as an amendment should we ever come to mark up; and that is, if you go, you pay for the price of the stadium that they built for you and you leave that behind.

No one is restricting the free market movement of these teams in and amongst the Nation. That is not what this legislation is about. This legislation is about exacting a price for that movement, a price that we have paid for by granting the antitrust exemption decade in and decade out over many years. That is where we are going with this.

So we are not involving ourselves per se into settling disputes over where teams go or where they should be. We have no interest in micromanaging the league insofar as saying you may move out of Cleveland or you may not. Certainly, you may move—the Bears may go to Gary or they may not, or whatever else. That is all in the good and responsible attitude of the teams and the communities in which they are coming from and going to.

All we are saying is that, if you are going to enjoy this antitrust exemption, there is a price to pay for it on the back end. I do not think that that is an overt interference by Congress. I think it is our proper role to behave that way, and hopefully I have opened your mind somewhat on the issue.

I must further observe that the necessity and the scope of the involvement of Congress in these matters is not insignificant. When you are dealing with really traditional—I hesitate to say values, but I guess I will—values involved in the warmth and affection one feels for a team, and it has risen to the level of congressional observance, an observance of the Supreme Court in the case of baseball, I don't know that our continued involvement in this is altogether inappropriate.

I must say that the history of sports being intertwined with communities, and the migratory nature of teams across State lines and throughout the Nation, certainly gives Congress the purview to at least examine this in some way.

I cannot imagine talking about Chicago baseball without speaking of it in historical terms, for there is nothing currently to be too excited about. You have to go back to Ernie Banks. You go back to Ron Santo. You go back to Tinkers to Evers to Chance. You go back almost a century with Chicago baseball, and you go back 80 years with the Cubs anyway. You go back to one of the oldest stadiums in Major League Baseball with the White Sox at Comiskey Park, which is only recently gone, and certainly you go back with the Cubs at Wrigley Field. You go back, as the chairman observed, in football, with the Cardinals who left Chicago and with the Bears who remain. You have the histories of the Sox, the Bulls, the Black Hawks, and the Cubs.

All of these are names, but they take on a special meaning when the word "Chicago" appears in front of them. If it were as fine a city as it is, the Los Angeles Bulls, it wouldn't mean the same thing. The people of Chicago have a vested interest in that team. The people of Los Angeles have a vested interest in the Lakers. The people of Ohio have a vested interest in the Browns.

Mr. HYDE. Could the gentleman on that——

Mr. FLANAGAN. With that, I will sum up——

Mr. HYDE [continuing]. On a high note.

Mr. FLANAGAN [continuing]. And say this gives us congressional purview. I thank you, Mr. Chairman. I thank you for your time. I thank the committee.

Mr. HYDE. Thank you, Mr. Flanagan. You are indeed Irish.

[The prepared statement of Mr. Flanagan follows:]

PREPARED STATEMENT OF HON. MICHAEL PATRICK FLANAGAN, A REPRESENTATIVE IN CONGRESS FROM THE STATE OF ILLINOIS

Mr. Chairman, thank you for giving me the opportunity to testify today on behalf of H.R. 2740, the "Fan Freedom and Community Protection Act of 1995," introduced by our Judiciary Committee colleague Representative Martin Hoke of Ohio. I am an original cosponsor of this legislation.

The thrust of this initiative is to support the fans and their communities. The fans are the ones who have given their loyalty to the teams in their cities and towns, from large urban areas like Chicago to small communities like Green Bay, Wisconsin. Without the fans and their support, the teams mean nothing, whether the sport be football, baseball, basketball, ice hockey or whatever. It is the fans who give the teams their die-hard emotional support and help. It is the fans who buy the tickets, the hot dogs and the programs and support their team and its community economically. It is these same loyal fans who are given short shrift when a team decides to relocate. When that happens, the fans and their community feel betrayed and abandoned, and rightly so.

When teams move away some of the magic of the community is gone forever. Even though they started out in Chicago, then moved to St. Louis and most recently to Phoenix, it is hard for any Chicagoan, and I am sure any St. Louisian, to relate to a team called the Arizona Cardinals. But, there are still many people in Chicago who nostalgically remember the Chicago Cardinals and there is a void there that has never been overcome. A little bit of Chicago left when the Cardinals moved. The void in St. Louis, however, was filled this past year by the relocation of the Los Angeles Rams to St. Louis and I am sure L.A. Rams fans have a hard time relating to a team called the St. Louis Rams. And now there is a void in Los Angeles, although the Seattle Seahawks are eyeing that territory for a possible move.

I cannot help but believe that we are today seeing the nucleus of sports franchise musical chairs. Remember that in addition to the Rams move, the Los Angeles Raiders moved back to Oakland, where they previously played, the Houston Oilers are going to Nashville, the Cleveland Browns to Baltimore, the Chicago Bears are seriously considering moving, the Tampa Bay Buccaneers considering moving to Orlando, or even perhaps to Cleveland, and so on. And that is just to mention some of the things happening in professional football. There could be no end to this hop scotching of professional sports team around the country.

When sports teams move, they usually take the team name with them. It is the name, however, that helps give the city where the team plays its games its unique identity. As Mr. Hoke's bill, H.R. 2740, states, "The name of a professional sports team is always linked to the name of the community in which it is located." It would be hard for me to ever conceive of a team called something other than the Chicago Bears, the Chicago Cubs, the Chicago Black Hawks or the Chicago Bulls. The city name gives out a certain ambience and vitality as well as a direct linkage to the community in which a team plays it games. It also connotes and denotes a usually long and illustrious history of a team. And in that history of a team is intertwined a large part of the history of the city where that team played its games. Let's admit it, sports histories and records don't quite have the same continuity and historical context when a team traipses all over the country. When a team moves, the city it played in loses a large part of its history.

Under H.R. 2740 cities don't lose their team name. The name stays in the city, provided the team has been there at least 10 years. This is how it should be. Would the name Packers mean anything to any other city than Green Bay? The answer begs the question. Obviously, the name Browns belongs in Cleveland, the names Bears and Cubs belong in Chicago. The "Fan Freedom and Community Protection Act of 1995" will ensure that these names never leave the cities that made the names famous.

Beyond the name, fans identify with the players on the teams. When teams move the linkage of players to the local community is broken. Fans in a team's new community have no real bond with the team's history or its players. For example, where I come from, Ernie Banks is still known as Mr. Cub, even though he retired long ago. But, if the Cubs ever moved to another city would the fans in the new area appreciate, and have any relationship to, Ernie's heroics during the many years he played on those terrible Cubs teams. They may know of them, but they would not be able to truly identify with them because they never saw those heroics in person or heard about them from relatives and friends who did. For those people in the new city, Ernie Banks would be simply a relic of a bygone era and the meaning of Ernie Banks being Mr. Chicago Cub would be greatly diminished. The same holds true for other names in other sports as well, Walter Payton and Gale Sayers will always be thought of as Chicago Bears, for example.

Just as Mr. Banks did, players on professional sports teams often become involved in the community during their careers. Many decide to stay in those communities even after their playing days are over. In the Chicago area, for example, Ernie Banks' teammate, the great Cubs third baseman Ron Santo has been a business leader and a community leader, especially in the area of fighting juvenile diabetes, even though he too retired long ago from baseball. And the fans still identify Mr. Santo with the Cubs. The point is that players often reciprocate fan support by staying in and helping the community economically and socially even after their playing days are over. So clearly there is a close link between players, the teams they represent and the communities where the teams play.

The "Fan Freedom and Community Protection Act of 1995" also helps protect communities by giving them some bargaining power should a team decide to relocate. Notice has to be given not later 180 days before the beginning of the season in which the team is to play in the new community to the appropriate authorities, including the local government for the community in which the professional sports team's stadium or arena is currently located. Thus, there could no longer be a clandestine midnight exodus to another city similar to the way the Baltimore Colts fled their home for Indianapolis one dank, dark and dismal night.

After a team has moved, the "Fan Freedom and Community Protection Act of 1995" requires the appropriate league to make an expansion team available to the community that has lost its team, provided certain criteria, such as finding a suitable investor, is met. Such an expansion team cannot relocate out of the area for at least 10 years. Thus, an expansion team will not be able to pack up and move out of town after only one or two seasons a la the old Seattle Pilots baseball team, who moved to Wisconsin and became the Milwaukee Brewers after only one season, 1969, in Seattle. Communities and fans need stability with their sports teams and they need to know for sure that any expansion team is going to be around a while. H.R. 2740 will ensure that this will happen.

In Chicago, Mayor Richard Daley is a strong advocate of having a sports franchise that relocates prior to fulfilling its contractual obligations, and which has received public financial assistance, pay the community back for its help. The team would have to pay back to the local government the benefit value of the public assistance the team received. This is an idea that has considerable merit, and I am working on an amendment to H.R. 2740 that will achieve this objective.

Mr. Chairman, without action on the part of Congress, for many cities with professional sports teams the tumult and the shouting will soon become the serenity and the silence of empty, stilled stadiums, and the loyal fans will continue to be deserted.

Mr. HYDE. The distinguished Senator from Ohio, Senator Glenn.

STATEMENT OF HON. JOHN GLENN, A SENATOR IN CONGRESS FROM THE STATE OF OHIO

Mr. GLENN. Thank you, Mr. Chairman. I appreciate very much the opportunity to testify here this morning. I would ask my entire statement be included in the record, if I might, please.

I am glad to be here with my good friend, Congressman Louis Stokes. He and I have companion pieces on this, the Fans' Rights Act in the Senate and in the House. His efforts on behalf of Ohio's sports fans, indeed all American sports fans, are invaluable.

I will skip over part of my testimony, Mr. Chairman, and say that the move of the Browns to Baltimore is what triggered off some of this activity. Of all the teams that have had loyal fan support, in the whole United States indeed, the cradle of football has been in that northeastern part of Ohio, and in Cleveland in particular. The National Football Hall of Fame is up there also.

Let me address Mr. Gekas's question a little bit here, because I think that does come into play. I believe that these sports teams have helped local communities rally and revitalize inner cities. They have created new sectors of economic opportunity. They are an asset to civic pride and spirit, and Congress does have an important role to play in giving fans and communities more of a say in franchise relocation. Why bother? It is a business. Let them do what they are going to do in business as we would any other business. But I think it does go far beyond that.

I don't think it is just a business per se, where you just look at the bottom line. You know, these teams are woven into the fabric of our communities. It is a matter that they are a rallying point. They are a symbol. They are civic pride. They are part of a can-do spirit. How do you put a value on something like that? I don't know the answer to that, and I don't know how you put a dollar value on it.

How do you put a value on it, what does the community spirit mean? How much is it worth? Is it important enough for us to address? Can football do all of this for community spirit? No, of course not. But are they a vital part of it in our communities? Yes, I certainly believe they are. If I did not believe that, I would not have helped put this bill together and have submitted it over in the Senate.

I do not want to take much of the time on other extraneous matters here. Let me get on to the Fans' Rights Act itself and make a few points about it.

First, in regard to our provision that would grant a limited antitrust exemption to sports leagues in relation to franchise relocation: this exemption is very narrowly drawn and would only come into play if a league, following the strict guidelines of our bill, votes against a team's relocation. Their own rules and guidelines right now say you have to have a three-quarter vote but teams ignore it. You are supposed to have a three-quarter vote of all league owners to permit a move, but it just doesn't work. They go ahead and move anyway, as the Oakland Raiders did when they went to L.A. and got $50 million in additional damages when they made that move against league rules. These are rules that all the NFL owners sign up to abide by when they come into membership in the league.

Some may argue that this exemption is not necessary. Leagues can already block a move. We thought we had that. It was true until the *Raiders* case, in which the NFL not only lost that antitrust case but also had to pay a $50 million suit brought by the Raiders because the league rejected this move. Even though the Raiders had agreed to these bylaws when they became a member of the league.

Our bill is called the Fans' Rights Act because it doesn't just give the leagues this exemption. We drafted very specific provisions that leagues and teams must follow in the event of a proposed relocation. It includes a 180-day notice of a relocation so that alternative offers can be prepared to keep the team in its present community. The bill has a requirement that any bona fide offer must be considered by the league.

The legislation also directs the league to take a number of factors, including fan loyalty and community support, into consideration when deciding to approve a move. And finally, the bill includes a fair play provision prohibiting an owner who wants to relocate from paying a so-called relocation fee, which some people have called a bribe, to the other owners for their vote prior to the vote. The bill prohibits that kind of a relocation fee to a league that is about to vote on a proposed move.

This is not an anti-owners bill. We don't intend it to be that. Our legislation will not prevent owners from making a profit on their investment, not even bar owners from moving their teams to other locations if there are legitimate reasons for doing so. It will not force a sports league to make a decision that might not be in its best business interest. I don't believe that Congress should just tie the hands of the owners or leagues so they are restricted in acting in their business interest.

It doesn't give a free ride to the sports leagues. The bill places very rigid requirements on sport leagues and how they decide relocation. The bill also lifts the cloud the Raiders' case has cast over how a league decides to approve or disapprove relocations. It gives the fans and communities a chance to be a part of that process.

Mr. Chairman, thank you very much for your kindness in letting me appear this morning. I would ask that the rest of my statement be included in the record.

Mr. HYDE. Without objection, so ordered. We thank you, Senator Glenn, for your contribution.

Mr. GLENN. Thank you, sir.

[The prepared statement of Mr. Glenn follows:]

PREPARED STATEMENT OF HON. JOHN GLENN, A SENATOR IN CONGRESS FROM THE STATE OF OHIO

Mr. Chairman and Members of the Committee, thank you holding this hearing and giving me the opportunity to address the serious problem of sports franchise relocation. This is an issue which has received a great deal of attention in Congress and I very much look forward to working with you on a solution. I'm also glad to see my good friend Representative Louis Stokes, the sponsor of the "Fans Rights Acts in the House, here today. His efforts on behalf of Ohio sports fans—and all American sports fans—are invaluable.

Sports team relocations are at an all-time high, especially in the National Football League. The Browns want to move to Baltimore. The Oilers want to move to Nashville. The Seahawks just announced they want to head south to play in the Rose Bowl. Last year we saw the Rams move to St. Louis and the Raiders return to Oakland. Teams from Chicago to Arizona to Tampa Bay are rumored to be packing up and heading for a new town. In baseball, the Pirates, Astros and Mariners have been reported as candidates for relocation in the past year. The Winnipeg Jets of the NHL are moving to Phoenix.

Mr. Chairman, as you well know, sports team relocation is an issue which hits very close to home for me. Last year, after quite a bit of speculation and reports in the media, the Cleveland Browns officially announced they planned to abandon their home of half-a-century and move to Baltimore.

This shocked the people of Ohio. It shocked football fans across America. The Cleveland Browns are a symbol of unwavering and undying fan support. Week in and week out, Lakefront Memorial Stadium has been packed to the rafters with fans rooting on the Browns. These fans didn't come to the stadium only when the Browns were winning, or only during the playoffs, they came every week—through 13–3 seasons and 3–13 seasons.

What could say more about American fan support than the dedicated followers of the Cleveland Browns? And, what could say more about the sorry state of franchise stability in sports than the Browns decision to abandon that support?

It's time that fans and communities begin to have more of a say in the future of their sports franchises. Professional sports teams are an important part of a city's economy. They have helped local communities rally and revitalize inner cities and create new sectors of economic opportunity. And, professional sports team are an immeasurable asset to civic pride and spirit. For these, and many other reasons, Congress has an important role to play in giving fans and communities more of a say in franchise relocation.

I don't want to take to much of the Committee's time this morning, so I'd like to submit a fact sheet on the "Fans Rights Act" for the record. But I do want to make a few points about the Fans Rights Act.

First, in regards to our provision that would grant a limited anti-trust exemption to sports leagues in relation to franchise relocation. Let me stress that this exemption is very narrowly drawn and would only come into play if a league, following the strict guidelines of our bill, votes against a team's relocation. Simply, this gives a league the ability to enforce its own rules.

Some may argue that this exemption is not necessary and leagues can already block a move. But the infamous *Raiders* case has created a great deal of confusion. The NFL lost an anti-trust case—to the tune of $50 million—brought by the Raiders because the league rejected its move. This has created a situation that when a team wants to move, the other owners in a league are not going to risk another lawsuit and will approve a move. The narrow anti-trust exemption granted by our bill is needed to correct this situation.

But our bill is called the "Fans Rights Act" because it doesn't just give the leagues this exemption. We drafted very specific procedures leagues and teams must follow in the event of a proposed relocation. This includes a 180-day notice of a relocation so that alternative offers can be prepared to keep the team in its present community. The bill has a requirement that any bona fide offer must be considered by the league. The legislation also directs the league to take a number of factors—including fan loyalty and community support—into consideration when deciding to approve a move. Finally, the bill includes a fair play provision prohibiting an owner who wants to relocate from paying a so-called "relocation fee" to a league that is about to vote on the proposed move.

As I've said many times before, the "Fans Rights Acts" is not an anti-owners bill. Our legislation will not prevent owners from making a profit on their investment. It would not even bar owners from moving their teams to other locations if there are legitimate reasons for doing so. Also, our legislation will not force a sports league to make a decision that might not be in its best business interest. I just do not believe that Congress should tie the hands of the owners or leagues so they are restricted in acting in their best business interests.

Yet, the "Fans Rights Acts" doesn't give a free ride to the sports leagues. The bill places very rigid requirements on sports leagues and how they decide relocations. The bill also lifts the cloud the *Raiders* case has cast over how a league decides to approve or disapprove relocations. It gives the fans and communities the chance to be a part of this process.

Mr. Chairman, thank you again for holding this hearing. I look forward to working with you and the members of the Committee on this issue.

FACT SHEET ON THE FANS RIGHTS ACT

Provides a narrowly tailored antitrust exemption shielding professional sports leagues from antitrust liability for blocking a team relocation. Provides no exemption in circumstances where a league approves a relocation.

Leagues would be required by law to base relocation decisions on set criteria that take into account fan loyalty, community support and bona fide offers to purchase a team and retain it in the existing community. This criteria is largely based on the current guidelines used by the professional sports leagues.

Requires teams that intend to relocate to give a community 180 days notice. During that time, the league would be required to hold public hearings on the proposed relocation. And the existing community would be given the opportunity to present bona fide offers to purchase the team or induce it to stay.

Includes a fair play provision prohibiting an owner who intends to relocate from paying a so-called "relocation fee" to a league that is about to vote on the proposed move.

Some may argue that leagues can already block a move and fight it out in court without antitrust protection. However, the infamous *Raiders* case has created confusion and unpredictability in this area of the law. In that case, the NFL paid close to $50 million in damages and legal fees when owner Al Davis sued the league for antitrust violations following a unanimous vote of the NFL to block his proposed move from Oakland to Los Angeles.

There have been other cases in the 9th Circuit, where the *Raiders* case was decided, in which that court indicated that the current NFL bylaws may take care of the antitrust issue. But that's just the 9th Circuit and if current litigation is any indicator, the law desperately needs clarification.

The NFL now faces another suit by Al Davis for delaying his move back to Oakland.

A former owner of the New England Patriots has filed an antitrust suit against the NFL claiming that they prevented him from moving.

And the NFL initially rejected the proposed move of the Rams from Southern California to St. Louis. However, after threats by the Rams and the Missouri Attorney General that they would seek billions in antitrust damages, the membership of the NFL reversed itself. In his November 29 testimony before the Judiciary Subcommittee on Antitrust, Commissioner Tagliabue indicated that this move would have been blocked had some antitrust protection been in place.

The Fans Rights Act seeks to restore some stability to professional sports and preserve its integrity. It makes sure that leagues have the ability to enforce their own rules and that a set process is followed before a relocation can occur.

Mr. HYDE. It is now a pleasure to recognize the distinguished gentleman from Cleveland, Mr. Louis Stokes, one of the most useful Members of the House and the dean of the Ohio delegation, for whatever that means. Mr. Conyers assures me it is a matter of high prestige.

So, Dean, you are on.

Mr. STOKES. Thank you very much.

Mr. GLENN. I agree with Mr. Conyers, I will tell you that.

Mr. HYDE. OK.

STATEMENT OF HON. LOUIS STOKES, A REPRESENTATIVE IN CONGRESS FROM THE STATE OF OHIO

Mr. STOKES. Thank you very much. Mr. Chairman and members of the committee, I appreciate the opportunity to appear before you to discuss a very pressing national issue, the challenges facing the future of professional sports.

As you have already stated, Mr. Chairman, and others have stated, I am sponsoring H.R. 2699, the Fans' Rights Act. This, of course, is also the companion legislation to the bill introduced in the Senate by Senator John Glenn, the distinguished Senator from my State and with whom I am very pleased and honored to be associated in this venture with the leadership he has given this legislation.

As a Representative of the 11th Congressional District in Cleveland, OH, I represent hundreds of thousands of avid sports fans who have a keen interest in the future and direction of professional sports. My constituents' interest in this important issue has been enhanced by a threat they now face, the sudden and unjustified attempt by the owner of the Cleveland Browns to move the team away from one of this Nation's greatest sports cities.

It is timely that this committee will address the challenges professional sports now face, because sports fans and nonsports fans alike have been concerned by several disturbing trends in professional sports. From last summer's baseball strike to the increased diversion of public funds, to support, maintain and attract professional sports teams, Americans have been asking tough questions about many of the disturbing trends in professional sports.

As a result of the proposed move of the Cleveland Browns, I am particularly concerned with the problem associated with the relocation of professional sports teams and more specifically the solutions available to rationally solve disputes arising from professional sports teams movement. It is my belief that the Cleveland Browns case is responsible for bringing to the Nation's attention some of the appalling inequities that exist in the professional sports industry.

The Cleveland Browns' proposed move to Baltimore extends far beyond the State of Ohio. This proposed relocation has and will continue to have repercussions in every community with professional sports teams. The clear message of the proposed Browns' move is that any community in America can fall victim to a bidding war in which the interests of loyal fans and communities are given little consideration. If it can happen in Cleveland, Mr. Chairman, where loyal fans supported the Browns for 50 years, it can happen anywhere.

In fact, news reports late last week confirm suspicion that the Seattle Seahawks are planning to leave Seattle to replace the recently departed Los Angeles Rams who just moved to St. Louis, MO. Despite substantial efforts by the Washington State Legislature and King County officials to raise over $400 million to make infrastructure improvements to the stadium that the Seahawks requested, the team is rumored to be packing its bags as we speak.

The Seahawks' planned move stands as another reminder of the need for congressional action on this national problem.

As a result of my concern over the dilemma in which the fans, municipalities, the sports teams are now placed, I have introduced in the House of Representatives the Fans' Rights Act. Senator Glenn has already explained the key elements of the Fans' Rights Act, so I will not take additional time repeating what he has already so ably stated.

Mr. Chairman, the balance and practical approach in the Fans' Rights Act to this longstanding problem will help ensure that reason prevails in the determination of when a professional sports franchise may relocate. This nonregulatory approach that incorporates the vital interests of all parties will certainly provide greater protection for the citizens and loyal sports fans of America.

I am committed to continuing my efforts to support the citizens of Cleveland and the millions of other fans throughout this Nation who are looking for rational and balanced solutions to the sports team relocation problem. I am also committed to pursuing this legislative remedy so that painful and costly disputes over sports team relocations can be resolved more effectively.

This should be our first step in our efforts to restore the Nation's faith in an industry that maintains a special place in American culture.

I thank you for the privilege of testifying this morning, and I yield back the balance of my time.

Mr. HYDE. Thank you very much, Congressman Stokes.

And I want to thank the panel for very illuminating testimony.

Mr. HYDE. Our second panel consists of several people who are deeply concerned about the issue of sports franchise relocation. From Cleveland, OH, we have John "Big Dawg" Thompson with us today. Mr. Thompson is an ardent Cleveland Browns fan and a founder of the "Dawg Pound." He has been very involved in Cleveland with the Save-the-Browns campaign. We know how disappointed he is at this proposed move to Baltimore, and we look forward to hearing from him.

Mr. Thompson, would you come up to the front.

From Hillsborough County, FL, we have Countywide Commissioner Joe Chillura here today. Commissioner Chillura has been very active in the Tampa Bay area on this issue as the owners of the Tampa Bay Buccaneers decide whether they will remain in that city. The Tampa situation is ironic because, among the rumors circulating, there have been reports that Tampa Bay Buccaneers might move to Cleveland.

We are also pleased to have with us today King County Executive Gary Locke. King County is the largest county in Washington State and includes the city of Seattle. The Seattle Seahawks recently announced their intention to relocate, and the King County government is actively involved in attempting to keep the Seahawks in Seattle.

Finally, we have Mayor Bob Lanier of the city of Houston, TX, with us today.

I am pleased now to turn to Congresswoman Jackson Lee from Houston, TX, to introduce Mayor Lanier.

Ms. JACKSON LEE. Thank you very much, Mr. Chairman.

It gives me great pride to acknowledge the city of Houston, the fourth largest city in the Nation. Mayor Lanier has had successful careers in law, banking, real estate and public service. He chaired the State Highway Commission, the Houston Metro, which gets around, and numerous other boards.

Mayor Lanier was born in Baytown, TX, he likes to tell you that, and he was educated at Lee College, University of New Mexico, University of Texas Law School, and is married to Alica Lanier, with seven children.

The one thing that we pride ourselves in, having a mayor like Bob Lanier, is that he places his emphasis on people. When he came into this office in the city of Houston in 1991, he talked about police protection. He has done it. He talked about improving the infrastructure. He has done it. Most of all, he has talked about promoting diversity, and we are doing it.

It is a pleasure now to indicate to you that the modus operandi of our mayor from the city of Houston is, "If it's good for Houston, let's do it." I have enjoyed working with him, and I am proud to introduce you to the mayor of the city of Houston, Mayor Bob Lanier.

Mr. HYDE. Mayor Lanier.

STATEMENT OF BOB LANIER, MAYOR, CITY OF HOUSTON, TX

Mr. LANIER. Thank you. Are these working all right?
Mr. HYDE. If you would push that microphone closer.
Mr. LANIER. Pardon me. Thank you very much, Congresswoman Lee. Ms. Lee and I served on the city council together so I have enjoyed working with her on the city council and again since she has been in Congress.

In addressing myself to this issue in front of us, pro football used to be a working man's sport, that is to say, a sport where working men and women enjoyed and could afford going out to a ball game. That is being taken away from them. What they are asked now to do is to support and pay for, as a consequence of the NFL's protection from the normal competitive laws that govern in this country, they are asked to support and pay for transfers to another city motivated almost entirely by the building of new luxury boxes, and the payment of moving expenses to the owner and the payment of transfer fees to the league.

The paradox is that this working guy, or lady, pardon my generation, that is asked to—take the case of Nashville where it looks like the Houston Oilers will go. They are building luxury boxes there. They are taxing the local taxpayer for it, and it costs $600 a seat to sit in that luxury box. They won't have anymore seats than they have in Houston. Houston sold out 105 percent of capacity over a 6-year period.

What they have is new luxury boxes built that the rich people can sit in, and they are taxing the pipefitter, the barber, the waitress, for the money to pay for it. He and she will never sit in it, and I think that is wrong. That bothers me in at a very visceral level.

And why does this come to pass? Because I am a disciple of, a product of the free enterprise system, admirer of the University of Chicago School of Economics, Milton Friedman. Why does that come about here, and why would I protest just the exercise of free enterprise?

Well, it is not free enterprise. The NFL came to Congress in 1961 and asked for a trust. They asked Congress to bestow a trust on them, that if they exempted them from the competitive laws of this country, that what you would have would be franchise stability; what you have would be a sport that working men and women in this country could enjoy.

And they came back a second time. We had the AFL in Houston and they merged with the NFL. At that time, if a team left a profitable city, the other league would pop a team in there overnight. There were no profitable cities left vacant. But the league said, "Trust us once more, Congress. Give us an exemption from these competitive laws that govern other people. We are sort of a house cat. We don't like to roam in the jungle. If you exempt this merger, which creates a monopoly in pro football, then you can trust us. We will have franchise stability and we will have competition."

It is my point of view that they have betrayed that trust; that instead of franchise stability, instead of competitive balance, what you have is owners sometimes leaving in the dead of night, not really for a better stadium. The Nashville stadium is no bigger than the Houston stadium, and the Houston stadium is sold out, but for luxury boxes.

The mayor of Nashville says, "OK, that's true. We may not be able to hire a few policemen. We may not be able to pave a few streets. Maybe we don't build a few more schools but, you know, we think pro football is worth it."

I don't think that pro football ought to enjoy an exemption from the competitive rules that relate to the rest of us, that related to me when I was in business, and be able to dog rob the working men and women of this country.

Let me just put it, for example, it would cost us about $200 million to have kept the Houston Oilers, city of Houston taxpayer money. That is the inner city. As Congresswoman Lee has said, we are rebuilding the inner city. We are building 14 neighborhoods a year, 20 parks a year. We have hired 1,300 extra police. We are now embarking on a program of looking at our intermediate schools and seeing if we can set up shares to give supplemental pay to teachers in those intermediate schools so we can attract excellence of education.

And I am asked, on the stadium that Pete Rozelle wrote just 7 years earlier when he put $100 million into it, it would qualify as a Super Bowl, be one of America's great stadiums, 7 years later it is no good. The stadium didn't change.

What changed is Bud Adams, the owner of the Oilers, got offered $28 million to move. For a guy making 3 million bucks a year to get 10 years' profit, cash in hand, that is pretty tempting. He got offered to build him luxury boxes that rich people could sit in at 600 bucks a copy, and the league gets a relocation fee, and it matters not that Bud Adams started in Houston with $25,000. It matters not he won't take $200 million from local people to sell his team. It matters not that they are profitable. Because they are protected from the rules of competition that govern us all, they will pick up and leave.

Now, let me tell you this: If they want to engage in free enterprise and repeal all this special protection they have, man, I will leave in a minute and I will not have another word to say to you. But they are not jungle animals that want to kill what they eat. They are house cats, and they like to be served up food by the political pros at the Jockey Club and places of that sort.

They wouldn't know a free enterprise competitor if they saw one. Pardon me. I see the red light is on. I am really for—I really support the——

Mr. HYDE. Go ahead and finish.

Mr. LANIER. Just two things. The mayors all came together and supported resolutions to give the people we represent some rights along with these owners. We particularly support the franchise expansion provision in Congressman Hoke's bill. We ask that it be mandated that we have the Green Bay type of ownership.

If Houston were offered an expansion franchise, we have told them we would have the same 75,000 seats that Nashville has. It could be financed with user pay, without a dime of taxpayer money. We would have local investors that would do it. The club has always been profitable but we are actually threatened, we are actually threatened publicly by the club that if we so much as speak out, so much as speak out, they will deprive us of a franchise forever.

And if we ask them to do the honorable thing of living out their lease, they say publicly, as Art Modell does, what they will do for the balance of the lease, paid for with public funds, $100 million, is they will give us a sorry product. They will let their best players go and play with their scrub team, as a punishment to the working men and women I represent for asking them to live up to their word.

Thank you.

Mr. HYDE. Thank you, Mayor Lanier.

[The prepared statement of Mr. Lanier follows:]

PREPARED STATEMENT OF BOB LANIER, MAYOR, CITY OF HOUSTON, TX

Mr. Chairman and Members of the Committee, I sincerely appreciate the opportunity to appear before you and to share with you the experience that the City of

Houston has had regarding its professional football team and my thoughts on the process and its effect on taxpayers.

The Houston urban area has supported the Houston Oilers since their infancy, causing a modest $25,000 investment to grow to a $100 million plus fortune. This support was for a team that has experienced both good years and bad. At the expiration of the 1994 season, the Oilers—coming off a 2–14 year—demanded (see attached correspondence) that the City of Houston choose between its priorities (neighborhoods, parks, police, youth programs, etc.) and transfer a minimum of $150 million plus of taxpayers' funds to the construction of a new stadium playground for the Oilers or face the loss of the team to Nashville.

In Houston, we have chosen the priorities of our youth programs (some 10,000 youngsters this fall are in City sponsored inter league soccer teams), but we do not think we should have been forced to do so.

We do not think in any other field would a business threaten to uproot itself and leave that city unserved where, as in this case, the business has been enormously profitable. That it is happening in Houston is caused only by the statutorily unregulated monopoly that the NFL owners and players' association enjoy and are now using to gouge their fans.

Harris County taxpayers built the Astrodome for the Oilers and the Astros about 30 years ago. In 1987, to meet a threat by Mr. Adams to move the Oilers, a mix of luxury box buyers and Harris County taxpayers paid in principal and interest another $100 million plus to hold the Oilers, gaining a ten year lease. After only seven years, and coming off a 2–14 season, the Oilers want to move to Nashville because Houston did not build a second domed stadium. The City responded that it had higher priorities: police, fire, parks, neighborhoods, youth programs. The Oilers' ultimatum and the City's response are attached.

The Oilers are, of course, a part of the National Football League monopoly. This monopoly protects owners, television networks and the players' union. It does not protect urban taxpayers. Indeed, it causes the taxpayers great harm. In no other industry would such a situation be allowed to continue.

The real demand is for luxury boxes, not more seats. So the average working person is asked to put a tax on their home or pay sales or some other consumer tax to build luxury boxes in which they cannot afford to sit. Frequently, the new stadium is smaller. The working person is asked to be satisfied with the "sense of pride" they get from this arrangement, which will last until another team bids more for their players, or until another city bids more for the team.

NATURE OF NFL MONOPOLISTIC PRACTICES AS IT RELATES TO URBAN TAXPAYERS

The League controls the number of franchises which it keeps artificially low. It is as though Congress gave the motion picture industry a monopoly and that industry then limited theaters to thirty cities. The Oscar would be the Super Bowl. Movie moguls would get even richer off taxpayers and call it free enterprise.

The League has a related practice of not allowing a new expansion franchise into a city losing its franchise so as to add to the pressure. It seems to matter not that a franchise is profitable, that fans are numerous or that the stadium is in good shape. It may be large, as in the case of the Los Angeles Coliseum. It may be one deemed but a few years earlier suitable for a future Super Bowl, as the Houston Astrodome. Or it may be Cleveland. Any other city could be next. No one is safe. No one is secure. It can happen without warning. The dollar rules, but it only rules because of special protection granted professional sports by previous federal legislation and practice.

LITIGATION POSSIBILITY

There remains a possibility that this unconscionable monopolistic practice will be successfully challenged in the courts under existing anti-trust laws.

When Al Davis sought to move from Oakland to Los Angeles and the owners tried to stop him, he sued successfully. The owners have treated this, not as a sign that agreements in restraint of trade are illegal, but as a case holding that owners can move whenever they want to. This has been parlayed to the extortionist practice of threatening moves unless taxpayers give them expensive stadium improvements or a new stadium. The League holds the number of expansion franchises below market demand, and the trap is complete. Encouraged, owners now demand and get millions in "moving expenses" and guaranteed ticket sales. Often, taxpayers are left with an empty stadium, having more money invested in the franchise than do the owners.

I understand that this lawsuit will be plowing new ground. However, it is a serious legal and social position. The amount of damages sought could be the value of a franchise lost, as measured by what the new team had to pay to get it. Interestingly enough, the new city might also sue since its price would have been unlawfully set. If one takes $200 million as a norm and say that only half the cities in the NFL are involved (15 out of 30) you come to the idea of $3 billion in damages which, when tripled, would amount to $9 billion.

SUGGESTED SOLUTIONS

Recently, Mayors from across the country, with teams and without, large cities and small, united to pass two resolutions as guidance for federal legislation to resolve this issue of national importance.

Some of the more important points for you to consider out of these resolutions are as follows:
1. Leagues should adopt objective standards and criteria in relocation rules which are subject to reasonable judicial review.
2. These relocation rules should include a public interest component which measures and considers fan loyalty, community support, and local offers to purchase and retain teams.
3. Franchises should be required to give the community adequate notice and hold public hearings prior to initiating any effort to negotiate a relocation.
4. Existing leases and the status of any other legal rationale which may affect the relocation should be strongly considered
5. Public ownership of a team similar to the local ownership structure of the Green Bay Packers should be allowed and indeed encouraged by the professional leagues.
6. Cities with a previously profitable team should be offered the first option on any league expansion without requiring payment of an expansion fee to the league.
7. All public debt issued to build a facility for a professional franchise must be retired by the franchise before relocation would be allowed. Failure to abide by this would subject the responsible parties to triple damages in the form of a federal excise tax or other federal penalty.

CONCLUSION

My conclusion is that the NFL has an unregulated monopoly that is broader than it deserves. Cities, as much as they may have professional football, should not be required to short what are surely higher priorities in order to fund increasingly expensive stadiums, luxury boxes and ticket sales. In no other entertainment industry would this situation be allowed to continue.

The monopoly protects the networks, team owners, the leagues and the players. And together they have made a handsome return.

Professional football is widely enjoyed in this country. However, most recently it has taken an ugly turn. Not satisfied with huge television and gate revenues, the teams have made hostages of urban taxpayers. This comes at a time when almost all observers feel our nations' cities are short of money and long on problems. Almost every city is undertaking as best as it can to treat its urban decay.

To take one facet of the entertainment business, widely enjoyed, and grant monopoly status which when exercised extorts money from working people to build luxury boxes that working people can't afford to sit in is, I think, unconscionable. Maybe there is a legal remedy. I do not think the taxpayers ought to have to wait for that. This is a national problem that affects many cities and we hear about more movements each passing day. I think Congress ought to address this problem. I hope you do.

Houston Oilers

PERSONAL AND CONFIDENTIAL

July 12, 1995

The Honorable Bob Lanier
Office of the Mayor
901 Bagby, 3rd Floor
Houston, TX 77001

Dear Mayor Lanier:

It has now been more than two years since our initial meeting where I expressed the necessity for a new stadium in Houston. I told you then that the Oilers would not remain at the Astrodome after the expiration of our lease following the 1997 season.

During the interim I have expended almost $1 million dollars on feasibility studies, economic impact reports, architectural and design work, financial consultation, marketing, legal and lobbying expense both in Houston and Austin.

In a little more than two years our lease with Astrodome USA expires and it is extremely important that I learn from you now whether you intend to take a leadership role in developing a business and political coalition to address the Oilers' stadium situation and provide solutions which will enable us to continue to remain competitive on the field and financially viable off the field.

The most recent projections on new stadiums and arenas which will become operational in the next five years only serves to confirm the judgment we made several years ago in determining the need for a new stadium designed for football. Almost daily there are newspaper reports on new stadiums being planned for cities throughout the U.S., but not in Houston.

It is now clear that if the Oilers were to remain in the Astrodome, the following facts would exist shortly after the turn of the century:

1. The Oilers would be playing in the second smallest stadium in the NFL.

2. The Oilers would be one of the two NFL teams sharing a stadium with Major League Baseball.

3. The Oilers would be playing in the fourth oldest stadium in the NFL.

4. The Oilers would be the only NFL team playing in a stadium designed for baseball.

5. The Oilers are, and would continue to be the only NFL team playing in a stadium controlled and operated by the owner of a competitive major sports franchise.

The Honorable Bob Lanier
July 12, 1995
Page 2

The sum total is that the Oilers would be relegated to a vastly inferior position in the NF and it would no longer be possible for us to avoid losing money regardless of how fisc y conservative the team was operated.

No prudent businessman, regardless of the industry, would allow a major asset to be placed in such an uncompetitive and financially disastrous position.

I remain optimistic that you will demonstrate leadership and vision in addressing the stadium problem and I will look forward to hearing from you in the very near future with your response.

With best personal regards, I remain

Sincerely,

Bud

K. S. "Bud" Adams, Jr.
Owner/President

KSAjr/bm

Mayor's letter attached

- S. BUD ADAMS
  President

Houston Oilers

PERSONAL AND CONFIDENTIAL

July 18, 1995

The Honorable Bob Lanier
Office of the Mayor
901 Rugby, 3rd Floor
Houston, TX 77002

Dear Mayor Lanier:

It comes as no surprise to me that I've not received any acknowledgment of my letter to yc of July 12, 1995. You have consistently displayed a cavalier attitude toward any sense of urgency in resolving the Oilers' stadium situation.

Accordingly, I am serving you with formal notice that I'm establishing a firm deadline of Friday, July 28, 1995 for you, in your capacity as Mayor of Houston, to respond in writing that you will either not support the construction of a new stadium for the Oilers, or your written commitment to the following:

1. Your unqualified public support of construction of a new stadium for the Oilers to be built and ready for occupancy by the 1999 NFL season.

2. Your written commitment that the City of Houston will enter into negotiations with representatives of the Oilers no later than August 15, 1995.

3. Agreement to a November 15th deadline for reaching a stadium agreement.

4. Your understanding that in the event an agreement for a new stadium requires a public referendum the cost of financing a media campaign to secure passage of the agreement will the sole responsibility of the private sector.

I want to emphasize that the conditions herein are non-negotiable and I trust you will assign top priority to this issue.

Regardless of any opinions to the contrary, since our initial meeting in June of 1993 I ha dealt in absolute good faith with you and the public officials of Texas. The results of efforts are well documented.

The economic forces which impact professional sports, and particularly the NFL, have chang dramatically in two years. You and others have chosen to ignore the stadium issue while public officials throughout the U.S. have responded in positive and affirmative manners wi olutions to stadium and arena problems.

The Honorable Bob Lanier
July 18, 1995
Page 2

There is no more vivid example of the looming financial crisis faced by the Oilers than the signing over the weekend of Kerry Collins, the Carolina Panther's number one draft pi. quarterback. The new 72,000 seat stadium rising in downtown Charlotte provides Carolina with significant stadium revenue streams enabling them to make lucrative long-term commitments which would be fiscally imprudent and unwise for the Oilers.

We now must sign Steve McNair and based on the realistic projections of the Oilers' revenue it will be done with great difficulty. I'm confident we will sign McNair, but less confident that without a new stadium we will be able to continue to compete for quality free agents necessary to field a competitive team.

I will look forward to hearing from you on or before July 28th!

Sincerely,

Bud

K. S. "Bud" Adams, Jr.
Owner/President

cc: Paul Tagliabue, NFL Commissioner

KSAjr/bm

CITY OF HOUSTON
Post Office Box 1562   Houston, Texas 77251   713/247-2200

OFFICE OF THE MAYOR

Bob Lanier, Mayor

July 19, 1995

Mr. K. S. "Bud" Adams, Jr.
Houston Oilers
6910 Fannin
Houston, Texas 77030

Dear Mr. Adams:

On returning from vacation I have read both your letters of July 12 and July 18.

I've enjoyed being a fan and supporter of the Oilers from the date that they first opened here with the AFL. I've been a season ticket holder and rarely miss a home game.

I supported the Domed Stadium at the time that the Oilers and Astros were its primary backers.

The Astrodome, of course, is a County facility. Currently, both the Houston Astros and the Houston Oilers are prime tenants there. Also, the Houston Livestock Show and Rodeo.

After looking at the new stadium issue during the course of about a year, it is my conclusion that the primary moving party on any new stadium should be Harris County Commissioners Court. They own and operate the Dome. Any possibility of remodeling the Dome to meet your requirements would rest with them. Any adverse effect of a new stadium on the Dome would need to be measured by them.

The opposite is true with respect to the Summit since that is a city facility. Also, in the course of discussion on a new stadium, the Oilers repeatedly advised me that it would only be feasible if connected with the Rockets. The Rockets have repeatedly and decisively said they did not wish such combination, pointing to the San Antonio experience.

Even if the Rockets were included in a new stadium financing proposal, there would still be a significant funding gap to be covered by the City. Legislation, which I supported, to close this gap through various "user pay methods", and state tax abatements did not pass this session. Therefore, we don't have a viable proposition to submit for voter approval, in my opinion.

As you know, our financing flexibility is limited. The hotel room tax is pledged to other debt service requirements. The county share of this tax, for example, is dedicated to pay off the bonds which financed over $100 million of Dome renovations during the 1980's. That is one reason why we don't have the financial flexibility available to some other communities.

Mr. K. S. "Bud" Adams, Jr.
July 19, 1995
Page 2

I have talked to Judge Robert Eckels and he said that he would be receptive to visiting with you.

I hope that you are able to sign McNair and he leads the Oilers to the Super Bowl.

Regards,

Bob Lanier

Bob Lanier
Mayor

RCL/bh

THE NATIONAL FOOTBALL LEAGUE

410 PARK AVENUE.   NEW YORK, N.Y. 10022 - 758-1500

October 29, 1986

Mayor Kathy Whitmire
City of Houston
P. O. Box 1562
Houston, TX 77251

Dear Mayor Whitmire:

It has been brought to our attention that Harris County voters will be asked early next year to approve a $60 million plan to expand and renovate the Houston Astrodome.

As you know, the current Astrodome capacity of less than 48,000 places it last among the 28 facilities in which NFL regular season games are played, some 16,000 below the median in the NFL, and well below the minimum figure needed to qualify a facility to serve as a potential host of a Super Bowl game.

This is our assurance that a firm capacity of 68,279, including auxiliary seating as contemplated, would be very adequate for a future Super Bowl site. Only one domed facility in which NFL teams play, the Silverdome in Pontiac, Michigan, exceeds that figure.

We would strongly endorse the planned expansion and renovation as outlined to us.

Sincerely,

PETE ROZELLE
Commissioner

PR:wdf

USCM POLICY RESOLUTION
AS ADOPTED ON JANUARY 26, 1996

BY: MAYOR BOB LANIER, HOUSTON
    MAYOR MICHAEL R. WHITE, CLEVELAND

PROFESSIONAL SPORTS FRANCHISE LOCATION AND THE
PROTECTION OF LOCAL GOVERNMENTS AND TAXPAYERS

1) WHEREAS, a total of 104 professional major league football, basketball, baseball and hockey teams are currently located within, and supported by, the citizens, fans and taxpayers of 45 American cities; and

2) WHEREAS, many professional sports teams are currently seeking to relocate to other cities or communities and others are rumored to be interested in relocating; and

3) WHEREAS, in order to attract or retain a professional sports franchise, cities are required to make substantial commitments of scarce public funds on a long term basis; and

4) WHEREAS, cities faced with the possibility of the relocation of a professional sports team are compelled to compete with cities desirous of obtaining a franchise, and all are required to make difficult financial decisions; and

5) WHEREAS, a balance must be established between the private interests of team owners to maintain a profitable business and the public interest of the various communities to enjoy the direct and indirect benefits of having a professional sports franchise; and

6) WHEREAS, it is essential to restore some stability to professional sports and preserve its integrity by ensuring that such leagues have the ability to enforce their own rules and the obligation to follow a set process before the relocation of a team is permitted to occur; and

7) WHEREAS, there is a high level of public interest in and support for professional sports for a variety of social, economic and political reasons, and Mayors desire to be responsive to the needs and demands of the public in this regard.

8) NOW, THEREFORE, BE IT RESOLVED that the United States Conference of Mayors endorses and supports federal and state legislation, as well as litigation where appropriate, that will protect the interests of the public, local taxpayers, fans and units of local government in those communities currently supporting, or attempting to attract, professional sports teams; and

BE IT FURTHER RESOLVED that any federal legislation addressing the issue of professional sports team relocations, including public financial or other support, include, at a minimum, provisions:

A. Requiring the leagues to adopt objective standards and criteria governing the relocation of professional sports teams that take into account the business interest of the owner and the public interest of the community; requiring the leagues to base relocation decisions on their set criteria; and providing the leagues with the ability to enforce their own rules; provided that the question of whether the league is following its own rules is subject to reasonable judicial review.

B. Requiring that the public interest component of the league's relocation criteria include consideration of fan loyalty, community support, and bona fide offers to purchase a team and retain it in the existing community.

C. Requiring teams that intend to relocate to give a community adequate notice, and further requiring that, during this period, the league hold public hearings on the proposed relocation.

D. Assuring meaningful protection to those cities or units of local government with existing stadium or facility leases with professional sports teams to prevent the loss of protection afforded such leases and requiring that any relocation decision by any professional sports league or similar organization be based, at least in part, upon consideration of the status of the lease of the city which is to lose its team, or the status of any other legal devices that may affect such relocation.

E. Allowing the use of public ownership of teams similar to the local ownership of the Green Bay Packers.

F. Requiring any professional sports league or similar organization to provide a city or community from which a profitable team has relocated the first option on any expansion the league would pursue exclusive of any expansion fees.

USCM POLICY RESOLUTION
AS ADOPTED ON JANUARY 26, 1996

BY: MAYOR RICHARD M. DALEY, CHICAGO

PROTECTION OF TAXPAYERS
IN THE EVENT OF SPORTS TEAM RELOCATION

WHEREAS, many professional sports teams are currently seeking to relocate to other cities or communities; and

WHEREAS, in many cities public financial support, such as publicly financed playing facilities, special tax treatment, foregone revenue and other forms of public assistance, has been used to attract and retain teams; and

WHEREAS, American cities have spent more than $1 billion building or renovating stadiums and arenas for professional sports franchises; and

WHEREAS, a number of cities are in various stages of completion of major stadium renovation projects with a total value of more than $475 million; and

WHEREAS, professional sports teams have benefited, directly or indirectly, from this public assistance; and

WHEREAS, taxpayers have provided this assistance in reliance on the team's commitment to the community;

NOW, THEREFORE, BE IT RESOLVED that if a team leaves a community prior to the expiration of a stadium lease, or breaks an agreement with a state or local government with respect to use of a facility, that team should retire the proportionate balance of any public debt previously created or incurred, and should repay the proportionate share of any public assistance granted by public entities for the benefit of that team.

BE IT FURTHER RESOLVED that failure to repay should result in the imposition of penalties under federal law. Options for such penalties might include imposition of a federal excise tax equal to three times the public assistance provided which would be rebated to the public entity; loss of tax advantages such as moving expense deduction, executive compensation deduction, deduction for ticket prices and sky boxes.

Mr. HYDE. The Honorable Joe Chillura, countywide commissioner of Hillsborough County, FL.

STATEMENT OF JOE CHILLURA, JR., COUNTY COMMISSIONER, HILLSBOROUGH COUNTY, FL

Mr. CHILLURA. Thank you, Mr. Chairman. I also want to thank Congressman Canady for his introductory remarks and his sincere interest in this issue.

Distinguished members of the committee, my name is Joe Chillura. I serve on the Hillsborough County Board of Commissioners, which represents a county of approximately 1 million people.

Joining me to help respond to questions you might have is Mr. Rick Nafe. He is my version of "Big Dawg," and Rick is right behind me here and will be happy to respond to any questions that you might have after I have completed.

On behalf of our community, I want to express my appreciation to you for scheduling this hearing, and I will do my best to present the views of the folks that I represent back home. The issue you are examining is not simply one relating to the location of an entertainment commodity or a sports team that might be nice to have in a community. Rather, it is one that relates to very real economic issues, and so it unquestionably merits review and action by the U.S. Congress.

Today I want to tell you a story I might find hard to believe had I not been part of it, a story of the Tampa Bay area and our 22-year relationship with our football team, the Tampa Bay Buccaneers. I said "our team" for reasons that will become clear to you as I unravel this story before that red light goes on.

Our team has struggled to be a winner on the football field. However, it has been a consistent winner for the owners. The people in the Tampa Bay area enthusiastically embraced the Buccaneers as a valuable partner that draws national attention, stimulates the economy, and provides exciting sports entertainment for our very dynamic area.

It took years of hard work and determination on our part to bring an NFL franchise to Tampa Bay. We built the 46,000-seat stadium in 1966, and we demonstrated this area was ready to be an NFL community by hosting 13 NFL exhibition games over the next 17 years with an average attendance of 41,000. In 1974, the Tampa Bay area was granted the NFL's 27th franchise.

As part of our pledge of support to the new team, we made a strong financial commitment and approved a major stadium renovation at public expense, increasing the capacity to 72,000. Over the years, our financial and fan support never wavered. Obviously the NFL believed our facility to be of high quality because it was selected to host Super Bowl XVIII in 1984 and Super Bowl XXV in 1991, just 4 years ago.

The people of Tampa Bay have kept the faith with the Buccaneers as they struggled on the football field. Through many lean years the community always remained supportive, perpetually optimistic and eternally expectant for the Bucs to have a winning season. When the new owner announced, quote, a new day in Tampa Bay, end quote, in January 1995, it was welcome news to a community that spent close to a year of suspense following the death of the team's original owner and amidst speculation that new owners would seek to move the team to another area. Palm Beach financier Malcolm Glazer told us, and I quote, the buck stops here, end quote, emphasizing that he was committed to keeping the team in Tampa.

The community responded, and a record attendance average of 59,000 fans supported the Buccaneers' home games in 1995. This is after 11 straight seasons of double-digit losses.

Now, however, our residents fear that the new day for the Buccaneers may not dawn in Tampa Bay but in some other community. The Tampa Bay area and its political and business leaders have done everything possible in the past year to accommodate the new owner and to see what could be done to satisfy him.

First, the Tampa Sports Authority voted to give the new owner the right to rename the existing stadium. The owner then promptly sold the naming rights to Houlihan's Restaurant chain for $10 million.

Secondly, changes were made in the stadium agreement to give the owner a large share of the profits from parking fees, concessions and other revenue.

State legislators, meanwhile, approved a bill that provides up to $60 million in State contributions for a new stadium or to refurbish an existing sports facility. This was a new piece of legislation enacted with the Tampa stadium in mind.

In addition, plans were prepared for the design of the new 65,000-seat stadium costing $168 million. The stadium was designed with amenities that would generate additional revenue requested by the owner. To date, more than $1.1 million has been spent by the good people of Hillsborough County to design and plan a new facility.

Last October, the community kicked off an innovative Bucs charter seat deposit program with an unprecedented pep rally broadcast by all area television stations. Our fans purchased more than 30,000 charter seat deposit tickets in just 1 month's period of time, representing a $20 million noninterest loan to the owner. This underscores the loyal support of our fans for the football team, win or lose.

When the owner said he would not wait for the State legislature to act on additional revenue sources, city and county leaders developed a creative plan to meet his time schedule for a new stadium.

Mr. Chairman, I have about 2 or 3 minutes. If you will give me that time, I would like to complete the statement.

With great optimism, community leaders announced this new financial plan on December 13, 1995, outlining how a new stadium could be built without new taxes, without the need of action by the Florida Legislature, and within a budget of $168 million for a new facility. Much of the funding would come from surcharges placed on all tickets, parking fees and concessions at the new facility.

This plan was rejected within hours after it was announced. Since then, team officials refused to negotiate, and reports in the media continue to show the owners shopping the team throughout the country and in other communities, so gross unconcern by the owner continues to cause unrest among the citizens of our community.

The Tampa Bay community actively sought an NFL franchise and has supported the Buccaneers for more than 20 years. We rightly believe that this is our team. Today our community is frustrated, hurt and angry over the possibility that we may lose this asset, whose economic impact is valued at more than $85 million annually.

That is why we strongly support and commend the efforts of our congressional leaders to protect communities like Tampa Bay when sports teams threaten to move.

We are especially pleased with the introduction of Ohio Congressman Martin R. Hoke's bill called the Fan Freedom and Community Protection Act. This bill would help protect communities like Tampa Bay from abusive actions of the owners of professional sports franchises when they attempt to move a team despite a community's demonstrated history of support.

However, I am compelled to state while we strongly endorse Congressman Hoke's bill in general, we must with all due respect express our strong opposition to one of the bill's provisions. Section 5 would exempt expansion requirements if a sports team relocates within 60 miles. We suggest this be changed to within the same metropolitan area, as in our case a team moving within 60 miles of Tampa may well be in a different community. Such a move would cause us to lose the financial and emotional investment made by the people of Tampa Bay.

We commend all of our congressional leaders who understand the serious and detrimental effects to a community when a sports franchise moves away. That is why we also want to acknowledge the work of Ohio Congressman Louis Stokes, who is sponsoring the Fans' Rights Act. It has many noteworthy provisions, and especially commendable is a provision that would require sports teams intending to relocate to give the community 180 days' notice.

Mr. HYDE. Could you bring your remarks to a close, Commissioner?

Mr. CHILLURA. Just about. I have two more paragraphs.

I suggest that the 180-day notice be changed from 180 days after a full session of the State legislature has taken place, to give State legislatures time to act to assist a local area, should it be necessary.

Our community deeply appreciates the work of this panel, and we look forward to working with you in every capacity we can to get this legislation approved by the House and hopefully the Senate. Thank you, Mr. Chairman.

Mr. HYDE. Thank you very much, Commissioner Chillura.

[The prepared statement of Mr. Chillura follows:]

PREPARED STATEMENT OF JOE CHILLURA, JR., COUNTY COMMISSIONER, HILLSBOROUGH COUNTY, FL

TAMPA BAY AREA AND THE TAMPA BAY BUCCANEERS: A LONG AND MUTUALLY BENEFICIAL RELATIONSHIP

The Tampa Bay Buccaneers professional football team has been a major asset for the Tampa Bay area, both on and off the field, for 22 years. The National Football League awarded the franchise to Tampa Bay in 1974, and shortly thereafter the team was purchased by lawyer-businessman Hugh Culverhouse for $16 million.

Although struggling to be a winner on the football field, the team nevertheless is a consistent winner for the community and the owners. The people in the Tampa Bay area have enthusiastically embraced the Buccaneers as a valuable partner that draws national attention, stimulates the economy, and provides exciting sports entertainment for our dynamic area.

It took years of hard work and determination to bring an NFL franchise to Tampa Bay. The city and county clearly demonstrated this area was ready to be an NFL community as early as 1966 by building a new, 46,000, seat stadium that would meet the needs of a professional football team. From 1968 until 1974, the stadium played host to 13 NFL exhibition games and attracted the attention of the NFL by consistent and enthusiastic attendance at these games.

Community pride was overwhelming in 1974 when the Tampa Bay area received word it would be home to one of the NFL expansion teams. As part of its pledge of support to the new team, the community made a strong financial commitment and approved a major stadium renovation, increasing its seating capacity to 72,000. Other improvements requested by the team ownership were approved as well.

Over the years, the stadium has been renovated at public expense to add more Lounge Boxes, install seat backs, and erect a Jumbo Tron scoreboard. Seating again was increased for a total capacity of 74,246. In addition, major road improvements were made surrounding the stadium. Because of these and other publicly funded improvements and the strong base of fans, Tampa Stadium was selected by the NFL to host two very successful Super Bowls, in 1984 and 1991.

The people of Tampa Bay have kept the faith with the Buccaneers as they struggled on the football field. Through many lean years, the community always remained supportive, perpetually optimistic, and eternally expectant for the Bucs to have a winning season.

Expectations did improve when a new owner was announced in January 1995 and he immediately pledged "A New Day in Tampa Bay!" It was welcome news to a community that spent a tense year following the death of the team's original owner and amid speculation that new owners would seek to move the team to another area. Palm Beach financier Malcolm Glazer, introduced as the new owner of the Tampa Bay Buccaneers at a press conference on Jan. 16, told the community that "The sue stops here," emphasizing that he was committed to keeping the team in Tampa.

The community responded, and a record attendance average of more than 58,600 fans supported the Buccaneers' home games in 1995. The team's win,loss record improved slightly, and now the community has given a warm and sincere welcome to Tony Dungy, the new head coach, who is well known and respected throughout the NFL. In many respects, therefore, the people of Tampa Bay expect the "new day" for the Buccaneers to begin next season. However, they are apprehensive that the new day may dawn not in Tampa Bay, but in some other community.

The Tampa Bay area and its political and business leaders have done everything possible in the past year to accommodate the new owner. One of the requirements to make the team a viable franchise in our community, according to Mr. Glazer, was a new stadium. As a result, business and political leaders rallied around him to see what could be done to make the sues financially viable.

First, the Tampa Sports Authority voted to give the new owner the right to rename the existing Tampa Stadium. Mr. Glazer has since sold the naming rights to the Houlihan's restaurant chain for $10 million. That is money that the Authority could have kept and used for other needs.

Then, the Tampa Sports Authority made changes in the stadium agreement to give Mr. Glazer a larger share of the profits from parking fees, concessions and other revenue. Other incentives also were approved, giving the team a break in stadium rent if attendance fell below 55,000 a game. (Happily, solid support by football fans kept average ticket sales higher.)

State legislators, meanwhile, approved a bill that is crucial to Hillsborough County's proposal to build a new stadium for the sues. The bill provides up to $60 million in state contributions over a 30,year period. The contribution comes in the form of a subsidy program that provides sales talc rebates to help build sports facilities or refurbish old ones. The $2 million per-year rebate is credited to the Tampa Sports Authority, which will use it for construction bonds.

Plans were prepared for the design of a new, 65,000,seat stadium with a price tag of $168 million. The stadium was designed with new club seating, additional skyboxes and other amenities that would generate additional revenue requested by the owner. Already, more than $1.1 million has been spent by the Tampa Sports Authority and the people of Hillsborough County on design and planning of the new facility.

In October, the community kicked off an innovative sues Charter Seat Deposit Program with an unprecedented pep rally broadcast by all area television stations and a goal of selling thousands of season tickets tied to a one,time seat deposit charge. The community responded with more than 30,000 charter seat deposits in one month's time, representing a $20 million commitment from sues fans to Mr. Glazer. This underscores the loyal support of the fans for their football team, win or lose. Mr. Glazer, meanwhile, offered to pay about half the cost of a new stadium.

Another source of revenue for the new stadium was presented a month ago when Tampa International Airport officials indicated their need to acquire Tampa Sports Authority land next to the stadium to control air space and offered to pay up to $25 million.

Throughout 1995 and into 1996, business and government leaders have been discussing a number of revenue options for a new stadium, all the while cognizant of the total economy of the community. Many of the revenue options will need the support of the State Legislature, which meets in the Spring. Because Mr. Glazer said he could not wait that long, city and county leaders developed a creative plan to meet his time schedule for a new stadium.

With great optimism, community leaders announced this new financial plan on Dec. 13, 1995, outlining how a new stadium could be built without new taxes, without the need for action by the Florida Legislature and within the budget of $168 million for a new stadium. Much of the funding would come from surcharges placed on all tickets, parking fees and concessions at the new facility.

This plan was rejected by the owner within hours after it was announced. Since then, team officials refused to negotiate, and reports in the media continue to show Mr. Glazer "shopping" the team in Orlando, Cleveland, Hartford, and Los Angeles. And so, the tension among the residents of our community continues.

The Tampa Bay community actively sought an NFL franchise and has supported the Buccaneers for more than 20 years. Today, the community is frustrated, hurt and angry over the possibility that it may lose this asset, whose economic impact is valued at more than $85 million annually.

That is why we strongly support and commend the efforts of our Congressional leaders to protect communities like Tampa Bay when sports teams threaten to move.

We are especially pleased with the introduction of Congressman Martin R. Hoke's bill, H.R. 2740, called the "Fan Freedom and Community Protection Act." This bill, if enacted, would help protect communities like Tampa Bay from frivolous actions of the owners of professional sports franchises, when they attempt to move a team despite a community's demonstrated history of support. The process which this legislation would establish for a league to use in determining whether to permit a relocation will protect communities against such moves, and the provision that would require a league to expand into an abandoned community would similarly help protect the interests of the community and the league by promoting a stable base of enthusiastic and loyal fans.

However, while we strongly endorse Congressman Hoke's bill in general, we must, with all due respect,express our strong opposition to one of the bill's provisions. Section 5(a) would exempt expansion requirements if a sports team relocates within 60 miles. While we recognize the intent of the provision to allow moves within a community, we believe that in some regions of the country, the provision would exempt moves between different media markets and different communities. For example, in Florida, a team moving within 60 miles of Tampa may well be in a different community, and so should be covered by all of the bill's provisions. Such a move would waste the financial and emotional investment made by the Tampa Bay community.

We also commend other Congressional leaders who understand the serious and detrimental effects to a community when a sports franchise moves away. That is why we also want to acknowledge the work of Congressman Louis Stokes, who is sponsoring the "Fans Rights Act." It has many noteworthy provisions, such as basing team relocation on fan loyalty, community support and bona fide offers to purchase a team and keep it in the existing community. Especially commendable is the provision that would require sports teams intending to relocate to give the community a 180-day notice.

The Tampa Bay community deeply appreciates the concern of Congressman Hoke and Congressman Stokes and their proposals to protect the fans and the communities which have pledged their loyalty and their tax dollars to sports teams, and we offer our enthusiastic support of this legislation and will work aggressively toward its enactment.

TAMPA BAY BUCCANEERS FACT SHEET

1966: October—Construction begins on Tampa Stadium, with 46,000 seating.

1968: August—First of 13 preseason NFL games played through 1974, with 41,000 average attendance.
1974: April—Tampa Bay is awarded the NFL's 27th franchise. December—Hugh Culver house purchases team.
1975: July—Ground broken for stadium expansion to 72,000 seats.
1976: July—Bucs first home game against Miami Dolphins.
1974: January—Tampa Bay hosts Super Bowl XVIII.
1991: January—Tampa Bay hosts Super Bowl XXV.
1994: August—Hugh Culverhouse dies; control of Buccaneers turned over to a three-person trust. November—Trust announces the team is up for sale.
1995: January—Malcolm Glazer agrees to buy the Buccaneers for $192 million. Glazer says new stadium needed. March—NFL officially approves sale of Buccaneers to Glazer. Tampa Sports Authority gives Glazer rights to rename the existing stadium. May—TSA says new stadium to cost $168 million. June—State lawmakers pass legislation making TSA eligible for tax break of up to $60 million over the next 30 years for a new or renovated stadium. TSA announces new financial deal more favorable to sues regarding concessions, parking, rents and other fees. August—Season ticket sales hit 32,000, the second largest single, season increase in Bucs history. Glazer announces he will pay for half of stadium costs. October—Stadium Task Force launches marketing blitz for Charter Seat Deposits. November—Community responds to Charter Seat Deposits, with more than 30,000 sold, representing a $20 million commitment to the Bucs. Community learns Glazer has sold stadium name to Houlihan's restaurant chain. December—Tampa Aviation Authority announces it will pay $2 million to purchase Tampa Stadium property for future airport expansion. City, County, TSA announce plan to finance stadium construction using surcharges on tickets, parking fees and concessions. Bucs say "no" to new financing plan within two hours.
1966: January—Bucs General Manager sends letter to Tampa Sports Authority Chairman criticizing community efforts.

Mr. HYDE. Now we will hear from John "Big Dawg" Thompson, the founder of the Save-the-Browns campaign and the number one fan in an area that has lots of fans. John "Big Dawg" Thompson.

STATEMENT OF JOHN "BIG DAWG" THOMPSON

Mr. THOMPSON. Good morning, Mr. Chairman. Thank you and all the members of the committee, for having me here today. It is really a pleasure to be here, and I want to thank you regarding this important issue to all of us.

The Cleveland Browns are a vital part of our history. Many things have changed over the past 50 years, but not the love and devotion of the fans to our football team.

My testimony is shared by many Cleveland Brown fans and NFL fans around our country. Our team's history is one of the NFL's very best and most important.

The great players, fans and coaches that have come and gone through the years have built this historic team, the Cleveland Browns. Our name, the Cleveland Browns, came from its very first owner, Paul Brown. What a tradition.

Many former players and coaches have made Cleveland their home, as well as many of the current players also make Cleveland their home. These guys are a big influence in our city because of their endless work with so many different charities. They are involved with kids' groups like the Big Brother program, Make A Wish Foundation, United Way, and so many others.

These players also work with the city's Muny Football League, which is very important to about 5,000 kids. You know, some of these inner city kids don't have the money to buy a football, but sponsored by the Cleveland Browns, they get cleats, socks, pads, pants, and they get to go out and compete every Saturday. That gives them self-esteem, responsibility and the stability that those children really need.

Mr. HYDE. John, I saw a commercial one time with Mean Joe Greene of the Pittsburgh team throwing a jersey to one of the kids, and Dennis Rodman with the Bulls does it all the time. Does anybody with the Browns give away their jersey?

Mr. THOMPSON. Yes. But, Mr. Chairman, was he drinking Coke or Pepsi?

Mr. HYDE. Well, it was a kid. It had to be a Coke.

Mr. THOMPSON. No, it is a big part of the players being tied with the children of the cities. I mean, it is just a major part of it.

But getting back to what I want to say today, and I appreciate that, not only does it give the children the self-esteem and the responsibility but, you know, it also tells you that, yes, the Cleveland Browns are a major source of civic pride, and we really don't want to lose that.

I have been a Browns fan for as long as I can remember. I have been a season ticket holder 18 years. The past 10 years I have been dressed like I am dressed today, as "Big Dawg" in the famous Dawg Pound, which is probably the most identifiable section of any stadium, ballpark or arena around the world today, and it was founded by the fans.

In these 10 years, I have been able to meet thousands of Cleveland Brown fans from all over the world. I have had a chance to visit a number of cities while attending Browns games, and at each one of those cities I was able to meet many of the Browns backers that are formed around the country. We have the largest fan-based organization in the world of any professional sports team, and it is pretty outstanding to be able to travel to Tampa Bay, to travel to Houston, to travel to all these cities, Cincinnati, which I have been to all of them, and know that when you get there there are, you know, 10,000 Cleveland Browns fans cheering and getting excited for the football game. We really don't want to lose that.

But, you know, the reason why the fans really need the rights is to protect our investment. And, you know, we paid for the tickets over the years, win or lose; paid for parking, win or lose. We bought the shirts and the caps and the hats, win or lose. We bought the hot dogs and the peanuts, win or lose. You know, we have been there. We have spent the money.

But you know what? That is really not the investment that this is all about. It is more about the investment like me trading NFL cards with my friends, trying to get my favorite Cleveland Browns players, or painting my little NFL electronic football pieces with the Cleveland Browns uniform on them, or entering the NFL's punt, pass and kick as a child and winning the 10-year-old group or, you know, just going around town in my Cleveland Browns jersey with No. 44 on it. That was for Leroy Kelly, and it was only because I couldn't get my favorite player Jerry Sherk's number. It wasn't available at the time. But it was all right because Leroy was my second favorite player.

Or the time as a kid playing grade school football, and having Charlie Hall and Bubba Bean, a couple of ex-Cleveland Browns, come out and, you know, get a chance to referee the game, and at the end have a chance to have them autograph my NFL Shell Oil stamp book from that year. Or when Don Cockroft, ex-Cleveland Brown, came to my grade school and talked to us, and I will never forget the story that he told us. It was about like after he kicks a field goal he would always raise his arms up, more or less to say that the kick was good, but he let us know that when he did that he really wasn't raising his arms up to say that the kick was good. He was raising his arms up to thank God for making the field goal.

Yes, these are the fans' investments that I am really talking about. Fans need rights to protect themselves from men who park on runways in Learjets waiting for secret knocks to sign secret deals, and take away our children's opportunity to have the same investments in the Cleveland Browns or any other football team.

Remember today, ladies and gentlemen and Mr. Chairman, that I am just one fan, and there are hundreds of thousands of NFL fans out there across this country that have the same investments that I do and also have the same feelings. Yes, I think we need rights as fans, but most of all I think we need to get the loyalty from the NFL back to the fans, and I would like to thank you very much.

Mr. HYDE. Thank you, Mr. Thompson, for your very important testimony.

[The prepared statement of Mr. Thompson follows:]

PREPARED STATEMENT OF JOHN "BIG DAWG" THOMPSON

Good Morning, Mr. Chairman and Members of the Committee, it is a pleasure to offer my testimony regarding this very important issue. The Cleveland Browns are a vital part of our history. Many things have changed over the past fifty years, but not the love and devotion of the fans to our football team.

My testimony is shared by many Cleveland Browns' fans and NFL fans across our country. Our team's history is one of the NFL's very best and most important. The great players, fans, and coaches that have come and gone through the years, have built this historic team, the Cleveland Browns. Our name Cleveland Browns came from Paul Brown our first coach. What a great tradition! Many former players and coaches have made Cleveland their home, as well as many of our current players today. These guys are a big influence in our city because of their endless work with so many charities. They are involved with many kids and groups like the Big Brother Program, Make A Wish Foundation, United Way and so many others. These players also work with the City's Muny Football league that is sponsored by The Cleveland Browns. This program gives about five thousand kids an opportunity they badly need. This program gives these kids self-esteem, responsibility and stability. Some of these city kids can not afford a football let alone spikes, socks. shoulder pads, jerseys or helmets. Yes! I think The Cleveland Browns are a source of civic pride that we should not lose.

I've been a Browns fan for as long as I can remember. I've been a season ticket holder for eighteen years. The past ten years I've been dressing like I am dressed today as Big Dawg #98 in the Dawg Pound. The Dawg Pound is probably the most identifiable section of any stadiums ball bark, or arena in the world that was founded by the fans themselves. In these ten years I have been able to meet thousands of Cleveland Browns fans from all over the world. I've also had the chance to visit a number of other football cities, while attending Browns away games. At each game I met thousands of Browns backers. Fans like these are what makes the NFL today. That is why we, the fans, desperately need rights to protect our investment.

Yes, we paid for the tickets year after year win or lose!
Yes, we paid for the parking year after year win or lose!
Yes, we bought the shirts or coats year after year win or lose!
Yes, we bought the hats and scarves year after year win or lose!

But you see ladies and gentlemen that is not the investment I'm talking about! I'm talking about fans personal investments like:

Trading NFL cards, trying to get my favorite Browns players!
Painting my NFL electric football games pieces with Cleveland Browns uniform!

Entering the NFL punt, pass and kick contest and being a winner in the ten year old group!

Wearing my Cleveland Browns' jersey with #44 on it, Leroy Kelly's number, only because my favorite player Jerry Sherk #72 was not available but that was ok because Leroy was my second favorite player.

The time ex-Browns Charlie Hall and Bubba Bean refereed one of my sixth grade football gamest and having them sign my collect able Shell Oil NFL stamp book!

When Don Cockroft came to my school to talk. I'll never forget the story that he told us about how after he would kick a field goal he would raise his arms as to say it was good, but he told us he really was thanking God!

These are the fans investments I'm talking about! Fans need rights to protect themselves from men who park on runways in lear-jets waiting for secret knocks to sign secret deals to take away our childrens' opportunity to have an investment in the Cleveland Browns or any other NFL team. Remember ladies and gentlemen and Mr. Chairman this testimony is of just one fan. There are hundred's of thousands of NFL fans across the country who have the same investments and feelings.

Yes, Fans Need Rights? But Most of All Fans Need Their Loyalty Returned by the NFL Now!

Thank You!

Mr. HYDE. The next witness is Gary Locke the county executive from King County in the State of Washington. Mr. Locke.

STATEMENT OF GARY LOCKE, COUNTY EXECUTIVE, KING COUNTY, WA

Mr. LOCKE. Thank you, Mr. Chairman and members of the committee. I want to thank you for the opportunity to testify and for your holding hearings on this very important issue of national consequence.

I have to say that when I was elected 2 years ago as county executive, I never thought that I would be completely embroiled in baseball stadiums and football stadiums. But King County is the home of Boeing and Microsoft, and Seattle is our largest city within King County.

It is time to bring honor and commitment back to the business of professional football. This chaos in the business of football is killing the sport of football, is betraying fans, hurting local economies and straining the budgets of local governments. It is robbing our communities of their sense of community. Just within the last year, five teams have moved or have announced plans to move. Enough is enough. This madness in football, of abandoning loyal fans and communities, simply must stop. We simply cannot continue to let owners pit one community against another in the endless pursuit of luxury skyboxes and Taj Mahal stadiums.

More communities deserve NFL franchises, but not at the expense of existing communities like Seattle, Cleveland, Houston, and Tampa Bay. If order is not restored, more local governments will be coerced into paying hundreds of millions of dollars of taxpayer money into new stadiums or improved stadiums out of fear of losing their existing franchises.

The Seattle Seahawks have been one of the more successful and exciting franchises in the last 19 years. The Seahawks reach a fan base in five States of the Pacific Northwest, including Alaska, as well as the Province of British Columbia.

For almost its entire history, the games have been sold out and there have been waiting lists for season tickets of almost 20,000 people. Our fans have made so much noise in our Kingdome that they have called the fans the 12th man on the team and a jersey in honor of the fans was retired.

King County has invested more than $100 million in improvements to the Kingdome since it was first built in 1976. As any good landlord, we want to continually upgrade our stadium, but we will not be coerced into making those improvements out of fear of the team leaving.

We have been negotiating in good faith with the Seahawks' ownership for improvements to the Kingdome, but their demands constantly changed. The Seahawks actually have a lease that runs for an additional 10 playing seasons in our Kingdome. Our contract with the Seahawks say that money damages are never adequate to compensate us for any breach of the contract and that the only remedy is specific performance, namely mandatory enforcement of the provision of the terms of the lease, that is, to play 10 more years in our Kingdome facility.

Yet as we speak, the owner of the franchise, Mr. Behring, is in southern California trying to find the highest bidder who will build him a new stadium with luxury skyboxes and club seats. He told us just five days ago that he had decided to take his franchise out of the Northwest and head south to his home in California, and there was nothing that we could offer him that would change his mind. Within 3 days, his moving vans were removing office records and training equipment. Fans were so caught off-guard and caught by surprise and felt such a deep sense of betrayal that they formed a human chain to try and stop the trucks from leaving.

This problem cries for national solutions. When teams feel free to leave communities that have invested emotionally and financially in them over the decades, something is clearly wrong.

Help us protect our communities which have invested hundreds of millions of dollars, public dollars, in the stadiums. Help the National Football League get its house in order by giving it a limited right to control the movement of franchises. Help our communities remain strong and vibrant by requiring owners to give us 180 days to find a local buyer to keep our teams within our communities.

In King County, we are not looking to the Congress to save the Seahawks. We have a valid lease and we have filed a lawsuit to enforce it. The Seahawks have actually offered our community a million dollars a year for the next 20 years or until a new NFL franchise comes to our town. They have asked us to negotiate a graceful exit. We said, no thanks. There simply is no grace in betraying the trust and the loyalty of fans and communities. We simply cannot be bought.

We can be a catalyst for change. We can be part of the national solution that comes from the Congress. We in the Seattle area are standing up for communities and sport fans across the Nation. If this team can leave Seattle with 10 years left on its lease, what is to stop any other team from betraying other communities across this Nation?

This is not just about football. This is about honoring commitments and contracts. It is time that we insist that football owners honor their contracts, honor their commitments to communities and fans across the United States.

Thank you very much, Mr. Chairman.

Mr. HYDE. Thank you, Mr. Locke.

PREPARED STATEMENT OF GARY LOCKE, COUNTY EXECUTIVE, KING COUNTY, WA

Mr. Chairman, and members of the committee, thank you for the opportunity to testify and for holding hearings on this important issue. It's time to bring honor and commitment back to the business of professional football.

This chaos in the business of football is killing the sport of football, betraying fans and hurting economies of ideal communities.

It's robbing our communities of their sense of community.

Within the last year, 5 teams have moved or announced plans to move.

Enough is enough. This madness in football of abandoning loyal fans simply must stop.

We simply cannot continue to let owners pit one community against another in the seemingly endless pursuit of luxury sky boxes, and Taj Mahal Stadiums.

More communities deserve NFL franchises but not at the expense of existing communities like Seattle, Cleveland, and Houston.

The Seattle Seahawks have been one of the most successful and exciting franchises in the league for 19 years.

The Seahawks reach a fan base in five states of the Pacific Northwest, including Alaska, as well as the province of British Columbia.

Our fans made so much noise rooting for the team they have been called the "12th man" in the Kingdome.

King County has invested more than $100 million in improvements to the Kingdome since it was first built in 1976.

The Seahawks have a valid lease that calls for ten more playing seasons in our Kingdome.

Yet as we speak, the owner of our franchise, Mr. Ken Behring, is in Southern California trying to find the highest bidder who will build him a new stadium . . . with luxury skyboxes and club seating.

Mr. Behring told us only five days ago that he had decided to take his franchise out of the Northwest and head south to his home in California.

Within 3 days, Mr. Behring's moving vans were removing office records and training equipment.

Fans were so caught by surprise, and felt such a deep sense of betrayal, that some formed a human chain to try and stop the trucks from leaving.

The problem cries out for a national solution.

When teams feel free to leave communities that have invested emotionally and financially in those teams over decades, something is wrong.

When children can no longer count on supporting the teams their parents and grandparents have supported for decades, Something is very wrong.

Help us protect our communities which have invested hundreds of millions of tax dollars into stadiums.

Help the National Football League get its own house in order . . . by giving it the right to control the location of franchises.

Help our communities be strong as communities . . . by requiring owners to give us 180 days notice to find a local buyer who will keep our team in our communities.

In King County we are not relying on Congress to save the Seahawks.

We have a valid lease, and we have filed a lawsuit to enforce it.

But we can be a catalyst for change, part of an enduring national solution that comes out of Congress.

We are standing up for communities and sports fans across the nation. If we let this team leave Seattle with ten years left on a valid lease, what is to stop any other owner from betraying any other community.

This is not just about football. This is about honoring your contract and your commitments.

It's time we insist that football owners honor their contract and honor their commitments to communities and fans all across our nation.

Mr. HYDE. Mr. Conyers.

Mr. CONYERS. Thank you, Mr. Chairman. These were illuminating statements from all of our distinguished witnesses. I am glad that they began this discussion.

Let's take a moment and go back to my friend from Wisconsin, Mr. Sensenbrenner's reminder to me that today's hearing has no relationship to the problems of baseball's antitrust exemption, and that their exemption has eliminated any relocation problems in that sport.

First of all, the title of this hearing is "Full Committee Hearing on Sports Franchise Relocation." It might interest the Members to know that baseball's antitrust exemption has not prevented 10 relocations since 1953, beginning with the former Brooklyn Dodgers and the New York Giants and continuing through the Washington Senators not once, but twice.

I would like to ask Mayor Lanier if he thinks baseball's exemption will ultimately keep the Astros in Houston, or whether it will be used to threaten the fans of Houston with possible relocation to northern Virginia?

Mr. LANIER. Clearly, the exemption would be used in the manner you suggest. As a matter of fact, it is my judgment that Major League baseball is just kind of watching what happens to the NFL right now. If the NFL gets away with it, the baseball owners are saying, you know, why shouldn't we get $200 to $300 million a copy from the taxpayers per franchise also? That is the very conversation that is going on as we sit here.

Mr. CONYERS. Well, they are looking and watching.

Commissioner Chillura may recall several years ago when the White Sox used the threat of moving to Saint Petersburg as leverage for building a new taxpayer-subsidized stadium in Chicago, and Commissioner Locke may want to discuss the difficulties Seattle has experienced when they lost the Pilots and almost lost the Mariners even with a baseball antitrust exemption. So let's not play football today and think that baseball isn't involved.

The whole sports industry is the subject of today's hearing. Sports franchise relocation, it is happening in one, it could happen in another. If any of you have any comments, I would be delighted to hear from you.

Mr. CHILLURA. Congressman Conyers, I guess you will recall in my testimony one of the real problems that we face in our community—

Mr. HYDE. Would you push the switch to turn on the microphone?

Mr. CHILLURA. One of the real problems we face in our community is the amount of time it takes to put a deal together to accommodate the ownership. We are now in the process of asking our legislature to give us enabling law to create new funding sources. They won't wait. So it is that leverage and that inability to respond in a reasonably timely manner that our plight is all about, and that is why we believe that Mr. Hoke's bill makes a lot of sense, particularly the retroactive aspects of it.

Mr. CONYERS. Good point.

Mayor.

Mr. LANIER. If I might say also, the cities have roughly 108 or a little over 100 Major League franchises. We think that because they have protection from being competitive, that we are looking at a demand of $200 to $300 million per franchise over the next several years, plus the abandonment of old stadiums.

That is a $20 to $30 billion tax or charge on our citizens to be able to enjoy something they love, and there is no reason for it. No other facet of the entertainment business charges that to come, because we sell out. We are a big metropolitan area. We grew 300,000 in the last 4 years, over 4 million people, the 10th biggest TV market. It is only because they are protected by law from competition that they are able to do that.

And we have terrible needs that you put alongside that $20 to $30 billion, and let me tell you, you can't manufacture money. The tooth fairy doesn't bring it. If you put it here you can't put it there, I don't care how you slice it, in order to try to, you know, not get run out of town by the voters.

Mr. CONYERS. Thank you very much.

Did Mr. Locke have a comment on this?

Mr. LOCKE. Yes. Congressman Conyers, I think part of the solution and the responsibility rests with the individual communities. We in Seattle, for instance, have specific clauses within our contracts, with the teams, that give us the right within so many days to find a local buyer. That was the case with the baseball team and we were able to secure local ownership, which saved the team for our community.

I do, however, believe that some of the provisions in Congressman Hoke's bill give incentives to communities and to the NFL to control the movement, and to say that if teams do move that there is an opportunity or first right for those communities to have another team. So I think it has to be a combination of a balance of incentives as well as responsibilities of local communities to have very tight contracts. But we also need the league to have the ability or the power to enforce those contracts for us.

Mr. CONYERS. I thank you very much for your testimony.

Mr. HYDE. The gentleman's time has expired.

The gentleman from California, Mr. Moorhead.

Mr. MOORHEAD. Thank you, Mr. Chairman. I sympathize with cities that are talking about losing a football franchise. We have lost two in Los Angeles. One of them left some time ago when they went to Anaheim, but I feel they had a right to leave. The Raiders had never brought their heart to Los Angeles. They had only brought the team there. They weren't loyal to the community, so why should the community be loyal to them?

If they won't build a coliseum or some other stadium fit to play football in, and if the owners cannot make that demand, I don't know how you are going to ever have decent places to play. The community owns the stadium and they have to make it such that people will want to play there.

My field is basically intellectual property and trademark so that is what I am interested in.

Mr. LANIER. What?

Mr. MOORHEAD. Trademarks, that is what I am interested in primarily. Is it fair to say that the trademark provisions of the bill will level the playing field for local communities by requiring by law what communities could not otherwise negotiate? In other words, is one problem that the only way that a city can negotiate the rights to a team name is by mandating it in Federal law for all cities and taking a property right away from the team owner? Mayor Lanier.

Mr. LANIER. Really and truly, I think I am sympathetic to that provision as it relates to the Browns because they seem to treasure the name "Browns." I am going to tell you today the name "Oilers" has less value in Houston, and if I gave it up I wouldn't be giving up a fortune.

Let me just say to you that the one provision of these bills that would protect Seattle, Cleveland, Tampa Bay, Houston, or L.A. is a provision in Congressman Hoke's bill that says if you do move out of a city, and particularly a city that is profitable, but if you do move out of a city then they need to offer a franchise, expansion franchise, to that city within a certain time length, provided we pay the regular price and we have people willing to come forward and invest $200 million. I don't think that is a hardship on the league, but it is the only thing that really protects cities where these owners already made up their minds to flee.

Mr. MOORHEAD. Later we will hear testimony from the International Trademark Association that the trademark provisions proposed are unconstitutional by taking property without compensation. If that is correct, do you believe that communities would be willing to pay the fair market value for the trademark team name when the team left and relocated?

Mr. LANIER. I would let the jury set that. Let me just comment, I would let a jury set the value of the Oiler name, and pay for it out of my pocket on a gamble that it would be low.

Mr. LOCKE. Well, that is really not a relevant issue in our case because the owners have said that they are willing to leave the name, the logo, the pictures and the trophies behind.

Mr. MOORHEAD. It is to the bill, however, that has been introduced.

Mr. LOCKE. Well, I have not had an opportunity to really review that portion of the legislation, but I clearly agree with Mayor Lanier that the most compelling part of the legislation is the requirement that the teams or the communities where the teams are vacating are entitled to another franchise at the earliest opportunity, if those communities are able to demonstrate their financial viability, and obviously they have been able to demonstrate that they were good markets for teams since they had teams in the past.

Mr. MOORHEAD. Mr. Chillura.

Mr. CHILLURA. Well, I do not get heartburn over a team taking the name and the logo with them as much as I do the inability to respond and to negotiate.

I, too, believe that the most salient aspect of the Hoke bill is the provision that, within 3 years, that you be afforded up to a year's period of time to present a viable offer to the NFL. I think that is the most important part of that legislation, and whether or not it dilutes the ability of the ownership to make the profits that they make is a question for this committee to debate.

I think that that provides an incentive, if you will, to stop the moving. I don't particularly like that aspect of it, but it is a good incentive to have the 30-some owners think twice about whether or not they are going to approve a move and then begin to dilute their ability to earn the billions that they do earn from television rights, for example.

Mr. MOORHEAD. Thank you.

Mr. HYDE. The gentleman's time has expired.

The gentleman from Virginia, Mr. Scott.
Mr. SCOTT. Thank you, Mr. Chairman.
Mayor Lanier, you kept talking about $600 per seat. Is that per season in these—not even close?
Mr. LANIER. No, I think that is per ticket, per game. I was told that with respect to the Nashville tickets.
Mr. SCOTT. The mayor of Hampton Roads has been toying with the idea of getting a major league franchise. We have got hockey and baseball in my district. But the public cost has—not major league but other teams—the public cost has gotten so big that it has been one that we haven't been able to get real strong public support for. In fact, we had a deal with the Redskins, but——
Mr. LANIER. I saw that.
Mr. SCOTT. But the support, local support or, excuse me, opposition got so strong that the deal couldn't go through. The Maryland Legislature is right now in a very contentious situation with both of the teams that they are trying to attract.
Mayor Lanier, you said there are other things you could do with the money.
Mr. LANIER. Yes, sir.
Mr. SCOTT. Now what would you do, if you lose the team, what would you do with the money that you didn't spend trying to get them?
Mr. LANIER. Pretty much our priorities are, we go into the inner city. We have stopped the exodus in the inner city. We are now gaining 5,000 population a year in the inner city. We completely rebuild 14 neighborhoods a year, with streets, streetlights, sidewalks, water, sewer, police; accompanying them, also, 20 parks a year. We have 100,000 youngsters in city-sponsored sports in those areas. We would add to and accelerate that program. We would go into the schools.
Mr. SCOTT. You would have to stop that program——
Mr. LANIER. No. We would have to take that amount of money from it. We wouldn't stop it. We would keep on. But we still have about close to a billion dollars of deferred maintenance to do, and if I had $200 billion, I would spend the $200 billion on that deferred maintenance in the neighborhoods and in the schools rather than on a football team, because without any tax money the football team is profitable, and they are doing it in a stadium the NFL claims they used to like.
Mr. SCOTT. Well, if it is so profitable, was there any willingness to have public funds, have public ownership, that is——
Mr. LANIER. Oh, yes. I think if——
Mr. SCOTT. That is a public offering.
Mr. LANIER. I think absolutely. What I like about the whole bill is——
Mr. SCOTT. I mean private but very broad ownership.
Mr. LANIER. But I think the mayors passed a resolution at the Conference of Mayors recommending that the Green Bay type ownership be allowed. I strongly support that. If we got an expansion team into Houston, I would propose that the ownership be distributed much along the Green Bay formula. Then I think you would have local ownership. You would have local pride and it would be

tied to the city. And Green Bay has been profitable all of these years.
  Mr. SCOTT. Mr. Locke, what financing did you get for the baseball team? Was that a broad-based or more individual-based ownership?
  Mr. LOCKE. Well, the owners are from the community and there is a large number of members in that ownership circle.
  Mr. SCOTT. Does baseball have the prohibition against public ownership?
  Mr. LOCKE. I am not familiar with the——
  Mr. SCOTT. The people behind you are nodding yes.
  Mr. LOCKE. All right. But, nonetheless, with respect to the funding that we were able to obtain for a new baseball stadium, our initial ballot on that measure for a general tax increase was narrowly defeated by a thousand votes. Had 600 more people voted affirmatively, or had the vote taken perhaps a week later, given the dramatic victories of the Seattle Mariners and Ken Griffey, Jr., I think it would have passed.
  But, nonetheless, the ultimate funding solution was not a general tax increase but primarily user fees and assessments and fees or taxes on discretionary spending, including vanity license plates; an increase in the sales tax on purchases for cocktail lounges and taverns and restaurants, as well as special lottery tickets and an admissions tax to the new baseball stadium.
  So most of the taxing for the new baseball stadium is really targeted at discretionary spending without a general tax increase. And we were proposing to look at ways to raise some funds for improvements to our Kingdome for the Seahawks, but Mr. Behring constantly changed the demands and I think was constantly upping the ante, almost forcing us to say no.
  Mr. HYDE. The gentleman's time has expired. The gentleman from Pennsylvania, Mr. Gekas.
  Mr. GEKAS. I thank the Chair.
  I suppose we all agree that the city of Baltimore, and the State of Maryland, made an economic decision in wooing or dealing with the Cleveland Browns's ownership to relocate to Baltimore. They did so ostensibly because of job creation, economic development, new revenues in thousands of different ways that would enure to the benefit, they feel, to the people and to the governments of the city, and of the State.
  My question to the gentleman from Houston is, that same consideration, it seems, looms over your head. In other words, your economic decision to preserve jobs, to preserve economic development, economic activity that comes along with the Oilers remaining there, would preserve the tax base, would it not? Are you not risking loss of a tax base in not meeting this $150 million or $200 million effort?
  Mr. LANIER. I don't think so. I think the economic benefit is marginal. I think it is a large emotional benefit that the citizens like. My objection, sir, is not competing in the free market. I grew up on that. I cut my teeth on that.
  My objection is that you have monopoly pricing. I have the same choices if you let the light company in and give them all exemptions. We have uniform electric companies throughout the country,

and they charge me a monopoly price. I either have to pay it or shut off the lights. That is what I object to.

Mr. GEKAS. I understand that you are saying to me that the decision, that the considerations back of the Baltimore, MD, decision, just for a moment, is not based on the prospect of great job creation?

Mr. LANIER. It is not one I would make, no, sir. If that is their judgment, I would respectfully disagree with it. And I don't think they acted lawfully, because at the time the Cleveland team was under lease, and I question whether they are not guilty of tortious interference with contract. There has been a $300 million lawsuit filed on that.

Mr. GEKAS. I am puzzled by that. I thought that some of the incentives to teams who go to cities or municipalities that want to attract the new team or an old team relocating is based on economic development and economic considerations. And the tax base—

Mr. LANIER. There are differences of opinion there.

Mr. GEKAS. OK. Let us move to Mr. Locke for a minute. You say that in the lease that is now obtaining between the Seahawks and the counties—is it the county?

Mr. LOCKE. Correct.

Mr. GEKAS. Provides for a 10-year lease, and you are applying for the courts for specific performance. Is the specific performance tied in with an injunction such that you would prevent the move or call for damages?

Mr. LOCKE. No. Actually ours is a lease that has 10 more years remaining on it to the end of 2005. The lease specifically says, if there is a breach by another party, compensation is not sufficient, and the only remedy is specific performance. So we have gone to court and obtained a preliminary restraining order with a preliminary hearing scheduled within the next 14 days to compel the team to abide by the terms of the lease and play its regular season games in our facility until the year 2005, as required by the contract.

Mr. GEKAS. I heartily endorse that effort on your part. If a lease calls for a team to remain there, and specific performance can apply, I support that fully.

Let me ask you, what are the lawyers for the Seahawks saying as to the efficacy of that lease? Undoubtedly they are saying that they can break it, but on what basis?

Mr. LOCKE. They are saying that because of seismic concerns of our facility, that Mr. Behring does not feel that he could morally allow or in good conscience allow fans to come into the Kingdome, given their belief that it is seismically unsound. That is why he is moving to L.A. to play in their stadium.

Mr. GEKAS. I respectfully suggest that we have another hearing on the seismic proportions of the west coast. I am hoping that a lesson will be learned by all with the success of such a preliminary injunction or injunction for specific performance that you have stated.

Mr. LOCKE. If I could add with respect to the economic impact. We have done some studies that show the economic impact of the Seattle Seahawks in our area is about $90 million. But half of that would be lost if the team left the area, primarily because in our situation we have a lot of people from out of state or out of country that come to our games.

But the real point is that you have to always question these economic values, and perhaps that is what Baltimore was looking at because, if I do not go to a Seahawks game or a football game, I may go bowling or shopping. So you have to question the total value of new money coming into a community because of the presence of professional sports. What happens is that oftentimes it is displaced money moving from buying a beer or pizza or going shopping and moving that money into going to a game. Therefore, if the team is lost, that money may remain within the community but in a different way.

Mr. GEKAS. I thank the gentleman and yield back the balance of my nontime.

Mr. HYDE. The gentlewoman from Texas, Ms. Sheila Jackson Lee.

Ms. JACKSON LEE. I thank the Chairman very much.

Mr. Locke, I don't know, from a Biblical perspective I would rather enter the kingdom. Maybe you might raise that point.

I think Houston had a lot of emotions. I think the mayor captured it. There were those who were frustrated, angry, charged up, and those who wanted to sit down at the bargaining table and pass any cup that they could in order to ensure that our Oilers stay. There is a great love for the team and its members, and I think the mayor made a very valuable point. There is history here, maybe not the 50-year history of the Browns, Mr. Thompson, but certainly starting out with $25,000 and having a team like the Oilers that we have loved through the good times and the bad times.

I think it is important to clarify why we are here today, to distinguish that we do have a compelling interest or a national interest that bears on economics and bears on fairness. We would hope that the Federal Government limits its intrusion, except for times when it is pervasive throughout our Nation.

Mayor, you mentioned, I am going to ask some general questions that I would like to pose to the collective panel, but I think it is important, Mr. Chairman, to note a letter in Mayor Lanier's testimony written to a prior mayor from Pete Rozelle. It notes the capacity of our Astrodome of 48,000 places. It cajoles and encourages us to become more competitive as it relates to NFL facilities, noting that we are some 16,000 seats below the NFL, and indicating that this is our assurance that a firm capacity of 68,279, including auxiliary seating as contemplated would be very adequate for a future Super Bowl site, one that we are still waiting on. Only one domed facility in which the NFL teams played, the Silver Dome in Pontiac, MI, exceeds that figure.

This, of course, is a letter that is about 10 years old, but it is still a letter upon which any local government would place reliance on. If we work toward this goal, we will be in good stead. So, the questions I would like to pose have to do with helping to define our national interest or concern on a national level.

First point: When we engage in trying to attract or keep our teams, there is a lot of public money that is offered. Construction, rehab, whatever else, infrastructure work that may be necessary, those are tax dollars. As I understand, we expend these dollars and in actuality have no investment rights in that business. That means that the city leadership, citizens, short of Green Bay, have no stockholder relationship. You have invested money, but we have no ownership rights.

I would imagine, if any major corporation comes into town, they build their infrastructure, their housing, their buildings. They may pay taxes, but they don't ask us to build their office buildings. So how do you respond to that? We pay our taxpayer dollars, and in essence do we have an investment? Are we part owners? Therefore, maybe there is that requirement or that study that we are now doing that that antitrust exemption is relevant because we do not have the investment product based upon the investment dollars.

The mayor made a very interesting point that I have a concern about, and that is again referring to the very narrowly directed antitrust exemption. If, for example, we had the technology industry come to Houston and they were not treated well, or a technology company, one, and they were not treated well for whatever reason, we didn't pave a street in front of their building for the employees to get in, and they decided to relocate to another area or another State. Could they organize all of the technological companies and say, Don't go to Houston? What I am hearing is that we have that situation with the NFL owners.

So the cities are being hit in both instances. I would appreciate it if the gentlemen collectively would answer that question, and, Mr. Thompson, you could answer it as well. I am going to go to Mayor Lanier first. The fans have invested money. What are they getting?

Mr. LANIER. Pretty much what current academics say, when you are putting taxpayer money into building a stadium, is, you are really not buying the stadium, because you don't have much use for it when they leave. You have an empty stadium that costs you something to keep up. What you are doing is renting a team. They have shown great skill in trying to break their leases.

We had to sue the owners to get specific performance for 2 years. They had to sue the Browns, and they are undertaking to get specific performance for 2 years. Seattle wants to breach; they have got 11 years. That is endemic, and they have fairly skilled—you are renting a ball club. You have no ownership interest.

On the second point, a very profound point, and that is in any other business that I am familiar with, if you have a profitable opportunity, the way the free market works is, somebody pulls up, you have a successor in there by nightfall exploiting that economic opportunity. I have been in business. In this business they tell you, unless you come with $200 million to $300 million of your taxpayer money, they will leave, even though the business is profitable. They tell you to your face, they will block another team coming in.

So there is no economic reality there. There is simply the protected people acting in that manner because they are protected from the normal rules and consequences of free market competition.

Mr. HYDE. The gentlewoman's time has expired.

Ms. JACKSON LEE. Mr. Chairman, would you allow just a brief word from the others? I asked a collective question. If they could

just briefly say yes or no on those two points, I would appreciate your indulgence.
Mr. HYDE. All right. For a yes or a no.
Mr. CHILLURA. I am a public official. There is no such thing as a yes or a no.
Mr. HYDE. That comes as a shock to me.
Mr. LOCKE. Congresswoman Jackson Lee, absolutely yes.
Mr. CHILLURA. My response very quickly is that I agree with everything you say. One of the advantages of the Hoke legislation is the definition of bidder. It gives—and I don't know if that was intentional or not, but it gives the community the opportunity to buy into the entire process and the system. In my community I believe that I could sell that concept if this legislation were a reality.
Mr. HYDE. The gentleman from Ohio, Mr. Chabot.
Ms. JACKSON LEE. If the fans have invested in these teams by your tax dollars and what you are willing to contribute.
Mr. THOMPSON. They have definitely, but it has been under their own choice to do that. They get a chance to vote on that, and I think that it is very important that basically the most important thing here is that the NFL does give, or the Major League baseball, who also has started this over 4 years ago with the Cleveland Indians when the American League President Bobby Brown came to Cleveland and said, either you folks are building a new open air stadium for baseball only or the Cleveland Indians are leaving Cleveland. That was not a point that came up before.
Yes, it is very important that the city that has a team has an opportunity to maybe purchase that team from the owner for whatever reason, its economical reason, for leaving be. Whether it is for mismanagement or whether it is for just to prosper more, he should give the rights to that city, in due time, instead of going out and signing a deal behind the city's back who actually did vote for a stadium to house his profits.
Ms. JACKSON LEE. I thank the chairman for his indulgence. Thank you very much.
Mr. HYDE. Mr. Chabot from Ohio.
Mr. CHABOT. Mr. Thompson, your testimony, I thought, was particularly moving. You are obviously an example of a loyal Cleveland fan who has given a lot of your time and a lot of your life to supporting a home team that means an awful lot to you and others in Cleveland. It is people like you who are really hurt the most when a team up and leaves, as the Browns are talking about doing in going to Baltimore.
As you possibly know, there was talk about the Cincinnati Bengals going to Baltimore. A deal was not struck, and apparently the emphasis shifted to Cleveland. Cleveland and Baltimore cut a deal.
Within our State, there now is some speculation about Cincinnati moving up to Cleveland at some point. I assume you talk to a lot of fans and a lot of other people up there. I would like to hear what your comments might be about that, knowing how moves have hurt you and other folks up in Cleveland.
Mr. THOMPSON. I have heard a lot of mixed emotions about that, but my particular feelings, and a number of other folks that I know, feel that would just be—the Cincinnati Bengals, who have become one of the Browns's major rivals. Due to the situation in

my testimony, reading about how the Cleveland Browns became the Cleveland Browns, by Paul Brown's name, and letting go of Paul Brown by Art Modell, which started the new franchise in Cincinnati.

So, personally I would not like to see that. I think it is important that the NFL really looks at their organization and sees that we cannot have teams moving from point A to point B just for money purposes. And just for, you know, new loges, new club seating, PSL's, and so forth.

I think that the proof that that is the reason for the moving is on the table. They really have to address their own organization, which to my feeling, if Cleveland were to lose the Cleveland Browns—and I really hope that they haven't lost the Browns, but if we were to lose the Cleveland Browns, that we would be given an expansion franchise immediately. And if not, we really don't want to see another team come into Cleveland from another city to go through the same heartbreak that we went through.

Although I listened to some of the panel—people up here say that the name doesn't mean much to them, the Oilers or the Tampa Bay Buccaneers. I disagree with that because I have been in both of those cities, and I know what those Oilers fans are like, and they love their blue.

I know what those Buccaneers fans are like. You go into a place like Tampa and people wonder—Tampa is a town where there are a lot of transplants. I can go to a Tampa football game, and it may not sell out just with Tampa fans, but you can go there to see the Chicago Bears. There are just as many Bears fans as Tampa fans because it is a transplanted area. But it is still an NFL city, and it supports the team that is there. And so it deserves the Tampa Bay Buccaneers. I think it is important that they keep the name Tampa Bay Buccaneers, and I know that the people of Tampa enjoy that.

Mr. CHILLURA. I take back what I said.

Mr. CHABOT. For the record, Mr. Thompson, we want to keep the Bengals, too, and, like you, we very much do not want them to move to Cleveland. We do certainly sympathize with you.

One of the key factors involved here is the element of greed. It is one thing when a team is not being supported in a city, and we have seen that in some instances where there hasn't been sufficient fan participation, where people are not buying the tickets and not going to the games. But Cleveland certainly was certainly not that type of case.

The thing that bothers me in the Baltimore case is that you have a city that had its team a couple of years ago go to Indianapolis in the middle of the night, and we know the trauma that that city went through, and now here we have the same type of trauma happening to Cleveland. I think every city would like to avoid that type of situation.

It is obviously a very unpleasant matter. The thing I wonder is, at what point do fans in this nation look at this as a plague on all your houses? We saw it in the baseball strike where they struck for a long, long time, and finally when they came back, people stayed away in droves. Attendance was 20 percent off in many cities, and even more in some cases.

At some point I think the NFL is going to have to get the message here and be aware that the patience of fans in this country is limited. I think we are coming very close to seeing that limit. I don't have too much time. I noticed that the mayor is nodding his head.

Mr. LANIER. I agree with that. After the Oilers announced they were going to leave, attendance fell off drastically, and I, as you, in Houston would prefer an expansion team. That is why I like the Hoke bill. We don't want to see another one of these renegade owners move. If it comes, it comes.

I will say it this way: You don't get the absolutely best class of owner moving. When you look at it, these are not the guys with a bunch of Super Bowl rings on their hands. These are the guys that are not making it where they are, and part of the reason is because they are not very good managers. If somebody offers them $35 million, they haven't made much operating, in moving expenses.

Mr. HYDE. The gentlewoman from California, Ms. Lofgren.

Ms. LOFGREN. Thank you, Mr. Chairman.

As I am listening to all of you, I am sorting through what the Federal Government could do that would make it easier for local governments not to be held up by sports franchises nationwide, not just the individual issues that you are facing in trying to deal with—I was in a local government for many years, and you have to cope with what is before you, I understand—but what could we do that would lessen this pressure, this craziness that requires cities and counties to have to compete and throw money at sports teams.

Mr. Locke, you are a county executive.

Mr. LOCKE. That is correct.

Ms. LOFGREN. In California it is an elected position. Are you elected or appointed?

Mr. LOCKE. In my county, it is elected. In most other counties in Washington it is appointed—there are three others that are elected executives.

Ms. LOFGREN. It may not be fair to ask this question to an elected official, which is why I asked. I did appreciate the mayor's comment that really the attachment to the team was emotional and really a financial case couldn't be made.

I know that in local government, and in my own community, the emotional attachment to sports is very high. I like the San Francisco Giants and watch them, and there was recently an issue where fans wanted to bring the Giants to San Jose. Elected officials are reluctant to speak out against that. Some do, or maintain their silence because it is such an emotional issue for fans.

And yet I wonder, Mr. Locke, if you would agree, if you had to choose between having your high school seniors be No. 1 in the Nation in SAT scores and No. 1 in the Nation in advanced placement tests versus your team being No. 1 in the Nation, which would be more important to your economic future as a community?

Mr. LOCKE. I have actually said it very publicly during the debate in the campaign for discretionary funding and tax increases for the baseball stadium. Clearly, if our football team or baseball team were to leave town, the economy of the Pacific Northwest would not fall apart. If Boeing left town, or Microsoft or the University of Washington left town, it would devastate our communities. Clearly, there are equally if not more compelling priorities facing our local governments by way of roads, bridges, mass transit, fighting crime, educating our children.

I would never profess to say that sports is the number one priority of our local governments, but it is of a national issue, given the investment communities with limited tax dollars have already put into our stadiums, hundreds of millions of dollars. For owners then to say, "Unless you put in another $200, $300 million, we will abandon you," that puts us into a very, very difficult position. That is why we have basically said we were willing to make some improvements to the Kingdome, but we would not do so with a gun to our head.

Mr. LANIER. We took essentially the same response in Houston, and said openly that neighborhoods and parks and youth programs and education were a higher priority to us than retaining the football team with extra money, with them wanting to break their lease, even though holding the team was important, and we were willing to be judged on that basis.

I think the public, although they love the football team, by and large supports those priorities. But your other question I would like to respond to is, what is the single most important thing that was treated?

I think the provision in Representative Hoke's bill that says if you leave a city, you provide an expansion team within a certain number of years, provided they are financially OK, and they put up close to $200 million or something like that for a new ball club. What that means is, an owner wanting to move cannot go and get the $50 million moving expenses. There will not be these transfer fees, and he will not get all of this money that doesn't relate to anything in terms of value for the citizens except his own avarice.

But that one provision, in a city like Houston, or I think the gentleman just said like Cleveland or like L.A., I talked to the mayor there, with all of this I would really prefer to wait for the expansion team to come and have a brandnew ball club. We don't like this process that is going on and would like to find a way out of it.

Ms. LOFGREN. My time has expired, and I have appreciated your input. Thank you.

Mr. HYDE. The gentleman from Florida, Mr. Canady.

Mr. CANADY. Thank you, Mr. Chairman. I want to thank each of the witnesses for their testimony. Each of you provided a very good perspective on this very important issue.

I would like to focus now on a particular point that was raised by Mr. Chillura. Mr. Chillura expressed support for Mr. Hoke's bill in general, but raised an issue about the 60-mile exception in section 5 of Mr. Hoke's bill.

I wonder if any of the other members of the panel have any thoughts about the 60-mile exception in that provision of the bill? That is the section which I think has been identified as the heart of the bill, which requires expansion teams to be made available to communities under certain conditions.

Mr. CHILLURA. My reason for asking that that be amended or deleted, we are in the situation now where adjoining areas are competing for the Buccaneers' attention. I could tell that you it would not be to the NFL's benefit if they approved a move to the Orlando area, primarily because we are the 13th television market in the country and Orlando is the 35th or 36th. Somebody might not agree with that, but that is the information that I have been provided by research.

I believe that provision in the bill would affect the Chicago Bears' move to Gary, IN, which I think is about 60 miles or less away. Admittedly, it is in another State.

In another particular instance, I believe that it would essentially nullify the amount of effort that we put into finding the time and the resources to save this team from moving, and that provision simply undermines our ability to continue with the time allotted to find a viable solution.

So the 60-mile limitation is one that we have expressed to Congressman Hoke, and we would hope that the panel would consider deleting that.

Mr. HOKE. I wonder if you would yield for just a moment?

Mr. CANADY. Happy to yield for your comments on that subject.

Mr. HOKE. The situation with respect to Tampa Bay, as well as the Chicago situation, was brought to my attention by Mr. Flanagan and Commissioner Chillura after we originally dropped the bill. I think the points they make are well taken and will be corrected at markup.

Mr. CANADY. Thank you very much. Again, I have no additional questions. I do appreciate each of you being with us. I would like to especially thank Commissioner Chillura for coming up for this hearing today, and for his leadership on this issue in Tampa Bay.

Mr. SCOTT. Will the gentleman yield?

Mr. CANADY. I would be happy to yield.

Mr. SCOTT. Mr. Chairman, I had one additional question I wanted to ask Mr. Thompson, if I could.

How do you get into the Dawg Pound? Are the seats reserved? Do you have to agree to be a dog to get in?

Mr. THOMPSON. They are sold as any other normal ticket. I personally have season tickets, but anybody who wants to go up to the ticket booth when tickets are available at the beginning of the year can purchase Dawg Pound tickets.

Mr. SCOTT. They are designated as Dawg Pound tickets?

Mr. THOMPSON. Well, they are now.

Mr. SCOTT. You know you are getting into the pound when you buy the ticket?

Mr. THOMPSON. Absolutely. It is a separate section of the stadium. It is basically the end zone, which would be the east end zone of Cleveland Stadium. It is a completely separate section of the stadium.

Mr. GEKAS. Will the gentleman yield?

Mr. CANADY. I yield to Mr. Gekas.

Mr. GEKAS. I too ask Mr. Thompson, on the question of loyalty, which you have exhibited to the nth degree here today, didn't Paul Brown go to Cincinnati?

Mr. THOMPSON. Absolutely.

Mr. GEKAS. If Jim Brown had been traded to X, would you have accepted that? I mean, these are questions of loyalties.

Mr. THOMPSON. Probably not. When Bernie Kosar was traded, we didn't take too good to that. I don't think that would have been acceptable at all.

Mr. GEKAS. So you would agree that the question of loyalties and all of this community spirit that is involved in the emphasis on one team has its exceptions. Like Paul Brown himself was an institution in Cleveland, and all of a sudden he appears in Cincinnati.

Mr. HOKE. Would you yield on that for a moment?

Mr. THOMPSON. Mr. Congressman, wait.

Mr. GEKAS. Mr. Canady has the time.

Mr. THOMPSON. I have an answer for that, and my answer is that coaches come, coaches go; players come, and players go.

Mr. GEKAS. But the teams you don't want to go.

Mr. THOMPSON. That is right. The teams don't come and you don't want them to go.

Mr. CANADY. I yield to Mr. Hoke.

Mr. HOKE. I think it is important to point out that there is a big difference between divorce and rearranging the furniture.

Mr. HYDE. In the nick of time, the gentleman's time has expired. The gentlewoman from Denver.

Mrs. SCHROEDER. Thank you, Mr. Chairman. I find this interesting, because bottom line is we are supposed to be trying to figure out is there something we can do here. So the question is, what can we do? Or are we just having a hearing?

I hear several things. In a way it is almost like sports fans have discovered there is no such thing as Santa, that sports are not about sports, they are about big bucks. I think we all know that the big bucks in sports come from TV, not from where they are located.

So I guess my first question, Mr. Thompson, what is going to happen to the people in the dog pound? Are they going to follow the Browns on TV once they move? What are you going to do?

Mr. THOMPSON. Definitely, my answer to that is no.

And I wanted to add to a point before, when I said that we would take a franchise, a new franchise, expansion franchise. But at this point the people that I have talked to, and a lot of them are loyal fans and have been loyal fans for a long time, feel that if we have to wait for something like that, that our loyalty has been thrown out the window by the league.

I think that we do realize that that aspect has come into play, and believe you me, there are a lot of other ways that we can spend our Sunday afternoons, and I am sure that is what we would do. Life goes on. Football is not our life. It is definitely a lot of fun and it is a major part of our life. We spend money, like I said, to go and enjoy ourselves and bring our kids and let them enjoy themselves, but if it is at those kinds of stakes it is not worth it. There is a lot more to life.

Mrs. SCHROEDER. So you are looking for a get-even time with these owners who have a heart the size of a swollen pea?

Mr. THOMPSON. No, I don't, Not at all. I disagree with that. Take Art Modell. I have heard a lot of negative things about Art Modell over the years. But, as I said, the Browns have done a lot. It was the Cleveland Browns who sponsored the Inner City League. That was Art Modell. He has done a lot for the city. I understand that he is in a financial crunch, or his situation, but he can get out of that real easy by selling the team to a local interest, and there are plenty of local interests who are willing to buy the Cleveland Browns from Mr. Modell.

My suggestion is that there should be some kind of a law or some kind of trust with the NFL to where if a situation like this comes up, that there is an opportunity for a city to put together—and obviously if it cannot be the city purchasing the team, the fans themselves, then a local owner would be willing to buy that team and keep it where it is. That is the way it should be, so the tradition goes on.

If you break the 50-year tradition of the Cleveland Browns, you are breaking the trust and loyalty of the fans and it cannot go on. That ends it. It ends everything. It may be good for the kids growing up to have a football team to watch and enjoy that fun. In Cleveland, football is a big part. We have the Hall of Fame down the road. You get a gene in Cleveland when you are born there. It is a big thing.

Mrs. SCHROEDER. It sounds like it might be shrinking, though. The thing that I think was interesting is that you were very consistent in saying "renegade teams" or "runaway teams" or whatever you want to call them. That is not what you want. You don't want to try and lure one away from another city.

Mr. THOMPSON. Absolutely not.

Mrs. SCHROEDER. There are two things happening here. Obviously this is a supply and demand type of thing. Once they come in, then a city has a reason to keep as few teams as possible because that means it is even better for their economic status, the fewer of them that there are. But it also means that they could be used more as a pawn in this game, and fans kind of get lost in all of that.

We sit here, we listen to the generic sports thing, whether it is baseball or anything else. The owners come in and say, "You know we made all of this money on TV, and so then we paid all this money for wages and everything, and now we are not making enough money, so now you have to find a way that we can make even more money," and we go round and round and round. I would just say as a policymaker I get very frustrated as to where does this all end and what is it that we are supposed to do. Do you see what I am saying?

Mr. THOMPSON. Absolutely.

Mrs. SCHROEDER. It is all very interesting, but are sports entitled to this very special exemption from antitrust? Should they be able to hold their monopoly that tight? How do we really talk about these things, or should sports fans all start boycotting TV and get them where they hurt?

Mr. THOMPSON. There is a real easy answer to that. They do deserve those exemptions if they prove they are going to use those in an honorable way. They said this in the beginning, they would run their organizations in an honorable way, and they are not doing that by what they are doing right now. The facts are on the table. It is up to them to make the decision, and if they are not willing to do it, that is basically why everybody is here today.

Mrs. SCHROEDER. That is the problem. If they played by their own rules, this would not happen. They are not. What can we do?

Mr. HYDE. The gentlelady's time has expired.

The gentleman from Ohio, Mr. Hoke.

Mr. HOKE. Mr. Chairman, I didn't get to the part in my testimony that described what is the most important part of my bill, and I want to describe it. I really appreciate your obvious thoughtful analysis of some of it already, and I want to get feedback.

First of all, I think it is important for everybody to know that nothing in the bill prevents owners from moving. There is nothing that says a team has to stay in a city, and I think Mr. Moorhead might have misunderstood that.

What the bill does provide is that if a team relocates, then the league has got to grant the abandoned city an expansion franchise if the city identifies a qualified investor, and the hurdles there are pretty high. If that investor is found, then the league has 1 year to provide a new expansion franchise. If the league refuses to do it, it loses the antitrust exemption that was granted by Congress in the 1961 act for 1 year, and pays a fine of treble damages.

Let me characterize what I think this means for communities with pro sports teams. First, it is going to give real leverage in negotiating with owners who threaten to leave because if the owner leaves, the community controls a replacement franchise. In other words, the owner's threat of "my way or the highway" becomes very hollow when the city can respond, "Fine, please leave. We have already been contacted by three investment groups who want to own your replacement franchise."

Pressure on the owner is going to be generated most persuasively not from his or her own conscience but from the other owners, because they are going to have now, for the first time, a direct personal self-interest in restraining expansion. With the expansion comes the dilution of their slice of the broadcast revenue pie.

Secondly, suppose that a community loses a franchise. Under my bill, instead of being pressed to steal a team from another city or made to compete in a bidding war to win a franchise, which we know can cost taxpayers hundreds and hundreds of millions of dollars, the community would in essence have control over a sports franchise provided that it can identify these investors who believe that the market is going to support a pro team. This will allow cities to entertain offers from various investors and strike the best possible deal for their fans and taxpayers.

One option that is contemplated by the bill is the Green Bay option. It has been a model franchise. There you have public money, private money, and you have an incremental approach to the improvement of their stadium over a period of time. They make money. Nobody goes to bed in Green Bay, WI, wondering whether the owner of the Green Bay Packers is going to steal their team overnight.

It is amazing to me as that as I watched the other people speak glowingly of the Green Bay model, I watched the representatives of the NFL behind you begin to look apoplectic about the possibility of that being the case nationwide in this league. But I have to tell you that the handwriting is on the wall. That is the better model.

I think, for the record, people should know that it is not public ownership in the sense that the city owns the team. They don't. There are 3,500 private shareholders in a public corporation, and that is the model for that ownership.

At the same time, my bill does not force leagues to put teams into communities that can't support them or won't support them, or don't, because the market test for the new investors is substantial. First of all, the investor has to pay 85 percent of the last franchise expansion fee to the league itself. In the case of the NFL, that was $140 million.

Second, the new owner has to capitalize the team in an amount sufficient to be financially viable. And the fact is that if a community has not supported the team in the past, it is going to be difficult to locate investors willing to take several hundred million dollars on a flyer. Maybe in the days when franchises cost less than 10 million bucks that would have been the case, but not at these prices in today's market.

In short, I think the provision puts the cities and the fans back in the driver's seat or at least levels the playing field with the owners. I think that a few moments of reflection shows how dramatically it changes the balance of power between the cities and owners. It is the only bill that provides a market-tested mechanism to restore a team to a city if an owner decides to skip town.

I wonder if you agree with this characterization of it. Commissioner Chillura?

Mr. CHILLURA. I totally agree. I said earlier that that incentive, if you will, built into the bill in itself should solve this problem. Once that bill passes, I think it creates a check and a balance between the NFL and the community and the community and the NFL. Hopefully, you would never have to exercise that, but I think that is the beauty of your proposed legislation, is that it builds in those incentives. Several have asked what can you do on this panel. Support this bill.

Mr. HYDE. The gentleman's time has expired. The gentleman from California, Mr. Bono.

Mr. BONO. Thank you very much, Mr. Chairman.

If I may address the mayor, thank you for coming.

Mr. LANIER. Thank you.

Mr. BONO. I just want to get a general picture, because this is relatively complicated. As far as, No. 1, how you feel about a lease, if you have a lease with a team and if that lease expires, do you have any objection to them, if they want to move on, moving on? Is that an issue?

Mr. LANIER. There are two issues. No. 1, when they have a lease, I think they ought to comply with it. And No. 2, if they don't, I think they ought to be subject to a specific performance lawsuit, and people that infer with it subject to tortious interference with the contract lawsuit.

If the lease expires, No. 2, I think since they enjoy this protection from competition and you have an undersupply of ball clubs, that the provision of Mr. Hoke's bill ought to apply. Right now they can leave if they wish. I think the provision of Mr. Hoke's bill that would let—for example, if the team did move from Chicago to Gary, instead of putting Chicago in the position of a predator with respect to its other sister cities, an expansion team would be provided to Chicago within a reasonable time if they pay the fee to the league and if they come up with owners.

Mr. BONO. Basically, as I understand it, if I can ask Mr. Hoke, in the lease situation, if it has expired, if the local city can match the bid of the new city, then what you are saying is then they should have the first option and stay where they are; is that correct?

Mr. HOKE. That is pretty much correct. What it really does is, it prevents the shotgun from being put to the old city's head in a "my way or the highway" type of approach. It really creates an atmosphere in which people have got to work it out together, and because there will, I think, probably reasonably be some public money in these agreements for stadiums. But at the same time, the balance of power now is so one-sided and so tilted that the cities have no way to protect themselves.

Mr. BONO. Yes. Mayor, being a mayor myself from a small city, Palm Springs, we had the Angels for 18 days every year. That was an agreement between the city, because Gene Autry lived in Palm Springs and he loved it, and so we built a little stadium and we had them every year for many years, 20 or 30. They would give us 18 days that they would play in Palm Springs.

When I was mayor, they wanted a bigger stadium, they wanted an improved stadium, and the improvements and what they requested, I knew I was looking at $25 million. They said $15 million, but it was $25 million, I guarantee you. I said, "I will see you later," much to their dismay and shock, because there was no way that the revenue that we would receive from having them play there on an annual basis would ever recoup that $25 million.

So ultimately, they left, and I took a lot of heat. But I didn't feel that I could justify that to the citizens of the community. I know that the big boys play hard ball, and cities are left with dealing with this hard ball.

It seems to me that if most of the projection could come on the front end of the lease portion, that it would be the best part of the negotiation. If you could get an agreement and pretty much stick to that, because we have got the question of free enterprise and having the right to do whatever you want to do, as well, regardless of whether they are making money or not. A lot of dollars.

I guess I am out of time, but just a couple more questions.

If a team is forced to stay in your town but can do much better somewhere else, do you still feel that they have to stay in this particular area if the price is matched? I mean, suppose they want to move to a different city, that they could double their income on a weekly basis or whenever they play at home.

Mr. HOKE. The bill doesn't prevent them from doing that.

Mr. LANIER. Tell them goodbye.

Mr. BONO. Tell them goodbye? I have no problem with that.

The last thing I am very sensitive to, I have been a song writer for many years and dealt with copyright and trademark, and when you build up a trademark, it has tremendous value. It appears to me that if I created that trademark, I owned it, perpetuated it, I marketed it, that it should be mine.

What happens with a trademark, because it is not tangible, so to speak, people have trouble with understanding that it is a chair or a table or a car—and who owns that? If the team indeed owns that, then how can you say, well, give us that trademark?

Mr. HOKE. Can I answer?

Mr. BONO. Sure.

Mr. HOKE. Very briefly, I promise. The only thing I would say is that it was never Los Angeles Sonny and Cher. It was never San Diego Sonny and Cher or Palm Springs Sonny and Cher. It is the Cleveland Browns, the Houston Oilers. Those names are connected inextricably every single time they are used, and the trademark becomes part of the city name. That is the real difference there.

Mr. BONO. Are the owners saying they want to keep the city name? Is that what is happening? Because when the Raiders left, they changed the city name but stayed the Raiders, so I guess that is the confusion I have here.

Mr. HYDE. I hate to break up this seminar, but the time is long expired.

The Chair recognizes Michael Patrick Flanagan for a brief 5 minutes.

Mr. FLANAGAN. Thank you, Mr. Chairman. I promise to take a brief 5 minutes.

Before we get lost in an emotional haze of who owns the team and who has a proprietary right in the name——

Mr. HYDE. Will the gentleman yield?

Mr. FLANAGAN. Yes, Mr. Chairman.

Mr. HYDE. You know, it is sad, but I haven't heard a word about the St. Louis Browns and their trademark and whatever happened to them.

Mr. FLANAGAN. My goodness, Mr. Chairman, I think that predates me. I am finding most things here do.

What I think we are dealing with here is a basic issue of contract law. I am compelled to offer this.

Because of the broadcast antitrust exemption granted by Congress and because of other nuances of trademark law, I believe that Congress has not only permitted, but mandated, that one of the parties in this local contract is an extremely unequal bargaining power, and consequently can compound particular issues in a contract, stadium rebuilding, short leases and other whatnots from a local government, in an interest to not only maintain whatever revenues come from a franchise being in that community or locality, but also in the interest, and the very sincere and warmhearted desire of fans like Mr. Thompson, to continue to have that particular team there.

Mr. Hoke's bill seeks to level that playing field by providing that with the antitrust exemption offered in the 1961 act, that the promise that was on the come at one time, which is that there will be stability in the league, which by any measure simply has not happened, that we will now compound that as a requirement for that exemption under contract law.

As participants in these local contracts, and gentlemen who make decisions about whether we will spend hundreds of millions of taxpayer dollars in order to lure a team or keep a team, I would like to have perhaps just a quick and brief discussion amongst, or by, each of you about the unequal bargaining power that you have endured, your difficulties in circumventing it and your frustration in trying to compound a good lease.

Mr. Locke, I guess you have been the most successful in propounding an excellent lease, despite having been in the position where the team did not have a warmth, largesse, or feeling for the community to offer a lease so the team might stay, gentlemen?

Mr. LOCKE. If I could start off, I would say that just as we have a lot of laws promulgated by the Congress to try and level the playing field with respect to consumers, with respect to rights of rescission, that clearly we are at a disadvantage, all local governments, in dealing with professional sports owners.

That is why the provision of Congressman Hoke's bill tries to level that playing field. It doesn't discourage owners from going someplace else but it provides some disincentives, or incentives to the league itself to compensate those communities that have invested hundreds of millions of dollars toward stadiums.

Mr. FLANAGAN. In your estimation, has the Federal Government of the United States, with its broadcast antitrust exemption or whatever else, placed you in this unfair bargaining position, is really the question I am asking.

Mr. LOCKE. No, I am not saying that the Federal Government has placed us into this difficult position, but we need that help and we would welcome that relief.

Mr. LANIER. I think without question the statutes have placed cities in an almost impossible bargaining position. First, television sharing rights allow them to amass billions of dollars of power from the television stations. Then, second, when they merged the two leagues, we had competition then between the AFL and the NFL. If they moved out of one good city, the other league would move back in. As a matter of fact, if you split them back into two leagues, I will go home happy; or you repeal all of the antitrust laws and let them compete, I will go home happy.

They have got over a billion dollars a year advantage in the first exemption, they are allowed to create a monopoly league in the second advantage, and they beat us over the head with it to where you have very little—this hearing here is one of the few places where we have any recourse at all or any voice at all.

Mr. LOCKE. If I could follow up with one point, the concern that we have and our frustrations or doubts are whether or not the league itself will sort of put its own house in order, and to the extent that the legislation gives greater authority to the league to control the renegade owners, then we would welcome it.

Mr. CHILLURA. Well, I think the legislation, every aspect of it, with the exception of the amendments, will create the level playing field. And I think my colleagues on the panel, it would be redundant to repeat what they said, but there is no question that Federal intervention should not occur until entities like this become abusive. I think they have become abusive and Federal intervention is necessary now to assist the cities and the communities that are literally coerced into submission.

Mr. FLANAGAN. I thank the panel, I thank the Chair, and I yield back the balance of my time.

Mr. HOKE. Mr. Chairman, I just wanted to particularly thank John Thompson for coming from Cleveland. I found out he is actually a constituent from West Park, OH, and I appreciate his——

Mr. HYDE. I hope he votes for you regularly.

Mr. HOKE. I hope he does, too. I didn't ask him. Maybe I should have.

Mr. HYDE. We are going to adjourn for luncheon and be back in 1 hour sharp. I said 1 hour, which will be 1:22, and we will start promptly. We have two distinguished panels left: Mr. Tagliabue, the commissioner of the NFL, Jerry Richardson, the new owner of the Carolina Panthers; and Prof. Gary Roberts, Prof. Andy Zimbalist, and Bruce Keller of the International Trademark Association.

However, before we break, Sheila Jackson Lee has a question she wishes to propound.

Ms. JACKSON LEE. Only to the mayor, because we mentioned the letter that Pete Rozelle signed to the city a few years ago. How many seats do we now have in the Astrodome?

Mr. LANIER. About 63,000, and there was an offer to the league to raise that number. We satisfied Rozelle's letter. It is the same number of seats they are proposing in Nashville, roughly.

Ms. JACKSON LEE. Thank you, Mr. Mayor. Thank you, Mr. Chairman.

Mr. HYDE. We will be back in 1 hour.

[Whereupon, at 12:22 p.m., the committee recessed, to reconvene at 1:22 p.m., the same day.]

Mr. HYDE. The committee will come to order.

Our next panel consists of National Football League Commissioner Paul Tagliabue and Mr. Jerry Richardson, owner of the new expansion team, the Carolina Panthers, in Charlotte, NC. Commissioner Tagliabue has been commissioner of the NFL since 1989. Prior to that, he represented the league as an attorney in several important areas, including expansion, franchise moves, and antitrust litigation. Of course, Commissioner Tagliabue's most outstanding achievement was playing basketball for the Georgetown Hoyas in 1961-62, following in my small footsteps.

Aside from being one of the two newest owners in the National Football League and a former Baltimore Colt, Mr. Richardson also chairs the stadium committee for the league. I understand Mr. Richardson will not be making a statement today, but will gladly answer any questions the committee may have.

And so, Mr. Tagliabue and Mr. Richardson, would you assume the table.

Mr. Tagliabue.

STATEMENT OF PAUL TAGLIABUE, COMMISSIONER, NATIONAL FOOTBALL LEAGUE, ACCOMPANIED BY JERRY RICHARDSON, OWNER, CAROLINA PANTHERS, CHARLOTTE, NC

Mr. TAGLIABUE. Thank you, Mr. Chairman. We very much appreciate your invitation to appear here today and the opportunity to address the legal and business uncertainties that continue to face professional sports leagues, particularly under the antitrust laws, which is the focal point of this committee's hearing today.

I am very pleased to have Mr. Richardson with me for many reasons, but I will just mention two briefly. No. 1, he is a former NFL player who played for the Baltimore Colts and I think other than Mr. George Halas, he is the first person to become a principal owner of an NFL team who started in the NFL as a player.

More to the point perhaps, he put together the expansion team in the Carolinas and they built a stadium with over $180 million of private funding, which is an indication of what is going on in the marketplace today as we strive to bring our stadiums up to current standards. And so he can speak to those issues very well.

There is a widespread perception today that perhaps there is an unprecedented level of financial stress and economic conflict in sports, what with work stoppages and franchise-hopping, player free agency and so on; and we submitted a 20-page statement which addressed many of those points. I would like to focus very specifically on the antitrust issue and try to explain it as simply as I can.

When Commissioner Rozelle was here before this committee in the early 1980's talking about the decision of the Federal court in Los Angeles, which had prevented the NFL from keeping the Raiders in Oakland, which in many ways is the source of the problem here, he was accompanied by George Halas, then the owner of the Chicago Bears. And I believe you were present, Mr. Chairman, when Mr. Halas said in very simple terms that a sports league is like a wagon wheel. The league itself is the rim; the teams are the spokes. They all have to be firm; they all have to be held together. They all have to be strong in order for the league to be effective, just as a wheel has to have a strong rim and spokes to roll.

What has happened in this particular area is that antitrust court precedents are treating the spokes of the wheel, namely the teams, as if they are independent competitors of each other, when they are not, in fact, independent competitors. They are business partners. So what has happened as a result is that the NFL's very strong record of franchise stability, from the late 1950's and early 1960's through 1980, has been eroded because of a growing uncertainty under the antitrust laws of the league's ability to deal with the issues that are presented in this area.

It is a clear issue. The source of the problem is clear from a legal standpoint. Teams are in the league as business partners, but the courts treat them, for purposes of section 1 of the Sherman Act, in an anomalous fashion, giving them the rights of independent business competitors. So a member of the league can turn around and sue the league and say the league's decisionmaking is restraining my ability to compete. It is as if the spoke is asserting the rim is restraining where I am in the wheel, and that is the source of the antitrust problem.

It is for that reason that we would support a narrow exemption from the antitrust laws which would recognize the league as the enterprise. It is not so much an exemption as it is a recognition that the league is the enterprise, not the individual teams.

I see that the light is on, and I will stop there.

Mr. HYDE. If you have—because of the prolixity of the previous witnesses, if you have something you really would like to add, please do.

Mr. TAGLIABUE. Well, the only other thing that I would add is that in addition to the legal issue, the antitrust issue which I have just identified, there are competitive issues here. We are operating in a very competitive sports entertainment marketplace, and secondly, there are economic issues here arising from cost escalation.

On the competitive side, it struck me this morning, and I don't mean to be critical because I understand very well the views of the Tampa Bay representative and other representatives, but in the west coast of Florida area, where Tampa Bay is located, one of the major problems that we face and they face is that they have gone from one major league team, the Tampa Bay Buccaneers of the NFL, to four. They added the Magic in Orlando and the NBA, which is 60 miles away, and they added the Major League Baseball and the National Hockey League in St. Petersburg. So an area which is not heavily populated is now seeking to support four franchises, not one. That is a very serious competitive environment and a major change in the environment.

In Cleveland, the city built $685 million worth of facilities for competing forms of entertainment—Jacobs Field for baseball, Gund Arena for the NBA, the Rock and Roll Hall of Fame, the Science and Technology Museum, and the Browns were left out. That is a major competitive disadvantage.

In Seattle, and I very well respect what the county executive said about the lease issue, which is a substantial issue, but by the same token, they built a new arena for the NBA and they have committed to a new stadium, $320 million for baseball. So those are competitive factors.

One final word on the cost side. Under our collective bargaining agreement, which we secured in order to have labor peace with our players—a long-term deal, and we did it to avoid a work stoppage, which we don't second-guess ourselves—we believe we did the right thing; but our costs have escalated dramatically with free agency.

Talk about the Green Bay Packers. They may not be viable, long term. It is a delusion to use the Green Bay Packers as an example. The Packers, in the new environment, have had a player cost increase in the last 2 years from $30 million a year to $45 million a year. If that continues, we are going to see tremendous pressures on a franchise like the Green Bay Packers.

The Packers have ceased operations in one of their markets for financial reasons, Milwaukee; they used to play three games there, as the chairman knows. They stopped that because they couldn't afford to get the low revenue that they were getting in Milwaukee compared to the higher revenue in Green Bay, and they couldn't continue the Milwaukee operations in the current economic environment.

So to sum up, I would say there are three things at work here. No. 1, the legal issue, which I identified as the section 1 Sherman act issue; No. 2, the competitive issues relative to other sports and other entertainment; and No. 3, the economic issues, particularly cost escalation, that are at work, creating the pressures we are all facing.

[The prepared statement of Mr. Tagliabue follows:]

Prepared Statement of Paul Tagliabue, Commissioner, National Football League

Mr. Chairman and members of the Committee, I appreciate your invitation and the opportunity to address the legal and business uncertainties that continue to face professional sports leagues, the communities in which they operate, and sports fans across America.

In many respects, those uncertainties are more profound—and more troubling—today than they were over a decade ago, when the Judiciary Committee last considered whether the internal decisions of a professional sports league—including a league's decision on where to locate its teams—should be treated for antitrust purposes as a "contract, combination or conspiracy" among independent economic competitors. Since that time, professional sports leagues have continued to be subject to antitrust concepts that, ignoring economic reality, ultimately undermine the public interest. Without a clarification of the governing antitrust principles by judicial decision or congressional action, that situation is bound to continue.

CURRENT CONDITIONS IN PROFESSIONAL SPORTS

Today there is a widespread perception—and sometimes deep concern—that professional sports involve unprecedented levels of financial stress and conflict, often reflected in complicated court battles or other dying legal disputes. The controversies include impasses as to planned or proposed new stadiums; concerns about "bidding wars" pitting community against community or "franchise hopping" in the location and relocation of teams; prolonged conflicts (including work stoppages) between leagues and their players' unions; and a steady diet of sports, business, and legal debate on related issues, all of which are of intense interest to fans and the public at large.

While the specific aspects of the stadium and team location controversies often differ by state or region, a number of considerations, in one measure or another, are generally involved in the mix.

First, there are obvious and significant differences in the size and characteristics of the communities or "markets" in which a league's teams operate. These produce significant differences in revenue potential among teams, no matter how well they are managed. In addition, at any given time, about one-half of a league's teams have below average won-loss records and are therefore vulnerable to declines in fan interest. (This requires a league structure that assures the stability of all teams even when they are in a losing cycle.) The differences in individual team revenue potentials are affected—and often aggravated by changes in larger economic circumstances (e.g., demographic changes, shifts of population, changes in industrial activity, plant closures, or "down-sizing"). Nonetheless, and despite differing market conditions and team revenue levels, in order to provide an attractive entertainment product, the members of a professional sports league must compete on the field with a reasonable degree of comparability or equality of opportunity.

Second, in the NFL there have been dramatic changes in the past three years in the terms and conditions of player employment. These changes resulted from player-sponsored antitrust litigation that challenged collectively-bargained limitations on "free agency" and player movement. The new provisions include a costly, League-wide commitment to revenue sharing with the players through their union and extensive, unrestricted "free agency" for veteran players. While this collectively-bargained agreement has brought "labor peace" to the NFL, these new operating conditions are presenting the NFL's teams, particularly those with average or below-average local revenues, with unprecedented and severe financial challenges.

Third, there has been a steady increase in the number of professional sports franchises operating in the various leagues throughout the United States. There is vigorous competition for the interest and spending of consumers on sports and entertainment generally. This competition is often intensified in particular markets by new teams, by the construction of new facilities with attractive fan amenities, and by other such factors. I will address this issue in more detail below.

Fourth, many of the professional baseball and football stadiums throughout the United States were constructed as dual-purpose stadiums during the 1960s when the nation witnessed an explosion of interest in professional sports. (During that time, for example, the American Football League emerged and, with the endorsement of Congress in 1966, ultimately merged with the NFL. The number of professional football teams therefore increased from 12 in 1959 to 26 in 1970.) Now, many of those stadiums are in need of extensive renovation or replacement.

Fifth, there have been significant changes over the decades in federal, state and local policies with respect to the use of tax receipts or tax exempt bonds in the financing of public facilities, including sports stadiums. These changes include the use of other sources of public funding, such as lotteries, for stadiums and the privatizing of stadium construction costs in some communities through various additional charges to fans in the form of seat "premiums" or "licenses." In addition, the occasional use of public funds on a selective or preferential basis for new stadiums or arenas in one sport has aggravated conditions for competing franchises that lack new facilities.

Finally, confusion, inconsistency, and uncertainty about federal antitrust standards as they apply to the location and relocation of sports teams continue to be a major problem. Coupled with the vagaries of venue as a factor in the outcome of civil litigation, this circumstance has left both sports leagues and communities seeking to retain such teams with difficult choices and little predictability in assessing the likely outcomes of alternative courses of action.

Because of the direct bearing of this latter issue on your inquiry, I will address it at some length below, followed by a discussion of the intense economic competition for the sports and entertainment dollar.

THE TEAM RELOCATION ANTITRUST ISSUE

A professional sports league is an unusual business entity because it creates and markets a single, jointly produced entertainment "product." The National Football League, for example, produces athletic competition among 30 separately owned clubs, none of which can produce and present that product on its own. The NFL's sports entertainment product competes in the marketplace with other sports leagues, each of which also creates a single, jointly-produced product, and with other entertainment producers of all kinds.

To encourage strong local ties and operations, and in an effort to ensure the integrity of their competitive performances on the playing field, each NFL franchise is held by separate ownership. A League franchise, however, entails a formal commitment to all other member clubs to operate in a particular home location, defined as "the city in which such club is located and for which it holds a franchise and plays its home games. . . ." Under the League's Constitution and By-Laws, the relocation of a team requires a three-fourth's vote of the League's membership.

A review of the NFL's operations over the past forty years demonstrates the League's firm commitment to competitive and geographic balance in the location of its franchises, to franchise stability, and to the protection of fan and community interests. Compelling evidence of that commitment is reflected, among other places, in the League's revenue sharing policies, which enable the League to conduct team operations on a nation-wide scale and in communities of vastly differing economic potential.

Approximately 55 percent of the revenues of the average NFL club today come from the joint presentation of NFL games on national television networks—both broadcast and cable. These revenues are shared *equally* among all clubs without regard to each club's market size or revenue potential.[1] As a result of the sharing of these and other revenues (including, for example, game receipts that are shared with visiting clubs), the economic advantages of the clubs in the better situated markets are balanced, albeit not always fully offset, by revenue sharing with the clubs in smaller communities (such as Minnesota, Green Bay, Buffalo, Kansas City, Cincinnati, and New Orleans) or less well-situated markets.

In the past decade, the NFL's member clubs have modified and focused their revenue-sharing policies to support new stadium construction and renovation. By deciding to waive a portion of the game receipts that otherwise would be shared by visiting clubs, all League clubs effectively contribute to the payment of stadium construction (or related financing) costs. Through this mechanism, the League's member clubs have collectively supported the construction of new stadiums in a number of communities (*e.g.*, Atlanta, Miami). The clubs are also collectively supporting the extensive renovation of existing stadiums in a number of communities, including Buffalo, New Orleans, and San Diego.

In this context, an *internal* decision of a professional sports league—whether it relates to funding stadium construction or determining where to locate its franchises—bears no resemblance whatsoever to a "contract, combination or conspiracy" among *independent* economic competitors that provides a coherent basis for applying the antitrust laws.

The Judiciary Committee's consideration of this issue in the 1980s was prompted by the Raiders litigation against the NFL, in which a federal court determined that Section 1 of the Sherman Act should apply to such internal league decisions. In that

---

[1] There is a short-term exception for the League's two new expansion franchise, the Carolina Panthers and the Jacksonville Jaguars.

case, a Los Angeles jury found that the NFL had acted "unreasonably" in reciprocating the loyalty of Oakland fans (reflected in twelve consecutive sell-out seasons) and denying the Raiders permission to move the Oakland NFL franchise to Los Angeles. As a result of that decision, the Raiders were allowed, over the NFL's objection, to abandon Oakland; and a new weapon—"antitrust brinkmanship"—was introduced into the relationship between sports leagues and the communities that they represent.

Prior to the Raiders litigation, a sports league franchise was viewed as a license to serve *the league's* fans and to play *league* games in a prescribed geographical area. A franchise was the means by which the *league* created a stable, continuous relationship with a community, subject to change only by *league* decision, ordinarily through a supra-majority vote.

This stable franchise concept reflected the courts' recognition that, in determining the location of a league's franchises, league members "are not competitors in the economic sense. . . . They are, in fact, all members of a single unit competing as such with other similar professional leagues."[2] Not coincidentally, prior to the *Raiders* decision, NFL clubs had been committed to and stable in their home territories for decades.

Since the *Raiders* decision, federal courts, seeing the Raiders precedent, have failed to recognize (and potential litigants have elected to ignore) the economic reality of a sports league—that league members are co-producers of a joint product, and thus together constitute a single league enterprise in competition with other entertainment providers. Instead, courts and others have tended to raise form over substance, viewing each team franchise as an independent competitive entity that is portable and transient without regard to its commitments as a member of the league enterprise, the needs and preferences of the league, or the interests of the league's fans.

As a result, some clubs—all of which had agreed to be bound by the league's internal procedures for determining franchise location—have been persuaded to abandon their commitments to *the league* and their fans, and unilaterally to move *the league's* operations to a new location. If a league seeks to enforce its contractual rights against such moves, it faces substantial antitrust risks, notwithstanding that every other business enterprise in America can decide without antitrust exposure where to conduct its operations.

The antitrust weapon has been claimed not only by clubs that seek greener pastures elsewhere; it has also been brandished by governmental agencies (including state attorneys general), stadium landlords (who assert that they compete in a "market" for club tenants), and former club owners as well. All such parties purport to find a basis in the *Raiders* experience to threaten antitrust litigation to influence or prevent *the League's* exercise of its business judgment—for or against—a proposed franchise move.

These threats necessarily affect League decision making. Regardless of its merits, each such threat raises the specter of burdensome, divisive, and costly litigation, similar to the *Raiders* case in the 1980s, that inevitably takes years to resolve. If such a suit is successful in establishing financial injury—a possibility that exists especially when the issues are litigated before a "home-town" jury (as in the *Raiders* case)—each plaintiff *automatically* receives *punitive* damages, three times the "injury" that the jury believes must have been proved.

The National Football League has experienced such threats numerous times over the last ten or twelve years, and it has paid the price, in litigation expenses and/or settlements, on several occasions. In an effort to keep the Raiders in Oakland, during the 1980s the NFL spent almost $50 million in legal fees and in ultimate settlement of the antitrust judgment. Ironically, the Raiders and the City of Oakland are currently suing the League for hundreds of millions of dollars because of the League's alleged refusal to allow the Raiders—the *Oakland* Raiders, as of September 1995—to return from Los Angeles to Oakland in 1994. The Raiders sued the NFL in the 1980s, claiming that the League was holding the club "hostage" in Oakland; now the Raiders are suing the NFL for holding the club "hostage" in Los Angeles and delaying its return to Oakland.

The recent Raiders' lawsuit, moreover, involves a situation where the club never sought—and the League therefore never held—a vote on the proposed 1994 move. Similarly, a former owner of the New England Patriots, even though he also never submitted a relocation proposal to the League, has filed an antitrust suit against the NFL claiming that the League diminished the value of the Patriots franchise

---

[2] *San Francisco Seals, Ltd.* v. *National Hockey League,* 379 F. Supp. 966, 969-70 (C.D. Cal 1974) (rejecting on summary judgment antitrust challenge to the NHL's denial of the Seals' request to move its NHL franchise from San Francisco to Vancouver).

by preventing him from moving the club out of New England in the early 1990s. (In separate lawsuits pending in Boston, New York and Philadelphia, *three* former owners of the Patriots are now suing the NFL for "antitrust" grievances, each allegedly arising from a different internal League rule or policy.)

Last year, the Rams and the City of St. Louis used the threat of antitrust litigation to force the NFL to acquiesce in the Rams' move from Southern California to St. Louis. By a vote of the League's members, the NFL initially rejected the proposed move based in part on a report that I, as Commissioner, filed with the membership finding that the proposed move did not satisfy the specific criteria of the League's guidelines for franchise relocation. The League's initial decision was immediately met with public and private threats—by the Rams and by the State's Attorney General—to seek "billions" of dollars in antitrust damages from the NFL in suits to be filed in St. Louis.

As a result, the membership eventually reversed its initial decision and reluctantly voted to permit the Rams to move. Even though we believed that we should have prevailed in any lawsuit, the NFL members were unwilling to endure years of antitrust litigation in a St. Louis court—not to mention the punitive nature of any errant treble damage judgment—in order to enforce their contractual right to require the Rams to remain in Los Angeles. In short, the League's judgment was understandably influenced by a preference for antitrust peace rather than war, especially in light of the legal conflicts that had recently plagued other sports and have been negatively viewed by millions of fans.

Even though the League allowed the Rams to move, St. Louis sued anyway. Their complaint, filed in St. Louis by the St. Louis Convention and Visitors Center, alleges that our franchise relocation rules violate the antitrust laws. That suit demonstrates that, in the absence of legislation, exploitation of the antitrust weapon against professional sports leagues will continue regardless of how the League resolves any particular franchise relocation issue.

Finally, after the League met for the first time to discuss the Browns' proposed relocation, the Maryland Stadium Authority sued the League in Baltimore, claiming in effect that our failure to vote on the proposal at that first meeting constituted a violation of the antitrust laws. Where will this sort of litigation end? And what public interest does it serve?

Now we face the prospect of additional team moves, with the earlier moves being viewed as indications that a League vote carries an unacceptable antitrust risk, or as "precedents" justifying additional moves, or as establishing a requirement of "equal treatment" enforceable with the threat of treble damage claims. In the absence of legislation addressing the application of the antitrust laws in these circumstances, the NFL's ability to exercise its business judgment with regard to these and other moves will inevitably be colored by the specter of antitrust litigation, threats of which have already surfaced.

In 1984, reviewing the trial court decision favoring the Raiders, a federal court of appeals suggested changes supposedly designed to enable the NFL's rules and procedures governing franchise relocation—and the NFL's reliance upon those rules—to pass muster under the antitrust "rule of reason." The NFL adopted the court's suggestions, as well as a set of objective business criteria for evaluating proposed franchise moves in the future. A copy of those procedures and criteria is attached.

Despite these provisions, misguided treatment of league members as independent economic competitors continues to confuse the antitrust analysis and to make any league decision susceptible to being characterized as an unreasonable restraint on "competition." Thus, we know that if we rely on those criteria to bar a proposed franchise move, the NFL can be involved for years in expensive and internally divisive antitrust litigation. The dispute would likely be litigated in an interested forum, as was the Raiders' case; and the potential damage exposure associated with a jury's second-guessing of the League's internal decision could be astronomical. Regardless of our confidence in the *propriety* of a decision barring a proposed move, the prospect of such litigation can understandably have a chilling influence on a league's willingness to enforce its contractual rights.

THE ECONOMIC ISSUES

A key factor driving clubs to seek to construct new stadiums or to renovate existing stadiums, with more favorable stadium financial terms, is intense competition for the sports and entertainment dollar.

Such competition exists in all American cities having major league sports franchises. In Cleveland, for example, the Browns compete with the baseball Indians and the basketball Cavaliers not only for fan support, but also for business and other support. In 1994, when the Browns' baseball and basketball counterparts received attractive new facilities built with major investment of public funds—Jacobs Field and Gund Arena—the Browns were not simply faced with intensified competition for fan interest; the Browns *lost* significant *existing* revenue streams. For example, a substantial proportion of the Browns' suite-holders cancelled their leases at Memorial Stadium, which was built in 1931, in favor of suites in the city's brand new, fan-friendly facilities built for the baseball and basketball teams. The following data, reprinted from materials recently submitted to the NFL by the Browns, illustrate the point.

Facility	Total Number	1993	1994	1995
Gund Arena	92	—	92 (100%)	92 (100%)
Jacobs Field	133	—	133 (100%)	133 (100%)
Cleveland Stadium	108	108 (100%)	82 (76%)	83 (78%)

LOGE OCCUPANCY RATE AT CLEVELAND SPORTS FACILITIES

The new baseball and basketball facilities in Cleveland also intensify the competition for potential sources of *new* revenues for the Browns, including advertising and naming rights, to identify just two examples. Similar competitive factors are now at work—or will soon exist—in Phoenix and Seattle, among other NFL cities.

Furthermore, in many American cities, there is substantial competition for dollars available to fund the community's participation in the public-private partnerships necessary to replace or renovate aging facilities. Cleveland again provides an excellent example. That community invested $175 million to build Jacobs Field and $152 million to build Gund Arena (as well as $92 million to build the Rock and Roll Hall of Fame); the funds necessary to complete proposed renovations of Memorial Stadium (or to construct a replacement stadium) will have to be developed from many of the same public and private sources.

Thus, it is not surprising that despite extraordinary fan loyalty and support—a factor that weighs heavily in our analysis of *the League's* interests with respect to any relocation proposal—*competition* on a variety of fronts has caused the Browns (after years of effort in pursuit of a new stadium in Cleveland) to consider—and ultimately to accept—an offer of alternative stadium arrangements in Baltimore.

These are different circumstances from those that existed only a decade ago in many NFL markets. The Washington Redskins, for example, who play in the League's smallest stadium and who have sought for years to build their own privately financed stadium, are already facing new, intense competition from the MCI Center, the publicly financed, state-of-the-art facility in downtown Washington that will be the new home of Washington's NBA and NHL clubs. The Tampa Bay Buccaneers, who for years were the only professional sports franchise on Florida's West Coast, today face competition from both an NBA club and the NHL, and will soon compete with a Major League Baseball team, which will play in a publicly financed stadium in St. Petersburg.

This intense competition for the local sports dollar comes at a time when player costs are escalating at an extraordinary rate. Even with a collectively bargained salary cap, during the League Year just ended, NFL clubs spent more than $1.4 billion on a cash basis on player compensation and benefits, nearly 45 percent more than the amount spent only three years before. In addition, signing bonuses involving large up front payments have become an increasingly important element in attracting and retaining free agent player talent in the NFL. Thus, despite extensive revenue sharing that provides even small-market clubs with a foundation on which to build a team, NFL clubs are now more than ever before dependent on the revenues generated by modern stadium facilities in order to field representative and competitive football teams.

In business and economic circumstances such as these, sports leagues face complex and difficult questions that require a balance of multiple interests those of fans in communities with teams, those of fans in communities seeking teams, league interests, and individual club interests—to arrive at sound decisions with respect to the location of league teams. In the NFL, the League itself has increasingly been involved both with its teams and with public officials in seeking to develop solutions to the stadium and facility challenges that are presented in the current environment.

Whatever the outcome of such efforts and decisions, a sports league cannot function in a responsible and predictable manner—and without a nearly paralyzing stream of actual and threatened antitrust treble damage claims—if its decision-making processes on team location matters continue to be subject to review by antitrust courts and juries under the "conspiracy" standards of Section 1 of the Sherman Act.

A STATUTORY APPROACH TO THE ANTITRUST ISSUE

My predecessor Pete Rozelle coined the phrase "franchise free agency" in the early 1980s in predicting the long-term consequences of the *Raiders* decision. Yet he was only one of many observers who recognized at an early stage the inappropriateness of treating internal league decisions on franchise relocation as "contracts, combinations, or conspiracies" subject to the restrictions and penalties of the antitrust laws.

In August 1982, for example, Senator Heflin addressed the Senate Judiciary Committee on this subject. He began by recognizing that the NFL "is not composed of economic competitors. They are engaged in a common business operation." He made clear that "[a]ntitrust policies which permit individual team owners to ignore the league's relationship and act as if they were sole proprietors do not reflect free enterprise principles, and they do not serve the public interest." Senator Heflin concluded that "league agreements voluntarily entered into by league members should be enforced according to their terms" and not subjected to the antitrust laws.

In June 1985, the then-Assistant Attorney General for the Antitrust Division of the Department of Justice, Charles F. Rule, testified on the same subject. Supporting "an antitrust exemption for league decisions to block franchise relocations," he urged on behalf of the Department of Justice that "a league's franchise relocation rule should be deemed *per se* lawful unless it adversely affects competition with other leagues or is merely a subterfuge to disguise some other egregious anti competitive conduct."

Indeed, over forty years ago, in the first in-depth antitrust analysis of the nature of a professional sports league, United States District Judge Allen K. Grim explained that the traditional premises for application of the antitrust laws do not apply to the internal decisions of professional sports leagues. He recognized that clubs in a professional sports league are not independent business competitors, and that treating them as if they were would lead to "first, the creation of greater and greater inequalities in the strength of the teams; second, the weaker teams being driven out of business; and third, the destruction of the entire League."[3] He concluded:

> The League is truly a unique business enterprise, which is entitled to protect its very existence by agreeing to reasonable restrictions on its member clubs.[4]

In the following quarter century, numerous jurists and distinguished academics concurred. Chief Justice Rehnquist, for example, observed:

> The NFL owners are joint venturers who produce a product, professional football, which competes with other sports and other forms of entertainment in the entertainment marketplace. Although individual NFL teams compete on the playing field, they rarely compete in the marketplace. . . . [Ordinarily,] the league competes as a unit against other forms of entertainment.[5]

Similarly, Judge Robert Bork has recognized:

> Some activities can only be carried out jointly. Perhaps the leading example is league sports. When a league of professional lacrosse teams is formed,

---

[3] *United States* v. *National Football League,* 116 F. Supp. 319, 324 (E.D. Pa. 1953).
[4] *Id.* at 326.
[5] *North American Soccer League* v. *National Football League,* 459 U.S. 1074, 1077 (1982) (Rehnquist, J., dissenting from denial of certiorari).

it would be pointless to declare their cooperation illegal on the ground that there are not other professional lacrosse teams.[6]

Notwithstanding these thoughtful views, when Congress considered these issues in the early- and mid-1980s, it was not accepted that the Raiders decision—which departed from the principles recognized by Chief Justice Rehnquist, Senator Heflin, Judge Bork, and the Department of Justice—would undermine the relationship between professional sports leagues and the communities that they represent. The Raiders, of course, had moved from Oakland to Los Angeles. And the Colts had moved from Baltimore to Indianapolis at a time when the NFL—engrossed in litigation with the Raiders—felt powerless to stop them. But to some in Congress, these moves appeared to be isolated and unrelated to any general or enduring antitrust anomalies that would affect league operations. The need to correct the anomalous consequences of the Raiders decision therefore did not lead to legislation at that time.

Today, however, there is an ample proof demonstrating that uncertainty over this narrow antitrust issue has had a substantial and deleterious effect. Congress now has an opportunity—and an ample record—to address this problem and to end the antitrust brinkmanship that (1) impedes a professional sports league's ability to make rational *internal* decisions and reasonable business judgments about its own affairs and (2) subjects communities to the vagaries of individual team decisions on the next best stadium offer without regard to a league's enforceable evaluation and decision on the proposed move.

Such legislation—to treat sports leagues as a single enterprise for internal decisions on such matters as franchise relocation—would not freeze the status quo. It simply would allow a sports league to exercise its reasonable business judgment without the threat of antitrust treble damage litigation and, in doing so, to take appropriate account of community interests and fan loyalties.

PROCEDURES FOR PROPOSED FRANCHISE RELOCATIONS

Article 8.5 of the NFL Constitution and Bylaws vests in the Commissioner the authority to "interpret and from time to time establish policy and procedure in respect to the provisions of the Constitution and Bylaws and any enforcement thereof." Set forth below are procedures and policy to apply to League consideration, pursuant to Section 4.3 of the Constitution and Bylaws, of any proposed transfer of a home territory. These provisions were established in December of 1984 and remain in effect.

Section 4.3 requires prior approval by the affirmative vote of three-fourths of the member clubs of the League (the normal voting margin for League business) before a club may transfer its franchise or playing site to a different city either within or outside its home territory. While the following provisions apply by their terms to a proposed transfer to a different home territory, a transfer of a club's playing site to a different location within its home territory may also raise issues of League-wide significance. Accordingly, the pre-Annual Meeting notification date prescribed in section (A)(1) below also applies to a proposed intra-territory relocation, and the Commissioner may require that some or all of the following procedures be followed with respect to such a move.

A. Notice and Evaluation of the Proposed Transfer

Before any club may transfer its franchise or playing site outside its current home territory, the club must submit a proposal for such transfer to the League on the following basis:

1. A club proposing a transfer outside its home territory must give written notice of the proposed transfer to the Commissioner no later than 30 days prior to the opening date of the Annual Meeting in the year in which the club proposes to commence play in a new location. Such notice will be accompanied by a "statement of reasons" in support of the proposed transfer that will include the information outlined in Part B below.

2. The Commissioner will, with the assistance of appropriate League committees, evaluate the proposed transfer and report to the membership; if possible, he will do so within 20 days of his receipt of the club's notice and accompanying "statement of reasons." The Commissioner may also convene a special committee to perform fact finding or other functions with respect to any such proposed transfer.

3. Following the Commissioner's report on the proposed transfer, the transfer will be presented to the membership for action in accordance with the Constitu-

---
[6] Robert Bork, *The Antitrust Paradox* 278 (1978).

tion and Bylaws, either at a Special Meeting of the League held for that purpose or at the Annual Meeting.

B. *"Statement of Reasons" for the Proposed Transfer*

Any club proposing a transfer outside its home territory must, in its accompanying "statement of reasons," furnish information to the Commissioner essential to consideration of whether such a move is justified and whether it is in the League's interest.

In this connection, the club proposing to transfer must present in writing its views to why its recent financial experience would support a relocation of the club. Such information would include a comparison of the club's home revenues with League averages and medians; past and projected ticket sales and other stadium revenues at both the existing and proposed locations; and operating profits or losses during the most recent four seasons. The club should also comment on any other factors it regards as relevant to the League's consideration of the proposed transfer, including but not limited to operations of other professional or college sports in the existing and proposed home territories, and the effects of the proposed transfer on NFL scheduling patterns, travel requirements, current divisional alignments, traditional rivalries, League-wide television patterns and interests, the quality of stadium facilities, and fan and public perceptions of the NFL and its member clubs.

To permit such a review, at least the following information will accompany the "statement of reasons" for the proposed transfer:

1. A copy of the club's existing stadium lease and any other agreements relating to the club's use of its current stadium (e.g., concession agreements, box suite agreements, scoreboard advertising agreements) or to a stadium authority's or municipality's provision of related facilities (e.g., practice facilities).

2. Audited financial statements for the club for the fiscal years covering the preceding four seasons.

3. An assessment of the suitability of the club's existing stadium, costs of and prospects for making any desired improvements to the stadium, and the status of efforts to negotiate such improvements with the stadium authority.

4. A description and financial analysis of the projected lease and operating terms available to the club in its proposed new location.

5. A description and financial analysis of the stadium lease and operating terms available to the club in its existing home territory, on a basis that permits comparison with the projected arrangements in the proposed new location.

6. A budget protection, using accepted League charts of account, showing a projected profit and loss statement for the fiscal years covering the first three seasons in the proposed new location.

C. *Factors to be Considered in Evaluating the Proposed Transfer*

While the League has analyzed many factors in making expansion and team-move decisions in the past, the Commissioner will also give consideration to the factors listed below, among others, in reporting to the membership on any proposed transfer outside a home territory. Such factors were contained in a bill reported by a Senate committee in 1984; they essentially restate matters that the League has considered vital in connection with team location decisions in the past. Accordingly, any club proposing to transfer should, in its submission to the Commissioner's office, present the club's position as to the bearing of these factors on its proposed transfer, stating specifically why such a move is regarded as justified on these standards:

1. The adequacy of the stadium in which the team played its home games in the previous season, and the willingness of the stadium or arena authority to remedy any deficiencies in such facility;

2. The extent to which fan loyalty to and support for the team has been demonstrated during the team's tenure in the existing community;

3. The extent to which the team, directly or indirectly, received public financial support by means of any publicly financed playing facility, special tax treatment and any other form of public financial support;

4. The degree to which the ownership or management of the team has contributed to any circumstance which might otherwise demonstrate the need for such relocation;

5. Whether the team has incurred net operating losses, exclusive of depreciation and amortization, sufficient to threaten the continued financial viability of the team;

6. The degree to which the team has engaged in good faith negotiations with appropriate persons concerning terms and conditions under which the team

would continue to play its games in such community or elsewhere within its current home territory;
  7. Whether any other team in the League is located in the community in which the team is currently located;
  8. Whether the team proposes to relocate to a community in which no other team in the League is located; and
  9. Whether the stadium authority, if public, is not opposed to such relocation.
  Any club proposing to transfer will have a full opportunity to state its position to the membership and to make its case for the proposed transfer. In order to fully assess a proposed transfer in light of the variety of League interests involved, and to fairly resolve the interests of all parties, it is essential that the membership be fully apprised of the relevant facts with respect to any proposed transfer. The procedures and policies outlined above are directed to that end.

Mr. HYDE. Well, I thank you very much, Mr. Tagliabue.

If Congress were to grant the NFL an antitrust exemption solely for its relocation rule, wouldn't this just immunize the owners from liability? How would the fans be protected?

That is, the antitrust exemption would not provide an absolute assurance to cities and States that their franchises wouldn't be relocated anyway; it simply would immunize the 29 owners against antitrust liability when an owner seeking to relocate his or her franchise sues. Isn't that so?

Mr. TAGLIABUE. Well, I would say two things most directly. No. 1, look at the league's record on franchise stability when it had the unquestioned authority to deal with these issues, before the Raiders' court rulings were entered. The NFL had an exemplary record in this area.

No. 2, I think we should recognize, and I identify very strongly with many of the statements that Mr. Thompson made as a fan, because at an earlier point in my life I was sitting where he was sitting. As someone, as you mentioned, who went to college because of an athletic scholarship, I was the kind of fan he was. The NFL has got an extraordinary record of recognizing fan loyalty, earning the respect of the fans, earning their loyalty; and we did it as a league when we were able to make league decisions.

What has eroded is the exposure of the—eroded that is the exposure of the league to antitrust liability. To give you an example, the New England Patriots owner told me several years ago that he wanted to leave New England, move the team out of New England. I told him I thought it was unwarranted for several reasons. No. 1, I thought the problems the team was having were largely of his own making; No. 2, it was contrary to understandings we had with NBC in terms of representation on national television; No. 3, his financial issues were primarily as a result of other business impacts from other businesses rather than from football. So he sold the team to an owner who was committed to keeping it in New England.

Now, as a result of those conversations with that owner and my unwillingness to support a move of the team, we are facing a $300 million treble damage suit in Federal court in New York. So it is not a question of power; it is a question of being powerless because of the courts coming in and tearing the league apart in terms of its ability to make decisions.

If we could make our decisions, I think we would have the kind of record that Mr. Thompson's admiration for the National Football League reflected. We know what fan loyalty is. We have got a tremendous record in earning it. But we have to be able to act as a league in order to do that. And we will do that.

Mr. HYDE. Is it true that the NFL has an uncodified policy against the sale of ownership interests in an NFL club to the public through stock offerings? Why hasn't community ownership like the Green Bay situation been encouraged?

Mr. TAGLIABUE. Well, again, I don't believe the community ownership such as Green Bay is a solution. It is not-for-profit ownership. It is historic anomaly. In the current environment, I don't believe it can be replicated.

First of all, you need to recognize what makes it work today: It is the equal sharing of all of our television revenue among the teams, so that Green Bay in Wisconsin gets the same slice of national television revenue as the New York Jets, the New York Giants, Chicago Bears and the biggest markets in the country. So that element of the league structure, which is without parallel in sports and which is under the 1961 act of Congress, is the most critical thing to the survival of the Packers.

No. 2, is their stadium. They have, as the Congressman from Wisconsin said, stayed ahead of the stadium curve in Lambeau Field. They have put in luxury suites, which others have been sitting here condemning. They have put in premium seats, which other people have been sitting here condemning. They have made it a 21st century stadium, so they are able to survive.

Thirdly, as I said before, in the current cost environment of free agency, their player costs escalating from $60 million in the two seasons before free agency to $90 million in the 2 years after free agency, I don't think we should delude ourselves into thinking the Packers are a slam dunk for the future. The Packers would be sitting right behind me here, I can assure you of that, urging that the league be given control of these decisions, because they recognize, as much as anybody in the league, that it is the league's ability to make decisions, the league's ability to enforce revenue-sharing rules, the league's ability to sell television and share it equally that is critical to the survival of the Green Bay Packers.

Mr. HYDE. Are you saying that professional football isn't so lucrative that the owners of stadiums cannot finance the construction of their own skyboxes without public funds?

Mr. TAGLIABUE. No, I am saying this: that in the current environment, in building stadiums, we face two or three major challenges. No. 1, is the cost of doing it in a market such as Los Angeles, where you have to build a state-of-the-art facility and you have to get supporting infrastructure, freeways and so on in the core of a major metropolitan area. That is a cost issue.

No. 2, is that we recognize we have to contribute, increasingly, private funds in a public/private partnership to make the economics work; and we are doing that. That is what Mr. Richardson innovated in the Carolinas, more than $180 million of private money from the fans in the nature of an investment by the fans for permanent rights to be seat-holders in the Carolina stadium. And the stadium, incidentally, is owned by a not-for-profit trust.

Mr. HYDE. They will be very unhappy when the Charlotte Panthers want to move somewhere.

Mr. TAGLIABUE. Well, they won't move because of the way they privatized their financing and the commitments they made to the fans in return for that privatization. So those—those are the key things: the cost, the need to privatize, a public/private partnership.

And then the third thing is whether a community makes a priority out of professional sports or whether it chooses to put its priorities in other sports or in other areas of investment.

We are dealing in a very difficult environment and the ability to get corporate support is, in effect, making the construction and renovation of these stadiums possible. If you would please, I might ask Mr. Richardson to comment on his experience in Charlotte, in the Carolinas, because I think it is very instructive on the privatization aspect of what is going on in the marketplace here.

Mr. RICHARDSON. Mr. Chairman, when we began the quest for an NFL franchise, as has already been stated, I was a former player in the NFL, and had it not been for the fact that I had been in the NFL and we had won a world championship, I would not have had the funds to invest in the business to allow us to take on this project. It was our thinking that in the Carolinas, the best way for us to deal with the stadium issue was to create what we call a private/public partnership. And the way—it has got four components to it.

The city of Charlotte made a decision. They came to us; we did not ask the city of Charlotte to do this. They had a quadrant of the downtown of the city that was unattractive. They said, if in fact we will lease this property to you, will you in fact build your privately funded stadium there? And the answer was, yes. We did that.

So, first, the city and the county came to us. Then when we got into the costing of the stadium, we thought originally the stadium would cost $85 million and we built that off of what had occurred down at Joe Robbie Stadium. That is the number we used. But as we got deeper into it, the costs continued to escalate because we felt it was important because the NFL is the most popular sport in America and we have very loyal fans, that we wanted to build the best facility we could for the Carolina Panthers and the NFL. We wanted it to be a benchmark for our fans.

So our cost, as the commissioner said, got up to $185 million.

Well, the reality of it is, somehow or another you have got to figure out how are you going to pay for it. In our particular case, we chose not to ask the taxpayers to invest more in the stadium than they had already—were willing to do. They had invested none in the stadium, but providing the land. So we came up with the idea, as the commissioner said, of a permanent seats license. We have already, to this date, paid $34,700,000 in Federal and State taxes on the PSL's that we have sold.

In addition to that, everyone that has bought a PSL, I assume, has paid taxes to net the money to buy the PSL's. I don't know what that number is, but in our case, it could not have worked if the business community had not leased all of the suites. The debt service on our stadium is $15 million a year, and that debt service is being serviced primarily by what we call premium seating, which is club seats and suites in our particular case.

So we had a partnership with the public. We had a partnership with our owner, our ownership group that was willing to make this investment, knowing it would be many years before we got a return on it. The business community supported it and our fans supported it.

Mr. HYDE. Well, that is very interesting. The league already allows the commissioner to sue in the name of the NFL. Why doesn't the league let the commissioner make the decision as to whether a move is justified or in the best interests of the league? The commissioner now enforces league rules. Why can't the commissioner make the decision on franchise relocation as well?

Mr. TAGLIABUE. Well, I will just give you our recent—most recent experience.

As you are well aware, when Commissioner Rozelle opposed the Raiders' move from Oakland in the early 1980's, the Federal courts ordered that the Raiders should be permitted to move; and also we ended up, as a league, paying more than $50 million in damages and costs for having tried to keep the Raiders in Oakland where they had the longest consecutive string of sellouts of any team at that time.

Last year, we were faced with a proposal of the Rams to move from the Los Angeles area to St. Louis. I found in a written report that they did not meet our guidelines for such a move. Initially, the membership declined to approve the move. We were then told by the Rams and by the authorities in Missouri that we would be sued for $2 billion under the antitrust laws—billion with a "B." And given this confused state of the law, given that the case would be litigated in an interested forum, namely in Missouri, given that it would go to a jury and given that the question is, has the league restrained the business opportunities of one of its members, treating the member as an independent competitor of the rest of the league under section 1 Sherman act standards, our ownership felt that they could not take that risk, with Mr. Richardson among them. The $2 billion has a heavy, persuasive impact on your thinking when you are trying to decide whether to approve or disapprove a move.

So I have a role in the process, but ultimately it is one that is chilled and disabled in many respects by the current antitrust precedents.

Mr. HYDE. Your written statement makes much of the uncertainty of antitrust litigation and the perceived problem of hometown juries. In the decade since the NFL adopted its relocation policy, has it ever received a court decision determining the validity of the policy in any of the countless relocation lawsuits? If not, why not? Why doesn't the league bring a declaratory judgment action against all of the owners who are threatening to move in a neutral venue to determine once and for all whether your relocation policy is valid under the antitrust laws?

Mr. TAGLIABUE. We have done that, Mr. Chairman. I authorized a suit last summer against the Raiders, a declaratory judgment action, in the Federal court in Los Angeles, seeking a declaration that we had the right to control team moves. Subsequently, the Raiders countersued us for a large amount of damages, filed their suit, I believe, in Oakland. So we are in such litigation right now.

But, again, I come back to the basic proposition, which grows out of the ninth circuit's own opinion in the *Raider* cases. The ninth circuit said that the members of the NFL, the member teams, are not true competitors, nor can they ever be. The ninth circuit recognized that we were a unique form of a business partnership.

Having recognized that, it turned around in the next part of its opinion and said, nonetheless, we are going to treat the plaintiff as if he is an independent business competitor of the other teams and of the league under section 1 of the Sherman Act, and we are going to allow juries to decide whether a league decision restrains the ability of that competitor to compete. So what we have is serious confusion in the court of appeals decisions, a premise which is inconsistent with what follows the premise.

But to your specific question, we have filed a declaratory judgment action in California. It is currently pending and has been met by a countersuit for damages by the Raiders.

Mr. HYDE. Would you suggest we forgo legislating pending the outcome of that litigation?

Mr. TAGLIABUE. I would not suggest that, because I think what the last 15 years of history have shown, beginning with the *Raiders'* decision in the early 1980's, is that by the Federal courts coming in and saying that a league member can act as an independent competitor and assert antitrust rights against the rest of the league when the league makes a decision, we have created an environment right now where, frankly, the league is regarded as being powerless.

I will give you an example with respect to the Los Angeles situation. I just mentioned that we are litigating with the Raiders over their moves—their move back to Oakland. When we approved the Rams' move and the Raiders' move, we adopted, as a league, a resolution which said that the reestablishment of an NFL team in the Los Angeles area will be the responsibility of the league.

We did it for two basic reasons, in my judgment. Number 1 was that we recognized that a major private investment by the league, including a commitment of Super Bowls in the Los Angeles area, was going to be critical to building a stadium with private financing in that marketplace. The league was going to have to step up and be a major investor in the stadium, so we wanted to control who would go in there.

Secondly, we wanted to avoid a situation where other teams would be tempted to abandon their existing markets and race pell mell for Los Angeles. So the membership adopted this with our three-fourths vote. It adopted it last April, it adopted it last July.

Now we have the Seattle Seahawks basically saying, the resolution be damned, we are going to Los Angeles. The reason is that some antitrust lawyer said the league cannot enforce its resolution.

Mr. Richardson is the chairman of our stadium committee, which is charged with implementing this resolution. We have been talking to private parties, such as the ownership of the Los Angeles Dodgers. We have talked to other private parties in the L.A. area. We have spoken with Mayor Riordan. We have had extensive meetings. We are trying to set up the conditions for a major NFL investment in a new stadium with major private funding in Los Angeles, and now we are being undercut by one of our own members out of the belief that we cannot control things because eventually they will have antitrust rights.

Mr. HYDE. Thank you.
Mr. Scott.
Mr. SCOTT. Thank you, Mr. Chairman.
Mr. Tagliabue, what are we talking about as the price for a new team? What would one—if a group in a city was trying to come up with some money, how much would they have to come up with to buy a new team or to be granted an expansion franchise?
Mr. TAGLIABUE. The two teams that were placed in Jacksonville paid $140 million over a period of years, and they also agreed to forgo some portion of their equal share of television rights. Now those—for a number of years, for 3 years.
Mr. SCOTT. That is kind of a franchise fee. They would have to build a stadium——
Mr. TAGLIABUE. Yes.
Mr. SCOTT [continuing]. In addition to that?
Mr. TAGLIABUE. Yes.
Mr. SCOTT. And those are going for what $150 to $200 million now?
Mr. TAGLIABUE. Mr. Richardson would put the cost of his stadium, I am sure, over $200 million if you included related infrastructure.
Mr. SCOTT. How much capital would the team have to start off the year with?
Mr. TAGLIABUE. I will let Mr. Richardson answer this. He has just done this on behalf of the Carolina expansion team.
Mr. RICHARDSON. Well, when you start from scratch—in our particular case, as the commissioner says, we have a reduced TV revenue share—your own income can come from season tickets that you sell in advance. That is one source of capital. But in our particular case, it cost us $75 million in cash to get into business.
Mr. SCOTT. Now——
Mr. TAGLIABUE. One thing I would add on the franchise price, from the standpoint of the existing 28 teams, it does not even offset the diminution of their own television revenue because, instead of dividing our TV 28 ways, we are now dividing it 30 ways by having added 2 teams. And over the course of the 7- to 10-year period, it actually costs the existing teams in order to engage in this expansion to Carolina and to Jacksonville.
Mr. SCOTT. OK.
Mr. Richardson—you said you have private funding, Mr. Richardson?
Mr. RICHARDSON. Yes.
Mr. SCOTT. You have private funding?
Mr. RICHARDSON. Yes.
Mr. SCOTT. Do you have one owner or a group of owners, a group of individuals?
Mr. RICHARDSON. I own 45 percent of the team, and I own 45 percent of the benefits that we get from the stadium, and I have other partners.
Mr. SCOTT. How many other partners? Is that public?
Mr. RICHARDSON. Excluding my family, there are, I think, 10 or 11.

Mr. SCOTT. Now, in Green Bay, I understand that—I think we are at 3,500 people who actually own the team. Is that right, Mr. Tagliabue?

Mr. TAGLIABUE. It is not exactly right because Green Bay does not have ownership as such. It is a not-for-profit foundation basically that owns the team. Those 3,500 people are basically nominees. It is a tax-exempt organization under the Wisconsin laws. It is not a true form of public ownership; it is a not-for-profit form of ownership with those people being representatives of a not-for-profit foundation. The team is basically owned, believe it not, by the VWF Foundation in Green Bay. That is why I say it is a historical anomaly.

Mr. SCOTT. Well, what is wrong with a group of investors, then, coming together and having a private/public—the word "public" is getting thrown around with two different meanings—broadly based investors, individual investors, for profit?

Mr. TAGLIABUE. Well, we have had a policy that has not allowed that. Other sports leagues have had policies which allow it. It has in fact not occurred very often.

Mr. SCOTT. Well, I——

Mr. TAGLIABUE. I just want to make one more statement, please.

Mr. SCOTT. On that point——

Mr. TAGLIABUE. We have a case——

Mr. SCOTT. Let me——

Mr. TAGLIABUE. We have a case on this very subject pending before a jury which is deliberating today as we speak. The judge in Boston has asked me not to comment on this matter publicly, or to limit my public comments. I would be glad to answer any and all questions, either in writing or at a later date, but this is under—this is a matter that is under deliberation by a jury today as we speak. It has been deliberating for 2 weeks.

Mr. HYDE. Mr. Commissioner, if the gentleman would yield, we would like to submit in writing questions subsequently that you would answer, as appropriate.

Mr. TAGLIABUE. I would be very glad to do that, Mr. Scott. But I would also like to abide by the suggestion of the Federal judge.

Mr. SCOTT. Without your answering, let me just ask you, and you can submit in due time, if there are any other teams in any other professional sports that are owned by large numbers of private investors?

Mr. TAGLIABUE. To my knowledge, the only one that exists in any of the other leagues is a minority interest in the Boston Celtics. That was done under provisions of the Federal tax law that have since been superseded and basically make that type of ownership impractical under the Federal tax laws.

But we can give you comprehensive information on that, as I say, hopefully, at a more appropriate time.

Mr. SCOTT. And as he answers that, what problems there would be with that, because I think as—that would eliminate a lot of the problems of—if somebody is going to lose a lot of money, it would be private investors and not the local jurisdictions.

Thank you, Mr. Chairman.

Mr. HYDE. Thank you, Mr. Scott.

Mr. Moorhead.

Mr. MOORHEAD. Thank you.

Mr. Tagliabue, one of the questions that has come up here today is whether a team owner, who has gotten a lot of good support from the cities and the fans, owes something to the city when they leave. What would your comment be on that? Do you think they are free to go, or free to pay whatever is left on their lease and go, or should be let out of their lease? Or what should the situation be?

Mr. TAGLIABUE. I think leases should be strictly enforced. Commissioner Rozelle repeatedly emphasized when he was before Congress in earlier appearances in the 1980's and 1970's, that the way for a city and a community to protect itself, in the first instance, is through a lease and a guarantee of use for the term of the lease.

In point of fact, most leases that have involved public funding have included such provisions. They have typically been 30-year bonds with a 30-year lease commitment, with the rental payments structured so as to pay off the lion's share of the bonded indebtedness. And we believe that is the first line of policy that a municipality should pursue. We will not do anything to short-circuit the terms of such a lease.

Secondly, as a league, we believe that this should be—team location should be a decision for the totality of the membership, and it should not be a decision taken out of our hands as it has been by the rulings of the Federal courts, which say that for purposes of moving, a member of a league becomes an independent competitor and can sue the league under section 1 of the Sherman Act at the same time that it is taking all the benefits, including an equal share of television, including other revenue-sharing, as a business partner.

You cannot simultaneously be a partner and a competitor, but that is what the Federal courts have ruled, which is why we have the current problems.

One of the reasons there is a spate of movement right now, in my judgment, in addition to the factors I mentioned earlier to the chairman, is that many of the stadiums currently occupied by professional football and baseball were built in the 1960's with 30-year leases that are now expiring. That is one of the reasons we have a problem in the mid-1990's: those leases are expiring.

The stadiums were built as dual-purpose stadiums for football and baseball. Start right here at RFK Stadium in Washington, Shea Stadium in New York, Three Rivers in Pittsburgh, Veterans Stadium in Philadelphia, Candlestick, Jack Murphy, Riverfront in Cincinnati, they were all built in the 1960's, usually with 30-year leases and 30-year bonded indebtedness, which is now expiring. It is one of the reasons we have got so much ferment.

But the lease is definitely a part of the protection for the investment here.

Mr. MOORHEAD. Some of the earlier witnesses have commented about the rights to the trademark of a team. Under trademark law, the person that applies for the trademark and has the trademark is the one that owns it. There has been some suggestion that that trademark is lost to the city that happens to have the team at the present time. A lot of people think that would be unconstitutional because it takes a property right away from the owner of the team and gives it to the city.

What is your comment about that and how valuable is that trademark, either to the city or to the team?

Mr. TAGLIABUE. Well, I am of the view that it is very valuable to the city, to the team and to the league. I think there are serious constitutional questions if you just take it from the owner of the mark who has built the value of the mark and transfer it to a city. But as a league policy, we are currently considering and we have considered in the past that the team name, colors, logos, history and tradition of a team should stay in a city in appropriate circumstances, as Mr. Thompson outlined, and not be moved.

On the other hand, I don't think that is much of a solution to say that we are going to keep the name, the logo and the history and let the team go, because people do not want to get up and look at the old logo and see the empty stadium. So it is only a part of the problem, obviously.

We are striving at the league level to respect that fan base that developed the value of that mark over time and to factor that into our thinking as we try to solve these problems that we have, such as the conflict between Baltimore and Cleveland over the Browns.

Mr. HYDE. The gentleman's time has expired. The gentlelady from Texas, Sheila Jackson Lee.

Mr. TAGLIABUE. But it would be private assignment, not directed by statute.

Ms. JACKSON LEE. Thank you, Mr. Chairman.

Mr. Commissioner, I raised a comment earlier referring to a letter that the city of Houston had received some years ago as we have continued to work diligently to secure a Super Bowl. I might add that the citizens are still looking to do that there in Houston. But we had gotten a letter from the former commissioner, Pete Rozelle, who mentioned improvements to be made, in capacity, which the city has diligently worked toward.

I think a question was asked by my colleagues, several of them, as to what grounds the Federal Government—Federal legislation would have in intruding in this process. And so I am trying to delineate in my mind the issues that would give us safe ground to be participatory in this process.

Certainly one of the issues seems to be the prolific nature of this movement of relocation and the enormous economic impact. But there is also a question of reliance, contractual reliance; and certainly Federal laws have protected contractual relationships in other instances.

So here we have a letter that indicates to a local entity that if you do certain things—certainly, I separate out the Super Bowl—but make improvements, you would be in line, the state of the art. My question to you would be, in terms of this legislation and in terms of commitments that are made or have been made to various jurisdictions—I think we heard Mr. Locke say that he has provisions in his agreement that might be challenged at this point— what are you doing to provide enforcement? And the owners in their collective governing of this issue, or these issues, are enforcing and giving protection to agreements, letters that are being sent by commissioners, to be able to feel comfort or a comfort level that we are all working on the same page.

Mr. TAGLIABUE. Well, the contract issues and the lease issues for the most part are controlled by State law. As I said before, it was Commissioner Rozelle's policy and it is my policy not to interfere in any way or support a rescission of a lease. Those are State law issues. They are contract issues, and if the parties are well advised, they should be able to protect themselves.

Our hands are tied in taking a more active role because of the decision adverse to the NFL in the *Raiders* case, which is a Federal antitrust issue. That is the problem.

It is very clear what the problem is here. The problem——

Ms. JACKSON LEE. But it——

Mr. TAGLIABUE. The problem is the rulings in the *Raiders* case and other cases interpreting section 1 of the Sherman Act.

Ms. JACKSON LEE. Say, for example——

Mr. TAGLIABUE. If the patient has got a 105 fever and we know the cause, that is the issue.

Ms. JACKSON LEE. If, for example, then, out of this hearing certain legislation was passed that provided for an exemption, would your owners and organization be in a position to provide enforcement, compliance at that level? Or would you be open to judicial review on this question?

Mr. TAGLIABUE. We think that our record of team stability before the *Raiders* case came down is very, very strong and that if we can function as the business partnership that we are, rather than having the partnership carved up, treating an individual team as an independent competitor of the other 29 members of the league, we can pursue very sensible and sound policies in this area.

I mentioned, I believe, before you were able to rejoin us, that Mr. Thompson's testimony about the NFL suggested what I think is clear. The NFL has had a uniquely strong record of earning the respect of fans and of their loyalty. That is why we are here, because we have done such a good job of it.

Ms. JACKSON LEE. I don't want to interrupt you, but I have some additional questions.

Let me just—I did not hear you say that you would be open to judicial review and maybe I can follow that up in writing, but let me find out as you move toward the meetings coming up this Friday, will you be making any recommendation regarding the proposed move to Baltimore, which is an opportunity for the owners to show, certainly, respect for their fellow owner, but also good faith on some of these questions that we are raising?

Some of the relocation guidelines you already have are being codified in Mr. Hoke's bill, and the question would be, if we simply codify them and you cannot follow them in this instance, how would you be able to follow them otherwise and what opportunities are there for minority participation, ethnic participation ownership?

And since I have asked the question, I would ask the chairman if he would allow Mr. Tagliabue to answer that question—those questions.

Mr. HYDE. Of course.

Ms. JACKSON LEE. Thank you, Mr. Chairman.

The first question was Baltimore, and the second question was minority participation in ownership throughout the country.

Mr. TAGLIABUE. On Baltimore, we are meeting on Thursday and Friday of this week to make recommendations. We have been sued by the State of Maryland, under the antitrust laws, with a claim that is going to run into the hundreds of millions, if not billions of dollars. That is going to be a factor in our decision, the antitrust uncertainty. It is part of the antitrust brinksmanship which brings us here.

On minority ownership, I believe Mr. Richardson has a minority owner in his group. There is a minority owner in the Jacksonville expansion team who is a former player, Deron Cherry. I have had a number of conversations in the past several years with minority groups, African-Americans, who are interested in buying a team. We have been encouraging them to talk to owners. Some of them have talked to existing owners about purchasing all or part interests in teams. That is something that we are in the—are currently encouraging.

Ms. JACKSON LEE. Thank you very much. I will pursue that with written questions.

Thank you, Mr. Chairman.

Mr. HYDE. I thank the gentlelady.

The gentleman from Pennsylvania, Mr. Gekas.

Mr. GEKAS. I thank the Chair.

Commissioner, I am still reeling from the testimony of the chief executive of Seattle's King County and the mayor of Houston, when they very blithely implied, if not stated overtly, that there is very little economic impact involved in a relocation move like the one contemplated between Cleveland and Baltimore. I felt that Baltimore and Maryland somehow discerned, in even entering into the fray, that for their area, for their city, for their citizens, for their taxpayers, there would be enormous beneficial economic impact visited upon their area. They tried to disabuse me of that. I would like to know if your decisions as a league and as commissioner take into account the economic impact that would occur should a relocation be approved.

Mr. TAGLIABUE. We definitely believe there is a positive economic impact in having an NFL team in a community. And certainly many, many public officials believe that. In front of the Senate committee several weeks ago, Mayor White of Cleveland and the representative of Baltimore were in agreement on one thing: that there is a very positive economic impact that justifies their investment—in the case of Maryland, the investment of lottery funds; in the case of Cleveland, the investment of tax funds.

Cleveland has invested, as I mentioned earlier, $685 million in the redevelopment of downtown Cleveland. In the Rock and Roll Hall of Fame, Science and Technology Museum, baseball stadium, NBA arena and now they are proposing to add to that with the NFL arena.

They believe, in their community, the business community as well as the city council and the mayor, that there is a very positive impact on that in the attraction of business, in the attraction of jobs that is part of the quality of life. I believe that Mr. Richardson had the same experience in Charlotte in the Carolinas in terms of the willingness of the city of Charlotte to step up to plate with land.

But obviously there is room for difference among local officials both in terms of the level of those benefits and whether they outweigh the costs. Those are local government decisions and not directly our decisions.

Mr. GEKAS. In your forthcoming discussions and eventual decision on Baltimore, will you have in front of you studies or statements or accounts rendered by the Maryland and Baltimore entities to demonstrate the safety of the move and the economic well-being of the team and the taxpayers and the citizens and the job creation that come with it? Will you have that as part of your documentation as you make that decision?

Mr. TAGLIABUE. Well, we are very well aware of how the Maryland authorities feel and the Cleveland authorities feel on that question. Whether we have specific studies as part of our presentation package, I would have to ask someone on my staff. But I have personally spoken to Mayor White in Cleveland about this issue and, as I say, he affirmed to the Senate committee that they believe there is a major payback for this community investment in Cleveland, and the Baltimore officials, including Governor Glendening, have told me that directly.

Mr. GEKAS. Well, then—then it goes without saying that the economic benefit that would inure to Baltimore is paralleled in a negative way by the loss to Cleveland?

Mr. TAGLIABUE. That is the Solomon's choice we are facing.

Mr. GEKAS. Which I tried to elicit from the mayor of Houston that when they in Houston rejected the opportunity to reinvest $150 or $200 million to retain a franchise which has economic benefits, tax-based jobs, all of that, that in their rejection of that, they were in the position of making a decision that there is no economic impact. It still astounds me.

Mr. TAGLIABUE. Well, my information on the Houston situation, which is certainly not as complete as the mayor's, indicates that there is a lot more to the recent history. There was reference to Commissioner Rozelle's letter some years ago, which had to do with the current lease which was basically a 10-year lease that runs, I think, through 1997 or 1998. There was a major effort between the Oilers in the city, including in the Texas Legislature, to get legislation passed on something called a sports team enterprise zone that would have recognized some of these aspects of public benefit that you are talking about, which was defeated in the Texas Legislature.

I wrote letters to the mayor within the last year or two indicating that we would make our best efforts to play our Super Bowl in Houston if they got that new stadium built, which they were talking about, which alone would have brought into that community an infusion of between $100 and $150 million of spending in Super Bowl week alone, as part of the justification for the new stadium. And we have that documented from the authorities in Miami, New Orleans, Los Angeles, and other places where we play the Super Bowl, that the infusion of spending in 1 week is between $100 and $150 million in a community.

Mr. HYDE. The gentlelady from California, Ms. Lofgren.

Ms. LOFGREN. Thank you, Mr. Chairman. I suppose reasonable people can and often do differ on their analysis of particular situations, but later in the panel following yours, Professor Zimbalist in his written statement reviews the information available on economic impact. It is really a very compelling analysis that seems to indicate, as the two local government officials indicated this morning, that the impact of professional sports is limited because there is only so much money that people are going to spend for entertainment and what they might spend on——

Mr. TAGLIABUE. That sort of assumes a static universe——

Ms. LOFGREN. If I may finish. I have only a few minutes; I don't want to engage in an argument because as I said reasonable people can disagree on the outcome. But having just been in local government, I think of sports as kind of like the military/industrial/sports complex, and for those of us who have served in local government recently, dealing with sports fans is kind of like having a meeting where you have the NRA, general aviation pilots and the Humane Society all in the same meeting, and it is very difficult in the local government environment to deal with it. I am sensitive to that.

So I guess one of the things we are here today to see is whether there is something we ought to do with the Federal laws. Now, certainly local governments have their own right to make their own decisions and we all recognize that, but we do not have the obligation to make it inevitable for local governments to be pushed around if they do not want to be. And I think most local governments are not very happy about putting out large amounts of funds for professional sports, especially when there are so many pressing needs in the law enforcement arena as well, and most compellingly in the education arena, and I think most local government officials and many citizens would rather have a great educational system than a great sports team. And the funds are limited in local governments.

So I guess what I am looking to either of you to say, and perhaps you, Mr. Commissioner, is, if you accept, just for discussion's sake, that we have an interest in making it less likely for local governments to feel compelled to put up funds for stadiums and the kinds of things that have been discussed here, what would your remedy be?

In a monopoly, either you introduce a lot of competition or you regulate against abuse. What would your remedy be if that was the problem that you wanted to solve?

Mr. TAGLIABUE. Well, our remedy would be to restore the ability of the league to make decisions in this area. We do not have any monopoly. We are competing—the biggest part of the problem that exists here today is from competition in the marketplace. We are competing—we all are competing for fan spending; we are all competing for public attention and public interest, with increasing saturation in some markets, in my judgment, oversaturation of professional sports teams. There is no monopoly here. This is competition that is driving the process.

But what would help, from our perspective, would be to restore the ability of a league to look at the total picture and to function as a league, which is what we do in most areas. We get a collective bargaining agreement as a league. We get a television contract as a league. We have revenue-sharing policies which subsidize our lower revenue teams from the higher revenue teams as a league.

And then we get to this particular area and our hands are tied by existing court precedents.

Ms. LOFGREN. Could I ask one more question? I am brandnew to the Congress, have been here only a year. Would you be willing to open up the books and the records of the league and its teams so we could review the minutes of your meetings about relocation matters and understand the kind of dynamics that you are dealing with, so that as we seek——

Mr. TAGLIABUE. I will be glad to—we gave the Senate committee the reports that I filed on the Raiders' and Rams' moves last year, which are the two most comprehensive reports that we have.

Ms. LOFGREN. So you would open up the records to this committee and their staff?

Mr. TAGLIABUE. Yes. We gave them to Senator Hatch's committee and we would be glad to furnish them to the chairman.

Ms. LOFGREN. Thank you. My time has expired.

Mr. TAGLIABUE. They deal with the application of our current policy guidelines to the extent we believe we are able to enforce them.

Mr. HYDE. Mr. Chabot, the gentleman from Ohio.

Mr. CHABOT. Thank you, Mr. Chairman.

Mr. Tagliabue, H.R. 2740, which is the Hoke bill, requires a league to award an expansion team to a community that loses a team if a financially qualified owner is identified. If the league refuses, then one of the consequences is that the league would lose its pooled broadcasting antitrust exemption for 1 year.

How would that provision affect small market teams like Cincinnati or Green Bay if it were implemented?

Mr. TAGLIABUE. The provision that says that if a team were to move, then another team would have to be replaced if there was a replacement buyer at 80 percent of the price?

Mr. CHABOT. Right. And then if they didn't get an expansion team, then the consequences would be that the league would lose its pooled broadcasting antitrust exemption for one year. I guess my concern, my community being Cincinnati, is that being a small market team, if we didn't have the pooled resources, the——

Mr. TAGLIABUE. The most negative thing that could be done, believe me, it is unquestioned, is to limit or take away the ability of the league to sell the television rights and to distribute the money equally to all the teams. That would undercut the stability of a large number of teams in the National Football League today, including the Bengals. For a lower revenue team in the NFL, our national television distribution today can be 60 or 65 percent of their total revenue, maybe even 70 percent—I would have to check—for the lowest revenue team.

That equal distribution of television to Green Bay, Cincinnati, Buffalo, Kansas City, New Orleans, those smaller markets, is their safety net.

Mr. CHABOT. So the——

Mr. TAGLIABUE. You create tremendous instability.

The beauty of the NFL in terms of what is left of our stability is that television pooling of the coverage and of the revenue equally to every team.

Mr. CHABOT. So just to paraphrase what I think you said, the small market teams, like Cincinnati, Green Bay and some of the others, would be the ones that would lose the most?

Mr. TAGLIABUE. It would be extremely counterproductive to tinker with that league sale of television, which gives us equal coverage, roughly, for all the teams. Every team is guaranteed exposure on all of its games, and it is—every team is guaranteed an equal share of the television revenues.

Mr. CHABOT. Thank you.

Another question: Could you comment briefly on what the rules are relative to the NFL and Major League baseball permitting the joint use of stadiums?

Mr. TAGLIABUE. We share stadiums with baseball in many, many situations, including Riverfront Stadium. In most instances historically, the baseball tenant was the prime tenant because they had 81 days, and our teams tended to be a subtenant or a subsidiary tenant; in terms of the dates, we get sort of second priority on dates, and we have to defer to their scheduling of their playoff games and their World Series in September and October.

So—and we have had to switch the location of some of our games probably, including Bengals games. We have had to schedule games on a contingent basis in order to deal with the uncertainty of whether a particular team was going to be in the playoffs or the World Series of baseball. We would just try to work it out on a case-by-case basis and sometimes we have had to switch games from one stadium to another to accommodate the baseball schedule.

Mr. CHABOT. OK. And finally, isn't expansion one solution to the problem of teams moving from one city to another: if there is such a strong demand for professional football why not allow more teams? And particularly when you look at the success of the Carolina Panthers' and the Jacksonville Jaguars' expansion franchises, doesn't that make a pretty strong case that there should be more expansion?

Mr. TAGLIABUE. My judgment is the opposite, frankly, as I suggested earlier. One of the marketplace problems we are all dealing with here, in my judgment, is oversaturation of teams. And we are dealing with markets that are having increasing difficulty supporting multiple franchises.

And again I am sympathetic to Tampa Bay's position, and I don't mean to disagree with anything that the witness said. I have had conversations with the mayor of Tampa Bay about their efforts to keep the Buccaneers. But the simple fact is that when the NFL put the Buccaneers on the west coast of Florida, it worked very well because we were the only team in town. Now they have acquired on that west coast of Florida, and I will include Orlando for present purposes, 60 miles inland from Tampa Bay, three additional major league franchises: The Orlando Magic in the NBA, a new baseball team about to start in the St. Petersburg Dome, and an NHL team.

Question, can an area which once well supported one team support four? I don't know the answer. It is an issue of oversaturation. They are all selling suites. They are all selling premium seats. They are all in the business of dealing with escalating player costs. They are all in the business of privatizing, to some degree or another, the cost of new construction of stadiums, renovation of facilities, et cetera. Facilities costs are now a major private cost in sports because of the limitations on the availability of private money. And where we had one, we now have four.

Denver, we started with the Broncos. It was great. We were the only game in the Rocky Mountains. Now they have the Rockies, 4 million fans a year. They have the Nuggets and they have the Avalanche. Is it going to work? I don't know. I have my doubts.

We are dealing with oversaturation. We are dealing with a glut of product in some markets, which is one of the reasons for the instability. At the same time as we have more people in the market chasing the dollars, we have escalating costs in every area. Our player costs in 1994 were $1.4 billion. Our revenue is $2.1 billion as a league. We pay 67 percent of our revenue to the players.

Mr. HYDE. The gentleman's time has expired. The gentleman from Florida, Mr. Canady.

Mr. CANADY. Mr. Chairman, I yield my time to Mr. Hoke.

Mr. HYDE. The gentleman from Ohio, Mr. Hoke.

Mr. HOKE. Thank you very much, Mr. Canady. I appreciate that.

I wanted to make a few observations before I asked several questions because I just feel the need to respond to some of the observations that the commissioner has made.

First of all, regarding the characterization of the competing forms of entertainment in Cleveland, OH, and that $685 million has been spent by the city on these competing forms, I think in the interests of just creating some balance and getting the record straight on this, there are a number of corrections that need to be made.

First of all, with respect to the Gateway project, the Jacobs Field and Gund Arena, about half of the money that went into those projects was private money. It was not public money. The balance of it came from the State and from the county, only a small amount came from the city.

The Rock and Roll Hall of Fame, for which I happen to be a member of the board of trustees, most of that money was non-Cleveland money. There is a substantial amount of private money, private foundation money, a substantial amount of State money, but very little money from the city.

I don't know the funding mechanism—well, I know a little bit about the Museum of Science and Technology funding mechanism, but there is a great deal of private money in that as well.

But I think that the point is that even with these competing forms of entertainment, and certainly it is arguable whether rock and roll is competing against the Browns. And as I am sure you know, Mr. Commissioner, the Museum of Science and Technology will not be open for another year. And to my knowledge, the NBA does not play on Sunday afternoons and there has been an attempt to not have games played simultaneously——

Mr. TAGLIABUE. We all compete. I can assure you of that.

Mr. HOKE [continuing]. Between Major League Baseball and football, at least in Cleveland. That did not prevent the Browns from selling out the stadium until Mr. Modell announced his move in early November, nor did it prevent the citizens of greater Cleveland from supporting a tax package that would, in fact, bring $175 million for renovations. So if your suggestion is that somehow these competing forms of entertainment are responsible for a lack of fan support, the facts simply do not indicate that.

Mr. TAGLIABUE. May I comment? I was not suggesting that at all. We have been working hand and glove with Mayor White since mid-November to keep the team in Cleveland.

Mr. HOKE. I am not sure what your point was, then.

Mr. TAGLIABUE. My point is that Mayor White has said——

Mr. HOKE. May I finish, please?

I am not sure what your point was about the $685 million in competing forms of entertainment, if in fact they have not eroded the popularity of the Browns.

Mr. TAGLIABUE. The point is that the city and the county said no more public money, because we have spent it all on baseball and basketball. That can be documented.

Mr. HOKE. The fact is that the county and the citizens of northeast Ohio came up with a package for another $175 million for football.

Mr. TAGLIABUE. Which is why we are working with the mayor very, very, very closely.

Mr. HOKE. Let me talk a moment about the Green Bay Packers. The fact is that the Green Bay Packers made a profit, according to their own published statements, of $3.5 million. They went to the championship game. They nearly went to the Super Bowl. They do have luxury seats. They do have premium seats. These things were not paid for only with tax dollars but in a private-public way. The private sector that is enjoying the benefits of that kind of business entertainment are paying the greatest share and bearing the greatest burden of those costs and that is completely appropriate. And they are not doing it in an environment in which a shotgun is being held to anybody's head with a threat that the team is going to move out of town. It seems to me that, in fact, they create a model which is extremely attractive.

The other thing I wanted to go to was the interpretation that we have of these ninth circuit cases, because it is absolutely crystal clear that we couldn't be farther apart in our interpretations of them.

What I find remarkable is that every time the NFL or its representatives talk about the inability of the league or leagues, professional leagues to restrict franchise movement, they always quote from what is commonly known as *Raiders I*, and yet, there is, as though a complete lack of memory or as though it never existed either the *Raiders II* case or the *Clippers* case. And I think to——

Mr. TAGLIABUE. I have written in the Antitrust Law Journal articles about *Raiders I*, *Raiders II*, and *Clippers* and I can give you a very simple comment. You and I are very far apart on what those cases mean. You read a statement this morning as saying the ninth circuit indicated that the league's rules on team relocation were not unlawful as a matter of law.

The court was there saying that they were not per se violations of the antitrust laws; that they were jury issues. As jury issues, the risks presented are unacceptable for a businessman because the issue that the jury is asked to decide is whether a league decision that says to a team you cannot move restrains the ability of that team to compete for a stadium. The question answers itself. It is like Mr. Halas' example: Does the rim of a wheel restrain the spokes? The answer is yes. So you go to a jury with a treble damage penalty in an interested forum with a rule of law that treats a member of the league as a business competitor of the other members of the league. It is a stacked deck. Believe me. I know the cases. I litigated the cases.

Mr. HOKE. I have to interrupt you. The idea of interested forums, particularly when we are in Federal court, is at least to me, who happens to be an attorney licensed in the State of Ohio, particularly offensive. This notion that somehow that kind of forum shopping, particularly when it comes to the Federal courts and the notion that they are going to stack the deck against the rule of law and in favor of the rule of popularity——

Mr. TAGLIABUE. The only thing I would say on that——

Mr. HOKE. I am not finished. Thank you—is I think extremely, extremely offensive to the Federal court system.

But what I cannot understand in this disagreement that we have is that you fail to actually see the outcome of the *Clippers* case. The *Clippers* case, which was the same ninth circuit located not in San Diego but in Los Angeles, found in favor of a $5 million settlement that ultimately was paid by the Clippers team to the NBA. Exactly the opposite result as in the *Raiders* case. And it seems to me that it is just common sense that indicates that while the ability to restrict the movements exist, it is not in the economic self-interest of the league to do that. I understand that; I don't particularly criticize it. I don't think that the owners are evil, although some of the behavior, particularly the behavior this past weekend and the behavior of Mr. Modell, is very unattractive when you consider the public statements made by those individuals.

But it is clear from the law itself that you can make those restrictions, you can enforce them if you care to. You have never tested that.

Mr. TAGLIABUE. Just a second, please. In the *Clippers* case, the NBA did not try to stop the Clippers from moving. They let them move from San Diego to Los Angeles. As corollary to that, they charged them a fee for the upgrade in the value of their franchise.

Mr. HOKE. They did not really let them move. The Clippers moved without permission. There was not the question of letting or not. It is sort of like, did you let the Seahawks move to Los Angeles? Did you let the Baltimore Colts move from Baltimore to Indianapolis?

Mr. TAGLIABUE. The Clippers moved because the NBA was unwilling to litigate the case.

Mr. HOKE. They set up the vans and they took their stuff.

Mr. TAGLIABUE. The Clippers moved because the NBA was unwilling to stop them in the light of the Raiders precedent in which we had been required to pay $50 million in damages to the plaintiff team, the Raiders, and the L.A. Coliseum. So the league took a litigation strategy of saying that we will let you move because of the antitrust risks; you can move from San Diego to Los Angeles, but we are going to charge you a fee for the upgrade in the value of your franchise now that you are a Los Angeles team rather than a San Diego team. That was upheld by the court. It was not a blocked move case. The damages are a key issue.

In the Rams' move from Los Angeles to St. Louis, they had signed a 30-year lease. They claimed, they and the State of Missouri claimed that the incremental value of the lease was $1 billion. We were going to face a $3 billion claim.

Mr. HOKE. I am just about out of time. Since you bring that up, I wonder, was any additional money paid by the owner of the Los Angeles Rams to the league after the first vote which prohibited the movement of the Rams from Los Angeles to St. Louis?

Mr. TAGLIABUE. Yes, that is a matter of public record. The owner of the Rams paid a sum of money to the league which was basically a disincentive to move, which was distributed to the low revenue teams in our league. We have a low revenue pool which we set up last year, and we are taking relocation payments and putting the money that comes from relocation of teams who are getting lucrative leases in new cities and distributing some incremental portion of that money to our low revenue teams who have difficulty surviving under our——

Mr. HYDE. The gentleman's 12 minutes have expired.

Mr. HOKE. I wanted to make the point——

Mr. HYDE. I am sure you do. Go ahead.

Mr. HOKE [continuing]. That the money was paid after a vote that went against the move. After the money was paid, the owners changed their votes and they allowed the move.

Mr. TAGLIABUE. But any suggestion that that was a significant factor is very misleading.

Mr. HYDE. The gentleman from Virginia.

Mr. SCOTT. Thank you, Mr. Chairman. Mr. Tagliabue has indicated that he has written law journal articles. I was wondering if we could get copies of those.

Mr. TAGLIABUE. Yes, sir, we would be pleased to provide them.

Mr. HYDE. Thank you.

[See appendix, page 228.]

Mr. HYDE. The gentleman from Chicago, Mr. Michael Patrick Flanagan.

Mr. FLANAGAN. Good afternoon, gentleman. Thank you for taking the time to come in.

Mr. Tagliabue, your testimony has been very enlightening. I have a logical problem, though, with where we have gone with this and I hope you can solve it for me.

I want to ask about the antitrust exemption that was granted 30 some years ago, the broadcast antitrust exemption that permits you to pool the money and distribute it out to lower level teams. In answer to Mr. Gekas you intimated it will provide stability to the league and will keep these other smaller market teams from moving on because they take a revenue share. Logically that seems correct and well, but it hasn't borne out.

Mr. TAGLIABUE. It bore out until the Federal courts subjected us to punitive damages for trying to stop a team from moving.

Mr. FLANAGAN. I think what we are seeing here is that you view the problem more as the fact that you do not have an a la baseball antitrust exemption to have an absolute power over movement or nonmovement by a mutual vote and, having that be the law, to use the term loosely, in whether a team can move or not, rather than being able to pool the money. Is it either or both or do they work together?

Mr. TAGLIABUE. I think if you look at it from a historical perspective, it becomes clear. Commissioner Rozelle testified in support of the broadcast legislation in 1961 and he said it was very important in order to assure the survival of teams in cities such as Green Bay and other small towns that the league be able to sell the television rights for all the members and distribute the revenue equally. He said then that that would support team stability. He reiterated that in 1966, at the time of the merger of the NFL and the AFL, and he made good on that commitment to team stability so long as he was the commissioner was in a position to have the league control the location of the teams. And the NFL had a terrific record of team stability. No team moved from 1960 until 1980. There was complete stability of franchises during that period of time.

Then when Commissioner Rozelle tried to—when he opposed the Raiders' move and the membership voted down the Raiders' move from Oakland to Los Angeles at a time when they had 12 consecutive seasons of sellouts, much like the Browns do now, a court in Los Angeles ordered that the Raiders, A, were entitled to move, and, B, the league was going to pay approximately $50 million in treble damages for having tried to stop them.

The erosion in our record on franchise stability begins with that decision and it has continued since then. And so it is not inconsistent; it is just the historical sequence of events.

Mr. FLANAGAN. I did not say it was inconsistent, I am just trying to find the root cause for the development of the movement of teams today. Is it because you cannot say no or is it because you distribute the money that comes in from a broadcast revenue-sharing plan, or is it both?

Mr. TAGLIABUE. The root cause is what I outlined at the beginning when the chairman was present. No. 1, it is the legal standards that have evolved under section 1 of the Sherman act and the *Raiders* case, and other cases.

No. 2, it is the competition in the marketplace for the sports dollar for fan competition and for the construction of new stadiums. And, No. 3, it is escalating player costs given the advent of free agency in the NFL. Those three things together are creating the pressures to pursue enhanced stadium revenue in new facilities.

Mr. FLANAGAN. I understand that, but the problem we are dealing with is not the economic survivability of football.

Mr. TAGLIABUE. Correct. As a league, we are in good shape. The problem is we have some teams that are not.

Mr. FLANAGAN. Dividing up $1.2 billion a year in broadcast revenues alone is survivability. No other form of business, industry, if you will, in this country enjoys the legal exceptions that sports do in one various form or another yet still we have the migration. General Motors doesn't move plants like football teams move, which have broad economic impacts.

What I hear you saying, if I am hearing you correctly, and I am asking, is for us to broaden your powers, to give you the powers that you exercised before Raiders I don't understand how giving you more powers solves the problem? To permit you to behave more in charge? I am confused.

Mr. TAGLIABUE. Right now we are powerless in this area because of the antitrust uncertainties. We are approaching the powerless. Believe me.

Mr. FLANAGAN. But pooling $1.2 billion like no other industry in this country can is not powerless.

Mr. TAGLIABUE. If you divide 1.2 by 30 teams, you have $40 million of revenue. That does not cover our current player costs.

Mr. FLANAGAN. Nor should it. You are a business as well.

Mr. TAGLIABUE. We have a collective bargaining agreement which forces every team to spend at a very high level in the free agent context. And we have some high revenue teams and then we have some medium and then some lower revenue teams.

Mr. FLANAGAN. Yes, of course.

Mr. TAGLIABUE. And as a league in the aggregate, we are healthy. What is not healthy is our lower revenue spectrum of teams. They fear—Minnesota Vikings are a good example and they have made an extensive financial presentation to a gubernatorial task force on their economics. They fear that in Minnesota, with their revenues being at the level of, say, 60 to 65 million total, when other teams have revenues in the range of 90 to 120 million, with 40 million of television being a common piece, but the Vikings' 40 million represents 65 percent of their revenue and the other club's 40 million represents maybe 40 percent of its revenue. They fear that they cannot compete in signing players and securing talent.

That is the dynamic which is at work in the league. We are trying to deal with it by a number of mechanisms. We have adopted new revenue-sharing in the last year. We are supporting the construction of stadiums now by having the visiting teams forgo some of the revenue that they would normally get, give it back to the home team and use it for debt service. We are going to do that with the Washington Redskins' new stadium. Visiting teams who come into that new stadium, if it gets built, will forgo a portion of their gate. They will turn it back to the Redskins who will use it on the private debt service on that stadium which is being privately financed by the ownership.

Mr. FLANAGAN. One last comment. I commend the NFL in finding the most creative way possible to maintain your economic viability, but I further must observe and I haven't heard an answer as to the complex paradigm we have of saying we make enormous amounts of money that we share in many wonderful different ways yet we have to compound huge amounts of money out of local governments to maintain our viability and to keep the markets trying to service fan interest. But, at the same time we are having to behave irrespective of it, because we don't have omnipotent power here, just colossal power. I continue to be confused.

Mr. TAGLIABUE. Again, I am beginning to be repetitive. But with respect to the particular subject at hand, we are becoming powerless because of the exposure to treble damage litigation. I told the story, perhaps you were not here, about the New England Patriots' owner who came to me in the last couple of years who said, I can't make it in New England, I want to move out of the market. I said, I don't think that is justified for three reasons. No. 1—and, believe me, my voice was a little louder than it is right now—No. 1, I think your problems are of your own making; No. 2, we have a commitment to NBC that we will have a team in New England; and, No. 3, some of your problems have to do with other businesses, not the NFL.

I said I cannot recommend that your team move. I think it has to stay where it is. That was your commitment when you came into the league, and if you wanted to move it, I would strongly oppose that.

He sold his team to a buyer who was willing to keep it in New England which is where it is now. As a result of that conversation or those conversations, we are now a defendant in Federal court in New York in a lawsuit in which he is seeking hundreds of millions of dollars of damages on the basis that I restrained his ability to compete because I told him he could not move his team. That is an intolerable state of the law.

And on the point of neutral venues, the only point I would make, Mr. Chairman, is that when the Senate Commerce Committee addressed these issues back in the mid-1980's and they reported a bill out that dealt with some of these issues, they saw merit in the neutral venue point and they included a provision that would provide for neutral venues because they felt basically that the litigation was between cities as much as it was between members of the league and that when cities are suing cities, there was sort of a unique basis.

Mr. HYDE. Mr. Commissioner, right up there with motherhood I rank neutral venues. They are not always available.

Mr. TAGLIABUE. The argument was not a shot at the courts, believe me, Mr. Hoke. It was the feeling that basically the litigation is not so much between the Browns and the NFL, or the city of Cleveland and the NFL, the litigation essentially pits Baltimore against Cleveland. And when you have those two types of municipalities, even if it is a Federal court, we would be better off at the Federal level having it in a neutral venue. That was the thinking.

Mr. HYDE. Everybody's time has expired but the chairman's, who has unlimited time. And I just want to say that it is my experience in many years of practicing law and living, that Federal judges are no different than other human beings, subject to the same pressures, and stimulus, and that search for the neutral forum is a worthy one.

I want to thank you, Mr. Commissioner, and you, Mr. Richardson, for the time you have invested helping us, and you have helped us. You have highlighted something that I think we understand more clearly than before, and that is that the uncertainties of the law disserve the sport and the communities involved.

It is one of the things that is our job, really, to try and resolve. Predictability in the law is very helpful, and no matter which way it goes at least you would not be groping in the dark. So we will take that to heart, and we thank you for your great contribution by being here today.

Mr. TAGLIABUE. Well, I appreciate the opportunity to be here, and I get a little emotional on some of these points because we do feel strongly about fan loyalty. Believe me. But we hope we can strike a sensible balance and go forward in a constructive way, and I am sure Jerry would echo those sentiments.

Mr. HYDE. Thank you.
Our final panel consists of three public witnesses who have varying perspectives on these bills. First, we have Prof. Gary Roberts from Tulane Law School. Since 1983, Professor Roberts has been a professor of law at Tulane where he directs the Nation's only sports law certificate program. He has written several articles focusing on sports, antitrust, and business issues. He is also the current president of the Sports Lawyer Association.
We also have Prof. Andy Zimbalist of the economics department of Smith College with us today. He has published several books and articles on the issue of sports economics, and he acted as a consultant during the litigation of the NFL players' association's efforts to obtain free agency rights. He is also the cofounder of the United Baseball League and has previously testified before Congress on baseball's antitrust exemption.
And finally we have with us Mr. Bruce Keller, who represents the International Trademark Association. Mr. Keller is a partner in the law firm of Debevoise & Plimpton where he focuses on trademark, unfair competition, and copyright law.
We look forward to hearing from all our witnesses this afternoon on this issue. And we commend from the bottom of our collective hearts your patience. Thank you.

STATEMENT OF BRUCE KELLER, ESQ., DEBEVOISE & PLIMPTON, ON BEHALF OF THE INTERNATIONAL TRADEMARK ASSOCIATION

Mr. KELLER. Thank you, Mr. Chairman. I have submitted to the committee a prepared statement which I request be made part of the record, so let me address a couple of points in that statement.
Let me emphasize as I start out that the International Trademark Association's concerns with the legislation before the committee are limited solely to the trademark issues raised by H.R. 2740. It has no position on the complex antitrust issues that are before the committee.
The International Trademark Association does believe, however, that those provisions of H.R. 2740 that require a relocating sports team to forfeit its trademark are seriously flawed both as a matter of public policy and as a matter of law.
INTA's policy concerns are triggered by the fact that, if enacted, H.R. 2740 would be an unprecedented effort by the Federal Government to compel privately owned assets, trademark assets which are owned by the owners of the team, not the league or the public, to be dedicated to a perceived public good. Frankly, I don't know of a more delicate way to put this. This legislation, if enacted, would align Congress with a series of actions by totalitarian regimes, such as Cuba and in Eastern Europe, that have seized private property assets in the name of the public good because particular industries were deemed to be particularly important, as the rum and cigar trade were to Cuba and as other industries have been offered up as particularly important in other countries.
Now, INTA recognizes that the bill which has been carefully thought through, offers some rationales for taking these assets away, and the rationale as we understand it is that the business

of sports is somehow different from the other businesses that exist in the American economy.

But when you read the findings of section 2 of the bill, I don't think that the findings support the distinction that is being drawn. I think that, as one of the witnesses earlier today from King County said, it would be as devastating, if not more so for Microsoft to leave the Pacific Northwest or King County, in particular.

Yes, sports are popular and sports are businesses that are rooted for by fans in a way that Microsoft will never enjoy, but the other findings that are offered in support of the legislation simply do not draw a principled distinction, and INTA's principal concern here is that it is going to set a precedent which could be offered to seize the trademark asset of any significant relocating business.

A second major policy flaw with H.R. 2740 is the degree to which it could possibly undermine ongoing U.S. efforts abroad to harmonize and ensure uniform trademark and other intellectual property protection throughout the world with our global trading partners. The problems that the United States faces in this area are considerable as evidenced as recently as Sunday's front page report in the New York Times which disclosed that the United States is having some degree of difficulty in getting China to adhere to the trademark and copyright provisions of the recent trade accord that was negotiated last year. This is a serious problem, and to put it mildly, it would not be helpful to have the United States, when it sits down at the negotiating table arguing for uniform intellectual property protection, have a country on the other side of the table say "you can't really believe that; look how you treat certain trademark assets in your own country." The bill lacks any principled distinction. This will undercut U.S. efforts both domestically and abroad.

As Congressman Moorhead indicated in his opening remarks, this would be the first time that Congress would have enacted such legislation without more carefully considering the possible policy impact this would have on intellectual property protection.

Worst still I think are the legal flaws that H.R. 2740 has, and let me identify just two with the time remaining. First, the International Trademark Association cannot understand how legislation that literally would strip a relocating team of its trademark asset, an asset worth millions of dollars, and without compensating the owner of that asset, require that the mark be reserved for use by the public, the community from which the team is relocating? How that ever could be reconciled with the fifth amendment's prohibition on the taking of private property for public use without just compensation. The cases on this point are clear, they are uniform and are described in our statement, so let me move to the next problem that we have with the provisions.

H.R. 2740 really takes a hacksaw approach to amputating the trademark from a team and putting it somewhere else. By separating the mark from the team and by possibly precluding the use of that mark for years, and by requiring that the mark be reserved solely for use by the community, H.R. 2740 clashes with well-established principles of law that forbid assignments of trademarks without any aspect of the accompanying business and prohibit the cold storage or warehousing of trademarks.

Now, there may be ways, as the commissioner indicated, that as a private matter this can be done, but as legislation it clashes with well-established trademark law principles.

And to stretch the amputation metaphor for one more second, there may be ways to do careful surgical structuring in the private sector to accomplish just what Mr. Hoke hopes to accomplish, but it ought to be done as a matter of negotiation between private parties because the legislation cannot possibly take into account all of the particular factors that come into play. H.R. 2740 cuts across all sports; cuts across all the cities, it covers all trademarks and it simply paints with too broad a brush.

For those reasons, and particularly because Mr. Hoke eloquently described the other benefits of his legislation apart from the trademark provisions, and because this committee has before it another bill which attempts to address the problems, we would urge that you not adopt these provisions of H.R. 2740, and if you decide to act, take another approach to the problem.

Thank you.

Mr. HYDE. I thank you, Mr. Keller.

[The prepared statement of Mr. Keller follows:]

PREPARED STATEMENT OF BRUCE KELLER, ESQ., DEBEVOISE & PLIMPTON, ON BEHALF OF THE INTERNATIONAL TRADEMARK ASSOCIATION

I. INTRODUCTION.

Mr. Chairman, the International Trademark Association (INTA) (formerly known as the United States Trademark Association) appreciates the opportunity to testify today on legislation relating to the relocation of professional sports franchises.

INTA's interest in the bills before this Committee, the Fans Rights Act of 1995 (H.R. 2699) and the Fan Freedom and Community Protection Act of 1995 (H.R. 2740), is limited to those provisions of H.R. 2740 that address the trademark rights of sports team owners. INTA expresses no view on the antitrust exemption issues raised by these bills or on any other proposal intended to discourage sports teams from relocating so long as they do not upset existing principles of trademark laws. As detailed below, INTA's review of the trademark provisions of H.R. 2740 has led it to conclude that, if enacted, they would: (a) unconstitutionally deprive the owner of a relocating team of property rights protected by the Fifth Amendment; (b) result in the unlawful warehousing and possible abandonment of those trademark rights; and (c) otherwise conflict with and undermine the basic goals and principles of trademark law. For these reasons, INTA respectfully urges this Committee not to adopt those provisions.

My name is Bruce Keller. I presently serve as counsel to INTA. I am a partner with the law firm of Debevoise & Plimpton, where I practice in the fields of trademark, unfair competition and copyright law. From time to time in my practice, I also have represented the National Football League, National Football League Properties, Inc. and National Football League Enterprises. I want to make clear that my appearance today is solely as a spokesperson for INTA.

INTA is a 118-year-old, not-for-profit membership organization. Since its founding in 1878, its membership has grown from twelve New York-based manufacturers to approximately 3,100 members that are drawn from across the U.S. and from 115 countries.

Membership in INTA is open to trademark owners and to those who serve trademark owners. Its members are corporations, advertising agencies, professional and trade associations and law firms. INTA's membership is diverse: it crosses all industry lines, spanning a broad range of manufacturing, retail and service operations. All of INTA's members share, however, a common interest in trademarks and a recognition of the importance of trademarks to their owners and to the general public.

INTA is extremely interested in seeing that the United States maintains its worldwide leadership role in ensuring that trademarks and trademark protection are recognized as essential elements of a free and open global economy. For example, INTA actively assisted Congress's landmark overhaul of federal trademark legislation in 1988[1] and its recent passage of a federal trademark dilution bill a few weeks ago.[2] The dramatic and adverse implications of H.R. 2740 for trademark law require INTA to speak out on the problems that bill would create.

II. TRADEMARKS ARE PROPERTY

For more than a century, Congress and the courts have recognized and treated trademarks as private property.[3] Congress passed the first federal trademark act in 1880,[4] and in 1946 enacted the present, federal trademark law, commonly known as the Lanham Act.[5] During the last 50 years, Congress also has recognized the strong, dual role trademark assets play in the U.S. economic system. They protect consumers against potential marketplace confusion and, at the same time, encourage businesses to invest time and money in developing marketplace recognition.[6] For these reasons, Congress consistently has acted to strengthen and expand the scope of trademark rights and restrictions—most notably in 1988 by the Trademark Law Revision Act,[7] and most recently in 1995.[8]

Courts also have recognized the valuable role trademark laws play in the American economy. For example, in 1942, the U.S. Supreme Court wrote:

> The protection of trade-marks is the law's recognition of the psychological function of symbols. If it is true that we live by symbols, it is no less true that we purchase goods by them. A trademark is a merchandising shortcut which induces a purchaser to select what he wants, or what he has been led to believe he wants. The owner of a mark exploits this human propensity by making every effort to impregnate the atmosphere of the market with the drawing power of a congenial symbol. Whatever the means employed, the aim is the same—to convey through the mark, in the minds of potential customers, the desirability of the commodity upon which it appears. Once this is attained, the trade-mark owner has something of value.[9]

More than 50 years later, these same two concepts continue to guide our nation's trademark law. The Supreme Court recently stated that trademark law:

> quickly and easily assures a [consumer] that this item . . . is made by the same producer as other similarly marked items that he or she liked (or disliked) in the past. At that same time, the law helps assure a producer that it (and not an imitating competitor) will reap the financial, reputation-related rewards associated with a desirable product.[10]

In addition to these legislative and legal perspectives, the importance of trademarks is a fundamental, business place reality. Trademarks often can be a company's most valuable asset. For example, the Coca-Cola® trademark has been valued at more than $39 billion, the IBM® trademark at more than $17 billion and the Kodak® mark at more than $11 billion.[11] The Lanham Act expressly codifies the principle that this valuable property, although intangible, is as capable of ownership as tangible assets like land or equipment.[12] It provides for a federal scheme that allows trademark owners to protect this property through federal causes of action for infringement or dilution of both registered and unregistered marks.[13]

---

[1] S. Rep. No. 100–515, 100th Cong., 2d Sess. 2 (1988), *reprinted* in 1988 U.S.C.C.A.N. 5577, 5578.
[2] Federal Trademark Dilution Act of 1995, Pub. L. No. 104–98.
[3] *See* Restatement (Third) Unfair Competition, § 9 cmte. (1995) (hereafter "Restatement"); *Trade-Mark Cases*, 100 U.S. (10 Otto) 82, 92 (1879).
[4] S. Rep. No. 100–515, 1988 U.S.C.C.A.N. at 5578.
[5] 15 U.S.C. § 1051 et seq.
[6] In 1988, the Senate Report on the Trademark Law Revision Act noted that "[t]rademarks encourage competition, promote economic growth and can raise the standard of living of an entire nation." They also serve "the public by making consumers confident that they can identify the brands they prefer and can purchase those brands without being confused or misled." S. Rep. No. 100–515, 1988 U.S.C.C.A.N. at 5580.
[7] Trademark Law Revision Act of 1988, Pub. L. No. 100–667.
[8] Federal Trademark Dilution Act of 1995, Pub. L. No. 104–98.
[9] *Mishawaka Rubber & Woolen Mfg. Co. v. S.S. Kresge Co.*, 316 U.S. 203, 205 (1942).
[10] *Qualitex Co. v. Jacobson Prods. Co., Inc.*, 115 S. Ct. 1300, 1303 (1995). *See also Two Pesos, Inc. v. Taco Cabana, Inc.*, 505 U.S. 763, 774 (1992) (extending Lanham Act protection of trade dress as consistent with legislative goals of securing the good will of owner and protecting consumers); *Inwood Labs., Inc. v. Ives Labs., Inc.*, 456 U.S. 844 (1982) (recognizing goals of Lanham Act to protect good will that proprietor possesses in mark).
[11] K. Badenhausen, "Brands: The Management Factor," *Financial World* (Aug. 1, 1995) 51.
[12] 15 U.S.C. § 1057(b).
[13] 15 U.S.C. §§ 1114 and 1125(a) and (c).

III. LEGISLATION THAT DEPRIVES AN OWNER OF THE USE OF PRIVATE PROPERTY WITHOUT JUST COMPENSATION IS UNCONSTITUTIONAL

The Fifth Amendment to the United States Constitution prohibits governmental abuse of due process of law and the taking of "private property . . . for public use, without just compensation."[14] Any governmental action that denies the owner of substantially all the economic benefits of the property taken is unconstitutional unless just compensation is paid. It does not matter that the property taken is intangible; courts have found an unconstitutional taking in a wide array of cases involving intangible property.[15] It does not matter that the property right is affected, or even protected by, a federal statutory regime; where a party has a reasonable expectation of a property right under existing law, the Fifth Amendment is violated when government takes new steps to confiscate that property.[16]

For over 80 years, U.S. courts have protected trademarks using the same constitutional takings analysis that applies to tangible and other types of intangible property,[17] and repeatedly have recognized that a governmental taking of a trademark would "violate bedrock principles . . . embodied in the Fifth Amendment to the Constitution."[18] In fact, this constitutional principle is so well established that U.S. courts never have faced an attempted seizure of trademarks by any U.S. governmental entity. Previously, the issue has arisen only when foreign governments, often communist or totalitarian regimes, have attempted to expropriate the U.S. trademark rights of multinational companies doing business both in the U.S. and abroad.[19] The consistent rulings of these cases put beyond dispute the principle that U.S.-based trademark rights are fully protected as private property under the Fifth Amendment.

Section 3 of H.R. 2740 is in complete conflict with this well established rule of law because it provides that if certain professional sports team relocations are approved:

(1) *the registered mark* that is used to identify the professional sports team becomes *the property of the League;*
(2) the League shall reserve the registered mark . . . for use only by the community from which the team is relocating;
(3) the registered mark . . . may not be used [by the relocating team]. (emphasis added). By expressly requiring that a trademark owner transfer its trademark to a League and that the League hold the mark for use by the public, there simply is no way to characterize these provisions of H.R. 2740 as anything other than a taking of "private property" for "public use." Without either establishing the compensation to be paid, or at the least, a mechanism for arriving at such compensation, the provisions are unconstitutional.

---

[14] U.S. Const. amend. V.
[15] *See, e.g., Webb's Fabulous Pharmacies,* 449 U.S. 155, 164 (1980) (interest on interpleader fund); *Kaiser Aetna v. United States,* 444 U.S. 164, 179–80 (1979) (right to exclude public from navigable waters); *United States v. Causby,* 328 U.S. 256 (1946) (air space over chicken farm).
[16] *Lucas v. South Carolina Coastal Council,* 505 U.S. 1003, 1029 (1992) ("confiscatory regulations . . . cannot be newly legislated or decreed (without compensation), but must inhere" in existing law); *Cabo Dist. Co., Inc. v. Brady,* 821 F. Supp. 601, 609 (N.D. Cal. 1992) (holding the trademark and trade dress of "Black Deaths vodka, as well as the certificates of label approval for imported liquor issued by Bureau of Alcohol, Tobacco and Firearms, property protected under Fifth Amendment).
[17] *Baglin v. Cusenier Co.,* 221 U.S. 580, 596 (1911). In *Baglin,* the Court analyzed the validity of France's expropriation of the U.S.-registered trademark "Chartreuse," used for a French liqueur, and refused to strip the trademark rights from the French monks who manufactured the liqueur.
[18] *Maltina Corp. v. Cawy Bottling Co.,* 462 F.2d 1021, 1027 (5th Cir.), cert. denied, 409 U.S. 1060 (1972) (citing *Republic of Iraq v. First Nat'l City Bank,* 353 F.2d 47 (2d Cir. 1965), cert. denied, 382 U.S. 1027 (1966)) (Cuban expropriation of plaintiff's business did not cause divestiture of plaintiff's trademark "Malta Cristal" used for malt beverage).
[19] *E.g., Baglin,* 221 U.S. at 593–94; *Carl Zeiss Stiftung v. V.E.B. Carl Zeiss, Jena,* 433 F.2d 686, 703 (2d Cir. 1970), cert. denied, 403 U.S. 905 (1971) (Soviet seizure of plaintiffs photographic equipment business did not affect plaintiffs ownership of U.S.-registered "Zeiss" trademark); *Maltina,* 462 F.2d at 1027; *Zwack v. Kraus Bros. & Co.,* 237 F.2d 255, 259 (2d Cir. 1956) (Hungary's seizure of plaintiffs liquor exporting business did not affect plaintiffs ownership of U.S.-registered trademarks); *F. Palicio y Compania, S.A. v. Brush,* 256 F. Supp. 481, 488 (S.D.N.Y. 1966), aff'd, 375 F.2d 1011 (2d Cir.), cert. denied, 389 U.S. 830 (1967) (Cuba's seizure of plaintiffs' cigar manufacturing businesses did not affect ownership of plaintiffs' U.S.-registered trademarks); cf., *Williams & Humbert Ltd. v. W. & H. Trade Marks (Jersey) Ltd.,* 840 F.2d 72, 75 (D.C. cir. 1988) (United States recognized Spain's rights to expropriate the mark "Dry Sack," for sherry, because Spain had attempted to compensate plaintiff for the expropriation).

IV. THE TRADEMARK PROVISIONS OF H.R. 2740 ARE INCONSISTENT WITH ESTABLISHED PRINCIPLES OF THE LANHAM ACT

H.R. 2740 has several other flaws as well. It conflicts with principles of existing trademark law; weakens the U.S. trademark position internationally; and sets bad precedent for the business community.

A. *The Trademark Provisions Conflict with Principles of Existing Trademark Law*

As noted above, Congress and the courts long have recognized the value and importance of trademarks to our national economy. The trademark provisions of H.R. 2740 ignore this settled law, and the rationale behind the Lanham Act, in at least three important ways: (1) they are based on the fundamentally flawed notion that trademarks can be separated from the businesses with which they are used; (2) they permit the unlawful "warehousing" of trademarks in violation of the Lanham Act; and (3) they are contrary to the broad protection Congress consistently has given trademarks.

1. *The Trademark Provisions Separate Trademarks From Their Use in Commerce*

It is important to recognize that although Congress has enacted trademark legislation pursuant to the Commerce Clause,[20] this federal legislation largely is a codification of trademark principles that have an independent existence at common law.[21] This common law tradition of trademark law in the U.S. is critical, because trademark rights are created upon use of a mark, and exist completely independent of any additional rights protected or awarded under the Lanham Act. It is because of the strong common law tradition that there can be no trademark rights without actual use of the mark [22] that Congress, in the Trademark Law Revision Act of 1988, emphasized "the central role that use continues to play in U.S. trademark law."[23]

Trademark rights may not be acquired or maintained without their use in commerce in connection with goods or services. The Lanham Act embodies this principle by providing that a trademark is "assignable only with the business or goodwill attached to the use of the mark,"[24] and is consistent with numerous judicial opinions to the same effect.[25] The trademark provisions of H.R. 2740, however, would force the owner of a relocating sports team to divorce the business operation of its team from the trademark under which it has operated and to assign that mark to a league. This is completely inconsistent with existing law. There can be no assignment of a mark "in gross," *i.e.*, apart from the accompanying business with which it is used.[26]

This bedrock principle of trademark law effectively serves as a consumer protection statute because it ensures that a trademark always will be used with the same business that consumers have come to recognize as being symbolized by the mark. That is one reason that the federal courts, in a recent sports franchise relocation case, rejected the argument that a Canadian Football League ("CFL") team could enter Baltimore and adopt the name "Baltimore Colts." The CFL's "Baltimore Colts" contended that they were entitled to that mark because the former Baltimore Colts, which left Baltimore in 1984 and now are know as the Indianapolis Colts,® no longer were linked to, or owned any rights in, their prior name. The Court of Appeals for the Seventh Circuit held that under well-established trademark principles:

---

[20] U.S. Const. art. I, § 8, cl. 3.
[21] Restatement, Foreword ("For the most part . . . both federal and state unfair competition statutes generally rely . . . on concepts derived from common law . . . Except as otherwise noted, the principles discussed in this Restatement are applicable to actions at common law and to the interpretation of analogous federal and state statutory codifications.")
[22] *United Drug Co.* v. *Theodore Rectanus Co.*, 248 U.S. 90, 97 (1918) ("There is no such thing as a property right in a trademark except as a right appurtenant to an established business . . . with which the mark is employed.")
[23] S. Rep. No. 100–515, 1988 U.S.C.C.A.N. at 5586.
[24] 15 U.S.C. § 1060; S. Rep. 100–515, 1988 U.S.C.C.A.N. at 5594.
[25] *Mister Donut of America, Inc.* v. *Mr. Donut, Inc.*, 418 F.2d 838, 842 (9th cir. 1969) ("The law is well settled that there are no rights in trademark alone and that no rights can be transferred apart from the business with which the mark has been associated.") (citation omitted); *see also* Restatement § 34.
[26] Restatement § 34 ("An assignment of ownership that does not maintain continuity . . . can result in abandonment"); *Clark & Freeman* v. *Heartland Co.*, 811 F. Supp. 137, 140 (S.D.N.Y. 1993) (the assignment of a mark for women's boots is invalid because the assignee's use of that mark for men's shoes and hiking boots was not substantially similar to the original use).

The Colts were Irsay's team; it moved intact; there is no evidence it has changed more since the move than it had in years before. There is, in contrast, no continuity, no links contractual or otherwise, nothing but a geographical site in common, between the Baltimore Colts and the Canadian Football League team that would like to use its name. *Any suggestion that there is such continuity is false and potentially misleading.* [27]

Section 3 of H.R. 2740 would force a valid trademark to be used, if at all, only with a completely new and different team, despite that new team's lack of continuity with the original franchise. For this reason, it is completely inconsistent with and dramatically undermines fundamental principles of trademark law that exist to ensure business continuity.

2. *The Trademark Provisions Permit "Warehousing" of Marks in Violation of the Lanham Act*

A corollary of the principle that trademark rights must be based on actual use is that "token" use of a mark cannot establish trademark rights. Token uses do not qualify as *bona fide* uses in commerce because they are not actual, commercial uses of a trademark in connection with a specific product or service that will allow the public to identify the mark with the good or service. For that reason, when the Trademark Law Revision Act of 1988 was passed, the definition of "use in commerce" was "[r]evised to eliminate the commercially transparent practice of token use."[28]

This concept is not new. Courts always have frowned on tactics that constitute token use, such as "warehousing," that are designed to allow a party to acquire and reserve rights in a mark without actual use.[29] Section 3 of H.R. 2740 violates this principle. It would bar a team owner from using its mark in connection with the sports entertainment services on which its entire business is predicated. It requires that mark to be held in reserve until—and if—another team owner brings an entirely new team to the abandoned locale. Section 3 thus legislates a form of warehousing that, under established law, could result in complete abandonment of the trademark at issue.[30]

Because H.R. 2740 undercuts such well-established principles of trademark law, it runs counter to Congress's longstanding practice of strengthening, rather than weakening, protection for trademarks and other intellectual property rights. Recognizing the importance of strong trademarks to the U.S. economy, Congress consistently has acted to broaden trademark protection, and actively has monitored judicial applications of the Lanham Act, even nullifying court decisions that would narrow trademark protection.[31] H.R. 2740 represents an unprecedented attempt to use federal legislation to deny a rightful owner his or her trademark rights, rather than protect such rights.

B. *The Trademark Provisions Undermine the U.S. Trademark Position Internationally*

In addition to the mischief H.R. 2740 would cause domestically to our trademark laws, it also would undermine the U.S. trademark position internationally. During the 1994 session of Congress, the House debated and passed certain amendments intended to conform the Lanham Act with the standards for the protection of intellectual property agreed to by members of GATT, as set forth in the Uruguay Round Agreements Act.[32] The U.S. played a leading role during the GATT negotiations in seeking the highest level of protection possible for intellectual property.

The addition of the Federal Trademark Dilution Act of 1995 was "part of our effort to improve intellectual property protection around the world."[33] A further impe-

---

[27] *Indianapolis Colts, Inc. v. Metropolitan Baltimore Football Club,* 34 F.3d 410, 414 (7th Cir. 1994) (emphasis added).
[28] S. Rep. No. 100–515, 1988 U.S.C.C.A.N. at 5607.
[29] *See Exxon Corp. v. Humble Exploration Co.,* 695 F.2d 96, 101 (5th Cir. 1983) ("The Act does not allow the preservation of a mark solely to prevent its use by others."); *Procter & Gamble Co. v. Johnson & Johnson Inc.,* 485 f. Supp. 1185, 1207 (S.D.N.Y. 1979), *aff'd,* 636 F.2d 1203 (2d Cir. 1980).
[30] *E.g.,* 15 U.S.C. 1127 ("Nonuse for three consecutive years shall be prima facie evidence of abandonment."). H.R. 2740 contemplates a period of perhaps four years or more of trademark nonuse. Because abandonment can occur much sooner, these provisions cannot be reconciled with existing trademark principles.
[31] *See* S. Rep. No. 100–515, U.S.C.C.A.N. at 5578 (discussing Lanham Act amendments, and noting amendments in response to *Fleishmann Distillery Corp. v. Maier Brewing Co.,* 386 U.S. 714 (1967) and *Anti-Monopoly, Inc. v. General Mills Fun Group, Inc.* 611 F.2d 296 (9th Cir. 1979)).
[32] Pub. L. No. 103–465.
[33] 141 Cong. Rec. S519,312 (daily ed. Dec. 29, 1995).

tus for the 1995 amendments was the desire to "assist the executive branch in its bilateral and multilateral negotiations with other countries to secure greater protection for famous marks owned by U.S. companies."[34] H.R. 2740 is inconsistent with these expressions of U.S. policy. The retaliatory seizure of well-established trademark rights will not escape the notice of our trading partners and has the obvious potential to undermine the long and difficult efforts of the United States Trade Representative, the United States Patent and Trademark Office and others to achieve increased protection for U.S. intellectual property rights around the world.

C. *The Trademark Provisions Set Bad Precedent For the Business Community in General*

INTA is particularly troubled that, were H.R. 2740 to become an expression of Congressional policy, the logic of its provisions could not be limited to the sports team relocation context. For example, each of the findings set forth in Section 2 of H.R. 2740 equally could apply to the numerous major businesses that have enjoyed a long relationship with their particular community. It is equally true of General Motors, Ford and Chrysler as it is of the Detroit Lions, Pistons, Red Wings and Tigers that they always are linked to Detroit, "the name of the community in which" they are headquartered.[35] It also is as true that the Detroit population has made "a substantial and valuable financial, psychological, and emotional investment" in these auto manufacturers.[36] Further, even more than the Detroit sports teams, these companies "generate jobs, revenues, and other local economic development,"[37] and their closure would be far more disruptive to both the local economy and psyche.[38]

There is no principled reason for treating sports teams any differently than business corporations in this context. The rationale justifying the application of the trademark provisions contained in H.R. 2740 to sports teams equally could be cited in an attempt to strip any of these companies of their valuable trademark assets should they decide to relocate. Surely, that is not the intended purpose of the congressional members who introduced the trademark provisions of H.R. 2740. Nevertheless, it is a logical, and perhaps inevitable, extension of the legislation.

V. CONCLUSION

In INTA's view, the trademark-related provisions of H.R. 2740 are superfluous. There already are pending a number of other bills that share the same legislative goal of preventing the relocations of professional sports franchises that neither upset settled fundamental principles of trademark law, raise substantial constitutional concerns, nor undermine U.S. creditability on international intellectual property issues.[39] Should Congress ultimately act to address the problems of sports team relocations, INTA urges that any approach it adopts be more carefully crafted to reflect a precisely defined solution that legislates no more broadly than necessary. H.R. 2740 is not such an approach.

Mr. HYDE. And let me say that the statements of all three of you will be put in the record in full, because while we have had interesting aspects of this, we are down to the nitty-gritty with you, gentlemen, in terms of the policy aspects of this legislation, so what you have to say is very important and your statements will be in the record and studied.

Mr. ROBERTS. Is that why everybody leaves when we get up here, Mr. Chairman?

Mr. HYDE. No. Unfortunately, it is time. People get worn out as the day moves on. But there is no way to hurry up the process. I tried to start early and tried to limit the questions, but this is too important to short-circuit.

---

[34] *Id.* at S519,310.
[35] Section 2(1).
[36] Section 2(2).
[37] Section 2(3).
[38] *See, e.g.,* Bob Drogin, *Labor Day Lesson: Horse Dies in One-Horse Steel Town,* L.A. Times, Sep. 1, 1986, at I (reporting devastating effect on communities in which major industry leaves); Philip Dine, *Shattered Lives: Layoffs Take Toll,* St. Louis Post-Dispatch, May 28, 1990, at 1B.
[39] *E.g.,* S. 1529, 104th Cong., 2d Sess. (1996); S. 1439, 104th Cong., 1st Sess. (1995); H.R. 2699, 104th Cong., 1st Sess. (1995).

Mr. ROBERTS. I once suggested to Senator Metzenbaum that he move the academics first on the program, but that fell on deaf ears.
Mr. HYDE. Like the wedding feast at Cana, we save the best for last.
Mr. KELLER. Nice to be elevated to the status of an academician.
Mr. HYDE. Professor Roberts.

STATEMENT OF PROF. GARY R. ROBERTS, TULANE LAW SCHOOL

Mr. ROBERTS. Well, I, too, want to thank the committee for this opportunity.
Briefly, I believe that sports leagues are, and in this respect I agree with Mr. Tagliabue, they really are single firms, that is, a group of partners who cannot produce anything of value independently of one another. Thus, league decisions about the conduct of the partners' inherently joint business should be regarded as the unilateral action of a single firm and not a conspiracy of independent business competitors that are subject to the standardless and highly political ad hoc review by courts.

The reasons for this are complex and compelling. I have written about five law review articles and I have spelled it out in great detail in the written statement that I have submitted, so I submit all of that to you.

This being so, all league governance decisions should be outside the scope of section 1 of the Sherman Act and shouldn't need an exemption. The Sports Broadcasting Act itself is simply correction of a mistake that the Federal courts had made earlier.

Unfortunately, courts have not accepted the single entity position, although the seventh circuit has hinted in a currently pending case that it might be the first to do so. The only plausible justification for this judicial reluctance to accept the single entity position is that sports leagues often appear to enjoy substantial and in some cases even monopoly market power, which I agree that they do because I believe they are inherently natural monopolies. But thus the argument goes, since they have inherent market power, it is better to have standardless, unpredictable and unprincipled ad hoc regulation by courts under section 1 than to have no regulation at all.

I reject this view, because I think it contributes to illegitimate result-oriented jurisprudence that causes confusion and causes the public to lose faith in our legal system. But even if you do accept the argument, applying section 1 to internal league decisions should at least be limited to those cases where there is some type of economic competition among teams that would arguably enhance consumer welfare and the public interest and, thus, where some rational standards where judging what is lawful can be articulated. In fact, there is no reasonable or even rational argument that meaningful intraleague competition is affected by league decisions involving where a fixed number of franchises play their home games or who will own the teams. These are simply internal partnership decisions that have nothing to do with restricting output or increasing prices which are the concerns of antitrust law.

To be sure, there is a structural problem that has enabled franchise owners to extract huge subsidies from communities; namely, that there are far fewer franchises than there are communities that want and can support one. With the supply of franchises well below the demand, something that natural monopolies can pull off, communities are forced to bid up greatly the price of franchises. But allowing an antitrust suit by an owner of one of the teams against the league that tries to block a purely self-interested move that does nothing to solve or mitigate the problem of too few franchises, and in fact it exacerbates the harmful effects by allowing a single owner to fully exploit the league's market power.

Of course, allowing leagues to have the final approval over franchise moves will not mean the end of franchise-free agency. No owner wants, as several have pointed out today, to eliminate a practice that drives up the value of every franchise. But as I describe in my written statement, all of the owners led by a nonowner commissioner will in each case have a much broader and longer term perspective than will a single owner who may reap a short-term windfall at the expense of some community's taxpayers. Thus, granting leagues an antitrust immunity for franchising decisions will mitigate the most harmful effects of a franchise-free agency. But simply if Congress will not regulate franchising matters directly, it is better to let the league control them than to let greedy individual owners exploit communities with their unchecked market power.

Such an exemption will have another beneficial effect. It will bar antitrust suits that always involve highly charged political issues and are heard by judges who use the lack of meaningful legal standards to benefit their hometown, so that the only governing principle in these cases is that the community in which the case is heard always wins. A good example is the infamous *Raiders* case which created the legal confusion that led to franchise-free agency and the milking of communities, and with a touch of poetic justice, where last year there were no teams in Los Angeles.

In the 22 years before the *Raiders* decisions, there were no NFL moves. In the 13 years since, there have been seven and now maybe eight with many more on the horizon. Thus, it is in the public's interest to let leagues with their broader and longer term perspective, rather than individual club owners driven only by short-term selfish interests, make the decision as to where and with whom the league partnership will conduct its business. Thus, I favor granting leagues the limited antitrust exemption from franchise location and ownership decisions.

If we are not going to treat leagues as the single firms they are because they have a lot of market power, then we should at least limit the application of section 1 to cases where there is some identifiable intraleague competition to promote that will reduce the effects of the owner's market power and not allow lawsuits that permit politically motivated hometown judges to pursue agendas that more often than not increase the ability of individual owners to exploit their market power to the detriment of the public interest.

Mr. HYDE. Thank you, very much.
[The prepared statement of Mr. Roberts follows:]

PREPARED STATEMENT OF PROF. GARY R. ROBERTS, TULANE LAW SCHOOL

I want to thank the Subcommittee for inviting me to share my views on a subject that has long been a focus of my professional work—the reasons for and legal implications of the decisions of professional sports leagues concerning the number, ownership, and location of their member team franchises, and particularly the application of section 1 of the Sherman Act to league decisions on franchise location and ownership.

I have been involved in litigating, teaching, speaking, and writing about sports legal issues, especially antitrust issues, for the better part of two decades. Since 1983 I have been a professor of law teaching sports law, antitrust, and business enterprises at Tulane Law School, where I founded and currently direct the nation's only sports law certificate program. I am also currently the president of the Sports Lawyers Association, on whose board of directors I have served since 1986. I am also the editor-in-chief of the SLA's bimonthly newsletter, *The Sports Lawyer*. I often speak at sports law conferences, have written several major law review articles (including four on the very subject of this hearing) and two book chapters on sports antitrust matters, and along with Professor Paul Weiler of Harvard Law School I have coauthored the leading sports law textbook and supplement used in American law schools, *Sports and the Law*, published by West Publishing Company. I also regularly work with and am cited by the print and broadcast media on sports legal issues and often author columns in publications like *The Sporting News* and *USA Today*.

I should also disclose that from 1976 to 1983 I worked at the Washington firm of Covington & Burling with, among others, now NFL Commissioner Paul Tagliabue. My primary client then was the National Football League, although I also did work for the National Hockey League, World Championship Tennis, and several nonsports clients. I was on the legal team that represented the NFL in the antitrust litigation involving the league's effort to block the Oakland Raiders' move to the Los Angeles Coliseum in 1982. However, I have had no formal relationship with, and have received no compensation from, the NFL or NHL since I came to Tulane in 1983, and I have no economic stake in the issues under consideration today.

Generally I am strongly of the view that professional sports leagues are partnerships for all practical business and economic purposes, and as such the purely internal rules and decisions of a league should not be subject to section 1's rule of reason as potentially illegal conspiracies. There simply are no rational doctrinal standards for identifying when partners in an inherently wholly integrated joint venture are or should be required by antitrust law to compete with one another in producing or selling their necessarily jointly produced product. Thus, trying to apply section 1 to purely internal sports league decisions inevitably creates ambiguity and confusion about what is or is not lawful that in turn results in distorted league decision-making, excessive costly litigation, and frequently bizarre court decisions that on balance injure the public interest and consumer welfare.

Thus, as explained in greater detail herein, I support granting professional sports leagues a limited antitrust exemption for decisions relating to franchise location or relocation (as well as for ownership restrictions), not because doing so will substantially eliminate the harmful effects of the underlying structural condition causing franchise relocations—namely the shortage of franchises in each league—but only because such an exemption is the only politically feasible way today to mitigate at all the public injury caused by the phenomenon of "franchise free agency." Certainly, allowing standardless antitrust litigation against leagues if they attempt to play a role in franchise location decisions serves no public interest, and in fact further exacerbates the harmful effects of the franchise relocation game on fans and taxpayers.

I. THE SINGLE FIRM NATURE OF PROFESSIONAL SPORTS LEAGUES

Section 1 of the Sherman Act proscribes every "contract, combination . . . or conspiracy" in restraint of trade. 15 U.S.C. 1. For many years I have argued often that sports league member teams are not the kind of independent horizontal economic firms that section 1 mandates must compete with one another, but rather are collectively the single relevant economic firm capable of producing the league's necessarily jointly produced entertainment product.[1] Thus, the league, as the lowest

---

[1] Because the product a league produces is high level athletic "competition," it is easy for casual observers to see only the public image of the teams as fierce competitors, an image the league's member clubs intentionally create to yield maximum customer loyalty to their favorite team and maximum interest in the league's entertainment product. While creating the reality

economic unit capable of producing its product, should not trigger section 1's threshold agreement requirement when its partners vote to adopt rules or make decisions with respect to the structure, governance, or operation of their joint venture partnership. See G. Roberts, *Professional Sports and the Antitrust Laws*, chpt. 7 in American Professional Sports: Social, Historical, Economic, and Legal Perspectives 135-51 (1991, Univ. of Ill. Press)[2]; Roberts, *The Antitrust Status of Sports Leagues Revisited*, 64 Tul. L. Rev. 117 (1989); Roberts, *The Single Entity Status of Leagues Under Section 1 of the Sherman Act: An Alternative View*, 60 Tul. L. Rev. 562 (1986); Roberts, *Sports Leagues and the Sherman Act: The Use and Abuse of Section 1 to Regulate Restraints on Intraleague Rivalry*, 32 UCLA L. Rev. 219 (1984). Other scholars have essentially agreed with this view. See Weistart, *League Control of Market Opportunities: A Perspective on Competition and Cooperation in the Sports Industry*, 1984 Duke L.J. 1013; Graver, *Recognition of the National Football League as a Single Entity Under Section 1 of the Sherman Act: Implications of the Consumer Welfare Model*, 82 Mich. L. Rev. 1 (1983).

Even if one believes that leagues are not single firms whose internal rules fail to meet section 1's "contract, combination . . . and conspiracy" requirement, the inherently integrated nature of a league and its jointly produced product should still render internal league decisions per se legal under section 1's rule of reason, either under the age old doctrine of ancillary restraints or because the league's partners are not business competitors and thus cannot internally reduce "competition" of the type section 1 is designed to protect. See Roberts, *The Evolving Confusion of Professional Sports Antitrust, The Rule of Reason, and the Doctrine of Ancillary Restraints*, 61 S. Cal. L. Rev. 943 (1988).

The reasoning behind the argument that leagues are single firms whose internal rules and decisions should not be reviewed by antitrust courts or juries emerges most clearly from the Supreme Court's landmark decision in *Copperweld Corp. v. Independence Tube Corp.*, 467 U.S. 752 (1984), which held that a parent corporation and its wholly owned subsidiary were together a single firm for section 1 purposes. In so holding, the Court articulated the test for whether two or more separate legal persons who act jointly constitute a single firm or a voluntary combination of competitors. The determining factor, wrote Chief Justice Burger, is not how the organization has chosen to structure itself or its decision-making process, for to make antitrust status turn on voluntary organizational choices would create incentives to structure businesses in ways not optimally efficient or good for consumers, but rather in ways that merely minimize antitrust risks. Making single entity status turn on voluntary structural choices "would serve no useful antitrust purpose but could well deprive consumers of the efficiencies that decentralized management may bring." 467 U.S. at 771. Instead, the deciding factor should be whether the inherent nature of the joint enterprise is such that its existence flows from a single source of economic power, or instead from inherently independent sources of economic power that have simply chosen to operate jointly—that is to say, if a joint enterprise "does not represent a sudden joining of two independent sources of economic power previously pursuing separate interests, it is not an activity that warrants § 1 scrutiny." Id.

While the parent-subsidiary relationship in *Copperweld* is obviously different from the sports league context, the test set forth therein for determining whether an enterprise is a single entity or a collection of competitors is valid and leads inevitably to the conclusion that leagues are single firms. While a parent-subsidiary organization derives from a single source of economic power because all subunits are commonly owned, a sports league derives from a different single source of economic power, namely the inherent reality that the league's product can only be produced through the total cooperation and integration of the member clubs, not independently by one team. Without doubt, the member clubs in a sports league are not "independent sources of economic power previously pursuing separate interests," for each has no capacity independently to produce anything of significant value, and thus cannot be an independent source of economic power.

To require the partners in an inherently joint venture partnership to compete against one another in some, but not all, economic respects is illogical and ultimately works to the detriment of consumers. General partnership/joint venture law reflects this by providing that partners not only are not required to compete against

---

and image of fierce athletic competition requires a high degree of decentralized decision-making within the league partnership, it does not mean that the league's member teams are not full partners in an inherently joint enterprise whose product none of them could produce without the full cooperation of each and every one of them.

[2] This chapter, which contains a somewhat condensed version of the single entity argument, is attached hereto.

one another, they have a *fiduciary duty not to compete* against the venture or one another with respect to the venture's business, and not to expropriate for individual gain an asset or prospective business opportunity of the joint venture,[3] absent express permission from the venture to do so.[4] See Uniform Partnership Act 21; Revised Uniform Partnership Act 404(b)(3); H. Reuschlein & W. Gregory, Agency & Partnership 267–68, 277–80 (West Pub. Co. 1979). Surely this rule should apply to the partners in a sports league at least as much as to partners in "voluntary" joint ventures.

A sports league, unlike most other joint venture partnerships, is not the result of wholly independent economic persons voluntarily joining their separate sources of economic power, but rather is necessarily a wholly integrated venture deriving from a single source of economic power that flows from the inherently joint nature of its athletic "competition" product. As such, the league's partners should not be required by antitrust law to do what partnership/joint venture law prohibits—to compete for individual gain against one another and the joint venture itself in ways related to the venture's business. As the *Copperweld* decision indicates, the internal business decisions of a venture representing a single source of economic power should not be subject to rule of reason review by judges and juries.[5]

The negative effect on consumer and public interests of requiring these league joint venture partners to compete in various ways can be seen in the very area the Committee is focusing on today—franchise relocation. Requiring league partners to compete against one another in the labor market for players naturally drives up costs and puts pressure on every team to pay players roughly comparable to what the highest paying team in the league pays. Then requiring the teams to compete against one another in various product markets allows some teams to exploit their natural market advantages or superior acumen and generate increasingly greater revenues than less well positioned or less well managed teams. The combination of growing revenue disparities and upward labor cost pressures, the effects of legally requiring intraleague competition, puts lower revenue teams in an untenable position and encourages them to seek new and greater revenue sources in other cities. Thus, applying antitrust to internal league operations and requiring the league

---

[3] In fact, the same Ninth Circuit panel that voted 2-1 to affirm a jury finding that the NFL's effort to block the Oakland Raiders move to Los Angeles in the early 1980s violated § 1, *see Los Angeles Mem. Coliseum Comm'n v. National Football League (Raiders I)*, 726 F.2d 1381 (9th Cir.), *cert. denied*, 469 U.S. 990 (1984), then turned around and recognized that the Los Angeles market was a league owned asset and thus that the league had the right to recoup the value of that market that the Raiders improperly expropriated from the league by moving there, *see Los Angeles Mem. Coliseum Comm'n v. National Football League (Raiders II)*, 791 F.2d 1356 (9th Cir. 1986), *cert. denied*. 484 U.S. 826 (1987). Both parties unsuccessfully petitioned the Supreme Court for review on the compelling ground that the two opinions were irreconcilable—it is nonsense for it to be an antitrust violation if a partnership prevents one of its partners from improperly expropriating a partnership asset.

[4] Significantly, the leading court decision recognizing this universally accepted rule, authored by then Chief Judge Cardozo, is one involving a joint venture, not a more traditional partnership. *Meinhard v. Salmon*, 249 N.Y. 458, 164 N.E. 545 (1928). In fact, Judge Andrews dissented in *Meinhard* on the ground that the venture involved there was a joint venture, not a more traditional partnership. Judge Cardozo and the majority regarded that distinction as irrelevant. Thus, while the basic law governing joint ventures is arguably different in some respects from that governing traditional partnerships, the rule requiring a duty of loyalty by partners (i.e., a duty not to compete against the venture or expropriate the venture's assets for individual gain without express permission by the venture) has been universally accepted as being the same for both since *Meinhard*. See D. Kleinberger, Agency & Partnership 208–09 (Little Brown & Co. 1995)("under the law of most states, joint ventures are analogized to partnerships and therfore governed by partnership law"). Thus, whether a sports league is more properly considered a partnership or a joint venture is of no relevance to the issue of whether the member clubs owe a duty of loyalty to the league. The clear answer is that they do.

[5] The fundamental "duty of loyalty" principle of joint venture/partnership law should insulate the internal business decisions of every such venture from case-by-case rule of reason review, not just those of ventures that are necessarily joint. This was the essence of Judge Taft's brilliant decision in *United States v. Addyston Pipe & Steel Co.*, 85 F. 271 (6th Cir. 1898), *aff'd*, 175 U.S. 211 (1899), which opined that internal decisions of legitimate joint ventures that were reasonably related to the business of the venture, so-called "ancillary restraints," should always be regarded as lawful under section 1. This interpretation of § 1 is the only one that has ever made sense of § 1's otherwise nonsensically broad condemnation of "[e]very contract . . . in restraint of trade." The wisdom of this decision was lost in the judiciary's subsequent unfortunate attraction to the rule of reason invented out of whole cloth in *Standard Oil Co. v. United States*, 221 U.S. I (1911), which has allowed courts to uphold some naked restraints as reasonable and yet to invalidate some ancillary restraints as unreasonable. *See* Roberts, *The Evolving Confusion of Professional Sports Antitrust, the Rule of Reason, and the Doctrine of Ancillary Restraints*, 61 S. Cal. L. Rev. 943, 992–1015 (1988). Nonetheless, the doctrine of ancillary restraints has compelling merit and is today fortunately making a modest comeback in the jurisprudence.

partners to compete against one another in labor and product markets creates the excuse, if not the reality, that drives many teams to seek lucrative stadium deals and other subsidies from new communities. Properly treating leagues as single entities whose partners are not required to compete against one another would allow leagues to minimize revenue and labor cost disparities between teams without fear of antitrust exposure and thereby greatly lessen the pressures on low revenue teams to seek greener pastures in new communities at taxpayer expense. Thus, while applying Sherman Act section 1 to league operations makes the unionized players and some particularly greedy owners much wealthier, it creates economic pressures that cause consumers to pay higher prices for tickets and TV rights and taxpayers to subsidize teams willing to abandon their traditional home communities.

To date, three circuit courts of appeal have addressed this single entity issue squarely, and all three have mistakenly held that sports leagues are not single firms, but rather a collection of separate competitors whose joint business decisions are subject to judicial "reasonableness" review. Two of these decisions predated *Copperweld* and relied heavily on cases that are easily distinguishable and today discredited (namely the *Topco Associates* and *Sealy* cases). *Los Angeles Memorial Coliseum Comm'n v. National Football League (Raiders I)*, 726 F.2d 1381 (9th Cir.), cert. denied, 469 U.S. 990 (1984); *North American Soccer League v. National Football League*, 670 F.2d 1249 (2d Cir.), cert. denied, 459 U.S. 1074 (1982)(Rehnquist, J., dissenting from denial of cert.). The third completely ignored the underlying test set forth in *Copperweld* and distinguished its holding on the superficial ground that *Copperweld* involved a corporate parent-subsidiary context. *Sullivan v. Tagliabue*, 34 F.3d 1091 (1st Cir. 1994). In the Seventh Circuit, however, Judge Easterbrook has strongly hinted in a recent case that the National Basketball Association might well be a single entity, and he encouraged the NBA to raise that issue back in the district court. *Chicago Professional Sports & WGN v. National Basketball Ass'n*, 961 F.2d 667 (7th Cir.), cert. denied, 113 S.Ct. 409 (1992). That case is now back before the Seventh Circuit and a decision is expected sometime this year.

Thus, the law, although not firmly settled, has so far been interpreted to render every internal decision by sports leagues subject to rule of reason review. The single entity nature of leagues has not been recognized. In my judgment, that is bad law and bad policy that has resulted in much confusion about what leagues may or may not lawfully do and has produced results that have injured the public interest and consumer welfare. Indeed, league fears of huge treble damages liability if they try to block franchise relocations, and the resulting game of franchise blackmail that teams have played against communities over the last decade, is the direct result of the confusing and contradictory opinions of the Ninth Circuit in the *Raiders* case in the early 1980s.[6]

II. THE LEAGUE AS A "NATURAL MONOPOLY"

The inherent joint venture nature of a sports league is obvious, even to the courts that have held league members to be a collection of horizontal competitors for antitrust purposes. Thus it is curious that the courts have so far not seen fit to recognize the member clubs' duty of loyalty not to compete independently against the league venture, nor to recognize internal league rules as being beyond the scope of case-by-case rule of reason review.

The explanation for this puzzling jurisprudence, I believe, lies in the fact that each major sports league is the only producer of its particular sports entertainment product at the major league level. While economists can debate endlessly how to define and identify monopoly market power and whether a sports league possesses such power in one or more of the many markets in which it operates,[7] most neutral observers sense that the tremendous attractiveness of each league's product to millions of rabid fans gives it substantial market power in many markets. The salaries

---

[6] See note 3, *supra*.
[7] The simplified classical economic definition of market power (i.e., the power to raise and maintain price above marginal cost or below marginal revenue product in an input market) by restricting output below levels dictated by supply and demand) is almost impossible to apply in the sports industry where average fixed costs are orders of magnitude larger than marginal costs. (This condition of fixed costs > marginal costs is usually indicative of a natural monopoly industry where competing firms price below average fixed costs and thus drive each other out of business until only one firm remains, which firm then has the power to charge enough to recoup its fixed costs.) Thus, it is meaningless to ask whether the prices of Redskins' tickets, the broadcast rights the NFL sells to NBC, the trademark rights NFL Properties sells to Coke, or the subsidies franchises extract from communities are far above marginal cost. Of course they are. But whether this means that the NFL necessarily has monopoly market power in each of these markets of a type antitrust law should seek to avoid is a much more subtle and elusive question on which volumes could be written.

that players and coaches command, the subsidies that teams can extract from local communities, and even the street value of a Super Bowl ticket all suggest that leagues exercise tremendous and arguably monopoly market power in several markets. In this respect, sports leagues are a greater threat to the public interest and consumer welfare than the typical partnership or joint venture that faces substantial "interbrand" competition and whose internal business decisions are presumably safe from case-by-case rule of reason review (*Topco Associates* and *Sealy* notwithstanding).

While subjecting internal sports league rules and decisions to ad hoc rule of reason review lacks theoretical justification and results in arbitrary, confusing, and unprincipled decisions that often work to the detriment of the public interest, there is a sense among many in the sports law field that even this arbitrary ad hoc application of section 1 deters leagues from fully exploiting their substantial market power at relatively little cost to the efficiency of the league. In short, so the argument goes, it is better to have unpredictable and unprincipled regulation of sports leagues through ad hoc application of section 1 than to have no regulation at all.

Frankly, I do not accept this argument because it tends to legitimize purely result oriented jurisprudence—the use of statutes in ways not intended in order to achieve a result in each case that the judge or jury generally thinks desirable.[8] This is a misuse of law and the legal process that in a single application or a limited context poses only a slight threat to justice. However, as yet another instance of courts claiming the legitimate authority to "govern" in unprincipled or arbitrary ways in order to achieve particular results that may or may not be in the general public interest, this approach contributes to the erosion of the integrity of the legal process and to the public's declining trust in our legal and political institutions.

Having said this, I recognize that leagues do appear to possess substantial market power of varying degrees in many relevant markets—the national player labor market (in which the counterveiling power of the union also exists), the national and local markets in which television rights and trademark licensing rights are sold, many local markets in which tickets to live games are sold, and, most relevant for this hearing, the national market in which professional franchises in each sport are distributed. I also recognize that it would be in the public interest for there to be some principled legal mechanism to reduce the ability of leagues fully to exploit their market power to the detriment of consumers and the public.

Some argue that Congress or the courts should require each league to split into three or more competing leagues that operate completely independently of each other, and that the resulting competition will greatly diminish any one league's market power. See Ross, *Monopoly Sports Leagues*, 73 Minn. L. Rev. 643 (1989). The underlying theory of this approach is reasonable and if it worked as planned the legal mechanism created would be principled and legitimate. The problems with this approach are that it is politically unfeasible and that as a factual matter it would not work over the long term. I believe that within a few years, inevitably one league in each sport would become perceived by the public as having the highest quality product, which in turn would result in that league generating much larger revenues, which in turn would result in the dominant league hiring the best players, expanding to fill the national market, and reestablishing the major league monopoly in the sport.

The more technical explanation for this likely phenomenon is that sports leagues face two economic circumstances tending towards a monopoly industry—average fixed costs that greatly exceed marginal costs in the product market and marginal revenue product numbers for many players that greatly exceed the average total revenue per player in their labor market. In highly competitive product markets, each league would thus price their output at levels just above marginal cost but well below average fixed costs, and in a competitive labor market would pay many of their players at levels just below marginal revenue product but well above average

---

[8] It is important to note here that what a judge or jury may believe to be the desirable result in any given case may or may not coincide with the goals of antitrust law or even the public interest. Sports cases are often highly publicized and politicized, and usually have substantial consequences for the community in which they are heard. It is almost axiomatic today that in sports franchise relocation cases, the principle of law that will govern is that the side wanting the team in the community in which the court is located will win. The fiasco of dueling state and federal courts in Minnesota and New Orleans over the 1993 relocation attempt by the NBA's Timberwolves amply demonstrates this. And it was clear in the *Raiders* case that the trial judge (a Los Angeles political insider who by the time of trial was on the Ninth Circuit, sharing chambers with the former lawyer who represented the L.A. Coliseum and the judge who later wrote the appellate opinion) had the singular agendum of making sure the Raiders played their home games in Los Angeles.

total revenue,[9] which means that the competing leagues would inevitably lose money and one-by-one go out of business until only one remained that had enough market power to charge prices high enough (and, if intraleague free agency is not legally required, to hold salaries low enough) to allow it to generate a profit. Thus, market realities suggest strongly that each major sports league is a natural monopoly whose market power in many markets cannot (and probably should not) be diminished for very long by forced market competition.

My own remedy for the natural market power that major sports leagues enjoy is to treat leagues in exactly the same manner that government treats all natural monopolies—that is, to regulate them. I believe Congress should create and empower a regulatory body to identify the markets in which sports leagues possess extraordinary market power and then to regulate what leagues may do in those markets so as to prevent exploitation beyond that necessary to guarantee a fair rate of return.

I made this same recommendation specifically in connection with Major League Baseball to this Subcommittee back on December 10, 1992, during hearings on the baseball exemption, and I was essentially told by then Chairman Metzenbaum that the idea of regulating baseball was too liberal for him. See *On Baseball's Antitrust Immunity, Hearing Before the Subcommittee on Antitrust, Monopolies and Business Rights of the Senate Committee on the Judiciary,* 102nd Cong., 2d Sess. 435 (1992). I quickly realized that if regulating professional sports is too liberal for Senator Metzenbaum, it is probably an idea whose time has not yet come (or perhaps has long since passed). But political difficulties aside, regulating natural monopoly power is far more principled, predictable, and rational than subjecting an enterprise to the vagaries of unprincipled, arbitrary, and unpredictable section 1 antitrust enforcement by courts, each of which has its own agenda—and I say this even after fully taking into account the dangers of incompetence, conflict of interest, and corruption that can plague government regulatory schemes.

Accepting that regulation, like breaking up the major leagues, is not a feasible option, and that for now the courts are intent on applying section 1 to internal sports league rules and decisions, the question for Congress today is how best to mitigate the effects of a league's substantial market power while at the same time allowing it to operate within a reasonably predictable and rational legal framework. It is in this context that I support adoption of a limited antitrust exemption for league decisions involving franchise location and ownership restrictions.

III. THE CASE FOR A LIMITED ANTITRUST EXEMPTION

If sports leagues are to be subject to anticonspiracy doctrines that will require the league partners to compete with one another in certain respects, then the contexts in which courts are allowed to engage in this ad hoc judicial regulation ought to be limited to ones in which it is likely that requiring intraleague competition will in fact mitigate the league's market power. It ought not to include contexts in which no rational theories of competition can be articulated and in which judges can thus be free to pursue their own political agenda.

One can make a rational argument that with respect to league restraints on member clubs' independent competitive conduct in the player labor market, or in the markets in which television or trademark rights are sold, requiring the league's member clubs to compete at least in some limited (albeit hard to define) ways would on balance benefit the public interest. Thus, if one rejects the various doctrinal variations of the single entity argument because leagues have too much market power, then league rules affecting these markets would arguably not be the best candidates for exemption from intraleague judicial section 1 regulation, even though exemptions already exist in significant respects in both the labor market, see, *e.g., Brown v. Pro Football, Inc.,* 50 F.3d 1041 (D.C. Cir. 1995), *cert. granted,*—U.S.—(1995)(scheduled for argument on March 27) and the television rights market, see 15 U.S.C. §§ 1291–94.

On the other hand, it is difficult to conceive of any rational argument for the proposition that the public interest or consumer welfare is enhanced by antitrust suits against league rules or decisions relating to franchise location or ownership. In fact,

---

[9] This is a phenomenon that currently can afflict even single monopoly leagues because section 1 has been applied to require league partners to compete against one another for players, pushing total player costs for some teams above levels justified by team revenues. Collective bargaining agreements setting a total team compensation cap at some percentage of total revenues can mitigate the effects of this phenomenon if all of the teams do not have grossly disparate revenues. Sports that do not cap total team compensation, however, like baseball and hockey, will likely always have several teams losing money as long as intraleague labor market competition is legally required.

it is quite likely that the public interest will be served by having leagues (the relevant productive firm) make such structural decisions instead of allowing individual club owners to make them based solely on their individual interests. For this reason, granting sports leagues an antitrust exemption for such decisions would at least marginally enhance the public interest, which is probably the most Congress can do if it is unwilling to make major substantive changes in the structure or governance of the sports industry.

The ability of major league franchise owners to extract huge subsidies of various kinds from communities by auctioning their teams to the highest bidder demonstrates enormous market power in the sports franchise market. By restricting the supply of franchises well below the demand for them, team owners can reap classical monopoly profits—driving up the value of a commodity by restricting output and forcing consumers to bid up the price for the scarce item. But the only way to mitigate significantly the monopoly wealth transfers from community taxpayers to individual franchise owners (and in turn to the players who share in the owners' largesse [10]) would be to create structures that would increase the number of franchises available so almost every viable community could have one, and this could only be accomplished through radical measures like direct government regulation or forced breaking up of each league, ideas which are apparently not politically viable. If Congress is not willing to regulate franchise matters through a neutral publicly accountable process, the next best alternative is at least to allow the league to exercise some regulatory restraint over individual owners.

If we must accept a fixed number of unregulated franchises in each sport, two things are inevitable. First, many communities that could support a franchise in a sport won't have one (a "misallocation of society's resources" effect). Second, in order to have a franchise, a community will be required to pay huge subsidies (a "monopoly wealth transfer" effect). So assuming a set number of teams, Congress' ability to mitigate the effects of the leagues' market power is quite limited. The question we are focussing on today is simply whether it is in the public's interest for decisions affecting franchise location to be made by individual franchise owners or by the full league/joint venture partnership. I believe that in virtually every case, the answer is that such decisions are better made by the league, and thus an antitrust exemption from section 1 suits should be granted in these types of cases.

We, of course, cannot expect the collective group of franchise owners comprising the league to act as a significant check on the league's exploitation of market power in order to protect the public interest.[11] This does not make them evil or immoral people, only business people who do what business people are expected to do, and what in many business contexts they have a fiduciary duty to their shareholders or partners to do—maximize profits. And it should be noted that it is not and has never been illegal for business people who lawfully possess market power fully to exploit it in the pursuit of profits. But even though the league partners are not likely guardians of the public interest, that interest will still be better served if the owners collectively make franchise location and ownership decisions than if single owners are free to pursue individual interests in individual cases.

In the first place, leagues will act from a broader perspective and thus will mitigate somewhat the most severe effects of market power exploitation by a single owner. Because all leagues equally share network television revenues, the effects of a move on viewership, which is directly proportional to market size and thus consumer welfare, will have minimal influence on an individual owner. However, stadium revenues are either kept entirely by the home team or shared somewhat with the visiting team. Thus, much smaller communities that can provide new state-

---

[10] This is a point that should not be ignored. Today, well over half of all revenues in every professional team sport goes to pay the salaries and benefits of the players. (In the NFL, the collective bargaining agreement mandates that at least 63% of all defined gross revenues go to the players.) Thus, while franchise owners are clearly economic beneficiaries of the enormous market power they enjoy in many relevant markets, the players, by virtue of the substantial market power they enjoy in the labor market because of protections accorded them under federal labor law, are also major beneficiaries of the owners' market power. It is inconceivable that average player salaries would be in the millions of dollars if the employer-owners were forced to operate in strongly competitive markets. When players and their unions decry the monopoly power of leagues (as they often do), what they really mean to criticize is the power of the leagues only in the labor market; the leagues' power in every other market undoubtedly suits the players quite well.

[11] Whether a franchise location decision is made by individual owners or the league, communities are still going to be subject to substantial market power and required to pay large subsidies to get or keep teams. The league, which is merely the collection of all the team owners, is unlikely significantly to discourage this process. When one team extracts huge subsidies from a community, it not only increases that team's revenue and value, but the value of every team in the league; and it creates the climate in which every other team can later do the same thing.

of-the-art stadia, luxury boxes, and a cadre of wealthy business leaders willing to fork over lots of money for box rentals and personal seat licenses can lure individual team owners to abandon much larger cities that cannot in the short term come up with similar financial guarantees.

With due respect to those who represent St. Louis, Nashville, and Baltimore, it is not in the interests of consumer welfare or the American public generally for NFL teams to be in those cities but not in Los Angeles, Houston, or Cleveland. There will be millions fewer NFL consumers because of the recent NFL franchise shifts (although the fewer will be wealthier people who are paying more for it—another symptom of the exercise of substantial market power), a fact which because of the way revenues are shared hurts the overall long term revenue and welfare of the league as a whole. If fear of antitrust litigation did not hang over the NFL, it is likely that some of these anti-consumer moves that benefit only the individual team owner would be blocked. Of course, as the NFL did with the St. Louis Rams, the league could condition approval of a move on the team's sharing much of its windfall with the rest of the league, which would somewhat diminish the beneficial effect of having league oversight,[12] but the overall principle that such league oversight is better than none at all remains valid.

Likewise, frequent franchise relocations undermine the image and credibility of a league as a whole and thus diminish the quality of the product in the eyes of consumers. This too is an injury to consumer welfare that league oversight might mitigate. Individual teams that get short term windfalls aren't deterred by subtle long-term image problems, but the league as a whole might be. In this way too, having league control of franchise location benefits the overall long-term public interest.

The bottom line is that if we assume a limited number of franchises, how the decision as to where they will be located is made is not an antitrust issue. No economic or business competition is diminished and no market power is enhanced or entrenched because the league decides where one team's home games on the league schedule are played instead of the team.[13] (And logically, why shouldn't a visiting team have the same right to decide where its road games are played, or the other league members whose television revenues are affected and whose jointly owned league trademark is exploited in every game?) These kinds of cases will virtually never implicate antitrust law or policy, yet leagues are always at treble damage risk if they get involved because of the highly political nature of the cases and the lack of meaningful legal principles.

As an illustration, there were very few inter metropolitan area professional sports franchise relocations prior to 1980. In the NFL, the last previous relocation had been the Chicago Cardinals move to St. Louis in 1960. However, after the highly political, result-oriented antitrust decision in the *Raiders* case in 1982, the ability of leagues to control franchise location without fear of antitrust litigation and liability disappeared. Since then, the Raiders have moved to Los Angeles and back again to Oakland; the Colts moved from Baltimore to Indianapolis; the Cardinals from St. Louis to Phoenix; the Rams from Los Angeles to St. Louis; the Browns are moving from Cleveland to Baltimore; the Oilers are moving from Houston to Nashville; and several other teams are reported to be likely to move in the near future. That's zero moves in 20 years before the *Raiders* decision, severe moves (and still counting) in the 14 years since. And several NFL teams that have not moved; like the Minnesota

---

[12] Curiously, the NFL's requiring the Rams to pay a relocation fee to the league as a condition for obtaining league approval for their move has itself recently become the target of a section I antitrust suit by St. Louis interests who claim that this "restraint of trade" caused them to have to pay more to attract the franchise. This is an absurd antitrust claim grounded on no logical or doctrinal foundation but one that the NFL cannot take lightly since it was filed, unsurprisingly, in St. Louis.

[13] Some facile plaintiff antitrust lawyers have concocted an argument in a few cases to the effect that member clubs in a league compete with each other to win more games so that they can sell more tickets and make more money, and thus league governance decisions like where teams play home games or who owns the teams can be anti competitive because they may cause some teams to be less effective at winning games. This is former New England Patriots owner Billy Sullivan's argument in his antitrust case that has just been tried a second time in Boston against the NFL alleging that the league's rule against public ownership of franchises violated § 1 because it injured the Patriots' ability to compete against the other NFL clubs. *See Sullivan v. Tagliabue*, 34 F.3d 1091 (1st Cir. 1994). This argument is preposterous because the competition it relies on is *athletic competition* on the field that is the product of the league itself. In every game, one team wins and one team loses, and antitrust law is indifferent as to which is which. To suggest that antitrust law, market power, or consumer welfare is implicated when league partners apply rules defining who their other partners will be is nonsense, a view that is shared by virtually every neutral expert of any political persuasion. That the *Sullivan* case was not dismissed on Rule 12(b)(6) motion is strong evidence of the need for a limited antitrust exemption in these types of league governance situations.

Vikings, New Orleans Saints, and Philadelphia Eagles, have used the threat of relocation as a negotiating ploy to extract huge subsidies from their home communities. One unprincipled decision by Los Angeles judges who wanted a second NFL team in Los Angeles unleashed the era of franchise free agency in the NFL that has greatly injured many consumers of NFL football and the taxpayers of many communities.[14] The possibility that the league could intervene to block a team from abandoning a loyal community would likely have materially diminished the unfettered power of individual owners to extract as much as they did, but that possibility was minimized because of the fear of antitrust litigation caused by the *Raiders* case.

CONCLUSION

Partnership/joint venture law recognizes that the efficiency and productivity of any joint venture is maximized if the partners are required to act with loyalty and good faith toward the joint enterprise and, unless the joint venture allows it, not to compete independently against the venture or to expropriate its assets. If antitrust law is going to ignore this principle and require sports league partners to compete independently against the league (and thus create the inefficiency that inevitably flows from such internal disloyalty) because the league partnership possesses market power, it should do so only in situations where requiring such "intraenterprise competition" will mitigate the effects of market power and benefit consumers. In cases involving franchise relocations or ownership, there is no intraleague competition in any meaningful sense implicated and the public interest will virtually never be enhanced by allowing courts to fantasize some imaginary type of intraleague competition and then to hold that the league illegally diminished it. In fact, particularly in the franchise location context, the most virulent effects of the league's strong market power on the public will actually be somewhat mitigated by allowing leagues to impose their broader and longer term perspective than by allowing individual owners to pursue their narrow short term interests with little fear of league intervention. The public interest and consumer welfare gain nothing and are actually diminished by allowing these types of nonsensical antitrust suits that unjustifiably enrich only the lawyers and disloyal plaintiff club owners and that greatly confuse and misdirect antitrust doctrine.

For these reasons, given that real structural reform or regulation is not feasible, the public interest and consumer welfare will be benefited by granting a limited section 1 antitrust exemption for professional sports league decisions involving franchise location and ownership.

---

[14] One cannot help but appreciate the irony that the unprincipled decision designed to get a second NFL team in the Los Angeles area unleashed a whirlwind that has today left Los Angeles with no NFL teams.

# Professional Sports and the Antitrust Laws 7

Gary R. Roberts

Perhaps no area of law has impacted professional sports more over these past twenty years than antitrust. Since 1966 the National Football League alone has had to defend over sixty antitrust suits. The National Basketball Association, and the National Hockey League, and even upstart leagues like the now-defunct World Hockey Association (WHA), American Basketball League, and the United States Football League (USFL), have also been frequently hit by such suits. Only major league baseball, which enjoys a broad antitrust immunity as a result of three U.S. Supreme Court decisions, has been able to operate without the substantial risk and expense of antitrust litigation.[1]

Although antitrust law seems mysterious and complex, its source is surprisingly simple. Except for the statute governing mergers of two firms, the overwhelming bulk of antitrust law derives from the first two sections of the 1890 Sherman Act. Section 1 prohibits "every contract, combination, . . . or conspiracy in restraint of trade or commerce," while section 2 makes it illegal to "monopolize, or attempt to monopolize, or combine or conspire . . . to monopolize" trade or commerce. Virtually all sports antitrust cases involve one or both of these vague statutory proscriptions—conspiracies to restrain trade and monopolization.[2]

Antitrust cases against professional leagues or their member clubs generally are of two types. The first involves disputes between two different leagues or between member clubs of different leagues. The second, and more significant, category includes all cases brought by anyone having a dispute with a league and alleging that a league rule or decision constitutes an unlawful section 1 conspiracy among the individual member clubs of the league. It is the second type of cases—those involving so-called intraleague conspiracies—that has been the most frequent and problematic, and it has had the greatest impact on professional sports.

The Interleague Dispute Cases

The interleague type of case is typically brought by a young struggling league claiming that an older and more established league monopolized or attempted to monopolize some part of the sports entertainment market in violation of Sherman Act section 2. To win such a claim the plaintiff must prove two things: (1) that the defendant has, or is close to having, monopoly market power in some relevant market or line of commerce, and (2) that the defendant has acted improperly in acquiring or maintaining that monopoly power. Because these issues are economically complex and often very difficult to prove, plaintiffs also often allege that the defendant league's conduct involved a section 1 conspiracy in restraint of trade. But regardless of the legal theory, the essential claim is always that a well-established league or its teams acted to cripple or destroy a rival league or teams in order to maintain a monopoly position.

As suggested above, antitrust cases between leagues have been few and have had relatively little impact on the structure or operation of professional sports. The most recent example is the highly publicized case the USFL brought against the NFL, which primarily claimed that the NFL's contracts with the three major television networks unlawfully monopolized professional football. After a lengthy trial in 1986, a Manhattan jury found that the NFL had monopolized professional football; however, apparently because the jury believed that the USFL went bankrupt primarily because of its own mismanagement, it awarded the USFL damages of only one dollar (which by law were automatically trebled to three). When the verdict was affirmed on appeal, the demise of the USFL became permanent (*USFL v. NFL*, 842 F.2d 1335 [2d Cir. 1988]). In a similar case in 1962, the old American Football League claimed that the NFL monopolized professional football by putting teams in Dallas and Minnesota and threatening to expand in other cities in order to disrupt the AFL's initial operations. The case resulted in a verdict for the NFL (*AFL v. NFL*, 205 F. Supp. 60 [D. Md. 1962], aff'd, 323 F.2d 124 [4th Cir. 1963]).

The WHA was more successful in its suit against the NHL in the early 1970s. The essence of this claim was that the NHL monopolized professional hockey by including a clause in all of its clubs' player contracts giving the club a permanent renewable option on the player when the contract term ended, which prevented a player from playing for any other hockey club until his NHL club no longer wanted him. Thus the WHA was unable to employ good hockey players if they had ever played in the NHL and, as a result, could never seriously compete with the NHL. In 1972 shortly after the case was filed, the district judge issued a preliminary injunction against the NHL's enforcement of these "lifetime reserve clauses" based on his finding that at trial they would probably be found to constitute unlawful monopolization (*Philadelphia World Hockey Club v. Philadelphia Hockey Club*, 351 F. Supp. 462 [E.D. Pa. 1972]). Unfortunately, the injunction was of little help to the WHA; by 1979 all of its clubs were insolvent and had disbanded except for the teams in Hartford, Winnipeg, Edmonton, and Vancouver, all of which joined the NHL. The case did, however, lead to a settlement between the two leagues and their player unions under which the NHL's lifetime reserve clause was replaced with a much less onerous "free agent compensation system" that allowed a player to sign with any hockey team when his contract expired, subject only to the new club giving some arbitrated compensation to the old club, but only if both clubs were NHL members.[3]

Another group of interleague cases has involved stadium lease or arena lease provisions that give the leasing club an exclusive right to use the facility for its sport. If a facility is realistically the only one in the area capable of housing a professional team, the exercise of the exclusive rights clause forecloses other leagues from putting a competing team in the city. Several cases have involved plaintiffs who were trying to obtain franchises in upstart leagues who alleged that such lease provisions allowed the established local team to monopolize the local market in its sport. These plaintiffs have generally been unsuccessful, either because alternative facilities were available or because the team could not show that they would have obtained a franchise in the new league even if the stadium had been available. The only such case to result in a published opinion was eventually settled for $200,000 after thirteen years of litigation. The ruling in this case makes it reasonably clear that the Sherman Act is violated if a new league is excluded from a city because of such a lease provision, at least unless very strong business justifications exist for restricting the newcomer's access to the facility (*Hecht v. Pro-Football, Inc.*, 570 F.2d 982 [D.C. Cir. 1977], cert. denied, 436 U.S. 956 [1978]).

Another interleague case involved a challenge by the North American Soccer League (NASL) to the NFL's proposed by-law that would have prohibited majority owners or chief executive officers of NFL teams from owning an interest in franchises of other sports leagues. Specifically at issue was the NFL's efforts to force Lamar Hunt, who owns the NFL's Kansas City Chiefs, and Joe Robbie, who owns the Miami Dolphins, to divest their interests (or in Robbie's case, his wife's interest) in NASL franchises. Because of the shaky financial position of the NASL, the divestment, combined with the paucity of non-NFL owners willing to invest in the NASL, might have pushed the NASL over the financial edge (over which it eventually went anyway). Curiously, the primary claim in the case was not that the NFL monopolized any relevant market, such as the league sports autumn entertainment market, but that the NFL clubs unlawfully conspired among themselves under section 1 to restrain trade. After the district court in New York granted a summary judgment for the NFL, the court of appeals reversed and entered a judgment for the NASL on the grounds that the NFL clubs had conspired to restrain the previously unheard-of sports capital investment market (*NASL v. NFL*, 670 F.2d 1249 [2d Cir.], cert. denied, 459 U.S. 1074 [1982]).

The *NASL* decision has been severely criticized, not only because of its result but because of its doctrinal justification. Justifying the decision on conspiracy grounds rather than monopolization grounds seems totally at odds with standard section 1 principles, which encourage vigorous independent competition between separate entities, such as two different leagues. Thus, although the decision clearly invalidated the NFL's cross-ownership ban when applied against the struggling NASL, it is probably limited to its specific facts—that is, the ban probably does not violate the law when applied by the NFL against cross-ownership in established sports leagues like the NHL, NBA, or major league baseball, or rival leagues in the same sport, like the WFL or USFL.

Generally, with the possible exception of the anomalous *NASL* case, the decisions in these interleague cases have been unsurprising and unremarkable, and they have had little impact on either the law or the structure of professional sports. Most doctrinal principles relating to monopolization are reasonably clear and have not changed, and in each of the cases the outcome primarily turned not on the interpretation or application of the law, but on what the juries believed were the real facts of the case. While jury findings of fact usually are significant for a particular case, they generally have little or no impact on future cases or the general state of the law.

The one legal issue in these sports monopolization cases that is problematic, and will probably remain so, is how to define the relevant market that the plaintiff claims has been monopolized. The market definition must include both a product and a geographic dimension—for example, professional football entertainment in the United States; ticket sales for football entertainment (high school, college, and professional) in the New York metropolitan area; network television rights for all kinds of entertainment in the United States; television rights for all sports entertainment in New England; and so on. The possibilities are almost endless. The general rule for making this determination is that the proper market includes all the different brands and products sold within the appropriate geographical area that are economically competitive with one another—that is, those that serve approximately the same purpose for the average consumer so that consumers can switch from one to the other if price or quality materially changes.

Defining the proper relevant market is extraordinarily difficult. For example, how can one identify everything that meaningfully competes with NFL football in a single market description? What percentage of people who now buy tickets to New York Giants football games would, if the Giants' ticket prices increased by a certain amount, spend their entertainment dollars attending college football games? Would they attend Yankee baseball games or Broadway shows or watch cartoons on television? Adding in the geographic dimension, how far would disgruntled Giants fans be willing to travel to find a substitute activity? How many would choose gambling in Atlantic City or skiing in Vermont? Then again, what effect would the amount of the ticket price increase have on all these factors? No one can possibly know. Nonetheless, based on whatever information is available, a plaintiff must establish that some group of actual or potential product alternatives exists that is generally substitutable to a sufficient number of consumers within an identified geographic area so that they comprise a relevant market that the defendant has monopolized.

The market definition problem is not unique to sports cases. Defining a relevant market is a nightmare in almost all monopolization cases. Because of the complexity and conceptual difficulty (if not impossibility) of doing the necessary economic analysis, courts generally either have reached a knee-jerk conclusion (camouflaged by confusing rhetoric), or have ducked the issue by leaving the question to juries to do what they instinctively feel is just. But the fact that a defined relevant market is an essential element of a monopolization case always injects a great deal of unpredictability into these interleague cases.

This problem could be greatly reduced in cases between two leagues in the same sport, like the USFL and the NFL, simply by identifying the relevant market as the labor market in which the leagues employ their players instead of focusing on some market in which the leagues sell their entertainment products against one another. The labor market is undoubtedly the proper market for relevant concern. If the NFL wanted to drive the USFL out of business, by whatever method, it was not because it was seriously concerned about NFL ticket buyers or television networks switching over to the USFL. It wanted to stop the rapid escalation in player salaries caused by the USFL's competition in the market for hiring football players. If the NFL was trying to monopolize anything, it was this labor market. This market is easy to define, and a plaintiff could probably prove that an established league like the NFL or NBA has enormous market power in it.[4] By focusing on the player market in cases between two leagues in the same sport, plaintiffs would greatly increase their chance of success.

Ultimately, however, these types of cases will probably never be very significant in altering the shape of professional sports because of the great likelihood that in each sport no more than one established league will ever exist for more than a brief period. Since World War II, one hockey, two basketball, and four football leagues have sprung up to compete against the

NHL, NBA, and NFL, respectively, and not one has survived more than a few seasons. The public's demand for a single acknowledged "world champion," and the need over the long run to control player costs and competitive balance among teams (which cannot be done effectively in either league if two are competing in the same sport), make it quite likely that the established league in each sport will never face permanent competition or be supplanted by an upstart league. Thus no matter what legal doctrines are developed or what the outcome of any interleague monopolization cases may be, it is unlikely that these cases will ever be of long-term or structural significance.

The Intraleague Conspiracy Cases

The second type of sports antitrust case involves challenges to any league rule, decision, or action ("league conduct") by some dissatisfied person claiming that the conduct constituted a section 1 conspiracy of the league's member clubs to restrain competition among themselves. These cases are by far more frequent, more unpredictable, and doctrinally more problematic than the interleague monopolization cases.

Cases in this category have involved virtually every type of league conduct. For example, league rules barring players from the league for a variety of reasons[5] and rules assigning each player to a specific league member (like the player drafts and reserve rules)[6] have been attacked by individual players, player unions, and rival leagues. Persons disappointed with not being able to own a team have brought cases challenging league decisions not to expand the league membership[7] and not to approve the sale of a franchise.[8] Stadiums seeking league tenants and even league members have challenged league decisions not to allow teams to relocate their home games to a new city.[9] The Justice Department, fans, and television stations have sued over league broadcasting contracts and practices.[10] Equipment manufacturers and players have even challenged playing-field rules.[11] In each case, the allegation was that the league's action had involved a conspiracy of the individual league members to restrain competition among themselves in some commercial market.

Although the defendant leagues have won the overwhelming majority of these cases, a few widely publicized cases in which leagues lost have had an enormous impact on the structure and operation of professional sports. The most notable are the *John Mackey* and *Yazoo Smith* cases from the mid-1970s, which invalidated respectively the NFL's reserve system and college player draft as they were then structured, completely altering the shape of labor relations in professional sports. In the infamous *Los Angeles Memorial Coliseum* case the court found the NFL's efforts to require the then

Oakland Raiders to play its home games in Oakland (as it had contractually agreed to do) instead of in Los Angeles to be an unlawful conspiracy of the other NFL clubs. What was so significant about these decisions was not only the way they dramatically and directly changed the face of the game but how they were based on legal principles that were confusing, aberrational, and inconsistent both with other antitrust decisions and with antitrust doctrine generally. The legacy of these cases is that today there is virtually no conduct of any sports league (other than baseball) involving any matter that cannot conceivably be challenged successfully in the right court.

In order to understand why these conspiracy cases are so doctrinally confounding and troublesome for league operations, it is necessary first to understand what section 1's condemnation of conspiracies is all about. The basic theory of free enterprise is that the products consumers want will be produced in the greatest quantity, at the highest quality, and at the cheapest price if production decisions conform to the dictates of supply and demand forces. This equilibrium will be achieved when independent producers of the same or functionally interchangeable products compete with each other to attract customers. It is through competition and each firm's desire to attract the greatest number of customers that prices are kept to a minimum and quality maintained. It is for this reason that antitrust law seeks to maximize competition by outlawing both (a) one firm driving all competitors out of business (monopolization) and (b) groups of competitors getting together to agree on the price or quality of their otherwise competing products (conspiracies).

But section 1's condemnation of "every conspiracy in restraint of trade" is not as simple as it might seem. Obviously, totally independent companies like General Motors, Ford, and Chrysler cannot agree on the price or design of pick-up trucks without illegally conspiring, but what about the Chevrolet, Buick, and Cadillac divisions of GM agreeing on the price of their cars? Because these are merely different divisions of the same company, it is undisputed that they constitute a single legal person whose internal actions are not "conspiracies." This distinction underscores a critical aspect of antitrust doctrine that many courts have failed to appreciate in sports league cases—namely that every type and form of cooperative action between separate persons cannot possibly be illegal.

It thus becomes crucial for section 1 cases that the law define in some rational way which persons or entities are to be considered independent of each other—or, put another way, which persons or entities the law will require to be competitors of each other. When such independent persons or entities, who ought to be competitors of each other, reach agreements on how to conduct their business or sell their products, they may unlawfully conspire to restrain competition. But when persons or entities that are merely employees, partners, or divisions of a single business firm make agreements or joint decisions in an effort to operate the firm profitably, their actions are clearly ordinary lawful cooperation.

In most factual contexts, making this distinction has not been a significant problem for courts. Clearly, the different employees of a single corporation cannot illegally conspire with respect to carrying on the corporation's business. The partners in a recognized partnership (whether individual people, corporations, or other partnerships) never illegally conspire when making decisions about the partnership's business. Different divisions, and even different subsidiary corporations that are wholly owned by the same parent corporation (since the Supreme Court's *Copperweld v. Independence Tube* decision in 1984), can never illegally conspire.[12] There is only one type of business entity that continues to give the courts fits—the joint venture. Unfortunately, this category includes sports leagues.

It is curious that for virtually every other legal purpose, joint ventures and partnerships are treated identically. In fact, under standard business organization law principles, joint ventures are merely a kind of partnership different from more typical partnerships only in that joint ventures are created by their partners for a narrow specific purpose or for a limited period of time. Thus the special fiduciary obligations of partners to the business, the liability of partners for the business's debts, and the authority of partners to bind the business and the other partners are all exactly the same whether the business is a joint venture or a more typical partnership. For seemingly arbitrary reasons, federal antitrust courts have singled out joint ventures and generally treated the internal business agreements of their partners as conspiracies subject to condemnation if found to be "unreasonable," whereas agreements among traditional partners have never been held to be unlawful conspiracies.[13]

From the standpoint of antitrust policy (namely, the advancement of consumer welfare), the distinction between joint ventures (like sports leagues) and traditional partnerships and corporations is not justified. It is simply nonsense to allow judges or juries unfamiliar with the industry to second-guess the wisdom of business decisions made by persons whose business is affected. When the members of General Motors' corporate board of directors collectively decide where GM's factories will be located, or when the partners in a law, medical, or accounting firm collectively decide where to locate their offices, nobody in his right mind thinks the decision should be considered a conspiracy and tested for reasonableness by some judge or lay jury. But when the governing board of the NFL collectively decides that eight league games every year will be produced in Oakland instead of Los Angeles, the decision is treated as a conspiracy, which a Los Angeles judge and jury can render illegal if they believe it to be unreasonable (as happened in the *Los Angeles Coliseum/Raiders* case).

This distinction also has been made with respect to the hiring standards and employment practices of corporations, partnerships, and sports leagues. If IBM (corporation) or a major national accounting firm (partnership) decided not to hire anyone who had not completed college or insisted that employee John Doe would have to agree to work at the company's Kansas City Office if he wanted to be hired, nobody would question the policy as a potentially unlawful conspiracy. But when a sports league declines to employ players who have not completed their years of college training or requires quarterback John Doe to play for the team in Kansas City, courts condemn these decisions as unreasonable conspiracies (as in the *Denver Rockets, Mackey,* and *Smith* cases).[14]

The reason generally given by courts and plaintiffs for this distinction is that, unlike corporations and partnerships, sports leagues are not really single business firms; they are a group of separately owned teams with distinct legal identities that maintain their own separate books and have different profits and losses. While these points are superficially true, they are wholly irrelevant to antitrust policy because they overlook the fundamental nature of the business of a sports league and the relationship among a league's member teams. In fact, the antitrust policy of maximizing consumer welfare can be furthered only by treating league conduct in exactly the same way as the law treats corporate and partnership conduct. To understand why this is so, one must first recognize that the unique product a sports league produces is athletic (not economic) "competition," which requires separate teams as a necessary camouflage for the inherent partnership nature of a league.

Sports leagues produce a unique type of entertainment product—team athletic competition. At a bare minimum two different teams are always necessary to produce this product. Every game is the product of at least a two-team joint venture. Although game tickets and television broadcasts are often marketed as, for example, "Washington Redskins football," this single reference is quite misleading. The Redskins team alone is incapable of producing any football entertainment; the proper designation is "NFL football."

Furthermore, although a single NFL game may be a discrete entertainment event for some marketing purposes, it is not a separate product for any meaningful economic or antitrust purpose. The product is actually the league's annual series of 224 regular season games leading to a post-season tournament and a Super Bowl champion. It is only because each game is ultimately connected to the championship that it has substantial value. An isolated scrimmage game between two teams that did not count in any league standings or statistical rankings would be far less attractive to consumers, and it certainly could not command millions of dollars in television fees or twenty or more dollars a ticket from tens of thousands of fans.

A league's product is thus jointly produced, and no team produces anything by itself. Furthermore, no individual game is solely the product of even the two participating teams; the value of every game is largely generated by the trademark and imprimatur of the league and the cooperation and participation of all league members, each of which must recognize and accept the results of every game. Each individual team's fortunes, no matter how the league elects to divide total league revenues and expenses, are to a greater or lesser extent inherently affected by the success or failure of every single league game. Thus decisions affecting the structure of the league or the production or marketing of any league game affect the entire league, and every member has a stake and an inherent right to participate in those decisions, just as a partner in a law firm has a stake and a right to vote in his firm's business decisions. For example, although the location of the Raiders' home games will most greatly affect the Raiders (but only because of the league's pragmatic decision to give the majority of locally generated revenues to the home team), it also affects every other NFL member.[15] Without the acceptance, recognition, and occasional participation on the field of the other NFL members, those Raiders home games would be of very little economic value.

Accordingly, no individual sports team is capable of any production without the full cooperation of the other league members, and each team's economic existence, as well as its profits, depends entirely on its being an integral part of the league. It logically follows that these members are all inherent partners in the business of producing the league's wholly integrated entertainment product, and thus the teams are not and cannot be independent economic competitors of one another unless they voluntarily allow themselves to be for practical business reasons.[16] In short, it is the league, not the individual club, that is the relevant business firm for proper economic and legal analysis, and cooperation or agreements among the members should be indistinguishable from those among the members of any partnership or the directors of any corporation.

From this perspective, a Minnesota Vikings home game is not a Vikings product that the team is entitled unilaterally to produce and market any way it chooses; it is always the product of at least one other team, and, as part of the integrated NFL season, it is also the joint product of every member club. If one league member has a right to determine when, where, against whom, or under what rules it will play home games, logically the same set of rights should exist for each team regarding road games. But obviously, under such a disorganized regime no league product could be produced. Only when all the teams agree to some method for deciding these production issues can there be a league schedule and a valuable entertainment product. Clearly, there is no economic justification for legally requiring any of these decisions to be made by individual teams unilaterally.

Because every NFL game is necessarily the product of the entire league, the structural, production, and marketing decisions about every game are by definition league decisions. The league may elect for pragmatic reasons to have some of these decisions made by the individual teams (e.g., setting home game ticket prices or player salaries); by the hired commissioner (e.g., hiring game officials, drawing up the schedule of games, or negotiating network television contracts); or by some percentage vote of the member partners (e.g., determining the location of teams, setting the size of team rosters, or agreeing to collective bargaining agreements). But regardless of what decision-making methodology the league elects to use for any given matter, it is undeniable that the inherently joint nature of the league and its product makes every decision, expressly or tacitly, a decision of the collective league membership. For example, when the Raiders decided to play its home games in Los Angeles, it necessarily imposed a leaguewide decision on every NFL team to play extra road games there and to recognize and accept the results of the relocated games.

Despite the inherently joint or partnership nature of a sports league, many are skeptical. The reason is, as noted earlier, that in some ways leagues do not look like typical partnerships because each club has its own owner(s), maintains separate books, and earns its own profit or loss. In short, the teams look like independent and vigorous competitors. It is difficult for many to believe that the owners and employees of the various league teams, who often publicly insult and deride each other and threaten to commit mayhem on one another, are really business partners. But the economic reality is that they are and that these appearances are merely deceptive reflections of the unusual nature of the league product—athletic competition.

Because the league's product is athletic competition, it must ensure at least the appearance of honest and vigorous athletic rivalry among league members. Thus member teams are allowed to operate with a great deal of autonomy. It would look very suspicious to many fans and greatly diminish their enthusiasm if the clubs were largely controlled from league headquarters and seemed to lack financial incentive to perform well on the field and efficiently in the front office. But the fact that the league must create both the appearance and reality of intense athletic competition does not lead to the conclusion that the teams should be treated under the law like unrelated business competitors, which they clearly are not.

The economic competition that many mistakenly think exists between the teams because of their separate identities and limited operational autonomy is not unlike the internal rivalries within any company operating through semiautonomous profit centers. The only real difference is that leagues openly advertise and promote this internal rivalry because they want to heighten the appearance of vigorous athletic competition, whereas more typical businesses have no incentive to create a public appearance of "infighting." But the law should recognize that deliberately created athletic competition and internal rivalry in the league does not mean that the league members must treat each other like independent business competitors who are engaging in a conspiracy every time the league acts.

Furthermore, the fact that the individual teams make different profits or losses is not material to the antitrust issue: if all league revenues were put in a single common pot and all league expenses paid out of that pot, with the remainder being distributed evenly among the clubs, nobody would doubt that the league was a true partnership. The reason leagues do not operate in that fashion is that it would destroy any incentive for the clubs to field a top-quality team or keep costs down. To run the day-to-day operations of every team from central headquarters would be foolish from a management standpoint because it would destroy the necessary appearance (and perhaps the reality) of honest athletic competition.[17] It is clearly good business for each club to be responsible for its own expenses and the quality of its team.

The practice of having many decisions made and profits determined at a decentralized level certainly should not distinguish leagues from partnerships or corporations, many of which have the same profit-center type of management structure. In a law firm, an unequal profit-sharing arrangement or one that allows the lawyer members great latitude to develop their own practices is not grounds for treating every decision of the firm as an internal "conspiracy" subject to review by a jury for reasonableness. The decentralized sports league structure should be treated no differently.

It should be clear that treating every league rule, decision, or act as a conspiracy of the member teams is pure folly. It is, of course, true that a league may make bad business decisions from time to time, just as any business might. A league may even act irrationally or with improper motives. In short, league conduct may occasionally injure consumers or be unreasonable. But the business decisions of every corporation and partnership are sometimes foolish or injurious to consumers, yet that does not mean that antitrust policy is furthered by treating their every decision as a conspiracy. If every time a business acts it is an antitrust conspiracy of the people making the decision, then every rule, decision, or act can be challenged by any disgruntled person. Business entities that are truly single productive firms simply could not survive the cost and uncertainty of a system in which they had to defend the economic reasonableness of every company decision to a jury whenever an employee, customer, supplier, or competitor did not like that decision.

This is the very reason why there is no question that the decision of a corporation or a partnership to locate a branch office in Oakland instead of Los Angeles, to require employees to have a college degree, or to require employee John Doe to work in the company's Kansas City office does not constitute an illegal conspiracy of the company's partners or board members. It is also the reason why a sports league decision to have its franchises located in specific cities, to require players to have exhausted college eligibility requirements, or to force its players to play for designated teams should not be considered an illegal conspiracy of the teams. It is simply preposterous to presume that juries can generally make such league business decisions more wisely than can the very partners whose profits depend on acting wisely. It is for this reason that the legal doctrine allowing every league action to be reviewed by a court as a Sherman Act section 1 conspiracy of the league partners is irrational and contrary to antitrust policy and should be permanently scrapped.

Nevertheless, a few remaining policy concerns cause some to insist that courts should continue to use anticonspiracy law to review the business decisions of sports leagues. These concerns flow from the fact that in each sport there has always been, except for brief intermittent periods, only one league. For many purposes, this situation allows the league virtually to dictate terms to many with whom it deals. For example, a player excluded from the league, assigned to a team he strongly desires not to play for, or paid a salary he believes is unfair may have no alternative except not to play at all. A stadium, city, or equipment supplier with whom a league decides not to do business is often simply out of luck. Few corporations or traditional partnerships have that kind of power to impact the lives of its employees, customers, or suppliers so severely. Thus the notion persists that courts should exercise authority to review the decisions of leagues under section 1 in order to ensure that league power is exercised fairly.

This concern is certainly not frivolous. The problem, however, is that the underlying cause of the ability of leagues to wield such power is that for some purposes, leagues usually possess monopoly power—for example, in the labor market for players. Monopoly power in any industry is problematic from the standpoint of social and economic policy, which is precisely why Sherman Act section 2 proscribes monopolization and attempts to monopolize. But the law does not, and should never, make it unlawful for a business firm that has lawfully acquired monopoly power to operate, and it should never subject that firm's every business decision to a review on vague reasonableness grounds by a judge or jury. What is illegal is conduct designed to achieve or maintain monopoly power, not conduct that merely exercises it.

If a league has acted unlawfully to become or stay the only major league in its sport, it can and should be found in violation of section 2. That is what the interleague cases have all been about. However, if a league has not improperly become a monopoly or improperly remained one (perhaps because it is a natural monopoly), the antitrust laws should leave it alone. To try to correct a problem of monopoly power by allowing courts to review every league business rule or decision under irrelevant section 1 conspiracy doctrine, and to strike down on an ad hoc basis any decision with which the court disagrees or which it believes to be unfair, inevitably engenders chaos and inefficiency. The rash of NFL franchise moves and the frequent threats of moving by individual NFL owners that have followed the *Los Angeles Coliseum* case, after decades of total franchise stability in the NFL, is a dramatic example. Such cases essentially have created a prescription for turning the business of running leagues over to hundreds of federal judges with vastly different philosophies and abilities. In the long run nobody gains from such an unpredictable and irrational system.

If leagues do exercise their market power in ways that are unfair or otherwise contrary to public policy, perhaps Congress should consider legislative solutions. For example, if unreasonable player practices cannot be corrected through collective bargaining or under existing labor laws, they could be corrected in the same manner that various types of unfair discrimination in employment have been dealt with in civil rights legislation. But such a decision to regulate league conduct must come from Congress if the regulation is to achieve established policy goals and still be fair and consistent. The courts should apply existing law vigorously and creatively to correct evils that Congress has declared should be corrected; they should not manipulate a law condemning conspiracies to set themselves up as the arbitrator of every dispute between a league and its actual or potential employees, customers, or suppliers, based on wholly unpredictable ad hoc standards. No other business firm in the United States, monopoly or not, is so saddled with such constant judicial interference (unless Congress has specifically given the regulators the power to further specific policies and to follow specific standards and procedures). Neither should sports leagues be.

NOTES

1. These three decisions were *Flood v. Kuhn*, 407 U.S. 258 (1972); *Toolson v. New York Yankees*, 346 U.S. 356 (1953); and *Federal Baseball Club v. Ntl. League*

Professional Sports and the Antitrust Laws / 149

of Baseball Clubs, 259 U.S. 200 (1922). The scope of the "baseball exemption" is somewhat unclear. See *Henderson Broadcasting Corp. v. Houston Sports Ass'n*, 541 F. Supp. 263 (S.D. Tex. 1982); *Twin City Sportservice, Inc. v. Charles O. Finley & Co.*, 365 F. Supp. 235 (N.D. Cal. 1972), rev'd on other grounds, 512 F.2d 1264 (9th Cir. 1975) (both cases limiting the exemption to league structure and operations and player rules). Generally the scope of the exemption is thought to be quite broad, and it clearly covers all cases involving alleged conspiracies between the member clubs in a league.

2. One exception is a group of cases brought against the NFL teams that included both regular season and preseason game tickets in their season ticket package. Season ticket buyers in several cities alleged that this practice violated section 3 of the 1914 Clayton Act, which prohibits selling one product conditioned on the buyer's purchase of a second product. Although the courts have not been uniform in their reasoning, these cases have all been won by the defendant teams. See *Driskill v. Dallas Cowboys Football Club*, 498 F.2d 321 (5th Cir. 1974); *Coniglio v. Highwood Services, Inc.*, 495 F.2d 1286 (2d Cir. 1974); *Laing v. Minnesota Vikings Football Club*, 492 F.2d 1381 (8th Cir. 1974); *Pfeiffer v. New England Patriots*, 1973-1 Trade Cases ¶74,267 (D. Mass. 1972).

3. The NHL reserve system that emerged from this settlement is described in detail in a 1979 antitrust case brought by a player who was awarded to the Los Angeles Kings as "compensation" by an arbitrator after his old team, the Detroit Red Wings, signed the Kings' star goaltender. The NHL eventually won the case on the ground that the reserve system had been agreed to by the union in a collective bargaining agreement and was therefore exempt from antitrust attack. *McCourt v. California Sports, Inc.*, 600 F.2d 1193 (6th Cir. 1979).

4. When a defendant has enormous economic power in a market in which it purchases inputs used to produce its product, as opposed to one in which it sells its output, it is said to have a "monopsony." Although a monopsony is conceptually somewhat different than a monopoly and is relatively rare in antitrust cases, the economic evil of misallocated resources in either case is essentially the same, and section 2 of the Sherman Act probably applies equally to both.

5. Examples include *Neeld v. NHL*, 594 F.2d 1297 (9th Cir. 1979) (ban on one-eyed players found legal); *Denver Rockets v. All-Pro Management, Inc.*, 325 F. Supp. 1049 (C.D. Cal. 1971); *Linseman v. WHA*, 439 F. Supp. 1315 (D. Conn. 1977) and *Boris v. USFL*, 1984-1 CCH Trade Cases ¶66,012 (C.D. Cal. 1984) (minimum age or college eligibility requirements found unlawful); *Molinas v. NBA*, 190 F. Supp. 241 (S.D.N.Y. 1961) (suspension of player connected with gambling found lawful); *Bowman v. NFL*, 402 F. Supp. 754 (D. Minn. 1975) (ban on WFL players coming into the NFL past mid-season found unlawful).

6. For example, see *Mackey v. NFL*, 453 F.2d 606 (8th Cir. 1976), cert. dismissed, 434 U.S. 801 (1977) (commissioner-determined compensation for free agents found unlawful); *Smith v. Pro-Football Inc.*, 593 F.2d 1173 (D.C. Cir 1979) (NFL draft found unlawful); *Kapp v. NFL*, 390 F. Supp. 73 (N.D. Cal. 1974) (draft and reserve rules were found unlawful, but the NFL eventually won a jury verdict on the grounds of no injury); *Robertson v. NBA*, 389 F. Supp. 867 (S.D.N.Y. 1975) (NBA reserve system found probably unlawful).

150 / ROBERTS

7. In *Mid-South Grizzlies v. NFL*, 720 F.2d 772 (3d Cir. 1983), cert. denied, 467 U.S. 1215 (1984), the court found the NFL's decision not to give a former Memphis team in the WFL an NFL franchise lawful.

8. In *Levin v. NBA*, 385 F. Supp. 149 (S.D.N.Y. 1974), the court found the NBA's decision not to allow a sale of the Boston Celtics to plaintiffs lawful.

9. See *Los Angeles Memorial Coliseum Commission v. NFL*, 726 F.2d 1381 (9th Cir.), cert. denied, 469 U.S. 990 (1984) (NFL refusal to schedule Raiders game in Los Angeles found unlawful); *San Francisco Seals v. NHL*, 379 F. Supp. 966 (C.D. Cal. 1974) (NHL's refusal to schedule Seals game in Vancouver lawful). Also see *NBA v. SDC Basketball Club*, 815 F.2d 562 (9th Cir.), cert. dismissed, 108 S.Ct. 362 (1987) (NBA has a right to consider and vote on whether Clippers could move from San Diego to Los Angeles).

10. In *United States v. NFL*, 116 F. Supp. 319 (E.D. Pa. 1953), the court found NFL blackouts of one team's games in another team's city lawful when the other team is playing at home but unlawful when not playing at home. In both *WTWV, Inc. v. NFL*, 678 F.2d 142 (11th Cir. 1982) and *Blaich v. NFL*, 212 F. Supp. 319 (S.D.N.Y. 1962), the courts ruled that NFL blackouts of television signals within a 75-mile radius of a game is lawful.

11. For example, the court in *Carlock v. NFL*, an unpublished decision in case SA-79-CA-133 (S.D. Tex., Aug. 13, 1982), found the NFL decision not to use the plaintiff's laser gun to spot the ball after each play to be lawful. In *Smith v. Pro-Football Inc.*, an unpublished decision in case no. 1643-70 (D.D.C., June 27, 1973), aff'd without opinion, case no. 74-1958 (D.C. Cir., September 25, 1975), the court found the NFL rule requiring the team of an injured player to take a time-out if there is over a one-minute delay to be lawful.

12. Although no one disputes that the internal cooperation of corporations and partnerships is not illegal, the doctrinal basis for this conclusion is not necessarily the same in both cases. Corporate behavior is lawful clearly because a corporation is a single firm incapable of conspiring with itself, and its employees and directors are considered merely parts of the same legal person. See *Copperweld*, 467 U.S. 752 (1984). Partnership conduct, on the other hand, is more probably immunized by a different legal explanation—that although partners may be legally separate persons, their cooperation in running the partnership is always per se lawful. This position is referred to as the doctrine of ancillary restraints. See *Rothery Storage & Van Co. v. Atlas Van Lines, Inc.*, 792 F.2d 210 (D.D.C. 1986).

13. Although Sherman Act section 1 expressly prohibits "every" conspiracy in restraint of trade, since the Supreme Court's *Standard Oil* decision in 1911 the courts have read this language to proscribe only unreasonable restraints. Thus, if an agreement between two persons or entities is considered to be a conspiracy, it is then subject to the so-called Rule of Reason and condemned only if it is found to be unreasonable. Although for decades courts believed this rule allowed them to make subjective assessments about what they intuitively felt was fair and unfair, the U.S. Supreme Court has made it clear since the late 1970s that antitrust reasonableness is a term of art defined as being whatever is beneficial for consumer welfare. Thus conspiracies that benefit consumers are not illegal; conspiracies that injure consumers are.

14. In many of the cases involving restrictions on players, frequently an overriding issue has been present that obscured the underlying antitrust issues. Courts have held that when the players' union agrees to a league rule in collective bargaining, the rule is then immune from antitrust attack because of the so-called nonstatutory labor exemption. See *Powell v. NFL*, 888 F.2d 559 (8th Cir. 1989); *Wood v. NBA*, 809 F.2d 954 (2d Cir. 1987); *McCourt v. California Sports, Inc.*, 600 F.2d 1193 (6th Cir. 1979); *Zimmerman v. NFL*, 632 F. Supp. 398 (D.D.C. 1986). While the precise scope and application of the labor exemption is far from clear and is a fascinating issue of great importance to sports leagues today, it is well beyond the scope of the present discussion.

15. All sports leagues allow their member clubs to keep a majority or all of the revenues collected from the sale of tickets to home games, although most leagues also require that some of this revenue be shared with other league members. Giving the home team, most of the locally generated revenue is done solely in order to create an incentive for each club to promote its home games vigorously and to develop an exciting winning team. But because each game requires the complete cooperation of the other league members, the league always has the inherent power to require that all gate revenues be divided equally (or any other way) among the members, just as the NFL divides the network television revenues from all NFL games equally. If any team refused, the other teams could simply refuse to play it or include it in the league standings. And if a league did require equal sharing of gate revenues, each member club would be indifferent as to which NFL game any fan attended since its share of the revenue would be the same either way. Any incentive the Raiders or any other team has to "compete" with other clubs or to move to a more lucrative market exists largely because the league allows home teams to keep most of their locally generated revenue.

16. This voluntary competition is not the type of competition required by the antitrust laws, and an entity's controlling such voluntary internal competition is not a "conspiracy" for section 1 purposes. This phenomenon is nothing more than internal firm rivalry similar to that encouraged by all companies between employees or divisions as an incentive for them to perform as efficiently as possible—for example, competition engendered by performance bonuses, sales awards, promises of promotion, and so on. But when internal rivalry between a company's employees or divisions becomes so cutthroat that it threatens to injure the company's profits, the company's efforts to control or eliminate the counterproductive behavior would never amount to illegal conspiracy.

17. Many decisions in any business are always better made at the local level, where people are best able to judge what is involved. For example, league executives in New York would be far less able than local executives to judge what an individual player is worth to a club, what rent is appropriate for each stadium, how best to market the local team, or how to cultivate good relationships with local political and business leaders.

Mr. HYDE. Professor Zimbalist.

STATEMENT OF PROF. ANDREW ZIMBALIST, SMITH COLLEGE

Mr. ZIMBALIST. Thank you, Mr. Chairman. We have been talking a lot today about the public interest. I wonder if we could get a staff member to bring us water and glasses in the interest of the panel members? I can go on before I have my water, though.

Mr. HYDE. Certainly. We have a plethora of water up here.

Mr. ZIMBALIST. I, too, have a written statement and I am glad to hear it will be entered in the record. I will highlight what I think are some of the economic controversies that have emerged in the very fascinating and substantive discussions so far today.

Sports teams move for two simple reasons: To increase their profits and increase their franchise value. And they are able to do this because each of the sports leagues is a monopoly and like any good monopoly they restrict their output or the number of franchises relative to the demand for those franchises from economically viable cities. So you have a steady situation in all the sports leagues where demand is greater than supply for franchises. It puts cities into competition with each other.

In the NFL, this has been particularly aggravated for several reasons. One, they only play 8 to 10 home games during the year, so there are not that many seats to fill during the course of a season. Two, they have extensive revenue-sharing which enables cities like Green Bay to play and succeed economically in the league, and that means that there are more cities which are potentially viable NFL cities. That increases still more or further exacerbates the standard imbalance between supply and demand for franchises. The result is that teams in all the leagues, but particularly in the NFL, are able to go to cities and get them to compete against each other and build new stadiums that bring $10 million to $40 million a year in additional stadium revenues to the teams.

These revenues go to two places: One, to the owner's pockets and, two, they go to the players. Ask any sports fan in America what the chief ills are of our sporting leagues and they will tell you the owners make too much profit and the players get paid too much. But it is the same fans, and worse, nonfans, who are forced to support with massive subsidies this activity.

Commissioner Tagliabue talks about the need for these subsidies because of rising salaries. He points to the rapid increase in the Green Bay Packers payroll from $30 million to $45 million. The simple fact is that salaries follow revenues. Salaries have been going up more rapidly in the last several years because they are in a catchup phase. Until the *McNeill* decision, you had plan B free agency in football, which was no free agency at all, so you had artificially restrained salaries that have been catching up.

For the future, NFL owners do not have a problem with revenues not going up as fast as salaries. In fact, now they have a salary cap now that sets salaries at 62 percent of revenues. Moreover, that 62 percent is of what they call defined gross revenues and, conveniently, that defined gross revenues completely excludes stadium revenues which is the most rapidly growing source of revenues today. So it is almost codified that salaries will go up in the future more slowly than gross revenues.

The NFL does have a problem with excess litigation. I can understand and sympathize with the sentiments of some of the Members of Congress that the NFL shouldn't be running away from litigation. If Mr. Murdoch did that, Fox TV certainly wouldn't be where it is today. But they seem to be running away and seem to have themselves in a deep pit right now with regard to this myriad of litigations.

And I think that granting the NFL, the NBA and the NITL a partial antitrust exemption pertaining to relocations would help reduce the volume of litigation and restore some sanity to the NFL. But at the same time that the partial antitrust exemption is granted, you have to realize that you are further empowering these already monopoly leagues and you need a countervailing measure.

There are two bills before you today that attempt to introduce countervailing measures, one of them through the right of first refusal provision in the Stokes bill and the other in the Hoke bill where a city that loses its franchise can recover it within 3 years through expansion.

By the way, I think that the Hoke bill stands perfectly well without the trademark provision, if you all decide that there are constitutional issues that are too problematic. But I also think that Mr. Hyde asked a very interesting question before about what happened to the St. Louis Browns. I believe they became the Baltimore Orioles. The trademark is not very valuable in another city and many times it is completely anomalous. But the basic instinct which is to provide cities with counterleverage to the sporting leagues and to the teams that attempt to put them into competition with each other is an excellent idea.

There are a few technical problems with the writing of the Hoke bill and I have worked with Mr. Hoke on them. I think that the notion of going towards a limited antitrust exemption for the sporting leagues as it pertains to franchise movements makes sense, but you need a countervailing power to do that. Either you go to right of first refusal or you go to a Hoke-type mechanism. In either case, you have to price the franchise in terms of its value in the original host city, not in the city that it is going to move to. By definition, if the owner wants to move to the new city, the new city is more valuable either because it has a new stadium or because of demographics, you can't expect the old city to pay the new city franchise value.

Finally, if you do move in this direction, I think it is a wonderful opportunity for Congress, which has been contemplating baseball's antitrust exemption since 1951, to move toward a symmetrical treatment judicially and legislatively of all the sports leagues in this country. The baseball exemption has done nothing but encourage arrogance and mismanagement, promote work stoppages in that industry, and frustrate the development of rival leagues.

Mr. HYDE. Thank you very much, Professor Zimbalist.
[The prepared statement of Mr. Zimbalist follows:]

PREPARED STATEMENT OF PROF. ANDREW ZIMBALIST, SMITH COLLEGE

Professional sports teams move for two very simple reasons: to augment their profits and to increase their franchise value. The fact that the NFl, the NBA, the NHL and MLB are monopoly sports leagues enables them to limit the supply of teams in their leagues below the effective demand for such teams from economically viable cities. This excess demand to host a professional sports team leads U.S. cities to compete against each other.

The tendency of sports teams to seek more hospitable venues has been exaggerated in recent years by the advent of new stadium technology. This technology replaces the cookie-cutter stadiums of the 1960s and 1970s with single sport constructions that maximize opportunities for revenue generation from luxury suites, club boxes, concessions, catering, signage, parking, advertising and theme activities. Depending on the sport and the circumstance, a new stadium or arena can add anywhere from $10 to $40 million in revenues to a team's coffers. In fact, the economics of new stadiums can be so alluring that demographically lesser cities (e.g., Memphis, Charlotte, Jacksonville) with new stadiums can begin to compete with larger cities with older stadiums. Thus, the new stadium technology creates new economically viable cities and, thereby, exacerbates the imbalance between supply of and demand for sports franchises.

This imbalance, in turn, leads cities imprudently to offer the kitchen sink in their effort to retain existing or to attract new teams. The cities build new stadiums costing in excess of $200 million, plus infrastructural expenditures and debt service obligations that often double the cost of the project. Furthermore, when the state government is involved in financially supporting the effort, it generally requires the approval of parallel pork projects elsewhere in the state to secure the necessary votes in the legislature. Frequently, the stadium lease is on such concessionary terms that the city cannot even cover its incremental debt service with rent and other stadium revenues. The public ends up paying for the stadiums, only to generate millions of extra revenue that inevitably is divided between higher player salaries and ownership profits.

While this line of reasoning applies to all the professional team sports leagues, it applies most forcefully today to the NFL for two reasons. First, the NFL relies less on regular ticket sales for revenue than the other sports because each team only plays between eight and ten home games each year. Smaller cities can fill a stadium of 60,000 eight times a year with relative ease. Further, in contrast to basketball, baseball and hockey where less than 25 percent of total revenues are shared among the teams, in football this proportion rises above 75 percent. Thus, there are more potentially viable cities in professional football. Second, because NFL teams must share 100 percent of their television, licensing and marketing revenues as well as 40 percent of their gate, NFL teams have a powerful incentive to maximize stadium revenues which are not shared at all. Although it might trouble Jerry Jones and some other owners, the NFL would be well served by sharing 40 percent of all stadium revenues.

ECONOMIC IMPACT OF SPORTS TEAMS ON CITIES

It is a common perception that sports teams have an economic impact on a city that is tantamount to their cultural impact. This is wrong. In most circumstances, sports teams have a small positive economic effect, similar perhaps to the influence of a new department store. First, individual sports teams are not big business. The average NFL team in 1994 grossed $65 million. Compare that to the 1993 Effective Buying Income (EBI) for the metropolitan limits of St. Louis of $21.1 billion. An average NFL would account for 0.3 percent of St. Louis' EBI, 0.6 percent of Jacksonville, Florida's EBI and just 0.05 percent of the EBI of the metropolitan limits of New York City. Before the 1994–95 work stoppage, the average Major League Baseball (MLB) franchise also had gross revenues of around $65 million, while the average revenues in the NBA were approximately $50 million and those in the NHL were closer to $35 million. In terms of permanent local employees, sports teams employ between 50 and 120 full-time workers, along with several hundred low-skill and low-wage, part-time and temporary stadium or arena personnel.

Second, economic studies have shown that most public stadiums and arenas do not cover their own fixed and operating costs. Operating and debt service deficits mean that city or state governments will have to levy additional taxes. Higher taxes, in turn, discourage business in the area and reduce consumer expenditures, setting off a negative multiplier effect.

Third, virtually all independent economic research has confirmed a diminutive or negligible economic effect from the relocation of a sports team in a city. For instance, Robert Baade looked at nine cities over the period 1965–83 and found no significant relationship between adding a sports team or a new stadium and the city's economic growth. In fact, he found that in seven of the nine cities, the city's share of regional income declined after the addition of a sports team or the construction of a new stadium. Mark Rosentraub studied Indianapolis, which put forth an integrated sports development strategy in conjunction with a downtown redevelopment initiative. The city was fortunate to be able to leverage only $436.1 million of its own funds to attract a total of $2.8 billion in private and public monies. That is, the city paid less than one-sixth of the total bill. Rosentraub's study found that, while the number of sports-related jobs increased, sports was too small a component of the local economy to have an appreciable impact. Indeed, most of the employment growth was in low-wage services and Indianapolis' share in the total county payroll actually declined from 1977 to 1989.

Fourth, dozens of studies have been performed by consulting firms under contract with the affected city or team. Predictably, most of these studies have concluded that there would be a substantial, positive impact from adding sports team. The main methodological problem with these studies is that they do not account for or do not sufficiently account for the difference between new and diverted (or gross and net) spending. People have only so much income that they will spend on leisure and entertainment activities. If they go to a ballgame, it generally means that they are not spending the same dollars locally to go to the theater, to the movies, to a concert, to dinner, to rent a video and so on. That is, the dollar spent at the sports event usually replaces the dollar spent elsewhere in the local economy. The net spending impact is nil. The main source of net spending is out-of-town visitors to a ballgame. With a few exceptions, such as Baltimore or Denver, this number is usually small for professional sports teams. It consists primarily of the visiting teams and out-of-town media.[1]

These same studies also tend to make favorable assumptions about the size of the area being impacted,[2] the share of executive and player salaries remaining in the local economy,[3] the interconnections between the sports team and the rest of the city's economy,[4] and the terms of stadium financing[5] as well as conditions of its lease. Depending on the assumptions made, one can get wildly different estimates. For instance, two studies were made about the impact of the Colts on the Baltimore economy in 1984. One study found an impact of $30 million and the other an impact of $200,000. The former estimate is wildly unrealistic, but even at such a level the benefits would have to be weighed against the costs of constructing, financing and possibly maintaining a new stadium. It would also be prudent for the city to recognize that after two decades a new stadium technology might come along and oblige the city to undertake yet another expensive construction project in order to keep the team in town.

Mayors, under pressure not to lose a city's historical franchise and cajoled by local contractors, unions, lawyers, hotel, restaurant and real estate interests, among other political powers, tend to look favorably upon new stadium construction. They invoke images of city grandeur and new corporate headquarters moving to town. While it is conceivable that some cities are on the threshold of recognition and a sports team could lift them over the hump, such an effect is highly speculative and there is no case where it has actually taken hold in a significant way. Moreover, corporate relocations rarely occur to cities whose fiscal situation is deteriorating.

To the extent that a new stadium (a) is a central element of an urban redevelopment plan and its location and attributes are carefully set out to maximizes,

---

[1] Hosting an all-star game in baseball or the Super Bowl in football provide an additional financial fillip to the fortunate city.

[2] The smaller the circle around the stadium that is chosen as the unpacted area, the greater percentage of attendees at the sports event that will be classified as out-of-town, and, hence, by assumption the greater will be the net spending. There is, however, little reason for public policy makers to endorse such a parochial view of economic impact, unless there is a clear intention to benefit one area at the expense of another.

[3] The more a team's owner and its experts (i.e., those with very high incomes) live in and spend their income in the host city, the larger will be the economic impact.

[4] The greater are these interconnections, the larger will be multiplier effect. Generally, the local area multiplier of sports spending will be between 1.5 and 2. That is, if one takes the first round local value added, that number should be multiplied by 1.5 or 2 to get the total annual effect on city income. Another error often made by these studies is that they take the first round gross value rather than the local value added. For example, if I buy a Samuel Adams beer at Yankee Stadium for $4.50, it is likely that almost $1.00 of that goes back to the manufacturer in Boston, another $2.00 goes to the concessionaire (which is based in another city) and, perhaps, the balance goes to George Steinbrenner and the other Yankees' owners. Since Steinbrenner maintains his primary residence outside of New York City, travels widely and saves a good portion of his income and since the concessionaire probably remits around half of its net sales to the home office (after paying the local personnel and other expenses), the local value added from this sale of beer is probably half or less of its $4.50 gross value.

[5] Since 1990, due to the 1986 Tax Reform Act, interest earnings on municipal bonds floated to finance a stadium (whose benefit is privately appropriated) generally are not exempt. This only raises the cost of new construction. The construction of a new football stadium for Baltimore was excepted from this provision. Cities can circumvent this restriction if less than 10 percent of the debt service is covered from private sources.

synergies with local business and (b) the terms of its lease are not negotiated under duress and are fair to the city, then the city may derive some modest economic benefit from a sports team. The problem, however, is that these two conditions rarely obtain when dealing with monopoly sports leagues. Cities are forced to act hastily under pressure and to bargain without any leverage. Properly reckoned, the value of a sports team to a city should not be measured in dollars, but appreciated as a potential source of entertainment and civic pride.

TEAM RELOCATIONS AND PUBLIC POLICY

Are sports franchises, such as the Browns, Rams or Oilers, so economically troubled that they need new stadiums for their survival? Definitively not.[6] Excluding the last two aberrant years in MLB, sports teams with very few exceptions are profitable or potentially profitable; indeed, well-managed franchises generally yield handsome returns to their owners.

On January 23, 1996, before the Senate Judiciary Committee, NFL Commissioner Paul Tagliabue was asked by Senator Arlen Specter why teams in the NFL required multimillion dollar subsidies annually from their host cities. The Commissioner responded that the short answer was rising player salaries. Senator Specter inquired what the long answer was because, he said, he didn't like the short answer. To be sure, municipal subsidies to NFL teams comfortably pre-date the emergence of modified free agency with salary cap in 1993. Football salaries have been in a catch-up mode over the last several years, making up for lost ground during the decades when no real free agency existed. Under the cap system, salaries will rise more slowly than revenues because stadium revenues, one of the most rapidly growing revenue sources in the NFL, are excluded from the 62 percent cap calculation.[7]

Generally rising player salaries follow rising revenues and are a sign of economic success, not a cause of economic decline. Nevertheless, sports leagues have different economic characteristics than other businesses. Teams in a league compete on the playing field, but they must cooperate as business entities. Audiovox might want Motorola to go bankrupt, but the Cowboys do not desire the same fate for the 49ers. When leagues have insufficient revenue sharing among the teams or define revenue sharing too narrowly, then the drive of individual teams to maximize profits can begin to have deleterious effects on the cohesion and stability of the league.

What can public policy do about footloose franchises jilting their fans and blackmailing our cities? Some in Congress have suggested extending antitrust immunity as it pertains to franchise movements to the NFL, the NBA and the NFL. On January 23, 1996, before the Senate Judiciary Committee Commissioner Tagliabue asserted the primacy of cooperation among teams in a sports leagues and argued that a sports league is really a single economic entity. If the NFL is a single entity, the reasoning goes, then its teams are like branches in the same company and there can be no conspiracy among them to restrain trade.

Thus, Tagliabue believes that the proper judicial context for the NFL is to have an antitrust exemption, just like MLB. In the absence of a blanket exemption, he would settle happily for an exemption pertaining to franchise relocations. He believes that the tendency for clubs and cities to litigate would be diminished if this partial antitrust immunity were extended to the league. While he is probably correct that there would be less litigation, MLB's experience suggests that litigation would not disappear. MLB's experience also suggests that there is another problem besides litigation and that is the financial exploitation of cities. MLB has managed over the past 23 years to maintain franchise geographic stability, but it has also managed to play the stadium extortion game most effectively. Over the past two-plus decades MLB teams have not moved, but they have used threats to move, often supported by statements from the commissioner, in order to extract extremely lucrative stadium deals. If Congress extends partial antitrust immunity to the other team sports leagues and does nothing else, it will make an already uneven playing field more imbalanced.

---

[6] *Financial World* magazine each year puts out estimates of operating income for all the franchises in the NHL, NFL, NBA and MLB based on figures and partial information provided by ownership. Their estimates tend to be conservative. For the 1994 season, *Financial World* estimated that the Browns had an operating income of $6 million, the Oilers had $2.8 million and the Rams had an operating loss of $1.8 million. However, *Financial World* estimated that the Rams had an operating income of $5.5 million in 1993.

[7] While it is true that individual teams can exceed the cap in some years by manipulating the timing of salary payments, eventually the same teams will be constrained to a tighter cap as the payments schemes catch up with them. The remaining NFL cap loophole (that it is not in effect for 1999) is expected to be closed when the current negotiations for a new collective bargaining agreement are concluded.

It is important to clarify that the 1984 decision of the Ninth Circuit Court of Appeals in the Raiders' I case did not state that sports leagues do not have a legitimate function in regulating franchise movements to promote league stability. It simply stated that the NFL's Rule 4.3 was too restrictive and it expressed concern that the league was trying to protect the Rams' monopoly in the Los Angeles market. The right of sports leagues to control franchise relocation was reaffirmed in the Ninth Circuit's 1986 decision in the Raiders' II case and the subsequent settlement between the NBA and the L.A. Clippers. To be sure, it was probably clear awareness of this judicial opinion that in 1995 led the NFL owners initially to deny the Rams' petition to move to St. Louis. It was not until a reported $46 million was proferred to the other owners (up from the earlier spurned $25 million) that the NFL permitted the move.[8] If the NFL had immunity in this case, the Rams probably would have moved anyway, but the extortion fee may have been even greater.

The root of the problem lies in the leagues' monopoly status and the solution must attack the root. This can be done either by engendering competition or by regulating the abuse. Competition could be created by breaking up each of the leagues into two or more business entities. The leagues would be permitted to cooperate in setting playing rules and schedules, but not in setting their business practices. In competition, each league would attempt to occupy all the viable cities available before their rival, and the supply and demand situation would balance out.

Regulating the abuse could take several forms. There are two bills before this Committee (H.R. 2699, hereafter the Stokes bill, and H.R. 2740, hereafter the Hoke bill) that attempt to deal with the franchise relocation issue. Each bill extends partial antitrust immunity to the leagues relating to franchise relocation, but to their credit each bill also recognizes the need to circumscribe the discretionary power of the leagues in these matters. In addition to establishing criteria which would govern a team's ability to move, the Stokes bill offers a right-of-first refusal to the host city or a local investor to buy the team. The bill stipulates that local government would have the right to own a major league team, an opportunity that has always been denied by the sports leagues. The first-refusal provision in Stokes, however, carries little enforcement power. This is because the bill leaves the franchise price open to negotiation between the existing and prospective owner. Under these circumstances, the existing owner will want a price for the team commensurate with its value in the new city. Since the owner wants to move, the new city is by definition more attractive, either by virtue of its demographic characteristics or a new stadium with favorable lease. Usually, these factors can increase the value of a sports team by tens of millions of dollars. Thus, the Stokes bill does little more than give the right to a prospective local owner to buy an asset for substantially above its value in the local market. It will offer little protection to the existing host city.

The Hoke bill ingeniously devises another mechanism for protecting host cities. It allows owners to preserve their "property right" to move their asset where they desire, but it allows for a vacated city to recover its team's name and obtain an expansion team within a three-year period. The Hoke bill also grants the sports leagues limited antitrust immunity for franchise relocations, but it circumscribes this power by requiring the leagues to provide expansion teams to the bereft cities. The leagues, thereby, will have a strong incentive and the muscle to limit team movements. The incentive comes from the fact that the league is allowing an individual owner to appropriate the extra value of a new city and stadium, while the league is left with a required expansion to a less desirable city (the previous host city presumably has less market value since the owner wanted to move the team). The weakness with the Hoke bill approach is that it stipulates that the price of the recovered expansion franchise to be "85 percent of the franchise fee charged by the league for the last expansion." This stipulation again runs the risk of offering the host city to buy back a team for a price well above such a team's local market value. Consider, for instance, the situation of MLB's Pittsburgh Pirates today. The Pirates are in the process of being sold for approximately $90 million, but the last MLB expansion fee was $130 million (plus another $20 million or so in foregone national television revenues). Taking 85 percent of the $130 million figures yields $110.5 mil-

---

[8] Two weeks ago, before the Senate Judiciary Committee Commissioner Tagliabue stated that the reason the Rams were allowed to leave Los Angeles was because Rams filed a triple-damage antitrust suit. It is hard to believe that the NFL owners did not anticipate such a suit before their initial decision. Further, if the antitrust suit was the sole motivation for permitting the move, why did the relocation fee jump by over $20 million? Tagliabue also indicated that a disproportionate share of this relocation booty was given to the NFL's low revenue teams. While this is a laudable use of the funds, it is still a payment to the NFL owners. Presumably, the greater use of relocation fees to aid low revenue teams obviates the use of other league revenues for this purpose. In any event, it would make sense for the Congress to request details on the distribution of relocation fees and new revenue sharing initiatives in the NFL.

lion. The Hoke bill would say to the city of Pittsburgh or to private investors who would keep the team in Pittsburgh that they have the right to reclaim their team with its name and trademark for a price that is at least $25.5 million above the market price. The problem, then, is that the 85 percent formula is arbitrary and may not offer any real protection at all.[9]

For either the right-of-first refusal or the Hoke approach to be meaningful, the team must be offered to the city for the team's market value in that city. Such a value could be reasonably established through an arbitration procedure. Another effective option, albeit one that goes against the prevailing ideological winds in Washington today, would be to establish a bipartisan National Sports Commission that would regulate the number and location of franchises in each league.

Finally, if Congress moves to grant partial antitrust immunity to the NHL, NFL and NBA, it would be well-advised to consider limiting MLB's presumed blanket exemption and bring symmetry at long last to the legislative and judicial treatment of team sports leagues in the United States. Baseball's exemption has done little more than to encourage arrogance, laxity and mismanagement, to promote work stoppages and to frustrate the emergence of rival leagues in that sport. Congress has been considering doing away with the baseball anomaly for forty-five years; it is now time for action.

Mr. HYDE. I am going to ask my colleagues if they would submit their questions in writing, because, frankly, it is late in the day and these folks have been here for a long time and they have distances to go.

However if someone has a question that is urgent, I don't want to foreclose anybody. I am just requesting that they withhold themselves unless they have a burning need to ask the question. And with that admonition, I yield—I hope I have transmitted enough guilt to inhibit a lot of prolix questioning.

Mr. Scott of Virginia, well-known for his brevity.

Mr. SCOTT. No, no, Mr. Chairman.

Mr. HYDE. You could submit them in writing if you have anything?

Ms. LOFGREN. Actually, the question I had was for Professor Zimbalist.

Mr. HYDE. The gentlewoman from California.

Ms. LOFGREN. It can be answered in writing later. He critiqued the bills before us. I wanted to invite him to provide any additional scheme that he could recommend for controlling the phenomenon that I think he is well aware of from his written statement, other than the bills before us and then his reasons for them. Thank you.

Mr. HYDE. The gentleman from Pennsylvania, Mr. Gekas.

Mr. GEKAS. Where am I?

Mr. HYDE. You are on the threshold of an open mind.

Mr. GEKAS. I want to say that the gentleman from Illinois, Mr. Flanagan, particularly, and Mr. Hoke companionably, have begun to gently open my mind. But it is not too far.

---

[9] Another weakness with the Hoke bill formulation is that it protects a ties that have hosted a team for ten years or more and it protects expansion franchise cities, but it does not protect a city that has received a relocated franchise within the last ten years. St. Louis is such a city and it deserves protection under Hoke as much as other NFL cities. Apparently, the new dome stadium in St. Louis cost in excess of $300 million. I would also suggest that the requirement that a prospective team owner put down 185 percent of the team's value is excessive and that the 60-mile limit should be rephrased to denote the same metropolitan area. Finally, while the constitutionality of limiting properly rights through the attachment of the trademark (and not permitting the fleeing team owner to retain half the trademark) is questionable, I think the Hoke bill is valuable without this provision. The sobriquet "Browns" has a good deal of value in Cleveland, but is not likely to have much value in Baltimore. Indeed, 43 years ago in baseball when the St. Louis Browns moved to Baltimore, this sobriquet was eschewed. In any event, the key mechanism in the Hoke bill is the right of the vacated city to purchase an expansion team within three years and this stands with or without the trademark provision.

Mr. HYDE. I thank the gentleman. The gentleman from Ohio, Mr. Chabot.

Mr. CHABOT. No questions, Mr. Chairman.

Mr. HYDE. I doubly thank the gentleman.

And now, if I have built up enough pressure, I doubt very much.

Mr. ROBERTS. Mr. Chairman, we actually like to perform once in a while.

Mr. HYDE. Do you really? I certainly will yield 5 minutes to the gentleman from Cleveland, because of your burning interest, which you have, in this issue.

Mr. HOKE. I don't think I can possibly take 5 minutes now, Mr. Hyde, but I really wanted to congratulate Mr. Keller. I was going to offer him a Cuban cigar, for his lively endorsement and great feeling for my bill. He obviously has a great deal of support for the trademark issues in it.

Mr. HYDE. Well, I didn't detect an awful lot of sympathy for obstructing the free transfer of trademarks. But I would—taking your side for just a brief second, and understanding fully where Mr. Keller is coming from—think that sports teams' names are not just private property. I think because of their appeal to the emotions of the city they become a quasi-public property.

I would think that such an emotional investment as we saw today from John Thompson, which is replicated in Chicago, the "bleacher bums" who used to inhabit the bleachers at Cubs Park, comes from people who live and breathe and die. They are not so different. They are normal human beings whose interest is not art or classical music, but football or basketball. It is just part of the human condition. Therefore, there is something public, something communal about that logo that doesn't seem to me something that the owner can easily put into his pocket.

Now, I don't know. I am not suggesting legislation on this at all, but there is an emotional investment that I think is ignored somewhat by all professional sports. The baseball strike last year was incredible. The shut-ins, the seniors who live for that baseball game, for that World Series, and to see millionaires fighting megamillionaires over additional millions, while the game, the game was just disregarded. That adds to the cynicism of people who, for God's sake, need their cynicism to be dispelled.

The same thing is true in football. A community that really gets involved with its team, waits all night for tickets in below-zero weather—something I don't understand but I admire—it just seems to me it is more than private property with all of the sanctity that we all attribute to private property.

Mr. KELLER. I think everyone in this room would agree with the Chair and other witnesses who have taken the same position. Our position is just this: Even though that is completely true, as a matter of law you have to separate out, as the law requires in a number of situations, the emotionality of this issue.

If there were not a whole body of trademark law that simply holds unequivocally trademarks are private property, I dare say INTA would not be here taking the position that it takes. But the disruption to trademark law, which this committee is extremely sensitive to and supportive of, as witnessed by the fine work of the subcommittee and the whole Congress in passing the Trademark

Law Dilution Act of 1995, is also a very important issue. I don't say that it is an easy decision to make, but I am very concerned that we not let emotionality run rampant and trample some well-established trademark principles, because in the long run that would be bad.

At the same time, I think the commissioner's olive branch, indicating that discussions are going on internally in the league to find the way to keep the Mr. Thompsons of the world happy, are exactly the sorts of discussions that ought to be encouraged by this committee and others, but I don't think that legislation is called for.

Mr. ROBERTS. One of the interesting trademark issues—and I might add that the trademark of the Browns for the last God knows how many years has been the Cleveland Browns. Does Mr. Modell have the right to move to Baltimore and call the team the Cleveland Browns? That has been his trademark. If he cannot take the word "Cleveland" with him to Baltimore, why can he take the word "Browns?"

Mr. HOKE. I want to make a serious observation with respect to what Mr. Keller was saying, because I really think that we need to point out two things. First of all, whatever property rights exist, and property rights do clearly exist, they were created by the Congress pursuant to article I, section 8: The Congress shall have the power to promote the progress of science, etc. That is a congressionally created power, and Congress has the power to modify that or abridge it or restrict it or reduce it or do whatever it wants with it.

I have heard the word "unconstitutional" used a number of times today, and I think that sort of begs the whole question. Clearly, this Congress has the right, in whatever limited laser-like way it wants to, to deal with that.

But probably more importantly, I want to just make one observation with respect to this antitrust issue, and it goes to what Mr. Roberts was saying and also Mr. Zimbalist, we spoke about it earlier, although I don't believe you spoke to it directly. As I think you all know because you have read the bill, I actually have no problem with codifying in black letter law what I already believe to exist in case law.

I was surprised that in your written testimony, Mr. Roberts, you do not mention Raiders II or Clippers. I am still convinced that the ability exists right now for the NFL or any other league to restrict the movement of a team, and that they are hiding behind that as a strawman to claim that they cannot do what they really deeply want to do.

My position is that they don't deeply want to do it at all because it is against their economic interests to do it. But bearing that in mind, I have no problem with the idea of codifying that so that they have the absolute ability to do that in black letter law.

My concern is not that they can or cannot do it; my concern is that they simply won't do it because it is against their economic interests to do that. And that, I guess I would ask each of you to just comment on that.

Mr. ROBERTS. I think you are wrong, Mr. Hoke. I mean, the way the *Raiders* case played out was in my judgment as close, if it didn't cross the line, to just judicial misconduct. It was a local judge who was, by God, going to see that that team got down there, and what went on in the chambers of the ninth circuit, where you had the trial judge who was on the ninth circuit, the guy on the ninth circuit who negotiated the contract with Al Davis on behalf of the Coliseum Commission, sharing chambers with the judge who wrote the ninth circuit opinion in the *Raiders* case.

There are no legal principles that came out of that case. If the law was as crystal clear as you think it is, you would not have the *Billy Sullivan* case in Boston, and you would not have the lawsuit in St. Louis right now, and you would not have the ability of the Raiders to threaten to sue the league.

Mr. HOKE. There are a lot of undecided lawsuits at this point, but the fact is that each of these professional leagues, all four of them, as soon as *Raiders* was decided, codified in their own rules and regulations the exact laundry list that was suggested there, and then *Raiders II* and *Clippers* said if you have that laundry list, if you have those criteria in your rules and regs, you can enforce, you can restrict team movement.

Mr. ROBERTS. I would ask you, if you were somebody who was threatened with a $2 billion lawsuit, and here is the NFL owners, and the league is faced with the unilateral move of a team from Los Angeles to St. Louis—which the league does not support, by the way, because it devastates their TV revenues over a period of time—

Mr. HOKE. Does that mean they do support the move from Seattle to Los Angeles?

Mr. ROBERTS. They want a team in Los Angeles. Whether they would support that move or not, I haven't studied it carefully enough. But with $2 billion at stake, would you put your trust in not having to pay a $2 billion judgment in a judge in St. Louis?

Mr. HOKE. The real question is, why didn't they bring the lawsuit when Baltimore moved?

Mr. ZIMBALIST. I think that Gary is pointing out one of the chief characteristics of a sports league, and that is that it does, to some degree, behave as a single entity. But it also behaves as individually profit-maximizing companies. The reality is simply more complex than Gary is allowing, in my view. I think it has both of those characteristics.

With regard to whether or not football would behave differently if they got a partial exemption, I think we can learn something from the experience in baseball. Baseball still has some litigations when they prevent teams from moving. We saw litigation from Tampa and we saw litigation from San Francisco. There are other litigations. They do have some, but a lot less than football has. That is an advantage.

But baseball still has cities vying against each other. They have had commissioners going to cities saying "You need to build a new stadium, because this stadium is not up to snuff and this town is not up to snuff, and if you don't do something, then we are not going to allow the team to move," and that is the same threat of extortion that you get in the NFL. They are able to parlay their imbalance of supply and demand to get new stadiums out of cities. I think that is the real issue.

Where Gary is right that it might not be in their long-run interest to have a team in St. Louis rather than Los Angeles, you are right that it would be in their interest to have it in Los Angeles rather than Seattle. So you will get some restriction of franchise movement but you will not get the desired level of restriction. So if you are going to move towards a partial exemption, that is fine, but you need have the countervailing measure.

Mr. HYDE. Again, I am going to request written questions from now on.

The gentlelady from Texas, I certainly don't want to short-circuit her. Do you have any questions that must be asked?

Ms. JACKSON LEE. Mr. Chairman, I thank you for your graciousness. You alluded to written questions, and I have just written a note about written questions that I will pose. I have one question that I would like to hear a response today, primarily because I have heard, in essence, seemingly conflicting themes.

I think I have been educated today to understand that there is an NFL and there are owners. For some of us, we have sensed an interlocking over a period of time: the NFL. But as I have heard the commissioner talk, it seems as if in that august body there is disagreement between the commissioner and this body called owners, which may be, I guess, considered as the board of directors.

The reason why I raise that is because I asked the commissioner about the potential of judicial review. Mr. Roberts, you testified that you believe it is in the public interest, as I understand your testimony, to provide the NFL with a narrow antitrust exemption.

My question would be, we have already heard that they have, generally speaking, criteria which the owners should use when they make determinations about relocation. There should be a vigorous debate about those criteria. This law will now attempt to codify that but, in addition, look at potentially an antitrust exemption.

Seeing that we apparently have these two prongs, the commissioner's office and the owners, would you have some suggestions to add in this legislation to prevent abuses by either group, keeping in mind as I understand that we as Americans have the right to pursue our grievances in the courts of law. But what would we need to do to get where we want to be, which is this even playing field with this antitrust exemption?

Mr. ROBERTS. Well, my position in my detailed statement, my position is that leagues are natural monopolies, single firms, and I think you ought to regulate them. But if Congress is not willing to set up a mechanism for regulating their conduct, then it is better to let the league control these decisions than it is to let individual team owners exercise the league's monopoly power unto themselves. That is what is going on now.

If you want, I think you could draft a statute that would create the criteria under which teams could move, and then set up a regulatory body of some type to make the judgment as to whether or not those criteria are met that would allow the team to move. That would take the decision out of the hands of the league and put it in the hands of an entity that is looking after the public interest. That is regulating a natural monopoly, which is what we do with natural monopolies. We regulate the electric companies and other natural monopolies.

But Congress has shown a political unwillingness to do that, and I doubt that it has the political will to do it now, particularly given the political direction the country is going in. So if you are not willing to do that, then the solution has got to be let the league exercise the power instead of letting an a individual selfish owner do it.

Ms. JACKSON LEE. And that would be, in the concept, the antitrust exemption to the league?

Mr. ROBERTS. Create the exemption for the league. The last thing you want is to let some judge who is sitting in the town whose team is at stake make the decision.

Ms. JACKSON LEE. Anyone else?

Mr. KELLER. I would like to respond in the following way, following up on the previous answer. You certainly could do a number of things by establishing legislative criteria. But following up on Representative Hoke's comments earlier, you could not make as a lawful criteria the requirement that a relocating team give up its trademark, for two reasons.

No. 1, it is incorrect that Congress finds its source of authority to enact trademark law in the copyright clause of the Constitution, which is what Representative Hoke referred to. In fact, there is a Supreme Court case on point that says that power resides solely in the commerce clause.

As a result of that particular gap in the Constitution, it is black letter law that trademark rights exist first as a matter of the common law of the United States, and because they exist as a matter of the common law and the Federal legislation is simply a codification, that is, the Lanham Act is a codification of the common law, that is a criteria that would result, if you enacted it, in an unconstitutional taking of private property.

There are lots of things you can do, and do not think, with all respect, you can do that constitutionally.

Ms. JACKSON LEE. Thank you for that.

Mr. ZIMBALIST. I agree with everything that Gary is saying, but I do not think he is saying enough. I think if you do take this position that you want the decisions to be in the hands of the league rather than individual selfish owners, then that is OK, give them the partial antitrust exemption. But what you are doing to the league as an entity is making a monopoly more powerful, and that is going to be bad for the consumer. So what you have to do is circumscribe that power. And there are two bills before you, each of which attempt to do it. I would only suggest that the proper way to approach this question of what price should the former host city have to pay to have its franchise, that should be based upon the market value of the franchise in that city rather than in some new city with a new stadium and different demographic characteristics.

Mr. HYDE. The gentlelady's time has expired.

Ms. JACKSON LEE. Mr. Chairman, I thank you. I think we have heard a myriad of positions throughout this day and I think our work is cut out for us and hopefully we can help work through this. I thank you.

Mr. HYDE. Well, I thank you. And I want to say that the grand finale, with emphasis on the word "grand," is to be presented by Michael Patrick Flanagan of Chicago.

Mr. FLANAGAN. Mr. Chairman, having been brought up in an Irish Catholic tradition and having been exposed to guilt merchants my entire life, I will be as brief as humanly possible.

Mr. HYDE. Will wonders never cease?

Mr. FLANAGAN. Thank you, Mr. Chairman.

I will ask just one question. In fact, I will happily accept a written answer because it is a very considered question, and it is on a deep legal issue. But most who have come before this committee who object to this legislation in one area or another point to the desire by the NFL to have the monopolistic powers that the NFL claims were pulled away by Raiders.

My question, on the specific issue of trademark, is if that monopolistic power were to be granted a limited or partial antitrust exemption, however the football exemption were to be granted, is that not in itself an obstruction to the free trade of a trademark, and consequently, is that not objectionable from a trademark standpoint all by itself?

If I tell you that you cannot move a name, is that not an equal infringement to saying you must leave a name when you go? That is a question I think that must be answered before it is over. I think the difficulty in observing the position of the NFL here is that—I do not want to use the term "power grab," but they are on a move to say if you trust us, and if you give us absolute power in this area, we will be good people and we will restrict movement and we will provide the fans the stability they need. We will do all these things.

My question is, and the base question of these entire hearings is, why not create equal bargaining power on a local level between local governments, local corporations and the NFL, or the individual teams, by limiting the NFL's power, not augmenting it?

Mr. ROBERTS. The rhetoric is what confuses me. If the NFL has monopoly power, it is better for that monopoly power to be exercised by the league than by a single team owner. You are not diminishing the league's monopoly power. You are just giving it all to Art Modell. It still has monopoly power. It is just you are giving one greedy team owner the ability to exercise entirely that monopoly power unto himself. You are not minimizing it at all. The cities are still hung out there to dry. You are better to give——

Mr. FLANAGAN. The cities are hung out to dry because the bottom line is paid for by the antitrust exemption given by Congress.

Mr. ROBERTS. That is just wrong, Congressman. It is just wrong.

Mr. FLANAGAN. $1.2 billion divided among 30 teams provides enough of a bottom line for people to move with impunity. If they did not have that amount of money——

Mr. ROBERTS. How could they do that?

Mr. FLANAGAN [continuing]. Sitting in the pocket for whatever team they go to, their ability to deal with the local government on an evenhanded basis would be very different.

Mr. ROBERTS. No, Congressman, what you would have is you would have wider revenue disparities between the teams which would create even greater pressures on teams to be constantly seeking new revenue sources.

Mr. FLANAGAN. Then we go back to the same question I had for Mr. Tagliabue. Which antitrust exemption do you need for stability? The one that will provide the antitrust exemption that will give the sharing of the broadcast powers, or do you need the a la baseball one that will give absolute right to the owners to control it? I am of the opinion you do not need both. You need one or the other, but you cannot have both.

Mr. ROBERTS. What you need is to treat the leagues like the single firms they are, instead of treating everything that they do as some kind of internal conspiracy regulated by legal principles that nobody can articulate.

Mr. FLANAGAN. My issue is not with any internal conspiracies. My issue is——

Mr. ROBERTS. Sure, it is.

Mr. FLANAGAN [continuing]. With $150 million that is going to have to be laid out by the taxpayers of the city of Chicago and the county of Cook to be able to build a stadium to keep the McCaskey family happy so the Bears do not move. If the McCaskey family did not have a piece of the $1.2 billion in revenue or had a larger piece without the exemption, their entire contractual negotiations at a local level would have a completely different flavor and a completely different aspect, and that is the problem.

If that playing field is leveled, Congress need take no other action for it becomes an internal and private matter between consenting, contracting parties. But because Congress has put them on a different plane with unfair bargaining power, it is up to us to level that playing field.

Now, we can do it by taking the exemption away and saying, have at it, boys; or we can do it by augmenting it in such a way as to bring the local communities to an even playing field level. We have a responsibility to do one or the other.

Mr. ROBERTS. I confess you completely lost me. And by the way, the Lakers belong to Minneapolis, not Los Angeles. I had to correct you on that one.

Mr. FLANAGAN. Thank you.

Mr. HYDE. Well, I want to thank again this very distinguished and helpful panel. You have made a contribution. Your statements and testimony will be studied and have an impact. We thank you.

Mr. ROBERTS. Thank you, Mr. Chairman.

Mr. HYDE. The meeting is adjourned.

[Whereupon, at 3:27 p.m., the committee adjourned.]

APPENDIX

Material Submitted for the Hearing

Statement of
Rep. Norm Dicks
RELOCATION OF PROFESSIONAL SPORTS TEAMS
February 6, 1996

Mr. Chairman:

I applaud the efforts of this Committee today to focus public attention on the issue of the relocation of professional sports franchises. This is, of course, a subject that has been discussed in the past, but the recent rash of sports teams abandoning their traditional communities has once again raised the question of whether professional sports franchises should be accorded a special status with respect to our nation's antitrust laws.

I am pleased that the National Football League (NFL) in a February 2nd statement said that "the team will remain in Seattle as far as the League is concerned," and I hope that pending litigation by King County will be successful in keeping the franchise in Seattle. These traumatic events in Seattle and in our communities around the country make it clear that Congress must act. We must act to give the League the legal authority to block a flagrant effort to move a team when it is unjustified.

In many ways, Mr. Chairman, sports franchises are different from traditional businesses, particularly because entire communities feel a sense of symbolic ownership of every aspect of the franchise. These sports businesses operate in a profoundly public environment, often in public facilities, and certainly with the assistance of local governments who benefit from the economic activity that these teams generate. They have a special place in the hearts of their fans, and it is up to this committee to determine if, in fact, they deserve a special place in American law.

My personal interest in this issue has been influenced by the middle-of-the-night move of the Baltimore Colts, the proposed transfer of the

Cleveland Browns franchise and, most recently, by the shocking announcement last week that the Seattle Seahawks owner was abandoning the Kingdome and planning to abscond with the team to the Rose Bowl in California. These are all business decisions made by the individuals who happen to have owned these teams at the time. But I agree with Congressmen Stokes and Hoke, as well as with Senator John Glenn, that these decisions are not just private decisions made by private business people: they involve many important public dimensions that should be considered as moves of this type are contemplated. Certainly there are thousands of fans who have been left powerless in the wake of these moves, but I believe there is also a question of the larger obligation to the public community in which these teams have thrived (and profited).

Since the announcement of the Seahawks move last week the outcry in the Pacific Northwest has been overwhelming, but there is little recourse for the fans to stop Seahawks' owner Ken Behring from relocating. The National Football League itself has been alarmed by the precipitous franchise changes, as well it should be. The League does not, however, have the legal authority to prevent teams from moving, no matter how strongly or weakly supported they may have been in their host city. The remedies suggested by Congressmen Hoke and Stokes are vital, providing limited anti-trust immunity for sports franchises, particularly with regard to the re-location of these teams. This is a very serious decision, but it is also intended to address what I consider to be a very serious problem today among sports franchises, and I believe it is time to act. Congress has considered this step before. In fact, a bill (S.950) providing broad anti-trust immunity was even approved by Senator Magnuson's Commerce Committee and by the full Senate in 1965. At the that time, even with fewer professional sports franchises, there was significant sentiment for the legislation which would have acted to "equalize competitive playing strengths" and clarified the rights to operate within specific geographic areas.

This is clearly an appropriate time for this Committee to revisit this important issue, and I look forward to the ideas that are generated from today's hearing. Thank you for this opportunity to endorse the proposals offered by Congressmen Stokes and Hoke, and to provide my encouragement to the Committee for pursuing an issue that means so much to sports fans in virtually every community in this nation. Thank you.

CITY OF CLEVELAND
Michael R. White, Mayor

Cleveland City Hall
601 Lakeside Avenue
Cleveland, Ohio 44114
216-664-2220

THE CASE AGAINST SPORTS FRANCHISE FREE AGENCY:
A STATEMENT FROM
THE CITY OF CLEVELAND
February 3, 1996

TO: HONORABLE MEMBERS OF THE HOUSE JUDICIARY COMMITTEE

I appreciate the opportunity to address your committee on the important topic of Sports Franchise Free Agency. The national media has identified Cleveland as the most obvious victim of NFL relocation practices to date. I believe our comprehensive attack of the Cleveland Browns' move to Baltimore will provide the framework for a federal solution to this problem.

This paper contains three sections. Part One discusses the origin of the problem, with particular emphasis on the NFL's 1993 Collective Bargaining Agreement. Part Two discusses the impacts of Sports Franchise Free Agency upon cities' treasuries and urban development policies. Part Three considers our proposed solutions to the problem.

I. **The Origins Of Sports Franchise Free Agency.**

The first wave of Sports Franchise Free Agency occurred in Major League Baseball from the mid 1950's to the early 1960's. The initial franchise shifts reflected cities' recognition that they could no longer support two baseball teams. The Boston Braves moved to Milwaukee in 1953; the St. Louis Browns moved to Baltimore in 1954; the Philadelphia Athletics moved to Kansas City in 1955. These were minor shifts when compared to the controversial 1958 moves of the Brooklyn Dodgers and the New York Giants to Los Angeles and San Francisco.[1] As stated by Gerald Astor in *The Baseball Hall of Fame 50th Anniversary Book* (1988):

> As in other cases, the proprietors could point to obsolete ballparks (Ebbets Field seated less than thirty thousand), deteriorating neighborhoods, and a drop in attendance. But the faraway new homes offered not only improvements in these areas but also vast untapped markets.[2]

Baseball expansions followed shortly thereafter, as new franchises were awarded to Minneapolis and California in 1961 and to Houston and New York in 1962.

An Equal
Opportunity
Employer

[1] Gerald Astor, *The Baseball Hall of Fame 50th Anniversary Book*, (Prentice Hall Press, 1988), page 254
[2] Id

Cleveland! the new American city

The period in baseball's history was a precursor to the trends we are seeing in the NFL in the 1990's. Then, as now, rapidly growing sunbelt cities were putting together extraordinary financial proposals in an effort to attract teams from more established cities. These newer cities regarded the attraction of a franchise as a validation of their national significance and were willing to offer attractive relocation terms to obtain this status.

Meanwhile, the NFL proceeded on a relatively ordered process of gradual expansion from the 1960's through the 1970's. In the early 1980's two franchise shifts disturbed the equilibrium. In 1982, the Raiders defied the NFL and moved from Oakland to Los Angeles. The NFL sued Raiders' owner Al Davis, but Davis parlayed court victories on antitrust claims into a substantial favorable settlement from the NFL. NFL owners have been reluctant to contest franchise moves ever since.

In 1984, Robert Irsay's Colts conducted the infamous "moving van" exit from Baltimore to Indianapolis (and a lucrative lease deal in the newly constructed Hoosier Dome). Both the Oakland and Baltimore moves tarnished the NFL's image. Oakland's rabid fan base had supported the Raiders' from their inception. Baltimore's Colts were an integral part of the NFL's heritage, and the city's fans had regularly filled Memorial Stadium until the last several years of Irsay's tenure in Baltimore.

However, neither Oakland nor Baltimore had developed significant stadium upgrade plans on the eve of the franchise moves.

The current reckless pattern of franchise shifts can be traced to two significant events; the 1993 expansion and the 1993 Collective Bargaining Agreement.

In 1993, the NFL narrowed its list of potential expansion sites to five cities: Baltimore, St. Louis, Charlotte, Jacksonville and Memphis. Significantly, each competing city had to demonstrate to NFL auditors the ability to finance a stadium and pay a one-time $150 million league entry fee. The NFL selected Charlotte and Jacksonville in late 1993, and ever since the Baltimore and St. Louis financing packages have remained as "ticking time bombs" threatening cities with existing franchises. Both bombs went off in 1995, with Los Angeles and (potentially) Cleveland as the victims.

The impact of the 1993 Collective Bargaining Agreement is explained in a recent Sports Illustrated article:

"As many as eight of the NFL's 30 teams are plotting moves to new cities or new stadiums. To understand why, it is necessary to understand recent NFL economics, particularly the impact Dallas owner, Jerry Jones has had on the way every pro-football team does business.

When the NFL and the player's union agreed to a six-year salary cap beginning in 1993, the league thought it had found the perfect solution to skyrocketing labor costs. Each team would spend about 63% of the teams' average gross revenue each year on the players. But while the average gross revenue in 1994 was about $62 million (meaning each team could spend, including benefits and pensions, about $39 million for players), there was a growing inequity. Jones... spent $40.5 million on signing bonuses for players in 1995. Because the "93" bargaining agreement allows teams to prorate signing bonuses equally over the life of contracts, only $14.6 million of that huge signing bonus pool counts against the Dallas salary cap in 1995..."Stadium deals have become important because economics in the NFL have changed", says Chicago Bear Vice President, Ted Phillips. "It used to be that what was important was market size. Now the determining factor between the haves and the have-nots isn't market size, it's stadium economics. That's why there are not teams in Los Angeles and that's why this is happening with the Browns." [3]

Although the NFL and the Players Association are reportedly discussing revisions to the 1993 Agreement, stadium economics will continue to drive franchise location decisions until changes are achieved.

II. **Impact Of Sports Franchise Free Agency Upon Municipal Finances And Urban Development.**

We have identified at least four significant impacts on American cities: teams are extracting exorbitant lease deals; shortening stadium lifespans place excessive demands on scarce tax dollars; cities economic development projects are imperilled; and moderate income fans are being priced out of the market.

A. **Teams Are Extracting Exorbitant Large Deals.**

In the 1990's, the intense competition for NFL franchises has resulted in truly extraordinary lease terms for expansion and relocation franchises. Zero rent is now the rule rather than the exception, and the stadium revenues are now almost exclusively earmarked to the teams. As a consequence, cities must devise tax sources to fund virtually all costs of new or renovated stadiums, and/or cities must face the possibility of franchise movement if they cannot keep up with the financial demands as a result of lack of stadium revenue sharing.

B. **Shortening Stadia Lifespans Place Excessive Demands On Scarce Tax Dollars.**

The 1990's have unveiled an alarming trend in stadium financing. For most of this century, cities only replaced stadia when the facilities became structurally obsolete. Recently, however, owners are deserting perfectly sound structures on the alleged grounds that they are economically obsolete.

---

[3] Peter King, "Down And Out" Sports Illustrated (November 13, 1995), pages 31-32

The trend is illustrated in the attached Table 1. Stadia constructed in the early decades of this century achieved useful lives of 50-75 years. However, recent developments in Cincinnati and Seattle suggest the complete abandonment of stadia with respective useful lives of 26 years (Riverfront Stadium opened in 1970) and 19 years (the Kingdome opened in 1977). Given that communities' scarce tax dollars are already stretched too far to fund schools and other public needs, it is our view it is completely inappropriate for team owners to demand new sports facilities when existing facilities have many years of potential use.

C. Cities' Economic Development Projects Are Imperilled.

Cleveland's case is illustrative of this significant urban development problem. Cities rarely base their stadium funding decisions solely on recreational grounds. Most cities try to use their stadium investments as catalysts for adjacent development.

Cleveland Stadium (the current home of the Cleveland Browns) is located on Cleveland's lakefront just yards away from the newly opened Rock & Roll Hall of Fame and Museum.

Given the unquestionable fan loyalty to the Browns (see Table 2 for attendance statistics), lakefront planners sought to enhance use of other nearby attractions based on a regular annual attendance of 550,000 - 600,000 at Browns games alone. The certainty of this attendance trend was recently acknowledged by *Sports Illustrated*:

> Even though at week's end the Browns were 38 - 51 in the 1990's, their average attendance since 1990 (70,407) is fourth in the league.[4]

It is one thing when a city "rolls the dice" in its economic development planning based on speculative attendance projections. It is quite another when - as in Cleveland - we based our plans on regular crowds of 70,000 since 1960, only to see the team attempt to break a lease and leave a huge hole in the city's lakefront development efforts.

D. Moderate Income Fans Are Being priced Out Of The Market.

Virtually every new stadium deal now includes a significant "premium seat license" ("PSL") financing component. Since the price of PSL's (ranging from $500 up to several thousand dollars) are beyond the reach of moderate income fans, the trend is toward homogenous, upper class stadium crowds in the late 1990's. Ethnic, racial and economic melting pots such as Cleveland Stadium's famed "Dawg Pound" will expire if current trends continue.

---

[4] Id at page 29

III. Proposed Solution.

I can not assure you that Congressional action can solve all of the problems cited in Section II above. However, we believe the following in the form of legislation can be a big part of the solution:

(1). **Due Process For Host Cities.**

Before relocating teams, owners would be required to give 180 days notice to their host cities. A host city would then have a right of first refusal to retain its team during the notice period.

(2). **Limited Antitrust Exemption For League Relocation Decisions.**

Notwithstanding antitrust laws, professional sports leagues could enforce rules prohibiting or restricting the relocation of member clubs. This provision would remove the anti-trust concerns that have troubled owners ever since their unsuccessful challenge of the Raiders' 1982 move from Oakland. The NFL's relocation rules would acquire real meaning for the first time since their adoption in 1984.

(3). **Prohibition Of Relocation Payments.**

League owners would be prohibited from sharing, directly or indirectly, in relocation payments. The $25 - 30 million "bribes" build into the Rams' relocation and the proposed Browns' relocation would be outlawed.

(4). **Retention Of Team Names.**

Relocating teams would be restricted in their efforts to take a team name with them when they relocate. This provision would recognize a longstanding team name as a protected community asset.

(5). **Elimination of Tax-Exempt Financing.**

The use of tax-exempt financing should not be available as a tool to entice owners to break leases and to abandon communities that have clearly supported their needs and desires. This provision would eliminate "rewards with public funds" for owners that forsake their host cities.

Admittedly, the above described congressional legislation cannot solve all of the public policy concerns associated with sports franchise free agency. In the case of the NFL, an amended Collective Bargaining Agreement (providing for sharing of stadium revenues) would further reduce the artificial franchise imbalances which are contributing to the problem.

Nevertheless, prompt Congressional passage of legislation would significantly stall the "musical chairs" game being played upon this nation's fans by disloyal owners. By forcing the NFL to return to fairer franchise relocation practices, Congress can eliminate most of "the franchise bidding wars", which are eroding communities' tax loses. The ultimate beneficiaries would be the loyal and deserving fan bases of communities such as Cleveland.

Thank you for your consideration regarding our position.

Sincerely,

Michael R. White
Mayor, City of Cleveland

TABLE 1
USEFUL LIVES OF STADIA

DECADE	NAME	CITY	OPENING DATE	CLOSING DATE	YEARS OF USEFUL LIFE
Prior to 1900	Sportmans' Park	St. Louis	1876	1966	91
	League Parks	Cleveland	1891	1946	56
	Polo Grounds	New York	1891	1963	73
				Average Years of Useful Life	73
1900 - 1909	Shibe Park	Philadelphia	1909	1970	62
				Average Years of Useful Life	62
1910 - 1919	Forbes Field	Pittsburgh	1910	1970	61
	Comiskey Park	Chicago	1910	1991	82
	Griffith Stadium	Washington	1910	1965	56
	Fenway Park	Boston	1912	open	84+
	Tiger Stadium	Detroit	1912	open	84+
	Crosley Field	Cincinnati	1912	1970	59
	Ebbet's Field	Brooklyn	1913	1957	45
	Braves Field	Boston	1915	1952	37
				Average Years of Useful Life	64
1920 - 1929	Keezar Stadium	San Francisco	1921	1970	50
	Los Angeles Coliseum	Los Angeles	1923	1994	72
	Yankee Stadium	New York	1923	open	73+
	Soldier Field	Chicago	1926	open	70+
				Average Years of Useful Life	66+

TABLE 1
USEFUL LIVES OF STADIA

DECADE	NAME	CITY	OPENING DATE	CLOSING DATE	YEARS OF USEFUL LIFE
1930 - 1939	Cleveland Stadium	Cleveland	1931	open	65+
	War Memorial Stadium	Buffalo	1936	1972	37
	Orange Bowl	Miami	1938	open	58+
			Average Years of Useful Life		53
1940 - 1949	Mile High Stadium	Denver	1948	open	48+
	Memorial Stadium	Baltimore	1944	open	52+
			Average Years of Useful Life		50+
1950 - 1959	County Stadium	Milwaukee	1953	open	43+
	Metropolitan Stadium	Minneapolis	1956	1981	36
	Lambeau Field	Green Bay	1957	open	39+
			Average Years of Useful Life		40+
1960 - 1969	Candlestick Park	San Francisco	1960	open	36+
	Dodger Stadium	Los Angeles	1962	open	34+
	RFK Stadium	Washington (D.C.)	1962	open	34+
	Shea Stadium	New York	1964	open	32+
	Astrodome	Houston	1965	open	31+
	Atlanta-Fulton County	Atlanta	1966	1996	31
	Busch Memorial	St. Louis	1966	open	30+
	Oakland-Alameda Coliseum	Oakland	1968	open	28+
	Anaheim Stadium	Los Angeles	1966	open	30+
	Tampa Stadium	Tampa	1967	open	29+

TABLE 1
USEFUL LIVES OF STADIA

DECADE	NAME	CITY	OPENING DATE	CLOSING DATE	YEARS OF USEFUL LIFE
	Jack Murphy Stadium	San Diego	1967	open	29+
	Sun Devil Stadium	Phoenix			
			Average Years of Useful Life		
1970 - 1979	Arlington Stadium	Arlington	1970	1993	24
	Riverfront Stadium	Cincinnati	1970	open *	26+
	Three-Rivers Stadium	Pittsburgh	1970	open	26+
	Texas Stadium	Dallas	1971	open	25+
	Foxboro Stadium	Boston	1971	open	25+
	Veterans Stadium	Philadelphia	1971	open	25+
	Arrowhead Stadium	Kansas City	1972	open	24+
	Royals Stadium	Kansas City	1973	open	23+
	Rich Stadium	Buffalo	1973	open	23+
	Exhibition Stadium	Toronto	1974	1989	16
	Superdome	New Orleans	1975	open	21+
	Pontiac Silverdome	Detroit	1975	open	21+
	Meadowlands	New Jersey	1976	open	20+
	Kingdome	Seattle	1977	open *	19+
	Olympic Stadium	Montreal	1977	open	19+
			Average Years of Useful Life		

9

TABLE 1
USEFUL LIVES OF STADIA

DECADE	NAME	CITY	OPENING DATE	CLOSING DATE	YEARS OF USEFUL LIFE
1980 - 1989	HHH Metrodome	Minneapolis	1982	open	14+
	Hoosier Dome	Indianapolis	1984	open	12+
	Joe Robbie Stadium	Miami	1987	open	9+
	Average Years of Useful Life				
1990 - 1999	Skydome	Toronto	1989	open	7+
	New Comiskey Park	Chicago	1991	open	5+
	Oriole Park	Baltimore	1992	open	4+
	Georgia Dome	Atlanta	1993	open	3+
	Jacobs Field	Cleveland	1994	open	2+
	Ballpark at Arlington	Arlington	1994	open	2+
	Coors Field	Denver	1995	open	1+
	Gator Bowl	Jacksonville	1995	open	1+
	St. Louis Dome	St. Louis	1995	open	1+
	Average Years of Useful Life				

* Tenants have requested a new facility.

SUMMARY BY DECADES

Decade	Years of Average Useful Life
Prior to 1990	73
1900 - 1909	62
1910 - 1919	64+
1920 - 1929	66+
1930 - 1939	53+
1940 - 1949	50+
1950 - 1959	40+
1960 - 1969	
1970 - 1979	
1980 - 1989	
1990 - 1999	

Source of Data:

Dean V. Baim, *The Sports Stadium As A Municipal Investment*, Greenwood Press (1994).

Lowell Reidenbaugh, *Take Me Out to the Ballpark*, The Sporting News Publishing Co., (1987).

TABLE 2
CLEVELAND BROWNS' RECORD/ATTENDANCE DURING ART MODELL'S OWNERSHIP

YEAR	REGULAR SEASON WON - LOST	REGULAR SEASON ATTENDANCE	GAMES	AVERAGE ATTENDANCE
1962	7-6-1	442,043	7	63,149
1963	10-4	487,430	7	69,633
1964	10-3-1	549,334	7	78,462
1965	11-3	557,283	7	79,612
1966	9-5	544,250	7	77,750
1967	9-5	544-807	7	77,830
1968	10-4	527,107	7	75,301
1969	10-3-1	578,360	7	82,623
1970	7-7	567,377	7	81,054
1971	9-5	541,505	7	77,358
1972	10-4	528,591	7	75,513
1973	7-5-2	490,406	7	70,058
1974	4-10	424,412	7	60,630
1975	3-11	390,440	7	55,777
1976	9-5	472,602	7	67,515
1977	6-8	480,805	7	68,686
1978	8-8	510,046	8	63,756
1979	9-7	593,821	8	74,228
1980	11-5	620,496	8	77,562
1981	5-11	601,725	8	75,216
1982	4-5	251,314	4	62,828
1983	9-7	564,639	8	70,580
1984	5-11	458,433	8	57,304

TABLE 2
CLEVELAND BROWNS' RECORD/ATTENDANCE DURING ART MODELL'S OWNERSHIP

YEAR	REGULAR SEASON WON - LOST	REGULAR SEASON ATTENDANCE	GAMES	AVERAGE ATTENDANCE
1985	8-8	535,752	8	66,966
1986	12-4	583,739	8	72,967
1987	10-5	492,939	7	70,420
1988	10-6	615,545	8	76,943
1989	9-6-1	613,415	8	76,677
1990	3-13	568,093	8	71,012
1991	6-10	571,752	8	71,469
1992	7-9	560,417	8	70,052
1993	7-9	568,474	8	71,059
1994	11-5	569,831	8	71,204

Years averaging over 80,000/game 2
Years averaging 70,000 - 79,999/game 20
Years averaging 60,000 - 69,999/game 8
Years averaging 50,000 - 59,999/game 2

Source of Data:

1994 Cleveland Browns Media Guide.

"Even though at week's end the Browns were 38-51 in the 1990's, their average attendance since 1990 (70,407) is fourth in the league." Peter King, "Down . . . And Out", Sports Illustrated, November 13, 1995.

TABLE 3
CLEVELAND BROWNS TV MARKET

As stated in the Browns November 4, 1995 relocation submission to the NFL:

The Cleveland/Akron ADI is ranked #13 with 1,460,420 television households.

The Baltimore ADI is ranked #23 with 979,410 households.

Moreover, Nielson ratings for the top 15 TV markets during the 1993 NFL season show Cleveland's household ratings for the Browns was **41.7** - second only to the Dallas Cowboys' rating of **43.3**. Note that the Cowboys went on to win the Super Bowl that season, while the Browns finished with a 7-9 record.

In the 1994 Nielson ratings, Cleveland took over 1st place with a **40** share; Dallas was second with a **39** share.

STATEMENT OF PROF. STEPHEN F. ROSS, UNIVERSITY OF ILLINOIS COLLEGE OF LAW, BEFORE THE HOUSE COMMITTEE ON THE JUDICIARY, FEBRUARY 6, 1996

Chairman Hyde, Mr. Conyers, and members of the Committee:

It is a privilege and honor to accept the kind invitation of the Chairman to submit testimony concerning H.R. 2740, the Fan Freedom and Community Protection. I regret that a combination of family and teaching responsibilities preclude my personal appearance, but I would be more than happy to work with you or your staffs in the coming weeks on this important issue. Chairman Hyde has acted judiciously in agreeing to allocate some of your scarce time to this important issue, because one of the most grievous abuses of monopoly power today consists of the exploitation of fans and taxpayers by monopoly sports league owners threatening to relocate sports franchises.

Last November, I had the opportunity to address similar issues in a general hearing before Senator Thurmond's Subcommittee on Antitrust, Business Rights, and Competition. Rather than repeating my testimony there, I attach a copy to this submission and incorporate it by reference. What follows is a very brief summary of the problem and specific comments on the solution proposed by H.R. 2740.

Introduction and Summary

In my opinion, the clearly optimal policy solution is to acknowledge that time has shown that the Act of November 8, 1966,[1] permitting a financially successful National Football League to merge with its financially successful American Football League rival, is now a mistake that should be corrected by Congress. If two or more rival major leagues made their own independent determinations concerning expansion and relocation, the result would be the end of "franchise free agency" and the end of massive exploitation of taxpayers.

---

[1] Pub. L. No. 89-800, 80 Stat. 1515 (1966).

Conventional wisdom is that this proposal is so radical that it is not a politically plausible alternative. Frankly, I would think that a new Republican Congress dedicated to free market principles would endorse a solution that limits government involvement (antitrust laws are always more deferential to joint ventures that do not possess monopoly power than those that do). In contrast, some will find H.R. 2740's provisions to be unduly regulatory, a criticism that could not be leveled at a proposal that simply undoes a monopoly created by Congress. Other legislators who represent markets that deserve new teams, and would potentially get them from one of two rival leagues, may be less than enthusiastic because H.R. 2740 will make it somewhat harder to lure existing teams from their current locales. As I detail in the Appendix, my proposal would seem to maximize the political interests of more members of this Committee than the alternatives.

However, I was not asked to testify as an expert on congressional politics but rather as one devoted to teaching and scholarship about sports and antitrust law,[2] and in that capacity I believe that the mandatory expansion provisions contained in section 5 of H.R. 2740 will indeed significantly restrain the exploitation of taxpayers and sports fans. As such, it represents a significant improvement over both the status quo as well as the initial proposal offered by Representative Stokes, which effectively grants the NFL an antitrust exemption for franchise relocation decisions without any significant limitations on their exercise of monopoly power.

---

[2] Because I have no particular expertise in trademark law, I do not address the provisions of §3 of H.R. 2740 concerning preservation of a team's name in its current home.

Mandating expansion to markets deserted by existing teams will significantly limit the monopoly exploitation of taxpayers and consumers.

The key to H.R. 2740 is section 5. This creative and thoughtful approach requires leagues to grant expansion franchises to markets deserted by existing teams. Knowing that the league will have to grant such expansion will make taxpayers feel less pressured to vote for generous tax subsidies in times of governmental fiscal crisis, will make leagues more hesitant to approve relocations, and will assure average fans that where they have demonstrated sufficient support for a major professional football team, their hopes and dreams will not be quashed because someone else put together a more lucrative package of luxury boxes. As such, it deserves your support.

Despite the current fiscal crisis affecting all levels of government, taxpayers are being asked to support massive tax subsidies to wealthy NFL owners. Cleveland area taxpayers, for example, recently approved a $175 million subsidy in an apparently vain effort to keep the Browns. In light of the great loyalty of Browns fans, some subsidy might have been forthcoming even if the provisions of H.R. 2740 were in place. However, it is probable that the size of the subsidy would have been quite smaller if Cleveland taxpayers knew that their failure to match Baltimore's bid would simply mean that they would have to root for an expansion franchise rather than Art Modell's team.

The current rash of actual and threatened franchise relocations in the National Football League is not due to antitrust liability. Rather, it is primarily due to the unique revenue sharing arrangements agreed to by the owners: revenue from tickets, broadcasting, and souvenirs are shared, but luxury box income or tax subsidies are not. As a result, individual owners may seek to relocate franchises even though the league would be better off if they remained in their present location.

There are several reasons why owners permit relocations that are not in the best interest of the league. The one asserted by Commissioner Paul Tagliabue in his testimony before Senator Thurmond's subcommittee was that the fear of antitrust litigation compels "franchise free agency." For example, Commissioner Tagliabue specifically stated that the Los Angeles Rams' relocation to St. Louis would not have been approved but for fear of antitrust litigation. In that case, an unpopular owner, whose mismanagement has contributed to the team's lack of success on the field (and consequent economic difficulties), sought relocation to a prime expansion opportunity from the second largest media market in the nation.

The Browns and Oilers cases are more typical. In these cases, popular owners with successful teams seek to relocate to somewhat smaller markets. Here, in my opinion, the owners are likely to approve a relocation even if they were to receive an antitrust exemption, for one simple reason: each owner would want the same courtesy from his fellow carteleers so he might at least offer a credible threat to move unless his own hometown provides massive tax subsidies.

In any event, H.R. 2740 deals with both cases. Section 6(a) provides a narrowly drawn antitrust immunity to permit owners to decide whether to approve specific relocations, so that owners may vote "No" without fear of litigation. But Section 6 has no effect on the second, and more typical, scenario when owners find it in their selfish economic interests to vote "Yes." Section 5's mandatory expansion gives them an incentive to vote against relocations that are not in the best interest of the whole league, by requiring them to admit additional venturers (and thus divide the network revenue pie into smaller pieces).

Section 5 would also give the owners an incentive to change their exploitive revenue sharing structure. The only logical reason why owners do not share revenues from luxury boxes and tax subsidies is so that each owner has a strong financial incentive to exploit local taxpayers. (Art Modell, Bud Adams, and Michael McCaskey would not be going through all this trouble to maximize luxury boxes if they had to share 29/30 of the revenue with their fellow owners.) If the incentive for taxpayers to approve publicly-funded luxury box construction was significantly lessened, as it would be under H.R. 2740, perhaps this inefficient system[3] would be discontinued.

Finally, H.R. 2740 is accurately titled as the "Fan Freedom and Community Protection Act of 1995" because it assures loyal fans that where they are in sufficient number to justify a major league professional franchise, their desertion by a greedy owner does not mean that they will be deprived of a new and more deserving team to attach their affections. The legislation's requirement of a substantial monetary investment by a new owner ensures that, in those cases where a market simply will not support a major league team at that point in time, the league will not be forced to admit a new investor "on the cheap."[4]

---

[3] The system is inefficient because the most profitable teams are those whose owners have done the best job of exploiting taxpayers, rather than those owners who have developed the best team on the field. As I detailed in my Senate testimony (at 19 n.21), in 1988 the then-inept Indianapolis Colts were the most profitable franchise due to non-shared income, while the Super Bowl champion Washington Redskins lost over $3 million, primarily due to the absence of luxury box, concession, or parking income.

[4] I detail some "quibbles" about this provision in the next section.

Short-comings and "quibbles" with H.R. 2740.

H.R. 2740 is not the perfect solution. Indeed, as I stated at the outset, I do not believe it is even the best one. This section of my testimony identifies some short-comings and technical problems with the legislation. On balance, however, these short-comings do not affect my conclusion that the bill is a substantial improvement over the status quo or legislation that simply immunizes NFL decisions.

1. *The bill does not affect relocations within a metropolitan area -- like the Chicago Bears' relocation from Solider Field.* As noted above, the key to this bill is section 5's mandatory expansion provision, and §5(e) provides that this does not apply to relocations within 60 miles of its existing locale.

Without creating a cumbersome regulatory apparatus, §5(e) is necessary. If the Cincinnati Bengals were to relocate across the Ohio River to Covington, Kentucky, it would be unrealistic to require the NFL to permit a new expansion team in Cincinnati. On the other hand, there are a few very large markets -- Chicago is certainly one of them -- that could support two major league teams. Unless the FTC or some other neutral body is given the broad regulatory power to determine when a metropolitan area can support two or more franchises, the mandatory expansion approach of H.R. 2740 will have to leave these large cities unprotected.

In contrast, I note that my proposal to create rival leagues would let the market determine whether Chicago or Los Angeles could support multiple franchises. If the NFL Bears had moved to Gary, the AFL would almost certainly move into Soldier Field in Chicago. If the AFL's Bengals moved to Covington, the NFL would doubtless leave them be.

2. *Public policy does not require the bill's detailed provisions concerning the identification of the expansion franchise owner.* Section 5(b)(2) requires a league to grant an expansion franchise to an investor whose name has been submitted to the league by "the community in which the team was previously located," at a statutorily determined price. The public benefits to the bill accrue from the creation of the franchise, not the selection of the owner. As long as the league creates a new franchise on the same terms as it would admit franchises through voluntary expansion, I see no need for government regulation of the process. Since the bill already provides Federal Trade Commission oversight, detailed regulatory provisions are probably unnecessary.

Section 9(2) defines "community" as the relevant "general function governmental unit established by State law." Presumably, the governing body of that governmental unit would make the submission. Although H.R. 2740 reflects the sound view that, if Congress is going to grant monopoly status to the NFL, some form of governmental regulation to prevent monopolistic exploitation is appropriate, it seems excessive to allow the Cleveland City Council to pick the new owner of the expansion franchise in Cleveland. There are serious risks that these decisions could result in an investor chosen on the basis of political connections rather than acumen in owning a sports franchise.

Professional sports leagues, in my opinion, don't do enough to screen out owners like George Steinbrenner of the Yankees and Georgia Frontiere of the Rams, who have neither the expertise to run a team nor the judgment to leave management to sports professionals. Leagues should be encouraged to ensure that new investors have the capital to compete in the free agent market and the business sense to be stewards of a product that remains, in almost all local markets, a monopoly.

Similarly H.R. 2740 seeks to assure that the investor is financially capable, and is not receiving a windfall, by requiring the owner to pay an expansion fee set at 85% of the most recent expansion, and demonstrate fiscal solvency through the deposit of a higher fee in an escrow account. This standard strikes me as overbroad and underinclusive. Cleveland, for example, is simply a more attractive market than Jacksonville, and -- assuming Congress wants to allow the NFL to preseve its monopoly status -- there is no reason it should not be able to receive what the market will bear for a franchise fee. At the same time, leagues have a legitimate interest in ensuring that new franchises are not unduly leveraged with debt, and that new owners will be effective stewards of the NFL product in their home community. Simply coming up with cash seems insufficient for this purpose.

Public policy should not be concerned with the identification of the investor, as long as the league approves one. Where the league improperly claims that no willing investor meets its criteria, the league could be found in violation of section 5(a), with the appropriate remedies as spelled out in section 7 of the bill.

3. Section 6 imposes no meaningful limits on the league's decision whether or not to approve of a franchise relocation. Because section 5 imposes a meaningful limit on monopoly sports leagues' power to exploit taxpayers and consumers, section 6(a), which confers a narrowly drawn antitrust immunity to allow the league to deny relocations on their own, will provide a modest additional benefit in cases where the league wants to be able to deny an incompetent owner the ability to move to new surroundings.[5]

However, the Committee should clearly understand that, while the "determination criteria" set forth in section 6(b) may serve some public relations benefit in a lobbying effort directed toward team owners, it provides no meaningful limit that would allow the league to do whatever it wants. The Browns move to Baltimore illustrates this point. Keeping in mind that the criteria are simply factors to consider, the NFL could find[6] that, per subsection (3), the Browns are a successful and well-managed team but the NFL's structure requires significant revenues from luxury boxes and concessions to compete; per subsection (4), the "extent" of public financial support for the Browns is lacking, relative to the promised support from Baltimore and, per subsection (5), Municipal Stadium is inadequate, and the local authorities in Cleveland have not been as willing to remedy any deficiencies as they would have been had their offer exceeded Baltimore's, and that these factors outweigh the other factors that might point against relocation.

4. *The bill doesn't protect new investors against discriminatory conditions.* As currently drafted, the NFL could exploit a loophole in the mandatory expansion provisions of

---

[5] The committee report should make clear that this exemption, like all antitrust exemptions, is to be narrowly construed. Specifically, as I testified in the Senate, I believe that a good argument can be made that the entire web of NFL revenue sharing rules constitute an unreasonable restraint of trade in violation of §1 of the Sherman Act. Because an attack on the entire revenue sharing structure would go far beyond "agreements authorizing the membership of such league to decide whether a professional sports team ... may relocate," such an antitrust challenge should not be barred by the exemption conferred in section 6(a).

[6] CAVEAT: In setting forth this argument, I don't necessarily agree that these findings are true, just that they are plausible and could be made by a skilled attorney such as Commissioner Tagliabue.

§5(a), by imposing so many onerous conditions on the new team that no investor would be willing to pay the required price. For example, nothing in the legislation would prevent the NFL from grudgingly accepting a new Cleveland expansion team with the provisos that (1) the team won't play any home games; (2) the team can't share any league revenues; and (3) there will not be an expansion draft that is typically used to stock new teams. The bill needs to be amended to require a principle of non-discrimination. I would recommend that disputes be subject to arbitration; alternatively a league that imposes discriminatory conditions could be found to violate §5 and be subject to FTC enforcement pursuant to §7.

5. *Mandatory expansion has an exclusionary effect on new rival leagues.* Despite my strong advocacy of rival leagues, I believe it is extremely unlikely for a new league to be able to enter and successfully compete against a 30-team National Football League. Unlike the 12-team league that was matched by its AFL rival three decades ago, there are too few open markets that remain lucrative, and it is too hard to oust an existing team from a market that will only support one franchise. Still, new leagues (like one just announced recently) would certainly want to start by looking at places like Los Angeles, Cleveland, and Houston as prime locations to build a new rival, and the NFL's addition of expansion franchises in those communities will make it not unlikely but impossible for these new leagues to compete.

Although the NFL's voluntary expansion to these markets would probably be lawful under the antitrust laws, there are some circumstances where such an expansion would constitute unlawful maintenance of monopoly power in violation of Section 2 of the Sherman Act. Under *American Football League v. National Football League*, 323 F.2d 124 (4th Cir. 1963), a plausible violation could be shown if a new league were to form next year based upon the ability to enter now-open markets in Los Angeles, Cleveland, and Houston, and it could be proven that the NFL preemptorily moved to expand into these markets even though it would not otherwise done so, in order to prevent the rival league from becoming established. Clearly, if the NFL were required to expand pursuant to §5 of the Act, it should not be liable under the Sherman Act. Thus, the disclaimer in section 8(5) of the bill that H.R. 2740 does not exempt any "conduct with respect to competing sports leagues which would otherwise be unlawful under the antitrust laws" needs to be clarified.

6. *Major League Baseball is not one league but rather an entity created by agreement of the National and American Leagues.* H.R. 2740 has been carefully drafted to avoid the current legislative and judicial controversy concerning baseball's judicially-created antitrust exemption.[7] Section 8(6) provides that the bill does not affect "the applicability or inapplicability of the antitrust laws" to any activity among persons engaging in baseball. However, in the event that baseball is considered subject to antitrust scrutiny for franchise relocation decisions, Section 9(4)(D) defines "league" to include "Major League Baseball."

As a matter of history and current practice, the primary decision makers concerning the relocation of a baseball team are the owners of the league in which the team is a member. For example, the effort of Tampa Bay investors to relocate the San Francisco

---

[7] Please note that I have testified before this committee urging that you enact legislation overturning the exemption; have successfully argued (*pro bono publico*, on behalf of the Consumer Federation of America) before the Florida Supreme Court that the current judicial exemption does not apply to franchise relocation issues, *Butterworth v. National League of Professional Baseball Clubs*, 644 So. 2d 1021 (Fla. 1994), and advocated in academic writings that the Supreme Court should reconsider and overturn baseball's exemption. Stephen F. Ross, *Reconsidering* Flood v. Kuhn, 12 U. Miami J. Ent. & L.J. (forthcoming 1996).

Giants was rejected by the National League, not all owners sitting as "Major League Baseball." Indeed, the Major League agreement specifically provides that approval must be obtained by a super-majority of the league in which the team is a member, followed by approval of a majority of owners from the other league. As such, this phrase should be redrafted to say "the National and American Leagues of Major League Baseball."

Conclusion

Because the mandatory expansion provisions of H.R. 2740 do not meaningfully protect against exploitation from intra-metropolitan relocations, and imposes a modest regulatory structure enforced by the FTC, the better course would be to let the free market work by repealing the 1966 monopoly-authorizing legislation and restoring two or more rival leagues to football. However, H.R. 2740 would significantly lessen the ability of professional sports leagues to exploit taxpayers and fans by threatened and actual relocation of franchises. As such, it deserves this committees serious consideration and support.

Thank you again for inviting me to participate. I would be happy to formally respond in writing to any official questions posed by the committee or its members, or to informally respond orally or in writing to any unofficial inquiries from you or your staff.

Appendix

ANALYSIS OF CONSTITUENCY AND IDEOLOGICAL INTERESTS OF HOUSE JUDICIARY COMMITTEE MEMBERS AND ALTERNATIVE SOLUTIONS TO FRANCHISE RELOCATION ISSUES

Four alternatives

I: **Competing Leagues**: repeal 1966 merger legislation, have FTC supervise creation of 2+ rival major professional leagues with freedom to relocate new and existing franchises and compete for taxpayer/fan support

II: **H.R. 2740**: immunize monopoly sports league franchise relocation decisions, but require expansion into communities capable of supporting franchises who have been deserted

III: **NFL *carte blanche*:** give monopoly sports leagues immunity to block or approve relocations as they see fit

IV: **status quo**: unchallenged monopoly sports leagues can exploit taxpayers and fans; case law permits sports leagues discretion to block relocations except in narrow circumstances, but leagues claim that treble damage threat deters them from exercising this discretion

SUMMARY OF RESULTS

PROPOSAL	STRONG SUPPORT	MODEST SUPPORT	???	MODEST OPPOSITION*	STRONG OPPOSITION
I	23	7	2	2	0
II	12	10	6	5	2
III	0	8	8	9	10
IV	0	7	4	13	11

CAVEAT: In 1966, anticompetitive NFL merger legislation was significantly aided by the strong support of Rep. Hale Boggs, following an explicit promise by then-Commissioner Pete Rozelle that New Orleans would get an expansion franchise. The following analysis does not take into account the potential for these specific private deals. For example, a guarantee that the Chicago Bears will not leave Soldier Field could switch Chairman Hyde's interests from supportive of Proposal I to opposition; similarly a guarantee that Los Angeles will quickly get an expansion team could affect Southern California representatives.

---

*This analysis assumes that a member would be modestly opposed to a proposal that did not adversely affect constituent interests but did absolutely nothing to further them, when alternative proposals would actually further constituent interests.

MEMBER-BY-MEMBER ANALYSIS

Chairman Hyde (suburban Chicago)

I: Bears' threat to move significantly limited because AFL would love opportunity to enter Chicago market and would be happy to agree to reasonable terms to play at Soldier Field; result is probably 2 teams in area, and reduced tax subsidies. **STRONG SUPPORT**

II: Bears' threat to move not subject to mandatory relocation provisions of bill because relocation will probably be within 60 miles of Soldier Field, so bill doesn't help Chicago interests. **MODEST OPPOSITION**

III: League immunity likely to have no effect; owners happy to allow Bears' owner to reach whatever deal maximizes his own profits. Legislation does nothing to protect interests of Bears fans and Illinois taxpayers. **MODEST OPPOSITION**

IV: Status quo leaves Bear fans and Illinois taxpayers subject to exploitation. **MODEST OPPOSITION**

Mr. Moorhead (suburban Los Angeles)

I: Rival leagues virtually guarantees L.A. one team anxious to play anywhere to get foothold in nation's second largest market; probably both leagues would sponsor franchises lest television viewers focus solely on one league. **STRONG SUPPORT**

II: Section 5 would result in a new team as a matter of right to replace Raiders; thus taxpayers less likely to be exploited. **STRONG SUPPORT**

III: Too late for L.A.: the teams have moved. Makes it easier for NFL to veto efforts by L.A. to lure existing team. **STRONG OPPOSITION**

IV: Status quo makes it easier for L.A. to lure existing team and Tagliabue claims NFL will be deterred from blocking move for fear of antitrust liability **MODEST SUPPORT**

Prof. Ross testimony, Appendix, Page 2

Mr. Sensenbrenner (suburban Milwaukee)

I: Rival leagues could potentially result in reduced monopoly profits in large markets, some of which are now shared with Green Bay Packers. Packers' unique corporate ownership poses no threat to relocate. However, if baseball antitrust legislation is passed, rival leagues will ensure continued Major League Baseball in Milwaukee <u>without</u> tax subsidy currently approved by legislature. **MODEST OPPOSITION**

II: Mandatory expansion will make Packers' slice of NFL revenue pie smaller, but will help protect Milwaukee's baseball interests. **???**

III: No effect on local interests -- Packers aren't moving and, liability or no, American League isn't going to block Bud Selig if he wants to leave Milwaukee **???**

IV: Same as III. **???**

Mr. McCollum (Orlando)

I: Rival league virtually guarantees hot new market in Orlando an expansion franchise. Like Houston in 1959, rival leagues will bid for rights to market, minimizing need for public subsidy for new stadium or renovated Citrus Bowl. **STRONG SUPPORT**

II: Harder to steal an existing team with league immunity and disincentive of mandatory expansion. **STRONG OPPOSITION**

III: Harder to steal an existing team with league immunity in place; if Orlando can lure a team, will come at a higher price than status quo, where league fears litigation. **STRONG OPPOSITION**

IV: Orlando is a better market than Nashville, if it's willing to pay price of franchise free agency. **MODEST SUPPORT**

Mr. Gekas (Harrisburg & Pennsylvania Dutch country)

I: Competition between leagues ensures that Philadelphia and Pittsburgh will continue to have major league teams; reduced ability to exploit taxpayers ensures that this is one metropolitan bill that residents of central Pennsylvania won't have to foot; rival leagues potentially can protect against Philadelphia teams demanding subsidies or a move across the Delaware to New Jersey; consistent with general regulatory reform philosophy of minimal regulation. **STRONG SUPPORT**

II: Mandatory expansion protects Philadelphia and Pittsburgh. Regulatory provisions of bill may prove difficult to reconcile with general deregulatory philosophy. **MODEST SUPPORT**

III: League immunity would protect Eagles/Phillies from moving out of media market, but wouldn't do much to protect Pittsburgh. **???**

IV: All PA teams at risk of relocation and all state taxpayers at some risk of exploitation. **MODEST OPPOSITION**

Mr. Coble (Greensboro/ central N.C.)

I: Rival leagues could potentially result in reduced monopoly profits in large markets, some of which are now shared with Carolina Panthers. New stadium means no immediate risk to relocate. However, rival leagues will also guarantee increased taxpayer leverage in stadium lease negotiations, and, if baseball antitrust exemption is inapplicable, rival leagues could result in team in Charlotte. Philosophically, reduced tax subsidies to sports franchises consistent with strong fiscal conservatism. **MODEST SUPPORT**

II: Mandatory expansion unlikely to affect Panthers soon; diminishes whatever chance that Charlotte could lure existing Major League Baseball team. **MODEST OPPOSITION**

III: League immunity might prevent Charlotte from luring baseball team from larger market if baseball exemption not applicable to franchise relocation issues. **MODEST OPPOSITION**

IV: No effect on Panthers; Charlotte would have to pay huge price to lure baseball team under current rules. **MODEST OPPOSITION**

Mr. Smith (suburban San Antonio/Austin)

I: Rival leagues will guarantee that Houston has a football franchise and significantly increases expansion chances for San Antonio. **STRONG SUPPORT**

II: Mandatory expansion restores team to Houston; makes San Antonio's ability to lure NFL team less likely, although would need to pay high price in any event. **MODEST SUPPORT**

III: No signs from NFL that immunity would result in owners standing in Bud Adams' way, so this doesn't help. **MODEST OPPOSITION**

IV: Same as III. **MODEST OPPOSITION**

Mr. Schiff (Albuquerque)

No proposal likely to directly affect constituents. **???**

Mr. Gallegly (Ventura Co. - exurban L.A.)

I: Rival leagues virtually guarantees L.A. one team anxious to play anywhere to get foothold in nation's second largest market; probably both leagues would sponsor franchises lest television viewers focus solely on one league. **STRONG SUPPORT**

II: Section 5 would result in a new team as a matter of right to replace Raiders; thus taxpayers less likely to be exploited. However, most if not all tax burden will fall on L.A. city and county, so tax aspect less important than for Mr. Moorhead's constituents. **MODEST SUPPORT**

III: Too late for L.A.: the teams have moved. Makes it easier for NFL to veto efforts by L.A. to lure existing team. **STRONG OPPOSITION**

IV: Status quo makes it easier for L.A. to lure existing team and Tagliabue claims NFL will be deterred from blocking move for fear of antitrust liability. **MODEST SUPPORT**

Prof. Ross testimony, Appendix, Page 5

Mr. Canady (Lakeland/ Tampa exurbs)

I: Bucs' threat to relocate significantly limited, as is opportunity to exploit taxpayers, because AFL would love opportunity to enter growing Tampa market. **STRONG SUPPORT**

II: Although, expansion fee for membership in monopoly NFL would be much higher than in one of two rival leagues and owner would probably want greater concessions from Tampa, Bucs' threat to move significantly limited by knowledge that Tampa could probably attract an expansion team under §5 of bill. **STRONG SUPPORT**

III: League immunity will not protect relatively weak franchise in Tampa if owner cuts profitable deal to move. Legislation does nothing to protect interests of Bucs fans and Florida taxpayers. **STRONG OPPOSITION**

IV: Status quo leaves Bucs fans and Florida taxpayers subject to exploitation. **STRONG OPPOSITION**

Mr. Inglis (Greenville/Spartanburg, SC)

No proposal likely to directly affect constituents. New-found Carolina Panther fans not likely to be affected anytime soon in light of new stadium in Charlotte. General free-market approach would be seem most consistent with proposal to restore competition. **???**

Mr. Goodlatte (Virginia Blue Ridge)

I: With Washington Redskins apparently now moving to suburban Maryland, risk of exploitation of Virginia taxpayers to support Northern Virginia stadium seems removed. If baseball antitrust exemption is narrowed/removed, rival leagues will ensure baseball for National Capital area without tax subsidy which might in part be borne by Virginia taxpayers if stadium located in suburbs. **MODEST SUPPORT**

II: Proposal unlikely to directly affect constituents. **???**

III: Proposal unlikely to directly affect constituents. **???**

IV: Status quo unlikely to affect football situation. Status quo in baseball subjects Virginia taxpayers to some risk of exploitation for new stadium if Major League Baseball decides to grant a franchise to National Capital region. **MODEST OPPOSITION**

Mr. Buyer (Hoosier heartland - No. Indiana)

I: Competition between leagues ensures that Indianapolis will continue to have major league teams; reduced ability to exploit taxpayers ensures that this is one metropolitan bill that residents of the Hoosier heartland won't have to foot. **STRONG SUPPORT**

II: Mandatory expansion protects Indianapolis. **STRONG SUPPORT**

III: League immunity won't protect Colts -- already complaining about inadequacy of Hoosier Dome -- moving out of media market. **STRONG OPPOSITION**

IV: Colts at risk of relocation and all state taxpayers at risk of exploitation. **STRONG OPPOSITION**

Mr. Hoke (Cleveland and suburbs)

I: Rival leagues not only guarantee franchise for Cleveland but, given strength of fan loyalty and media market, would probably permit local stadium authority to force leagues into a bidding war for the right to play in new stadium. **STRONG SUPPORT**

II: Section 5 would result in a new team as a matter of right if Browns left, so taxpayers less likely to be exploited. **STRONG SUPPORT**

III: Although owners likely to approve Art Modell's money grab in hopes of being allowed to do the same themselves, immunity would slightly increase chance of league veto. **MODEST SUPPORT**

IV: League claims it is deterred from blocking Browns' relocation because of fear of antitrust liability and no guarantee Cleveland will get a new team. **STRONG OPPOSITION**

Mr. Bono (Palm Springs- exurban L.A.)

I: Rival leagues virtually guarantees L.A. one team anxious to play anywhere to get foothold in nation's second largest market; probably both leagues would sponsor franchises lest television viewers focus solely on one league. **STRONG SUPPORT**
II: Section 5 would result in 2 new teams as a matter of right to replace Raiders and Rams; thus taxpayers less likely to be exploited. However, most if not all tax burden will fall on L.A. and Orange counties, so tax aspect less important than for Mr. Moorhead's constituents. **MODEST SUPPORT**
III: Too late for L.A.: the teams have moved. Makes it easier for NFL to veto efforts by L.A. to lure existing team. **STRONG OPPOSITION**
IV: Status quo makes it easier for L.A. to lure existing team and Tagliabue claims NFL will be deterred from blocking move for fear of antitrust liability. **MODEST SUPPORT**

Mr. Heineman (Raleigh, NC)

I: Rival leagues could potentially result in reduced monopoly profits in large markets, some of which are now shared with Carolina Panthers. New stadium means no immediate risk to relocate. However, rival leagues will also guarantee increased taxpayer leverage in stadium lease negotiations, and, if baseball antitrust exemption is inapplicable, rival leagues could result in team in Charlotte. **MODEST SUPPORT**

II: Same analysis as above-- mandatory expansion will make Panthers' slice of NFL revenue pie smaller, but mandatory relocation provision will give bargaining leverage to public. Could hurt ability to lure existing baseball team to Charlotte. **MODEST OPPOSITION**

III: Panthers aren't leaving so NFL immunity won't have any effect; if baseball exemption inapplicable, statutory immunity would hurt ability to lure existing baseball team to Charlotte. **MODEST OPPOSITION**

IV: No effect on NFL; current ability to attract baseball team only at a very steep price. **MODEST OPPOSITION**

Mr. Bryant (West TN, Memphis suburbs, Nashville exurbs)

I: Rival leagues maximizes chances for football teams in both Nashville and Memphis if markets can support them. **STRONG SUPPORT**

II: Mandatory expansion and NFL immunity jeopardizes Nashville bid for Oilers. **STRONG OPPOSITION**

III: NFL immunity gives owners more freedom to veto Oilers relocation and would allow Memphis to lure a team only by paying similarly exorbitant tax subsidies. **STRONG OPPOSITION**

IV: Threat of litigation will probably facilitate Oilers move to Nashville; any expansion to Memphis only via extortionate payments. **MODEST SUPPORT**

Mr. Chabot (Cincinnati)

I: Cincinatti's historic major league status and regional pull ensures that, with rival leagues, one of them would keep a team in this market; opportunity for expansion here by rival league would give city leverage vis-a-vis Bengals and Reds, although market not big enough for 2 teams so owners still have credible threat to relocate across Ohio River. **STRONG SUPPORT**

II: Mandatory expansion would provide some measure of protection against relocation, although would not prevent bidding war with Northern Kentucky. **STRONG SUPPORT**

III: NFL immunity unlikely to protect small-market team if lured by other market. **MODEST OPPOSITION**

IV: Fans and taxpayers subject to exploitation AND threat of litigation by owners seeking to leave. **STRONG OPPOSITION**

Mr. Flanagan (Chicago)

I: Bears' threat to move significantly limited because AFL would love opportunity to enter Chicago market and would be happy to agree to reasonable terms to play at Soldier Field; result is probably 2 teams in area, and reduced tax subsidies. **STRONG SUPPORT**

II: Bears' threat to move not subject to mandatory relocation provisions of bill because relocation will probably be within 60 miles of Soldier Field, so bill doesn't help Chicago interests. **MODEST OPPOSITION**

III: League immunity likely to have no effect; owners happy to allow Bears' owner to reach whatever deal maximizes his own profits. Legislation does nothing to protect interests of Bears fans and Illinois taxpayers. **MODEST OPPOSITION**

IV: Status quo leaves Bear fans and Illinois taxpayers subject to exploitation. **MODEST OPPOSITION**

Mr. Barr (Marietta/ West GA)

I: Although Georgia Dome and Ted Turner's Atlanta base make it unlikely that Falcons or Braves will relocate, threat to do so diminished if rival league can enter Atlanta market, thus reducing chance of state tax dollars being used for further subsidies. **MODEST SUPPORT**

II: Mandatory expansion, like rival leagues, modestly reduces chances of taxpayer exploitation. **MODEST SUPPORT**

III: League immunity of some value if owner seeks to relocate to smaller market. **MODEST SUPPORT**

IV: Taxpayers at small risk of exploitation; fans at small risk owner will move to smaller market. **MODEST OPPOSITION**

Mr. Convers (Detroit)

I: Although leaving such a major market would have been unthinkable until recently, Detroit more vulnerable than Cleveland. Rival leagues not only guarantee franchise for Detroit but, given strength of media market, would probably permit local stadium authority to force leagues into a bidding war for the right to play in new stadium. **STRONG SUPPORT**

II: Section 5 would result in a new team as a matter of right if Lions left, so taxpayers less likely to be exploited. **STRONG SUPPORT**

III: Although owners likely to approve money grab by William Clay Ford or his successor, in hopes of being allowed to do the same themselves, immunity would slightly increase chance of league veto. **MODEST SUPPORT**

IV: League would claim it is deterred from blocking Lions' relocation because of fear of antitrust liability and no guarantee Cleveland will get a new team. **STRONG OPPOSITION**

Ms. Schroeder (Denver)
I: Competition between leagues ensures that Denver will continue to have major league teams and threat of expansion by rival league reduces Broncos' ability to exploit taxpayers. **STRONG SUPPORT**

II: Mandatory expansion protects Denver. **STRONG SUPPORT**

III: League immunity won't protect against prospect, albeit unlikely, that Broncos move out of media market. **MODEST OPPOSITION**

IV: Broncos at some risk of relocation and all state taxpayers at real risk of exploitation. **STRONG OPPOSITION**

Mr. Frank (suburban Boston and southern MA)

I: Competition between leagues ensures that Boston will continue to have major league teams and threat of expansion by rival league reduces Patriots' ability to exploit taxpayers. **STRONG SUPPORT**

II: Mandatory expansion protects New England. **STRONG SUPPORT**

III: League immunity won't protect against Patriots moving -- especially if Massachusetts taxpayers don't foot the bill for luxury boxes. **STRONG OPPOSITION**

IV: Patriots at risk of relocation and all state taxpayers at risk of exploitation. **STRONG OPPOSITION**

Mr. Schumer (Brooklyn)

I: With rival leagues, Dodgers would have never left because leagues would have already expanded to L.A.! Today, rival leagues might well add a 3rd team to the NY Metro area, giving another option to Brooklynites dissatisfied with Giants, or Jets, or trip to Jersey. Most relevant, with rival leagues the ability to exploit local taxpayers would be zero -- indeed, leagues would bid for lucrative in-town locations. **STRONG SUPPORT**

II: Mandatory expansion protects New York fans against exploitation through threat of leaving area. **MODEST SUPPORT**

III: League immunity might be helpful if Giants or Jets follow Rams' lead. **MODEST SUPPORT**

IV: Monopoly leagues can exploit taxpayers and threat of litigation could lead to shift of franchise from largest market to tax-subsidized smaller market. **STRONG OPPOSITION**

Mr. Berman (Los Angeles)

I: Rival leagues virtually guarantees L.A. one team anxious to play anywhere to get foothold in nation's second largest market; probably both leagues would sponsor franchises lest television viewers focus solely on one league. **STRONG SUPPORT**

II: Section 5 would result in a new team as a matter of right to replace Raiders; thus taxpayers less likely to be exploited. **STRONG SUPPORT**

III: Too late for L.A.: the teams have moved. Makes it easier for NFL to veto efforts by L.A. to lure existing team. **STRONG OPPOSITION**

IV: Status quo makes it easier for L.A. to lure existing team and Tagliabue claims NFL will be deterred from blocking move for fear of antitrust liability **MODEST SUPPORT**

Prof. Ross testimony, Appendix, Page 11

Mr. Boucher (Southwest VA)

I: With Washington Redskins apparently now moving to suburban Maryland, risk of exploitation of Virginia taxpayers to support Northern Virginia stadium seems removed. If baseball antitrust exemption is narrowed/removed, rival leagues will ensure baseball for National Capital area <u>without</u> tax subsidy which might in part be borne by Virginia taxpayers if stadium located in suburbs. **MODEST SUPPORT**

II: Proposal unlikely to directly affect constituents. **???**

III: Proposal unlikely to directly affect constituents. **???**

IV: Status quo unlikely to affect football situation. Status quo in baseball subjects Virginia taxpayers to some risk of exploitation for new stadium if Major League Baseball decides to grant a franchise to National Capital region. **MODEST OPPOSITION**

Mr. Bryant (Dallas)

I: With newly refurbished stadia, Cowboys and Rangers aren't going anywhere. Rival leagues would diminish monopoly profits and lead to even more aggressive crack-downs on wealthy owners like Jerry Jones, possibly hurting Cowboy dominance. **MODEST OPPOSITION**

II: Although no relocation threat in short-term, mandatory expansion coupled with league immunity, like chicken soup, couldn't hurt. **MODEST SUPPORT**

III: Proposal unlikely to directly affect constituents. **???**

IV: Status quo unlikely to directly affect constituents. **???**

Mr. Reed (western RI)

I: Competition between leagues ensures that Boston will continue to have major league teams and threat of expansion by rival league reduces Patriots' ability to exploit taxpayers. **STRONG SUPPORT**

II: Mandatory expansion protects New England. **STRONG SUPPORT**

III: League immunity won't protect against Patriots moving -- especially if Massachusetts taxpayers don't foot the bill for luxury boxes. **MODEST OPPOSITION**

IV: Patriots at risk of relocation. **MODEST OPPOSITION**

Mr. Nadler (Manhattan/Brooklyn)

I: With rival leagues, Dodgers would have never left because leagues would have already expanded to L.A.! Today, rival leagues might well add a 3rd team to the NY Metro area, giving another option to those dissatisfied with Giants, or Jets, or trip to Jersey. Most relevant, with rival leagues the ability to exploit local taxpayers would be zero -- indeed, leagues would bid for lucrative in-town locations. **STRONG SUPPORT**

II: Mandatory expansion protects New York fans against exploitation through threat of leaving area. **MODEST SUPPORT**

III: League immunity might be helpful if Giants or Jets follow Rams' lead. **MODEST SUPPORT**

IV: Monopoly leagues can exploit taxpayers and threat of litigation could lead to shift of franchise from largest market to tax-subsidized smaller market. **STRONG OPPOSITION**

Mr. Scott (Newport News/ parts of Richmond)

I: With Washington Redskins apparently now moving to suburban Maryland, risk of exploitation of Virginia taxpayers to support Northern Virginia stadium seems removed. If baseball antitrust exemption is narrowed/removed, rival leagues will ensure baseball for National Capital area without tax subsidy which might in part be borne by Virginia taxpayers if stadium located in suburbs. **MODEST SUPPORT**

II: Proposal unlikely to directly affect constituents. **???**

III: Proposal unlikely to directly affect constituents. **???**

IV: Status quo unlikely to affect football situation. Status quo in baseball subjects Virginia taxpayers to some risk of exploitation for new stadium if Major League Baseball decides to grant a franchise to National Capital region. **MODEST OPPOSITION**

Prof. Ross testimony, Appendix, Page 13

Mr. Watt (Charlotte/Durham/Greensboro)

I: Rival leagues could potentially result in reduced monopoly profits in large markets, some of which are now shared with Carolina Panthers. New stadium means no immediate risk to relocate. However, rival leagues will also guarantee increased taxpayer leverage in stadium lease negotiations, and, if baseball antitrust exemption is inapplicable, rival leagues could result in team in Charlotte. **MODEST SUPPORT**

II: Same analysis as above-- mandatory expansion will make Panthers' slice of NFL revenue pie smaller, but mandatory relocation provision will give bargaining leverage to public. Could hurt ability to lure existing baseball team to Charlotte. **MODEST OPPOSITION**

III: Panthers aren't leaving so NFL immunity won't have any effect; if baseball exemption inapplicable, statutory immunity would hurt ability to lure existing baseball team to Charlotte. **MODEST OPPOSITION**

IV: No effect on NFL; current ability to attract baseball team only at a very steep price. **MODEST OPPOSITION**

Mr. Becerra (L.A.)

I: Rival leagues virtually guarantees L.A. one team anxious to play anywhere to get foothold in nation's second largest market; probably both leagues would sponsor franchises lest television viewers focus solely on one league. **STRONG SUPPORT**

II: Section 5 would result in a new team as a matter of right to replace Raiders; thus taxpayers less likely to be exploited. **STRONG SUPPORT**

III: Too late for L.A.: the teams have moved. Makes it easier for NFL to veto efforts by L.A. to lure existing team. **STRONG OPPOSITION**

IV: Status quo makes it easier for L.A. to lure existing team and Tagliabue claims NFL will be deterred from blocking move for fear of antitrust liability **MODEST SUPPORT**

Prof. Ross testimony, Appendix, Page 14

Mr. Serrano (Bronx)

I: Today, rival leagues might well add a 3rd team to the NY Metro area, giving another option to those dissatisfied with Giants, or Jets, or trip to Jersey. Most relevant, with rival leagues the ability to exploit local taxpayers would be zero -- indeed, leagues would bid for lucrative in-town locations. **STRONG SUPPORT**

II: Mandatory expansion protects New York fans against exploitation through threat of leaving area. **MODEST SUPPORT**

III: League immunity might be helpful if Giants or Jets follow Rams' lead. **MODEST SUPPORT**

IV: Monopoly leagues can exploit taxpayers and threat of litigation could lead to shift of franchise from largest market to tax-subsidized smaller market. **STRONG OPPOSITION**

Ms. Lofgren (San Jose)

I: Rival leagues would ensure that S.F. Bay Area would continue to enjoy 2 teams (and slightly increased chance that a brand new league could form would increase chances for team in San Jose area). Although San Jose/Santa Clara taxpayers might end up in bidding war with neighbors in S.F. or Oakland, leveraging is less likely because of presence of other league. **STRONG SUPPORT**

II: Definition of "community" in the bill would protect S.F. and Oakland, without giving San Jose a chance to enter the fray. **MODEST OPPOSITION**

III: Ability of league to keep 49ers and Raiders from moving from area (unlikely and unprecedented for league to keep either team from moving to South Bay) is a modest improvement. **MODEST SUPPORT**

IV: Raiders and 49ers at some small risk of relocation and taxpayers at risk of exploitation. **MODEST OPPOSITION**

Ms. Jackson Lee (Houston)

I: Houston is the one city in American that has demonstrably profited from rival leagues, when Bud Adams won bidding war in 1959 by giving city $150,000 for stadium renovation. Rival leagues not only guarantee franchise for Houston, but, given strength of market, would probably permit local stadium authority to force leagues into a bidding war. **STRONG SUPPORT**

II: Section 5 would result in a new team as a matter of right if Oilers left, so taxpayers less likely to be exploited. **STRONG SUPPORT**

III: Although owners likely to approve Bud Adams' money grab in hopes of being allowed to do the same themselves, immunity would slightly increase chance of league veto. **MODEST SUPPORT**

IV: League claims it is deterred from blocking Browns' relocation because of fear of antitrust liability and no guarantee Cleveland will get a new team. **STRONG OPPOSITION**

Prof. Ross testimony, Appendix, Page 16

STATEMENT OF PROF. STEPHEN F. ROSS, UNIVERSITY OF ILLINOIS, BEFORE THE SENATE COMMITTEE ON THE JUDICIARY, SUBCOMMITTEE ON ANTITRUST, BUSINESS RIGHTS, AND COMPETITION, NOVEMBER 29, 1995

Chairman Thurmond and distinguished Senators:

It is a privilege and a pleasure to appear before the committee for whom I had the honor of working as a staff counsel over a decade ago. A committee whose principal concern is antitrust law -- what the Supreme Court has described as a prescription for the welfare of consumers[1] -- is appropriately focusing its attention on one of the most grievous abuses of monopoly power in America today: the exploitation of fans and taxpayers by monopoly sports league owners threatening to relocate sports franchises.

Introduction and Summary

National Football League owners are not, to my knowledge, evil or nefarious people. They are simply monopolists, and they behave consistently with the way economic theory suggests monopolists will conduct themselves: they produce less of their product (too few franchises), charge more for it (obscene tax subsidies in this current era of government deficits), and operate inefficiently (franchises relocated from nation's second largest media market (Los Angeles) and one of the most popular on a percentage basis (Cleveland)). Fans in areas without teams suffer from the inability to see a major league professional team in their area; taxpayer suffer through these public stadium subsidies.

As I have previously written,[2] the clearly optimal policy solution is to acknowledge that time has shown that the Act of November 8, 1966,[3] permitting a financially successful

---

[1] Reiter v. Sonotone, 442 U.S. 330, 344 (1979).

[2] *Monopoly Sports Leagues*, 73 Minn. L. Rev. 699 (1979).

[3] Pub. L. No. 89-800, 80 Stat. 1515 (1966).

National Football League to merge with its financially successful American Football League rival, is now a mistake that should be corrected by Congress. If two or more rival major leagues made their own independent determinations concerning expansion and relocation, the result would be the end of "franchise free agency" and the end of massive exploitation of taxpayers.

In light of the many policies of the 1960s being reconsidered by the 104th Congress, I do not believe this proposal is too radical to be politically possible. Indeed, as I illustrate in Table 1 below, I believe that this proposal is not only good policy but good politics. After addressing why I believe the committee should seriously consider this proposal, this testimony will address why proposals to simply immunize NFL relocation decisions from antitrust scrutiny will not solve the real problems of the exercise of the NFL's monopoly power, why the cumulative effect of a number of NFL revenue sharing rules may result in an unreasonable restraint of trade that should not be immunized, and why fear of antitrust liability is not the principal cause of the recent rash of franchise relocations in the NFL. As I detail below, by requiring teams to share all revenues from live gate, television, and souvenirs, but permit teams to keep for themselves all revenues from local tax subsidies, the NFL owners have illegally channelled their entrepreneurial competition away from making their games exciting and entertaining to fans and toward exploiting taxpayers. Finally, I suggest that several second-best solutions deserve the Committee's consideration if the restoration of competition in major league professional football is not going to be possible. Specifically, I propose that you consider employing Congress' Commerce Clause power to condition the NFL's continued existence as a monopolist on their refusal to accept tax subsidies by state and local governments to lure or keep franchises from relocating to another state, and that you also consider specific legislation to outlaw, as an unreasonable restraint of trade, the NFL's current revenue sharing system that allows owners only one way to improve profits -- through taxpayer rip-offs.

I. **Restoring competition in the franchise market is the best solution to the current problems.**

In 1959, Bud Adams agreed to pay $150,000 of his own money to expand the seating capacity of a local stadium in order to secure a five-year lease, and obtain for his Oilers team in the American Football League the Houston, Texas, franchise.[4] This month, Mr. Adams announced he was moving his team to Nashville, Tennessee, in pursuit of a new stadium that will guarantee Adams $71.5 million in "personal seat licenses" and at least 82 luxury suites as part of a $292 million agreement subsidized by $55 million in state general obligation bonds, $18 million in cash for road improvements, and $4 million in local funds accumulated by the Nashville water department.[5] The principal explanation for the stark difference in Mr. Adams behavior is that in 1959 he was part of a competitive enterprise; today, he operates as a member of a monopoly cartel.

In prior legislative battles, senators from states that currently have NFL franchises skirmished with their colleagues from "have-not" states, preventing any legislation from

---

[4] *Houston Post*, Oct. 30, 1959, §5, at 2, col. 3.

[5] *Memphis Commercial Appeal*, Nov. 17, 1995, p. 7A; Christopher McEntee, "Nashville, Oilers Sign Pact to Bring NFL to Tennessee", *The Bond Buyer*, Nov. 17, 1995, p. 11.

passing. It is time for you to join together to accomplish a result that will benefit taxpayers and fans everywhere, and where the only losers are the monopolists. By restoring competition, the exploitation of taxpayers would cease. The NFL wouldn't think of abandoning Los Angeles or Cleveland, because the AFL would move right in, picking up a lucrative expansion opportunity, higher ratings for the AFL's network television rights, etc. If taxpayers in Baltimore or Nashville thought that creation of a publicly-funded stadium was critical, at least they would have the AFL and NFL bidding to pay more rent to defer some of the cost.

Creation of competing leagues would also reduce the antitrust uncertainty that NFL officials like to cite as a cause of the current problem. The Supreme Court has clearly suggested that where two or more rival leagues exist in a market, each league will have considerably more flexibility to make its own decisions free of review in antitrust litigation.[6] Moreover, modern antitrust law (which has, in fairness, become more sophisticated since Congress allowed the AFL-NFL merger in 1966) would clearly permit the NFL and its rejuvenated AFL rival to agree on a Super Bowl, inter-league play, and agreements ancillary to this cooperation.[7]

Some suggest that competing leagues are simply not possible in professional sports. I have dealt in detail with such a historical argument elsewhere.[8] For current purposes,

---

[6] National Collegiate Athletic Ass'n v. Bd. of Regents of the Univ. of Oklahoma, 468 U.S. 85, 115 n.55 (1984) (citing Continental T.V., Inc., v. GTE Sylvania Inc., 433 U.S. 36 (1979)).

[7] I discuss this point in detail in my article, *Monopoly Sports Leagues, supra* at 733-48.

[8] *Monopoly Sports Leagues, supra,* at 715-33.

suffice it to say that, although many attempts to challenge an established major league failed for economic reasons, in both baseball and football successful rival leagues were formed and succeeded in joining the established league in a cartel exempted either by the Supreme Court or Congress from antitrust scrutiny.[9] Moreover, repealing the 1966 legislation and establishing an orderly procedure for the recreation of the old AFL would involve, unlike prior cases, two rival leagues of equal strength. The law is also clear that a common draft, or even restraints on the ability of an AFL team to bid on the services of an NFL player, would be protected from antitrust challenge if they were embodied in a collective bargaining agreement signed by both leagues and the players' union.[10] Finally, the public will be well served even if I am wrong in my judgment that a recreated AFL could compete with the NFL.[11] Even if the players' union did not help preserve members' jobs by agreeing to restraints on competition for players services in a collective bargaining agreement, Congress

---

[9] Federal Baseball Club of Baltimore v. National League, 259 U.S. 200 (1922); Pub. L. No. 89-800, 80 Stat. 1515 (1966).

[10] *See* Reynolds v. NFL, 584 F.2d 280 (8th Cir. 1978). For example, when the American Basketball Association was heading toward bankruptcy, the players' union offered to support a common rookie draft among ABA and NBA teams if veteran players were able to receive competitive bids for their services. *Professional Basketball: Hearing Before the Subcomm. on Antitrust and Monopoly of the Senate Comm. on the Judiciary on S. 2373*, 92d Cong., 2d Sess. 295 (1972) (testimony of Lawrence Fleisher). (For a discussion of why the ABA's inability to sustain competition against the NBA was probably the result of predatory practices by the NBA, see *Monopoly Sports Leagues, supra*, at 725-30.)

[11] Economists and sports executives share my judgment that competition for players -- which in the past has been the principal cause of the inability of rival leagues to sustain competition with an established incumbent -- would taper off once it became clear that the rival league was not going to be driven out of business and that Congress would not permit a merger. *See, e.g., Professional Basketball: Hearing Before the Subcomm. on Antitrust and Monopoly of the Senate Comm. on the Judiciary on S. 2373*, 92d Cong., 2d Sess. 370 (1972) (testimony of leading sports economist Roger Noll); *id.* at 859 (testimony of Golden State Warriors executive Melvin Kratter).

could revisit this issue and re-enact merger-authorizing legislation a decade from now. Meanwhile, the public will receive the benefit of ten years worth of competition.

One benefit of a free enterprise system is that the market usually responds to increased consumer demand for a product by spurring increased output. Monopoly sports leagues, in contrast, exercise their power deliberately to hold down the number of available franchises: the fewer the franchises, the more incentive for have-not cities to provide tax subsidies like the ones lavished upon Art Modell and Bud Adams. Even owners with no intention of relocating their own teams want to suppress the number of franchises so that they may exercise a credible threat to relocate, and have no desire to share lucrative television revenue with another co-venturer.

If competing leagues existed, each league would have a greater incentive to expand to available markets. Each league would be eager to tap into new markets to attract new viewers to its own network television package, whose value would depend on how many fans viewed each leagues' games. For example, when the AFC-member Colts left Baltimore for Indianapolis, the Baltimore NBC affiliate (who broadcasts AFC games) saw its ratings fall, while the CBS affiliate (who used to broadcast NFC games) saw its ratings rise.[12] Faced with a potential move by another AFC team (the Browns) into Baltimore, the NFC would have a strong incentive to expand to that media market, an incentive that its current network, Fox, would probably be willing to pay for.

As a noted economist once wrote, one of the virtues of competitive markets is that

---

[12] *See* Arbitron Ratings (1983-84) (cited in *Monopoly Sports Leagues, supra* at 665 n.103).

they "solve the economic problem impersonally, and not through the personal control of entrepreneurs or bureaucrats. There is nothing more galling than to have the achievement of some desired objective frustrated by the decision of an identifiable individual or group."[13] The following table shows the benefits and costs of such restored competition. I remain optimistic that this Committee will be able to assert leadership in this area on behalf of all their constituents who don't happen to own NFL franchises.

---

[13] F.M. Scherer, *Industrial Market Structure and Economic Performance* 12-13 (2d ed. 1980).

TABLE 1
EFFECT OF LEGISLATION REPEALING THE NFL-AFL MERGER

INTEREST GROUP	PRINCIPAL EFFECT	WINNERS/LOSERS
Fans in cities without teams (football fans in Nashville, Baltimore)	Increased likelihood that each league will expand to gain new market and prevent rival from gains	WINNER
Taxpayers in cities without teams	Rivals leagues will bid for chance to play in new stadia, pay rent, etc.	WINNER
Fans in cities with franchises (e.g. Browns, Oilers fans)	Reduced chance that favorite team will leave, since most lucrative markets will be filled	WINNER
Taxpayers in cities with teams	Popular support for tax subsidies reduced since local team will lose credible threat to relocate to desirable market	WINNER
Elected representatives who do not depend on political support from NFL owners	Bi-partisan legislative solution shows problems can be solved in D.C.	WINNER
Television networks	Fees potentially reduced with rival leagues	WINNER
Average and young players	More jobs = greater opportunity	WINNER
Currently over-paid stars	With reduced monopoly income from league, deals like Deion Sanders' may suffer, but competition from leagues may prevent strikes	???
NFL owners	Lose ability to exploit taxpayers by threatening relocation	LOSER

II. **Granting antitrust immunity for NFL rules concerning franchise relocation is not a desirable alternative.**

Although I have not seen today's testimony from NFL officials, in the past they have suggested that the problem of "franchise free agency" would be significantly alleviated if only they were allowed to operate as they saw fit, free of any threatened antitrust liability. If the NFL were not a monopoly league, I believe that current interpretations of the Sherman Act would make it virtually impossible to win a case against one league's franchise location decision, and, for purposes of clarification, I can see little harm from affirmatively immunizing franchise relocations decisions made independently by one league where that league faced effective competition from one or more rivals. However, as long as the NFL remains a monopoly league, I do not believe that this Committee's response to the problem should be to grant such immunity. First and most fundamentally, such an immunity does nothing to prevent cities, fans, and taxpayers from exploitation when the league works in concert with a team owner to threaten or actually relocate. Second, depending on the language of the legislation, such immunity could block what I believe is a potentially viable antitrust challenge to the current problems in the NFL. Third, such immunity would also improperly immunize the inefficient and anticompetitive vote by a minority of NFL owners to block a desirable relocation solely to protect an existing owner from competition. Fourth, such an immunity is not really necessary to enable the NFL to effectively prevent franchise free agency if it chose to do so. Fifth, although on balance carefully drafted and narrow legislation might represent a slight improvement over the *status quo*, Senators representing states without NFL franchises (obviously including Senators Thompson and Heflin of this

Committee) are likely to come under tremendous constituent pressure to strongly oppose such legislation. If this Committee is determined to forge ahead with controversial legislation in this area, I strongly urge that you pursue the legislation advocated in Part I of my testimony despite the opposition of the NFL, rather than legislation discussed in this part of my testimony, despite the opposition of have-not cities and their representatives.

Legislation that would immunize NFL decisions to prevent a franchise from relocating would obviously have an effect only when NFL owners chose to block a relocation. Although allegations of bad faith concerning Mr. Modell's negotiating tactics have made Cleveland's case a particular *cause celebre*, even here Commissioner Tagliabue made it clear that the league would welcome Modell's relocation if Cleveland taxpayers did not come up with a sizable subsidy package to attempt to meet Baltimore's offer.[14]

For example, almost all legislative proposals I have seen, as well as current NFL rules, permit the league to consider among the relevant factors the "adequacy" of the existing stadium and the willingness of local taxpayers to support any efforts to remedy any inadequacies. As a good lawyer, Paul Tagliabue would have no trouble defending a league decision that any stadium without substantial luxury boxes was "inadequate," and that any locality whose taxpayers were unwilling to provide significant subsidies to be insufficiently supportive, so that a relocation would be justified. Indeed, since adequacy and support are relative concepts, even the Browns relocation could be approved by league owners, if they so

---

[14] *See* Timothy Heider, "Sin Tax Wins Big; Three of Four Voters Say 'We Want a Team,'" *Cleveland Plain Dealer*, Nov. 8, 1995, p.1A (NFL Commissioner Paul Tagliabue told [Cleveland's Mayor] White in a meeting last Sunday that there would have been no hope of keeping the Browns in Cleveland - or luring another NFL franchise here - had the referendum been defeated).

chose, because the proposed new stadium in Cleveland is arguably inadequate relative to the new stadium in Baltimore, and the degree of taxpayer support is similarly inadequate -- if it were not, Mr. Modell would not have bothered to move to Baltimore! The real problem is not individual owners like Mr. Modell, or Al Davis before him -- even Pete Rozelle went to Minnesota and threatened to support relocating the Vikings if the state legislature did not construct the Humphrey Metrodome at taxpayer expense. The problem is that NFL owners want to be able to threaten to relocate in order to maximize taxpayer subsidy, and as long as they have a monopoly it is most difficult to prevent them from doing so.

Depending on the breadth of the exemption, immunity legislation could unjustifiably eliminate what I believe to be a viable cause of action that could be brought under current law by taxpayers and fans in Ohio and Texas against the entire system of NFL rules that, in my opinion, unreasonably restrains and channels trade and competition among NFL owners away from an exciting product on the field and toward exploitation of local taxpayers. The NFL has a number of rules that require teams to share revenue from live gate, television, and souvenirs. Taken in isolation, the rules are probably reasonable. The NFL also permits teams to keep for themselves income from luxury boxes and other stadium revenues and does not require any pooling of costs of leasing facilities. The combined effect of these rules is to dampen incentives to increase live gate income, broadcast ratings, or popularity of team jackets and other paraphernalia, while maximizing incentives to relocate or otherwise exploit local taxpayers. In my opinion these rules, together, fall within the Supreme Court's definition of unreasonable trade restraints in the sports area: prices are higher and output is lower than would otherwise be the case, and both are unresponsive to consumer preference.[15] It is clear, for example, that Mr. Modell would not bother moving to Maryland if he personally would pocket only 1/30 of the subsidy. Less clear, Mr. Modell might not have moved even if he were able to keep the subsidy but would have to substitute the revenues from Baltimore's television market for the revenues from Cleveland's television market. Only because tax subsidies are not shared while other revenues are can the current situation flourish. It would be unfortunate if this legal theory were wiped out by Congress.

Not only would immunity legislation do little to solve the real problem of taxpayer exploitation, but it might facilitate some real injustices. Recall that the Cardinals franchise left St. Louis for Phoenix without great controversy, because the fans were not supporting the team and there was little support for a new stadium. Suppose, however, that based on objective market factors Baltimore was a stronger candidate for the Cardinals' franchise than Phoenix, but a minority of league owners, organized by the Washington Redskins' Jack Kent Cooke, prevented the selection of the superior Baltimore market? In such a case, I believe, fans are entitled to some protection from anticompetitive decisions by a minority of monopoly sports league owners.

This Committee should recognize that NFL officials seriously overstate the legal risk in blocking franchise relocations under current antitrust law. (Of course, were the NFL to appear in court, they would plainly support the narrow interpretation of existing case law that I set forth below.) The only case to find a professional sports league liable for refusing to

---

[15] National Collegiate Athletic Ass'n v. Bd. of Regents of the Univ. of Oklahoma, 468 U.S. 85, 107 (1984).

allow a franchise relocation was the NFL's rejection of the Oakland Raiders relocation to Los Angeles. In the *Raiders* case,[16] the plaintiffs presented evidence found credible by a jury that (1) the L.A. market could easily support both the Raiders and the Los Angeles Rams; (2) the NFL had failed to show any harm to the league, in terms of network television exposure, regional balance, or travel costs, as justification for refusing to permit the relocation; (3) the NFL rules permitting 8 owners to veto the move, combined with evidence that the Rams strongly objected, supported the conclusion that the leagues' motivation was to protect the Rams from competition rather than to enhance the quality or marketability of NFL football; and (4) the league's most persuasive argument -- that it had a legitimate interest in recognizing the loyalty of Oakland fans -- was undercut by its lack of any criteria for evaluating relocations and significant evidence that, in other cases, the league was willing to overlook fan loyalty in order to permit teams to credibly threaten to move unless they received public stadium subsidies. Moreover, the court of appeals subsequent opinion on damages confirmed that leagues may legitimately impose a significant fee upon the relocating team to compensate the league for the lost opportunity to obtain expansion fees from a new team in the new area.[17]

In my judgment, this means that the NFL could have legally barred the Rams from relocating to St. Louis. The league's claims of effect on regional rivalries (e.g. with the San Francisco 49rs) and television exposure (losing the second largest media market) would have

---

[16] Los Angeles Memorial Coliseum Comm'n v. NFL, 726 F.2d 1381, *cert. denied*, 469 U.s. 990 (1984).

[17] Oakland Raiders, Ltd. v. NFL, 791 F.2d 1356 (9th Cir. 1986), *cert. denied*, 108 S.Ct. 92 (1987).

been legitimate. Most significantly, the Rams had no plausible claim that a refusal would be based on any anticompetitive motive. This also means that the only way that Messrs. Modell or Adams could prevail in an antitrust suit should their fellow owners reject their relocation proposals would be if their attorneys could persuade a *reasonable* jury that, like the *Raiders* case, the league was not interested in saving television dollars, regional rivalries, or fan loyalty but rather was interested in protecting the Washington Redskins or some team somehow viewed as nearby to Nashville from competition.

Most significantly, I read the *Raiders* decision as permitting a league to adopt a strong and consistent policy of rewarding fan loyalty -- demonstrated by live gate attendance, television viewership, and souvenir purchases, as opposed to public stadium subsidies -- as a long-term business strategy. The NFL is not going to adopt such a policy however, because the owners don't want to deprive themselves of the ability to threaten teams with relocation. Indeed, if legislation conditioned antitrust immunity on the league's adoption of such a policy, and prevented a league from permitting teams to relocate because of insufficient tax subsidies, it would be a significant improvement over the *status quo*. Similarly, legislation that, for example, granted immunity to the NFL for ten years, conditioned upon an expansion of at least four teams during the next six seasons, might approximate the results of a free market, and would make it very difficult for teams to credibly threaten to leave existing metropolitan areas.[18] I have seen no serious proposals along these lines.

I have yet to see any proposed statutory language that would effectively protect

---

[18] No legislation being discussed today, other than my proposal for competing leagues, would affect threats to relocate within a metropolitan area, such as the Chicago Bears threatened move to Gary, Indiana.

against real or threatened relocations because the league believes that taxpayers in the current location have not provided a sufficiently large subsidy. At the end of the day, however, the number of cases where the league might want to prevent an individual owner from exploiting taxpayers is probably greater than the cases where the league might inefficiently protect one owner from intra-territorial competition. Thus, legislation carefully drafted to immunize specific relocation decisions, while still permitting antitrust challenges to the overall system of league rules that facilitate taxpayer exploitation, would probably mark a very modest improvement in the *status quo*.

However, such legislation is likely to provoke strong opposition from key interest groups, as Table 2 demonstrates. If this Committee is going to draft legislation that offends an interest group, it makes better sense, better policy, and better politics to take on 28 owners of NFL teams rather than millions of sports fans in Los Angeles, Nashville, Baltimore, Birmingham, Portland, Sacramento, and other communities that fancy themselves worthy of an NFL franchise.

TABLE 2
EFFECT OF LEGISLATION PRESERVING NFL'S OPTION TO EXPLOIT TAXPAYER

INTEREST GROUP	PRINCIPAL EFFECT	WINNERS/LOSERS
Fans in cities without teams (football fans in Nashville, Baltimore)	Decreased chance of outbidding existing teams for franchise if NFL owners wish to avoid P.R. "hit"	BIG LOSER
Taxpayers in cities without teams	Somewhat decreased chance of exploitation if relocation barred by owners	MODEST WINNER
Fans in cities with franchises (e.g. Browns, Oilers fans)	Reduced chance that favorite team will leave, if can convince owners	MODEST WINNER
Taxpayers in cities with teams	Still required to support tax subsidies or league will allow relocation	LOSER
Elected representatives who do not depend on political support from NFL owners	Have-not cities pressure their representatives to oppose bill, so legislation unlikely	PROBABLE LOSER
Television networks, average and young players, over-paid stars	No effect	???
NFL owners	Preserve ability to maintain good P.R. while continuing to exploit taxpayers by threatening relocation	BIG WINNER

16

III. Legislative solutions if merger-repealing legislation is deemed unacceptable.

Thus far, I have attempted to demonstrate that the best solution would be to restore competition between competing leagues by repealing the 1966 merger legislation, and that granting the NFL greater antitrust immunity while enabling owners to both maintain their monopoly powers and their freedom to exploit taxpayers would do little to improve the current problem. If the Committee's judgment is that your limited time should not be spent on this issue unless a consensus can be reached and legislation could be passed with at least the acquiescence of the NFL, I would urge you to turn to other matters immediately. Unfortunately, this issue involves a zero-sum game. As demonstrated in Part II, any legislation that would likely be supported by the NFL will not solve the real problem of taxpayer exploitation. Moreover, as shown by Table 2 on the next page, it is likely to hurt strong interest groups, and thus is unlikely to pass anyway. If you are willing to take on the NFL, my proposal to repeal the 1966 legislation seems the cleanest. However, in this Part of my testimony, I offer two other suggestions that would significantly improve the status quo and defer to your political judgment if they are more politically palatable.

A. Prohibit tax subsidies to lure or retain franchises

Although restoring competition to professional football and allowing the marketplace to allocate franchises would be most consistent with general public policy, one legitimate congressional response to the immediate problem of franchise free agency would be to directly target the social harm caused by this process -- the exploitation of taxpayers -- by prohibiting special tax subsidies to lure or retain franchises from leaving a state.

As you may know, the European Community has historically prohibited these "state aids," as well as tariffs and other negative barriers to the free flow of commerce. In the United States, special tax breaks have been held not to interfere with interstate commerce.[19] Whatever the merits of this aspect of American federalism generally, it seems entirely appropriate for the same national legislature that granted a special antitrust exemption to allow the creation of a monopoly football league to insist that such a league not play one community off against another through tax subsidies. If federalism concerns are perceived to prevent Congress from limiting the ability of states to use their spending or taxing authority in a way that Congress believes is inimical to interstate commerce,[20] legislation could be drafted that would provide that, notwithstanding the 1966 merger legislation, the NFL would be subject to a monopolization challenge under §2 of the Sherman Act if it or its member teams accepted tax subsidies as a lure to remain or relocate a franchise.

---

[19] As my colleagues John Nowak and Ronald Rotunda explain in *Constitutional Law* 296 (5th ed. 1994), state legislation unconstitutionally interferes with interstate commerce only when it discriminates against out-of-state business and thus forces outsiders to bear the costs of state policy. Tax subsidies, in contrast, are paid for by the same voters who elect the legislature doling out the benefits, and thus the costs and benefits of such a policy can be weighed by democratic processes.

[20] In New York v. United States, 112 S. Ct. 2408, 2423 (1992), the majority wrote that Congress did not have the power "to regulate state governments' regulation of interstate commerce." This language could be interpreted to preclude congressional limits on tax subsidies. However, commentators have suggested that the case "involved a very limited ruling that federalism principles, and the Tenth Amendment, prohibited Congress from directly ordering states *to take governmental actions*." Nowak & Rotunda, *Constitutional Law* 189 (emphasis added). It is not clear whether the case extends to congressional *prohibitions* on state governmental actions that are inconsistent with national policies against monopoly exploitation.

B. *Require luxury box income to be shared by all members of the league.*

As noted earlier, the structure of NFL rules requiring sharing of all income the Browns and the Oilers derive from live gate, television, and souvenirs, but allowing Messrs. Modell and Adams to keep for themselves the benefits of local taxpayer subsidies, has unreasonably channelled competition away from activities that make NFL football the most marketable product possible and toward techniques to further exploit consumer. As a result, for many years now the principal difference between the most profitable and least profitable franchises was not the quality of the organization or the team but the success of the team owner in negotiating a lucrative stadium deal.[21] One way to correct this problem, and take away a significant incentive for owners to relocate, would be to require that stadium-related income be shared with co-owners to the same degree as other principal sources of revenue.

As explained above, these owners would simply not have gone through the trouble of becoming exiled from their hometowns for 1/30th of the proceeds of the move to Baltimore or Nashville. Moreover, consider the impact this has if we assume that these owners are knowledgeable about the sport in which they operate. For the past few years, the Houston Oilers have had their ups and downs amid several coaching changes, novel offensive

---

[21] This data is not publicly available and thus is hard to come by absent subpoena power (which this committee may wish to consider). In 1988, a detailed report showed that the most profitable team in the NFL was the Indianapolis Colts. As a reward for jilting Baltimore's loyal fans, the Colts' owners earned considerable profits despite a mediocre on-field product because of $4.5 million in luxury box income and $2.6 million in concession/parking income, leading the league in both categories. In contrast, the Super Bowl champiion Washington Redskins lost over $3 million that year, primarily due to no income from luxury boxes or concessions and parking. See "The Pluses and Minuses of the NFL," *Los Angeles Times*, Jan. 25, 1988. This cannot be an efficient way to run a sports league, unless the goal was to maximize taxpayer exploitation at the expense of a quality on-field product.

strategies, and decisions about whether to keep old and popular veteran players. Should Mr. Adams have been spending more time focusing on these issues, or trying to figure out ways to exploit taxpayers? Under NFL rules, clearly the latter. If the Oilers win big on the field, they might have many sell-outs and ticket prices at the Astrodome could rise considerably, but Mr. Adams will have to share 40% of this source of income with the visiting team. If the Oilers' players are popular, Oiler jackets, hats, helmets, and other paraphernalia might become big sellers, but Mr. Adams simply shares 1/30 of all profits from NFL Properties. If the Oilers' design an exciting offense that attracts major television ratings, both in Houston and across the country, Mr. Adams simply shares 1/30 in the profits. However, if Mr. Adams can get a multi-million tax subsidy, he keeps it himself. This is not the way that free enterprise is supposed to work in this society, and this Committee is the appropriate body to call a halt to these practices.

Again, I appreciate the opportunity to appear before you today.

Antitrust Law Journal

35TH ANNUAL MEETING

San Francisco, California
August 10-12, 1987

SECTION OF ANTITRUST LAW
AMERICAN BAR ASSOCIATION

Volume 56, Issue 2

CONTENTS

FOREWORD	ix
MINUTES OF COUNCIL MEETING, AUGUST 9, 1987	xiii
MINUTES OF COUNCIL MEETING, AUGUST 13, 1987	xxi
MINUTES OF COUNCIL MEETING, AUGUST 14, 1987	xxix
MINUTES OF BUSINESS MEETING, AUGUST 12, 1987	xxxv

35TH ANNUAL MEETING
SAN FRANCISCO, CALIFORNIA
AUGUST 10–12, 1987

DEVELOPMENTS 1986–87

INTRODUCTORY REMARKS	285
James F. Rill and Michael Denger	
SUPREME COURT REVIEW: 1987	289
Michael Malina	
HOW MUCH IS ENOUGH? DEVELOPMENTS AFFECTING MERGERS AND ACQUISITIONS	303
Bruce J. Prager	
ANTITRUST DEVELOPMENTS IN SPORTS AND ENTERTAINMENT	341
Paul J. Tagliabue	
DEVELOPMENTS IN THE *NOERR* DOCTRINE	361
Lawrence A. Sullivan	
LEGISLATIVE DEVELOPMENTS	371
Ky P. Ewing, Jr.	

ANNUAL ANTITRUST SECTION LUNCHEON

INTRODUCTORY REMARKS	383
Mark Crane and James F. Rill	
ADDRESS	387
Senator Howard M. Metzenbaum	

ANTITRUST DEVELOPMENTS IN SPORTS AND ENTERTAINMENT

PAUL J. TAGLIABUE[*]

I. INTRODUCTION

In this review of antitrust developments in sports and entertainment, I will treat three subjects: (1) certain issues arising out of economic changes in the entertainment industry that may portend changes in customary legal analysis of motion picture distribution and exhibition practices; (2) the need for coherent antitrust principles for evaluating intra-league agreements among the member clubs of professional sports leagues, particularly ancillary restraints principles; and (3) the labor exemption from the antitrust laws as analyzed in a recent Second Circuit decision involving professional basketball.

At its meeting yesterday, the Antitrust Section's Sports and Entertainment Industry Committee, in cooperation with the Forum Committee on the Entertainment and Sports Industries, presented an outstanding program by four experienced members—Gerry Phillips, Tim McCoy, Jim Selna, and Gary Roberts. The best way for me to start my review is to summarize very briefly what they reviewed.

Gary Roberts, a professor at Tulane Law School, commented on the antitrust labor exemption in sports, and particularly the Second Circuit's recent decision in the *Leon Wood* case,[1] an important decision by Judge Winter, the author of an important article on this topic in the *Yale Law Journal*[2] almost twenty years ago. Gary also touched on the implications of the Supreme Court's decision in the *NCAA* television case[3] for other aspects of amateur and college athletics.

Gerry Phillips, Chairperson of the Forum Committee, who has long been involved in the motion picture business, reviewed the origins of

---

[*] Member of the District of Columbia Bar and Chairman, Sports and Entertainment Industry Committee, Section of Antitrust Law.
[1] Wood v. National Basketball Ass'n, 809 F.2d 954 (2d Cir. 1987).
[2] Jacobs & Winter, *Antitrust Principles and Collective Bargaining by Athletes: Of Superstars in Peonage*, 81 YALE L.J. 1 (1971).
[3] NCAA v. Board of Regents, 468 U.S. 85 (1984).

the *Paramount* case,[4] the terms of the *Paramount* decrees, and a recent proceeding before Judge Palmieri in the Southern District of New York applying those decrees.

Tim McCoy, a practitioner in Los Angeles, reviewed the recent vertical and horizontal acquisitions of theaters and exhibitors; he discussed the videocassette explosion and its implications for product market definition in the entertainment industry; and he commented on some of the positions taken by the Department of Justice on various Herfindahl issues in the entertainment industry.

Jim Selna, also a practitioner in Los Angeles, reviewed the implications of recent Supreme Court decisions on the analysis of certain motion picture distribution practices, such as block booking. He touched particularly on the Court's decisions in the *Jefferson Parish* case,[5] including Justice O'Connor's concurrence, which criticized *Paramount*'s treatment of block booking.[6] He also discussed the Court's decisions in *Monsanto*,[7] *Matsushita*,[8] and *NCAA*[9] in terms of their potential impact on entertainment industry issues.

II. ECONOMIC AND ANTITRUST DEVELOPMENTS IN THE ENTERTAINMENT INDUSTRY

The entertainment industry is in the process of some remarkable changes. From an antitrust perspective, one of the most notable is the recent acquisition of exhibitors—that is to say, theater circuits—by motion picture producer-distributors. For example, Paramount Pictures now owns the Mann Theater chain, as well as the Festival and Trans-Lux Theater circuits; MCA, which is Universal's parent, owns a fifty percent interest in Cineplex-Odeon, one of the largest theater chains in the United States.[10]

---

[4] United States v. Paramount Pictures, Inc., 66 F. Supp. 323 (S.D.N.Y. 1946), 70 F. Supp. 53 (S.D.N.Y. 1947), aff'd in part and rev'd in part, 334 U.S. 131 (1948), on remand, 85 F. Supp. 881 (S.D.N.Y. 1949), aff'd, 339 U.S. 984 (1950).
[5] Jefferson Parish Hospital Dist. No. 2 v. Hyde, 466 U.S. 2 (1984).
[6] Id. at 38 n.7 (O'Connor, J., concurring).
[7] Monsanto Co. v. Spray-Rite Serv. Corp., 465 U.S. 752 (1984).
[8] Matsushita Elec. Indus. Co. v. Zenith Radio Corp., 475 U.S. 574 (1986).
[9] NCAA v. Board of Regents, 468 U.S. 85 (1984).
[10] As further examples, Columbia Pictures acquired and subsequently resold the Walter Reade chain. And to make something of a circle from recent developments, Warner Brothers is trying to obtain Justice Department approval to acquire some portion of Paramount's interest in its theaters.

At the same time, the national theater circuits have themselves grown, often by merger and acquisition in recent years. For example, Cineplex-Odeon has acquired ownership of major theater chains in recent years.

Variety estimates that in 1986 alone some 4,300 movie screens changed hands, at a cost of $1.6 billion.[11] That is about twenty percent of the total number of motion picture screens in the United States changing hands in one year. In another context, Gerry Phillips has commented on the implications of these developments:

> The recent buying spree of theater circuits by the major motion picture producer-distributors ... and the growth of the large circuits are reminiscent of the mad dash to own theaters by the major producer-distributors in the 1920s and 1930s.
>
> The current wave of acquisitions by major distributors, which appears to be just beginning, may well bring about a restructuring of the industry. It is also bound to have an enormous impact, both on theater's competing for the motion pictures of the integrated companies and on competing distributors who seek to license their films to all theaters.[12]

These developments have prompted many observers to question the continuing vitality of the famous *Paramount* decrees entered between 1948 and 1952.[13] To review the decrees in simple terms, they required what were then the five major integrated motion picture companies—Paramount, Loew's, RKO, Warners and Fox—to divorce production/distribution from exhibition.

The decrees also contained certain conduct provisions. They required these companies, plus three others that did not own theaters—Columbia, Universal, and United Artists—to abstain from certain specified trade practices, such as fixing admission prices and making franchise agreements. All eight companies were required to license their film product on a so-called "theater-by-theater" basis, without discrimination in favor of affiliated theaters.

Until the recent re-entry by producer-distributors into exhibition, the *Paramount* decrees seemed to symbolize a governmental admonition against mixing these functions in an integrated company. For many years, such integration was considered likely to instigate a new round of gov-

---
[11] Variety, Jan. 7, 1987.
[12] Phillips, *The Recent Acquisition of Theatre Circuits by Major Distributors*, 5 ENTERTAINMENT AND SPORTS LAWYER 1 (Winter 1987).
[13] 1948-1949 Trade Cas. (CCH) ¶ 62,335 (RKO); 1949 Trade Cas. (CCH) ¶ 62,377 (Paramount); 1950 Trade Cas. (CCH) ¶ 62,573 (Columbia-Universal and UA); 1951 Trade Cas. (CCH) ¶ 62,765 (Warner); 1951 Trade Cas. (CCH) ¶ 62,861 (Fox); 1952 Trade Cas. (CCH) ¶ 67,229 (Loews).

ernmental and, perhaps, private litigation, possibly resulting in expanded or new *Paramount*-like decrees.[14]

At present, though, both vertical and horizontal integration appear to be occurring in the motion picture business at the producer/distributor and exhibitor levels. This does not necessarily mean that there has been increased concentration, and some have argued that there is less concentration now than there was even a few years ago.

The recent acquisition of LTM Holdings, which is the successor of the Loew's interests, by TriStar Pictures, is instructive because it provides insight into some current thinking on these issues by both the Justice Department and by Judge Palmieri, who has been supervising the consent decrees for the past three decades. TriStar is a film producer and distributor and a relatively new entrant into the entertainment industry. LTM is a successor to certain of the Loew's companies, originally subject to a decree that resulted from the *Paramount* case.[15]

At the time of the *Paramount* decrees, Loew's, Inc. agreed to divest its exhibition function, and a separate theater circuit came into being as a result of the Loew's decree, which was known as the "New Theater Company." The New Theater Company was not originally subject to the conduct provisions of the *Paramount* decrees; it was, however, prohibited from engaging in the distribution business, absent court approval. Loew's Theaters, Inc. (LTI) became the successor to this New Theater Company that was set up as a result of the decree.

In 1980, LTI petitioned Judge Palmieri for relief from its consent decree to enable it to enter the motion picture distribution business in addition to the exhibition business. That motion was granted subject to a number of conditions, two of which are particularly important: (1) LTI could not exhibit any of the pictures that it distributed or in which it had a financial interest; and (2) in its capacity as a distributor, it was bound by a set of restrictions virtually identical to the so-called conduct restrictions of the original *Paramount* decrees.[16]

When TriStar acquired Loews in 1986, in the absence of relief from the *Paramount* decree and from the judge's order entered in 1980, TriStar would have been subject to two restrictions: (1) it would have been prohibited from exhibiting its own films to Loews theaters, and (2) it was

---

[14] Technically, Paramount and Universal are free to acquire theater chains because for historical reasons the specific provisions of their decrees did not require court approval before such an acquisition.

[15] United States v. Paramount Pictures, Inc., *supra*, note 4.

[16] 1980–81 Trade Cas. (CCH) ¶ 63,692, 1980–2 Trade Cas. (CCH) ¶ 63,553.

subject to restrictions in its overall distribution business that were materially identical to the conduct restrictions which bound the original *Paramount* defendants.

In November of 1986, as part of the acquisition, Loews and TriStar applied to the court for interim relief in two respects: (1) to permit TriStar's films to be exhibited in Loews theaters over the lucrative Christmas release period; and (2) to be free of the trade practice injunctions in its dealings as a distributor with exhibitors other than Loews. Judge Palmieri granted this relief, but only on an interim basis.

In March of this year, Loews and TriStar sought permanent relief from the *Paramount* consent decree and from the 1980 order. The Justice Department came out in strong support of TriStar's application, and in doing so it set forth what it considered to be the proper analytical framework for analyzing the competitive effects of a vertical merger, at least in the motion picture business. The Department of Justice's approach was derived from its analysis of Clayton Act cases and its own 1984 Merger Guidelines,[17] and might be described as a six-part test, consisting of the following elements:

First, did the contemplated relief—in this case, permitting TriStar to show its films in Loews theaters—significantly foreclose other exhibitors from access to motion pictures or access on competitive terms?

Second, did the contemplated relief significantly foreclose other distributors from access to theaters, or a substantial portion of them?

Third, if actual competitors of TriStar and Loews are not likely to be foreclosed, did the requested relief nonetheless effectively force actual or potential competitors to enter or continue in the distribution or exhibition business on a vertically integrated basis?

Fourth, if vertical integration is effectively required, how difficult is it to achieve?

Fifth, if vertical integration is required, and if there are "significant barriers" to such integration, is the market "otherwise conducive to noncompetitive performance?" According to the government, "[i]n a market not otherwise conducive to single firm market power or coordination among several firms ... even significant increases in barriers to entry are unlikely to affect competitive market performance adversely."[18]

Sixth, and finally: Does the vertical merger have offsetting positive benefits for the economy by creating efficiencies?

---
[17] 2 Trade Reg. Rep. (CCH) ¶ 4490.
[18] Brief of Department of Justice at 15.

The government seemed to have no trouble concluding that actual competitors of TriStar and Loews were not likely to be foreclosed by letting these firms operate on a vertically integrated basis. Indeed, the Antitrust Division went so far as to state that it believed that "competition in distribution or exhibition would not be unreasonably restrained, even if TriStar and Loews dealt exclusively with one another...."[19] This is an interesting observation for the government to have made, since that question was not even before the court.

Nor, apparently, was the government concerned that future entry into or expansion in the market might have to occur on an integrated basis. According to the government, even if the relief sought by TriStar and Loews was granted, "a substantial amount of unintegrated exhibition and distribution capacity would be available in all the relevant markets and ... integrated entry would therefore not be required."[20]

Given these views, the government's analysis did not even require resort to assessment of the last three elements of the government's six-prong test: (1) ease of integration, (2) whether the market was conducive to concentration of economic power, and (3) whether any beneficial results would flow from the proposed vertical integration.

Based on this analysis, the government concluded that the relief sought would "neither create market power in TriStar or Loews, nor significantly enhance the ability of distributors and exhibitors collectively to exercise market power."[21] Interestingly, the government was not concerned, at least so it seemed, that market power should be presumed from the fact that the product involved, namely, motion pictures, was copyrighted. Additionally, in assessing market power, the government did not take into account whether videocassettes should be included in the relevant market. Videocassettes are now becoming available in the marketplace much more quickly after the release of films to theaters, and in some cases, films are apparently released simultaneously to theaters and via videocassette distribution. This particular issue is likely to be a hotly contested issue in future analysis of market power in the motion picture industry. Suffice it to say that, in the TriStar case, the Antitrust Division was satisfied without the need to expand market definition to include videocassettes that the relief requested by TriStar and Loews would not create any dangerous market power.

Although the government relied on an assessment of market share in evaluating the effect of the proposed relief, its analysis reflects a sharp

---
[19] *Id.* at 17.
[20] *Id.* at 18.
[21] *Id.*

focus on the perceived economic effects of the practice in the marketplace as it currently exists and as it seems to be developing.

The next hearing on TriStar's application may reveal that the government is willing to endorse a future application by TriStar and Loews to permit dealings between these firms free of the conduct restrictions to which they are currently bound. If so, this may reflect a willingness by the government to reexamine the entertainment industry as it exists today, rather than to assume that it continues to operate as it did when the *Paramount* decrees were originally imposed. This view may already have been expressed to some extent by the government's support of TriStar's request to be relieved of the conduct provisions in its dealings with other exhibitors. In that context, the government noted that certain of the conduct provisions entered against the original Paramount defendants, such as franchise agreements, are not necessarily anticompetitive. While the original participants in the Paramount conspiracy may have needed so-called "fencing in" with provisions of this type, companies that were not involved, such as TriStar, do not.

Presumably, the business practices of these firms will be assessed against the realistic economic effects in today's evolving market. Logically, the same standard should come to apply to all firms in the entertainment market as the passage of time casts doubt on any notion that the original Paramount defendants are more likely than other firms to operate anticompetitively in today's entertainment environment.

In granting the TriStar and Loews motion, Judge Palmieri observed that, in agreeing to be bound by the licensing injunctions in its dealings with Loews, TriStar has made an appropriate concession. Judge Palmieri also responded to the claims of certain exhibitor amici who opposed the application by telling the Justice Department—and this has received considerable media attention in the entertainment industry—that it should give "serious consideration to these complaints" by these exhibitors, who contended that some of the original *Paramount* defendants were violating the conduct provisions, "and act vigorously to vindicate their rights if the complaints are valid."[22] The Antitrust Division has publicly indicated that it will look into this and is prepared to act on Judge Palmieri's direction.

At this time, it does not appear that Judge Palmieri is abandoning the *Paramount* decrees, notwithstanding a liberalizing trend and apparent recognition of the current economic realities in the entertainment industry. Clearly, this is a business that is changing; it is equally clear that

---

[22] Order of Judge Palmieri, June 18, 1987.

the changes in the business will influence future legal developments. As to what those legal developments will be, I am reminded of what Professor Bickel said in another context, that you will all have to remember the future, imagine the past, and act accordingly.[23]

III. DEVELOPMENTS IN ANTITRUST PRINCIPLES CONCERNING PROFESSIONAL SPORTS LEAGUES

When horizontal business competitors agree not to compete against one another and to that end allocate marketing territories and/or customers, their agreements ordinarily constitute classic cartel arrangements and are routinely condemned.[24] However, when the parties to such an agreement are combined by contract into a partnership or other form of lawful joint venture, it should be evident that different rules apply.[25]

A number of decisions in the sports field demonstrate, however, that when non-price agreements among the members of an integrated joint venture such as a sports league are put in issue, confusion reigns and the principles are not so clear.

Professor Areeda has commented that the courts have not developed "comprehensible guides to 'reasonableness'" in reviewing sports league agreements under Section 1 of the Sherman Act. Judges and juries often "venture beyond competition into management discretion" in such cases because the existing "substantive rules" do not guide judges or juries "very reliably or consistently."[26]

There are four decisions that illustrate this point. The first is the Ninth Circuit's decision earlier this year in *National Basketball Association v. San Diego Clippers*,[27] involving the San Diego Clippers' move from San Diego to Los Angeles. The second and third are the two decisions by Ninth Circuit panels issued in mid-1986 and in 1984 in the litigation surrounding the move of the Oakland Raiders from Oakland to Los Angeles, *Los Angeles Memorial Coliseum Commission v. National Football League*.[28] The fourth is the 1986 opinion of the District of Columbia Circuit, written

---

[23] A. BICKEL, THE SUPREME COURT AND THE IDEA OF PROGRESS 102 et seq. (1970).
[24] See, e.g., National Soc'y of Prof'l Eng'rs v. United States, 435 U.S. 679, 692 (1978).
[25] As to price restrictions, see, e.g., Broadcast Music. Inc. v. Columbia Broadcasting System, Inc., 441 U.S. 1 (1979); National Bancard Corp. (NABANCO) v. VISA, U.S.A., Inc., 779 F.2d 592 (11th Cir.), cert. denied, 107 S. Ct. 328 (1986).
[26] 7 P. AREEDA, ANTITRUST LAW ¶ 1478 at 359 (1986).
[27] National Basketball Ass'n v. SDC Basketball Club, Inc., 815 F.2d 562 (9th Cir. 1987).
[28] 726 F.2d 1381 (9th Cir.), cert. denied, 469 U.S. 990 (1984); 791 F.2d 1356 (9th Cir. 1986) (opinion on damages).

by Judge Bork, in *Rothery Storage & Van Co. v. Atlas Van Lines*,[24] which involved agreements among the members of an enterprise integrated by contract

In early 1980, the Raiders were operating in the Bay Area alongside the San Francisco Forty-Niners, when they announced that they would unilaterally move to Los Angeles. The Raiders' agreement with the other NFL teams was that they would present NFL football in Oakland, not elsewhere. The NFL Constitution provides for League decision-making on the relocation of member clubs, and specifically states that no member club may "transfer its franchise or playing site to a different city" without approval by a vote of three-fourths of the members of the League.[30] The League disapproved the Raiders' announced move under this by-law provision.

The case was bifurcated, with issues of liability to be tried first and then, if the Raiders prevailed, a later trial would be held on damages. In the second trial of the violation issues (the first having ended in a hung jury and a mistrial), the jury found that the NFL's decision requiring the Raiders to adhere to their agreement and to continue to operate in Oakland was an unreasonable restraint in violation of Section 1, with the jury apparently finding that the League's decision unreasonably restrained potential competition between the Raiders and the Los Angeles Rams in the Los Angeles area.[51]

On appeal, a divided Ninth Circuit panel affirmed.[52] The panel majority held that the issue was properly submitted to the jury under the rule of reason as it has been elaborated in *Professional Engineers*[53] and in *Chicago Board of Trade*.[54] While so holding, however, the majority of the panel reached some interesting conclusions: First, it said, "The NFL teams are not true competitors, nor can they be."[55] Second, it said that the NFL was an exceptional and unique horizontally integrated enterprise to which it is difficult to apply standard antitrust principles.[56]

With respect to the League agreement on the location of teams, the panel majority concluded that "the agreement creating the NFL is valid and the territorial divisions therein are ancillary to its main purpose of

---

[24] 792 F.2d 210 (D.C. Cir. 1986), *cert. denied*, 107 S. Ct. 880 (1987).
[30] National Football League Const. & By-Laws § 4.3 (quoted at 726 F.2d at 1385 n.1).
[51] 726 F.2d at 1395.
[52] *Id*.
[53] National Soc'y of Prof'l Eng'rs v. United States, 435 U.S. 679 (1978).
[54] Chicago Bd. of Trade v. United States, 246 U.S. 231 (1918).
[55] 726 F.2d at 1391.
[56] *Id*. at 1394, 1404.

producing NFL football."[37] The panel majority further concluded that "the nature of NFL football requires some territorial restrictions in order both to encourage participation in the venture and to secure each venturer the legitimate fruits of that participation."[38]

With respect to ancillary restraints, the Ninth Circuit rejected the League's contention that the agreement on team location was inherent in the League's joint venture structure and, therefore, lawful as a matter of law as an ancillary restraint.[39] Reliance on ancillary restraints, said the Ninth Circuit, was "inventive," but this was described as a little used area of antitrust law.[40]

The majority further found the jury's verdict warranted because the League had failed to observe procedural safeguards in evaluating the Raiders' move. It thus concluded that "some sort of procedural mechanism . . . may also be necessary, including an opportunity for the team proposing the move to present its case."[41]

More than the result itself, the majority's analysis of antitrust principles is of interest.

First, the panel reasoned that, since the NFL teams were legally separate entities, the League by-law provision on the movement of teams was a combination or conspiracy under Section 1. The League could, thus not be regarded as a unitary actor or as a single economic enterprise.[42] For this conclusion, the panel relied on the Supreme Court's intra-enterprise conspiracy decisions,[43] which were subsequently overruled in *Copperweld*.[44]

Second, the panel majority reasoned that the pro- and anticompetitive effects of the League's by-law could be assessed under standard rule of reason principles. For this, it reasoned by analogy to decisions such as *Sealy* and *Topco*.[45]

Finally, as already suggested, the majority relied upon the antitrust procedural due process analysis that had emerged from the Supreme

---

[37] *Id.* at 1395.
[38] *Id.* at 1396 (emphasis added).
[39] *Id*
[40] *Id.* at 1395.
[41] *Id.* at 1397.
[42] *Id.* at 1387–90.
[43] Perma Life Mufflers, Inc. v. International Parts Corp., 392 U.S. 134 (1968); Timken Roller Bearing Co. v. United States, 341 U.S. 593 (1951).
[44] Copperweld Corp. v. Independence Tube Corp., 467 U.S. 752 (1984).
[45] United States v. Topco Assocs., Inc., 405 U.S. 596 (1972); United States v. Sealy, Inc., 388 U.S. 350 (1967).

Court's decision in *Silver v. New York Stock Exchange*[16] and certain lower court decisions. These decisions were effectively wiped from the books by the Supreme Court's subsequent decision in *Northwest Wholesale Stationers*.[17]

With these points in mind, let me turn to the second *Raiders* decision[18] and then to the *San Diego Clippers* case,[19] which was decided in April of this year.

In the second *Raiders* case, the damages trial resulted in judgments for the Raiders and the Los Angeles Coliseum totaling approximately $50 million after trebling. On appeal, the Ninth Circuit did three things: (1) it affirmed the judgment for the Coliseum; (2) it vacated the Raiders' antitrust judgment, remanding for a determination of what it called the windfall benefit that the Raiders received by seizing the League's opportunity to franchise a second team in Los Angeles; and (3) it reversed a judgment for the Raiders on a pendent state law claim that the League had dealt with the Raiders unfairly and in bad faith. Cross petitions for certiorari are now pending in the Supreme Court.[50]

In the second opinion, the court of appeals made it even clearer that the NFL's agreement on the location of teams was not the action of competitors, but of co-owners of a jointly held property right. It ruled that "the NFL as a whole owned the right to expand into the Los Angeles area."[51] Accordingly, when the League would place an expansion team in Los Angeles or any other city, the League would be entitled to charge "the new expansion owner for the expansion opportunity."[52]

In spite of these further conclusions about the legitimate joint property rights of the members of the League, the court adhered to its prior ruling that the League's decision had been an unlawful trade restraining decision in keeping the Raiders from competing with the Rams in the Los Angeles market.[53]

---

[16] Silver v. New York Stock Exchange, 373 U.S. 341 (1963).
[17] Northwest Wholesale Stationers v. Pacific Stationery & Printing Co., 472 U.S. 284 (1985).
[18] 791 F.2d 1356 (9th Cir. 1986).
[19] 815 F.2d 562 (9th Cir. 1987).
[50] Los Angeles Raiders v. National Football League, No. 86-1968; National Football League v. Oakland Raiders, Ltd., No. 86-1972. Both petitions have since been denied. 56 U.S.L.W. 3243 (Oct. 6, 1987).
[51] 791 F.2d at 1371.
[52] *Id.*
[53] *Id.* at 1369.

Now, in 1987, comes the *Clippers* case. In its essentials the issues in *Clippers* are indistinguishable from those raised in the *Raiders* case. A League team wanted unilaterally to move from a city, this time San Diego, to Los Angeles. The League team would operate alongside another League team, this time the Lakers. The NBA allowed the Clippers to move, but sued for a declaration that it was entitled to compensation from the Clippers for the difference in value between the San Diego NBA franchise and a second Los Angeles NBA franchise. The district court concluded that the result was controlled by the decisions in the *Raiders* case, granted summary judgment for the Clippers, and dismissed the NBA's complaint.

The Ninth Circuit, in April, reversed and reinstated the NBA's complaint.[51] In doing so, the Ninth Circuit said again that the teams in a sports league "are not true competitors, nor can they be." This time, however, the remaining analysis of *Raiders I* was either ignored or rejected. With respect to procedural due process, the court explained that this had not been the basis of the *Raiders* decision, although the opinion does not so state.[52] It seems evident that the Supreme Court's intervening decision in *Northwest Wholesalers* made the procedural due process theory less than compelling.

Second, in *Clippers*, the panel did not discuss or rely on the intra-enterprise conspiracy cases, which is not surprising, since they may no longer be on the books in the wake of *Copperweld*.

Finally, in *Clippers*, the panel made no mention of *Sealy* or *Topco*, for reasons which one can only surmise.

So, what is the law now and where is it heading?

As to what it is, with some risk of understatement, I will say it is unsatisfactory. In trying to counsel a client as to what is permissible in a professional sports league, you cannot be confident of any advice.

The NBA tried to meet the Ninth Circuit's criticisms of the NFL transfer rule by adopting elaborate procedural mechanisms, including hearings, and written objective standards to guide decisions and to identify the basis on which moves would be approved or disapproved. After doing so, it learned that procedural due process was apparently irrelevant to the antitrust analysis.

Before commenting on where the law is going or may be going, it is worth observing the anomaly of these decisions in terms of the purposes

---
[51] 815 F.2d 562 (9th Cir. 1987).
[52] *Id.* at 568.

of the antitrust laws, which are to protect, promote, and encourage true business competition.[55] It is anomalous that parties that are not true competitors, nor can they be, and that have a legitimate joint property interest in the location of their business units can nonetheless have their joint decisions on the location of such units found unlawfully to restrain required competition.

Moreover, the notion of restraint of competition that emerges in these cases tends to turn antitrust on its head. The suggestion in the cases is that if two teams in a single market will not hurt each other financially, then the League must permit the move into that market; but, if two teams in a market will hurt each other financially, then the League can block the move. Reduced to simple terms, the standard is this: If the two teams do not compete and if customers will not switch, then it is an illegal restraint on competition to prevent them from being in the market; if the two teams will compete and customers may switch, then it is legal to prevent them from both being there and competing.

A related point is relevant to *Professional Engineers*, which talks about net anticompetitive effects under the rule of reason. In cases like these it is very difficult to analyze the net anticompetitive effects. The NFL started with two teams competing in the Bay Area and a one-team market in southern California. It was said to be illegal to continue that location of teams, that what was required was two teams in a market in southern California and a one-team market in northern California. The net elimination of competition is difficult to fathom when the two markets are examined in the aggregate.

The need for clarification is illustrated by testimony of the Antitrust Division before Congress. There the Division expressed the view that decisions under League relocation rules "should be deemed per se lawful."[57] The Division urged that antitrust "courts should defer" to League decisions under rules of this type, at least if they were made in a bona fide fashion, because "the League's choice is highly likely to be procompetitive or competitively neutral" and "because of the difficulty of assessing the net competitive effects in the two cities involved."[58] While this statement describes why the rule of reason does not provide a workable test, it does not state a test of legality, and the Division did not cite any case authority for its view.

---

[55] *See, e.g.*, Parker v. Brown, 317 U.S. 341, 351 (1943); Apex Hosiery Co. v. Leader, 310 U.S. 469 (1940); Appalachian Coals, Inc. v. United States, 288 U.S. 344, 359–60 (1933).
[57] *Hearings on S. 298 before the Senate Committee on the Judiciary*, 99th Cong., 1st Sess. 379, 390 (1985) (testimony of Charles F. Rule).
[58] *Id.* at 388–90.

As to where the law is heading, the principles of ancillary restraints may offer a solution. Judge Bork's decision in *Rothery* is suggestive of this approach.[59] In *Rothery*, the court examined the status under Section 1 of an agreement among separate members of an interstate trucking system not to compete against the members of the system.[60] The affiliated trucking companies were parties to an enterprise that Judge Bork said was "identical in economic terms to a partnership formed by agreement"[61] — it was a contract integration. The contracts provided that no member could use the facilities and the name of the joint venture to compete against the members of the venture. It was, in short, an agreement limiting intra-venture competition in the sale of the product, as in the *Rothery* case.

The D.C. Circuit held that the integration was lawful and that the restraint on competition between members of the venture was "ancillary to the integration [and]... should also be lawful."[62] As Judge Bork made clear in that opinion, this ancillary restraints analysis was based directly on Judge Taft's analysis in the *Addyston Pipe* case.[63]

The applicability of *Addyston Pipe*'s ancillary restraint analysis to sports leagues formed one of the bases of then Justice Rehnquist's dissent from the denial of certiorari in an NFL case involving cross-league ownership.[64] There, Justice Rehnquist first relied upon the Court's decision in *BMI-ASCAP*[65] in analyzing joint production within the NFL: he stated that "NFL football is a different product from what the NFL teams could offer independently" and that the NFL has "made a market in which individual [teams] are inherently unable to compete fully effectively."[66] *Addyston Pipe* was thus dispositive: the challenged league agreement was "a covenant by joint venturers who produce a single product not to compete with one another."[67] Accordingly, the agreement challenged in that case could not be analyzed under general rule of reason standards as if the NFL members were horizontal competitors.

---

[59] Rothery Storage & Van Co., v. Atlas Van Lines, Inc., 792 F.2d 210 (D.C. Cir. 1986), cert. denied, 107 S. Ct. 880 (1987).
[60] *Id.* at 217.
[61] *Id.*
[62] *Id.* at 230 n.11.
[63] United States v. Addyston Pipe & Steel Co., 85 F. 271 (6th Cir. 1898), aff'd as modified, 175 U.S. 211 (1899).
[64] National Football League v. North American Soccer League, 459 U.S. 1074 (1982) (Rehnquist, J., dissenting from denial of certiorari).
[65] Broadcast Music, Inc. v. Columbia Broadcasting System, Inc., 441 U.S. 1 (1979).
[66] National Football League v. North American Soccer League, 459 U.S. 1074, 1077 (1982).
[67] *Id.*

The conflict between the Ninth Circuit's approach in these cases and the D.C. Circuit's decision in *Rothery* is striking For the Ninth Circuit, ancillary restraints principles were inventive and little used; for Judge Bork, and perhaps for Judge Easterbrook in the *Polk Brothers* case in the Seventh Circuit,[68] ancillary restraints are alive and well. Judge Bork concluded that the intra-venture agreement was lawful because ancillary to a lawful contract. In addition, while the Ninth Circuit decision in *Raiders* was heavily influenced by *Sealy* and *Topco*, Judge Bork in *Rothery* considered both of these cases to have been effectively overruled,[69] which is a position that spokesmen for the Antitrust Division have also put forth.[70]

It will be necessary at some point for the Supreme Court to review and clarify the law as to joint ventures, such as sports leagues and similar organizations that are integrated by contract. At present, the cases are in conflict, and there is little in the way of predictability.

IV. DEVELOPMENTS IN THE ANTITRUST-LABOR EXEMPTION IN SPORTS

During the past two decades there have been a series of decisions involving the scope of the non-statutory labor exemption in professional sports leagues. While some of the initial suits were pending, the issue was addressed in a seminal article in the *Yale Law Journal* by then Professor Ralph Winter.[71] Winter expressed the view that the antitrust laws would essentially be supplanted by the labor laws in their application to terms and conditions of professional athlete employment by reason of the unionization of professional athletes.

A year later in its decision in *Flood v. Kuhn*,[72] the Supreme Court rejected a player challenge of the baseball reserve clause, reaffirming its earlier decision that major league baseball is not subject to the Sherman Act. In dissent, Justice Marshall stated that baseball should be subject to the Sherman Act and that the dispositive issue might well be whether baseball employment terms and conditions qualified for the labor exemption to the antitrust laws.[73] In offering this suggestion, Justice Marshall cited Professor Winter's *Yale Law Journal* article.[74]

---

[68] Polk Brothers, Inc. v. Forest City Enters., Inc., 776 F.2d 185 (7th Cir. 1985).
[69] 792 F.2d at 226.
[70] Rule, *The Administration's View of Joint Ventures*, 54 ANTITRUST L.J. 1121, 1123 (1985).
[71] Jacobs & Winter, *supra* note 2.
[72] Flood v. Kuhn, 407 U.S. 258 (1972).
[73] *Id.* at 293-96 (Marshall, J., dissenting).
[74] 407 U.S. at 295 n.8.

Thereafter, the scope of the labor exemption was litigated in professional basketball, football, and hockey. In two opinions involving interleague competition in basketball and hockey, the courts held that the challenged practices of the established league with respect to players did not qualify for the labor exemption.[75] In each case, the principal effect of the employment practices related to business competition between the two leagues in business markets, not to restraints on competition for employee services in a labor market.

Subsequently, the labor market issue was directly addressed in three leading decisions—two by the Eighth Circuit in NFL cases and one by the Sixth Circuit in an NHL case.[76] In *Mackey v. National Football League*,[77] the Eighth Circuit fashioned a three-part test from earlier Supreme Court decisions on the labor exemption, particularly the Court's 1965 decision in the *Jewel Tea* case:[78] (1) the trade restraint must primarily affect only the parties to the collective bargaining agreement; (2) the agreement must concern a mandatory subject of bargaining; and (3) the agreement must be the product of bona fide arm's length collective bargaining.[79]

While a number of scholars thereafter addressed these issues, there were few significant court decisions until early this year—when the Second Circuit issued an important labor exemption ruling in a case involving the NBA.[80]

The Second Circuit's decision, in *Wood v. National Basketball Ass'n*,[81] is of broad significance because it analyzes the labor exemption in terms fundamentally different from the earlier decisions, and it provides an approach for analyzing some difficult labor exemption issues that are on the horizon in professional sports. The decision is also of interest because its author is now Judge Winter, the same author of the 1971 *Yale Law Journal* article.

---

[75] Robertson v. National Basketball Ass'n, 389 F. Supp. 867 (S.D.N.Y. 1975); Philadelphia World Hockey Club, Inc. v Philadelphia Hockey Club, 351 F. Supp. 462 (E.D Pa. 1972).
[76] McCourt v. California Sports, Inc., 600 F.2d 1193 (6th Cir. 1979); Reynolds v. National Football League, 584 F.2d 280 (8th Cir. 1978); Mackey v. National Football League, 543 F.2d 606 (8th Cir. 1976), cert. dismissed, 434 U.S. 801 (1977).
[77] 543 F.2d 606 (8th Cir. 1976), cert. dismissed, 434 U.S. 801 (1977).
[78] Amalgamated Meat Cutters v. Jewel Tea, 381 U.S. 676 (1965).
[79] 543 F.2d at 614.
[80] Wood v. National Basketball Ass'n, 809 F.2d 954 (2d Cir. 1987). A recent NFL case, Zimmerman v. National Football League, 632 F. Supp. 398 (D.D.C. 1986), is also of some interest because it carefully considers whether an identifiable quid pro quo must be found in order to conclude that a provision of a collective bargaining agreement is exempt from antitrust challenge.
[81] 809 F.2d 954 (2d Cir. 1987).

In *Wood*, a talented rookie player challenged certain provisions of the collective bargining agreement between the NBA, its teams, and the NBA players union, including the provisions authorizing the league to hold its draft of college players and requiring league teams to operate under certain "salary caps." Wood contended that these provisions had sharply reduced his salary; that they were horizontal agreements among competitors to eliminate competition for the services of basketball players; and that they were per se violations of Section 1.[82]

The Second Circuit assumed (1) that Wood would have obtained more favorable salary terms without the draft and salary cap and (2) that the challenged agreements would violate the antitrust laws "in the absence of a collective bargaining *relationship*" between the NBA teams and the NBA players union.[83] The Second Circuit held that the challenged employment terms were entirely lawful under the labor laws and exempt from antitrust challenge.[84]

This holding itself is not surprising. The challenged employment terms were set forth in a valid collective bargaining agreement and many decisions, including the NHL *McCourt* decision,[85] hold such agreements to be exempt from antitrust challenge.[86]

Nonetheless, the *Wood* decision is a very significant development, since it outlines a labor exemption concept broader than that found in any earlier decision. As Judge Winter put it, 'Virtually all of the courts that have addressed the present issues have reached a conclusion similar to ours, *although on somewhat different grounds*.'"[87] That is a considerable understatement.

While the earlier decisions put great emphasis on the need for an agreement negotiated at arm's length (relying on the Supreme Court's decision in the *Jewel Tea* case), Judge Winter regarded *Jewel Tea* as essentially irrelevant, rejecting its application as follows: "[T]hese cases are so clearly distinguishable that they need not detain us. Each of the decisions involved injuries to *employers* who asserted that they were being excluded from competition in the product market."[88]

---

[82] *Id.* at 958.
[83] *Id.* at 958–59.
[84] *Id.* at 962–63.
[85] McCourt v. California Sports, Inc., 600 F.2d 1193 (6th Cir 1979).
[86] *See also* Reynolds v. National Football League, 564 F.2d 280 (8th Cir. 1978).
[87] 809 F.2d at 962 n.6. (emphasis added).
[88] *Id.* at 963 (emphasis in original).

While this may seem obvious, it is a radical new insight in a sports labor market case. A court of appeals—guided by a labor law expert—has recognized that *Jewel Tea* required a *balancing of antitrust and labor concerns* because of product market effects that do not exist in cases such as *Wood*.[89]

In this respect and others, the Second Circuit's reasoning—its analysis of the labor statutes, of the authorities that are relevant, and of the authorities that are not relevant—properly identifies the doctrinal basis of the labor exemption.

In the Second Circuit's analysis, the fact of an arm's length bargaining agreement clearly is not the dispositive consideration; it is almost beside the point. Where product market competition is constrained, as in *Jewel Tea*, the fact of a union-management agreement and the character of the bargaining leading to the agreement are relevant in assessing whether the restraint is merely a union-approved cover for management.

In contrast, in the typical sports league case, where the challenged restraints only affect competition in the labor market for player services, such considerations are of little or no moment. For this reason, the Second Circuit found other factors to be dispositive: (1) the "collective bargaining *relationship*" between the NBA employers and the union;[90] (2) the statutory function of the union as the exclusive bargaining representative of all its members;[91] and (3) the federal labor policy of freedom of contract between the parties to collective bargaining agreements.[92] As to this latter point, the court stated:

> Freedom of contract is particularly important in the context of collective bargaining between professional athletes and their leagues. Such bargaining relationships raise numerous problems with little or no precedent in standard industrial relations. As a result, leagues and player unions may reach seemingly unfamiliar or strange agreements. If courts were to intrude and to outlaw such solutions, leagues and their player unions would have to arrange their affairs in a less efficient way. It would also increase the chances of strikes by reducing the number and quality of possible compromises.[93]

---

[89] The analytical approach of Judge Winter reflects his own considerable understanding of the federal labor laws, labor policy, and the purposes of the labor statutes. In its essential elements, the *Wood* opinion also reflects the approach of preeminent labor law experts, such as former Justice Arthur Goldberg, who brought his labor law experience to bear in urging a broad labor exemption in his concurring opinion in the *Jewel Tea* case. *See* 381 U.S. at 676, 697-735 (1965) (Goldberg, J., concurring).

[90] 809 F.2d at 959.

[91] *Id.*

[92] *Id.* at 961.

[93] *Id.*

This analysis has important implications for the major labor exemption issue that remains to be settled in professional sports (and perhaps other entertainment industries): whether collectively bargained terms of employment continue to be exempt from antitrust challenge even after the formal expiration of the bargaining agreement establishing the employment terms.

In both the NBA and the NFL, collective bargaining negotiations are currently in progress. In both leagues, collective bargaining agreements have "expired" or will shortly reach their formal expiration dates. At least in the NFL, there have been reports of possible antitrust litigation challenging the post-expiration operation of employment terms previously bargained between the teams and the union.

The Second Circuit's analysis in *Wood* plainly suggests that the labor exemption would not expire or lapse immediately upon formal expiration of a collective bargaining agreement. All of the federal labor statutes and policies identified by Judge Winter—exclusive bargaining representative, freedom of contract, avoidance of strikes, maximizing the solutions that can be developed in collective bargaining, encouraging good faith bargaining on mandatory subjects, and other considerations—support the conclusion that employment terms and conditions remain exempt from antitrust challenge even after formal expiration of a collective bargaining agreement.

When a union-management collective bargaining *relationship* exists, what is exempt from antitrust review are the subjects of collective bargaining and the bargaining process, not merely agreements reached through such bargaining.

NATIONAL FOOTBALL LEAGUE

Paul Tagliabue
Commissioner

February 13, 1996

The Honorable Henry Hyde
2110 Rayburn Bldg.
Independence and S. Capitol St., SW
Washington, D.C. 20515

Dear Congressman Hyde,

We are pleased to enclose a copy of the <u>Interim Agreement</u> reached last week between the City of Cleveland and the NFL.

We believe the agreement resolves a unique set of issues. It is a compromise on both sides, but it preserves the Cleveland Browns tradition, history and heritage for the citizens of Cleveland and Northeast Ohio. It also restores an NFL team in Baltimore.

We also hope that you will support legislation regarding a limited exemption for sport leagues' internal business decisions on proposed franchise relocations. While we have resolved the Browns matter, we continue to face threatened moves by the Seattle Seahawks and others.

I appreciated the opportunity to appear before your Judiciary Committee on February 6. As I testified that day, the NFL needs to decide these matters as a League without the continual threat of antitrust litigation and treble damages.

I hope we can discuss a legislative approach in person later this month.

Sincerely,

Paul Tagliabue

PAUL TAGLIABUE

encl:
PT/bhc

410 Park Avenue, New York, New York 10022   (212) 758-1500   FAX (212) 758-1742

2/8/96

INTERIM AGREEMENT

This interim agreement will be the basis for a final, written agreement ("Agreement") to be prepared on or before February 23, 1996 and thereafter signed and delivered by the City and the NFL as a binding and enforceable agreement pursuant to appropriate authorizing resolutions to be adopted on or before March 8, 1996.

- In consideration of binding NFL commitments that an NFL franchise will be located in Cleveland and that the NFL will make the contributions for construction costs as described below, Cleveland will construct a new stadium to be available for League play for the 1999 NFL season at the latest.

- The new stadium will be owned by the people of the City of Cleveland.

- NFL will deliver to Cleveland, no later than the first season of play that a new stadium is constructed, an expansion franchise or existing franchise from another city. The first season of play will be the first full season after stadium completion.

- NFL will make every effort to notify Cleveland no later than November 15, 1997 if it elects to provide Cleveland a franchise by expansion.

- If an existing team is to be relocated to Cleveland, NFL will notify the City of the identity of the team in sufficient time to permit the team to play the 1999 season. However, even if the NFL does not notify Cleveland by November 15, 1997, of its intention to provide Cleveland with an expansion franchise, the NFL will award an expansion franchise to Cleveland for play in the 1999 season if a suitable team for relocation is not identified by the NFL to Cleveland in time to play in the 1999 season.

- If an existing team is to be relocated to Cleveland, NFL must determine in its sole discretion that the relocation is justified based on application of the NFL relocation criteria. The City communicated its position to the NFL that it is opposed to relocation of a team that is supported by its home city through fan loyalty and competitive economic support. Moreover, in no event will the City accept, nor will the NFL permit, the relocation of an existing team in breach of that team's extant lease obligations without the consent of the host city.

- Upon execution of this Interim Agreement, Cleveland will not negotiate or enter into agreements with other owners of NFL franchises to relocate their franchises to Cleveland.

- Assuming a project budget of up to $220MM for construction of a new open-air stadium (inclusive of all soft costs, including architect, engineering and construction manager fees, contingency and financing costs), City will fund $182 MM from public sources, Cleveland Tomorrow will fund $10MM and NFL will fund the balance up to $220MM. In the event the project budget exceeds $220 MM: NFL will fund first $10MM increase over $220MM; City and NFL will share equally the funding of any increases between $230MM and $250MM; and City will fund any increases over $250MM.

- Sources of the public funds for construction will be: $140MM from proceeds of a tax-exempt borrowing (inclusive of investment earnings on unexpended proceeds during construction); $6MM from City utilities; $3M from RTA; and 15% of the project budget from the State.

- The City will make deposits to a Capital Repair Fund for the stadium in the amounts set forth in the City's 11/8/95 proposal to the Cleveland Browns except that the following amounts may be redirected to pay costs of construction of the new stadium, as follows. In the event the project budget for the new stadium exceeds $230MM but does not exceed $240MM, up to $5MM may be taken from the Capital Repair Fund deposits to fund the City's contribution to the incremental costs over $230MM. In the event the project budget for the new stadium exceeds $240MM, up to an additional $2MM may be taken from the Capital Repair Fund deposits to fund a portion of the City's contribution to the incremental costs over $240MM, with the balance of the City's obligation to be funded by State appropriations or other available public funds.

- NFL currently anticipates funding its contribution from a variety of sources, including premium seating. However, its contribution will be an obligation of the NFL and will not be conditioned on marketing to, or collection from, other parties.

- In the event permanent seat licenses (PSLs) are marketed to fund the NFL's contribution to costs of construction of the new stadium, special consideration shall be given in the terms of any PSL program for long-time season ticket holders, and PSLs will not be utilized for seating in a new Dawg Pound of approximately 10,000 seats. All net proceeds from the sale of any PSLs must be applied to costs of construction of the stadium. Any such PSL program will be structured to ensure that the stadium is funded in the most efficient manner. If PSLs are marketed and amounts in excess of $35MM are collected from that marketing, any amounts in excess of $35MM will be applied to reduce the City's contribution to costs of construction of the new stadium. Consideration will be given by the City to using such amounts to replenish any amounts in the Capital Repair Fund redirected to pay costs of construction.

- The NFL Executive Committee will adopt a resolution authorizing the NFL to enter into the Agreement specifically stating that unless specific revenue streams are committed to funding the NFL's contribution under the Agreement, the amount of the NFL's contribution will be a League assessment (or, in the event that committed revenue streams do not fully fund the contribution, the amount of the shortfall will be a League assessment) and setting forth a payment schedule under which (i) the first $5MM of the NFL's contribution will be paid in cash as a lump sum on or before April 15, 1996, to be used, together with an advance from Cleveland Tomorrow of $5MM of its $10MM to be paid following expenditure of the NFL's $5MM contribution, to fund architect and engineering services relating to the design of the new stadium, (ii) upon the successful marketing of premium seating at the levels described in the Agreement, another $5MM will be contributed by the NFL to reimburse Cleveland Tomorrow for its $5MM advance; and (iii) the balance of the NFL's contribution (determined as of the date the City ascertains the guaranteed price of the general contract for construction) will be paid in cash as a lump sum on or before the date the City enters into a contract for construction of the facility.

- In the event that the City publicly markets securities to fund its financial contribution to the costs of construction prior to the date the guaranteed price of the general contract for construction is determined, the NFL will provide a letter of credit or other credit facility to evidence and secure its financial contribution to the costs of construction provided that the credit facility will provide that it cannot be drawn upon until the premium seating condition to the NFL's funding obligations (described below) has been satisfied or waived by the NFL.

- If for any unforeseen reason the project does not go forward and the NFL has funded any of the architectural and engineering services to develop design drawings for the stadium, the NFL will be the sole owner of the design drawings and any unexpended funds contributed by the NFL will be returned to the NFL.

- Amounts contributed by the NFL for construction will be deposited in a segregated account and disbursed for project costs. Contributions by the NFL following the completion of the design phase of the project for costs of construction based on the $220MM budget will be disbursed pro rata with the City's contributions.

- Any change orders that increase the cost of the project above the guaranteed price of the general contract for construction awarded by the City and that are a financial obligation of the NFL (in whole or in part) are subject to joint approval by the City and the NFL.

- In the event that the costs of the stadium exceed the amount determined at the time the City enters into the general contract for construction and the price is in the range where the NFL is contributing to the payment of those additional costs, the NFL's contribution for those additional costs shall be paid in cash as a lump sum within 30 days of invoicing.

- The obligation of the NFL to contribute to the costs of construction of the new stadium (exclusive of $5MM to be applied to the costs of design development) is subject to receipt by the NFL of pledge agreements from business organizations and individuals to lease private suites and club seats in the new stadium. The Agreement will establish the percentage of suites and club seats to be secured by pledge agreements, the average term of the leases, the amount of funds to be deposited to secure the pledges and the date by which those pledge agreements are to be received by the NFL. The NFL has informed the City that it believes the sale or lease of 75% of 108 suites and 80% of 8,000 club seats at "base case" prices specified in WJC Howell's 12/7/95 study for a period of ten years represents an appropriate level of business community commitment.

- The City shall have the right to specific performance of the NFL's obligations under the Agreement to place an NFL franchise in Cleveland for play by the 1999 season and to deliver to that Cleveland NFL franchise the Cleveland Browns heritage, intellectual property and records, including without limitation, the name, uniform designs, logo, colors, trademark, tradenames, copyrights (including films, photos, artwork and publications), history, playing records, statistics, retired jerseys, trophies, memorabilia, banners and pennants and the season ticket and premium seating sales records. The NFL acknowledges and agrees that the damages incurred by the City as a result of any breach of those obligations are not readily ascertainable, that money damages or other legal relief will not adequately compensate the City for any such breach, and that the City is entitled to injunctive relief compelling the specific performance of those obligations under the Agreement.

- There will be prepared and attached to the Agreement the form of lease ("Lease") to be entered into by the NFL and the City, and assigned by the NFL to the owner of the Cleveland franchise. The Lease will contain all material terms to which the NFL and its assignee will be bound for the lease by the City of the new stadium.

- The Lease will obligate the NFL to cause the owners of the Cleveland NFL franchise to assume the obligations of the NFL under that Lease as assignee of the NFL. The Lease will be for a term of 30 years, and the lessee will agree, among other things: that the Cleveland NFL franchise will play all regular season home games in the new stadium to be constructed by the City except for not more than one special game event every two years that may be located outside of the City (e.g. international site for a regular season game); that the damages incurred by the City as a result of any breach of that agreement are not readily ascertainable; that money damages or other legal relief will not adequately compensate the City for any such breach; and that the City shall have the right to specific performance of the Cleveland NFL franchise's 30-year playing obligation and the right to enjoin the Cleveland NFL franchise from breaching that obligation.

- The Lease also will contain the terms of Cleveland's 11/8/95 proposal to the Cleveland Browns, except the City will redirect to costs of construction certain up-front payments that then had been identified to reimburse the Browns for certain capital improvements ($4MM from the 1996 Capital Repairs Fund deposit and $10MM to be loaned by Cleveland Tomorrow) and a portion of the deposits scheduled to be made to the Capital Repairs Fund after 1996 (in an aggregate amount not to exceed $3MM as described above). Those terms consist of the following:

    - No rental payments to City by team

    - Team receives revenues from all Stadium operations, including:

        - Ticket sales

- Advertising
- Food, drink and other concessions
- Novelty sales
- Private suite lease payments
- Club seat lease payments
- Team receives naming rights
- Team pays operating and maintenance expenses
- City pays property taxes
- City funds Capital Repairs Fund in amounts set forth in Cleveland's 11/8/95 proposal less the amounts described above to be used to fund the City's contribution to any costs of construction in excess of $230MM.
- Amounts in the Capital Repairs Fund will be applied solely to pay costs of capital improvements to the new stadium. In the Agreement, the NFL and the City will establish criteria and procedures for determining the timing and necessity of expenditures from the Capital Repairs Fund to maintain the stadium in an appropriate condition.
- NFL will hold the Cleveland Browns heritage, intellectual property and records in trust pending identification of, and transfer by the NFL to, the owners of Cleveland NFL franchise. That will include without limitation: the team name, uniform designs, logo, colors, trademarks, tradenames, copyrights (including films, photos, artwork and publications) the history, playing records, statistics, retired jerseys, trophies, memorabilia, banners and pennants, and all season ticket holder information and premium seating sales records.
- NFL will have access to all records of Cleveland Stadium Corp. and the Cleveland Browns Football Company relating to the operations and activities conducted at Cleveland Stadium.
- Efforts will be made to include individuals who reside in northeast Ohio among the owners of the Cleveland franchise.

- The parties contemplate that the training facilities in Berea will be available to the NFL and the Cleveland NFL franchise under terms and conditions substantially the same as the current terms and conditions enjoyed by the Modell-owned organizations.

- Cleveland will consult with the NFL concerning the architect, engineer and construction manager for the project, and Cleveland will select such firms or individuals for those services who are mutually agreeable to the City and the NFL. Such agreement shall not be unreasonably withheld. If the NFL or the City objects to the selection of a particular firm or individual, the objecting party will state the basis for its objection in writing and only objections based on the qualifications or experience of firms will be considered. The City will control construction contracting and the selection of contractors, consistent with applicable laws. The NFL may, at its own expense, retain a consultant to review construction matters and the City will cooperate with the NFL to permit access to the construction site and records by that consultant.

- The new stadium, if an open air facility, will have a natural grass playing field, approximately 72,000 seats, approximately 8,000 club seats and approximately 108 private suites. It will be a facility that can function for NFL football games and any large scale seating event typically held in an outdoor stadium (e.g., soccer, concerts, motor events). The program requirements for construction will be substantially those set forth as generic stadium guidelines by Hellmuth, Obata & Kassabaum, Inc., Sports Facilities Group in its "NFL Stadium Facility Program" dated December 15, 1994.

- The design of the new stadium will include a masonry facade acceptable to the City and the NFL and will provide for the replication of the bleacher area known as the "Dawg Pound".

- City will secure a commitment from Cleveland Tomorrow that the proceeds of its $10MM loan (that was to fund a portion of up-front payments to Modell in City's 11/8/95 proposal) may be used instead to pay costs of project design or construction of the new stadium as set forth in the Agreement.

- City may determine to construct a domed stadium or a domed multiplex facility, in lieu of an open air stadium, and apply the above-described NFL contribution to either such facility. The decision on the type of new stadium facility to be constructed must be made by the City on or before March 24, 1996.

- In the event the City constructs a domed stadium facility and meets the NFL's other site selection criteria for hosting a Super Bowl, the Commissioner will recommend Cleveland as a site for the Super Bowl.

- The City and NFL will explore the feasibility of locating in Cleveland as a permanent installation the NFL theme park known as the "NFL Experience" that has been staged in the past as a temporary installation at Super Bowl events.

- The Agreement is subject to ratification by the Executive Committee of the NFL and approval by the City Council required by the Cleveland City Charter. In order to proceed in an expeditious manner and assure the location of a team in Cleveland for the 1999 season, and to commence the design and engineering of the new stadium as soon as possible, it is necessary that final action be taken by the City of Cleveland on or before 5:00 p.m. on March 8, 1996 to ratify the Agreement and that final action be taken by the NFL on or before the annual meeting of the NFL owners on March 11, 1996, to ratify the Agreement.

- Upon the signing of this Interim Agreement by Commissioner Tagliabue and Mayor White, and approval of this Interim Agreement by the members of the NFL, the City will join with the Cleveland Browns related defendants in the pending actions in Cuyahoga County Common Pleas Court and the United States District Court for the Northern District of Ohio in seeking an immediate stay of such litigation pending completion and execution of final documents and completion of the procedures necessary to authorize the signing and delivery of the Agreement and the form of Lease as binding and enforceable agreements of the NFL and the City. Upon the completion and execution of the Agreement and the Lease and the receipt of all necessary approvals by the Executive Committee of the NFL and Cleveland City Council, and upon the execution of appropriate mutual general releases by all of the parties to the aforesaid litigation along with those Maryland persons and/or entities identified as potential defendants in the City's motion for leave to amend the Cuyahoga County Common Pleas Court action, said cases will be dismissed by the City with prejudice, costs to be borne by the defendants.

- The NFL will cause the Cleveland Browns to pay in a timely manner, to the City and to the City's legal counsel, Squire, Sanders & Dempsey, the actual City administrative costs and expenses (in an amount not to exceed $500,000) and the actual legal and other professional fees and expenses (in an amount not to exceed $1,750,000), respectively, incurred in connection with the Cleveland Browns controversies. That payment will be made within 30 days of submission of documentation evidencing the actual amounts so incurred or expended.

- The NFL will cause the Cleveland Browns to pay in a timely manner, damages to the City in the amount of $9.3MM. Payment will be made to the City in four equal annual installments of $2,325,000 on January 1 in each of the years 1997, 1998, 1999 and 2000.

This Interim Agreement is approved by the undersigned this 9th day of February, 1996.

CITY OF CLEVELAND

By: _____
Mayor Michael R. White

NATIONAL FOOTBALL LEAGUE

By: _____
Paul Tagliabue, Commissioner

LAW OFFICES OF
JOSEPH L. ALIOTO
650 CALIFORNIA STREET
TWENTY-FIFTH FLOOR
SAN FRANCISCO, CALIFORNIA 94108
(415) 434-2100
TELECOPIER (415) 434-3277

January 25, 1996

VIA FEDERAL EXPRESS - AB NO. 8327816630

Honorable Henry J. Hyde
Chairman - House Judiciary Committee
2110 Rayburn Building
Washington, D.C. 20515

Dear Congressman Hyde:

You may know that Al Davis, owner of the Oakland Raiders, and I appeared before the Senate Antitrust Committee on September 20, 1982 to argue against a concerted but unsuccessful attempt by the National Football League to secure a retroactive exemption from the antitrust laws which would have nullified our judicial victories in the Los Angeles litigation.

Since that time to the present, I have represented the Oakland Raiders in many cases, including a sneak lawsuit filed by Commissioner Tagliabue two days before our opening 1995 home game, to the surprise and consternation of many NFL owners. No approval was sought from the owners. The suit represented a rush to Court with forum-shopping motives. Only after this sneak attack did the Raiders and the City of Oakland file their suits against the National Football League. Mr. Tagliabue, without disclosing the total circumstances, had the temerity in his testimony before the Senate Judiciary Committee on November 29, 1995 to complain of the existence of this litigation!

Mr. Davis was asked by administrative assistants of Senator Strom Thurmond to appear at the hearings to discuss franchise relocation. He was compelled to decline because of the day-to-day demands of the ongoing NFL professional football season. We trust further hearings in both Houses of Congress will be held after the season to permit his appearance.

We believe this will be helpful because Commissioner Tagliabue's testimony before the Senate Committee was replete with misrepresentations, nuanced distortions and concealment of material facts. In his testimony, the Commissioner referred to the Raiders so many times, we feel compelled to write this letter.

Joseph L. Alioto

Honorable Henry J. Hyde
January 25, 1996
Page 2

The Commissioner's complaint about the "Raider lawsuit" of October 5, 1995 is a case in point. Immediately before the NFL vote on the Raiders relocation to Oakland, Mr. Davis, in unequivocal language, made crystal clear in July, 1995 to all NFL owners, that a condition of the vote permitting the Raiders' move was that the Raiders would not pay any tribute for the relocation such as had been exacted from the now St. Louis Rams. The Commissioner, both orally and in writing, told the League that the Raiders met the NFL Guidelines for Relocation. The Rams did not. The Raider move received the unanimous approval of the owners, with the conditions.

Moreover, the NFL gratuitously attached to the Resolution "authorizing" our relocation a provision that the Los Angeles area was the exclusive domain of the League and no member could undertake even an exploratory negotiation with any stadium owner or buyer in Southern California. Needless to say, we immediately dissociated ourselves from this obviously *per se* violation of the antitrust laws. Simultaneously we called attention in writing to our stated condition that the vote of the owners on July 19, 1995 carried the express condition that we would not be subjected to a monetary shakedown ala the Rams.

This covenant was breached by a surprise letter the very next day from the Commissioner, with the backing of the Finance Committee, demanding a form of tribute in the millions from both the Raiders and the City of Oakland. We promptly rejected the demand. The NFL retaliated by filing the surprise suit for millions in a Los Angeles court on August 31, 1995 - an obvious and invidious forum-shopping maneuver. Thus, the NFL started the current litigation just as they started the litigation in 1980.

Only then did we and the City of Oakland sue. The circumstances are undisputed. Yet Commissioner Tagliabue deliberately conveyed the false impression that the Raiders started this latest round of litigation.

We call attention as well to the Commissioner's testimony about the League's "Objective Relocation Guidelines" which were forced on the League by the earlier successful *Raider* lawsuit. But these "guidelines" are cosmetic. The Rams admittedly did not meet them, but for an exchange of money were permitted to move anyway. Further, the Commissioner advised the NFL owners that they could base a vote approving or disapproving a team relocation on any "business" reason, irrespective of the guidelines.

JOSEPH L. ALIOTO

Honorable Henry J. Hyde
January 25, 1996
Page 3

The role of the Finance Committee in relocations was another area touched on by Commissioner Tagliabue, with serious omissions from "the whole truth." He failed to tell the Committee that the Finance Committee is made up of seven members, all appointed by the Commissioner to do his bidding. Leading the charge were Chairman Bud Adams of Houston, Art Modell of Cleveland, David Behring of Seattle, Mike McCaskey of Chicago, Carmen Policy of San Francisco, Lamar Hunt of Kansas City, and Bob Tisch of New York. Most of these members had and have vested interests, and made public utterances that rules must be followed.

The Oilers' Bud Adams used his position as Chairman of the Finance Committee to secretly promote his abandonment of Houston for the siren sounds of Nashville. Another member, Art Modell, who can certainly be "trusted" to be objective about "Objective Guidelines" as he prepares to take the road to Baltimore, is in clear violation of these Guidelines. Also to be trusted are the Seahawks Ken Behring and Mike McCaskey of the Bears - both threatening moves in violation of the self-same Guidelines. Two other members - the '49ers Carmen Policy and Lamar Hunt - have admittedly been granted or seized exemptions from the ownership rules of the NFL. Yet these six of seven members are the principal trumpeters of the clarion call that "the NFL rules must be obeyed," as though they were sacred icons instead of malleable putty to be utilized for conspiracy, collusion and favoritism.

The covert and sinister actions employed by members of the Finance Committee who clandestinely shopped for venues throughout the country to see what they could extract, will be soon revealed, as will the vast and varying ramifications of those clandestine operations.

The clamorous public outcry and outrage over the desertion of Cleveland by Art Modell was not anticipated by the Commissioner, Mr. Modell or the Finance Committee members, who were quite prepared to grease the skids for Mr. Modell to slide down from Cleveland to Baltimore in violation of the "Objective Guidelines." When questioned by another owner as to what he would do if he did not receive the approval of the owners, Modell replied that he would move anyway. Taken aback, this coterie of insiders is simply attempting to divert attention from its anticompetitive perfidy by pious psalm-singing testimony before the Congress, and may also well be attempting to extract from Cleveland a "Baltimore-like" deal for the Browns and Modell.

JOSEPH L. ALIOTO

Honorable Henry J. Hyde
January 25, 1996
Page 4

Neither Cleveland nor Houston remotely meet the guidelines for relocation.

We are hopeful that a hearing before your Committee can be held after the football season ends so that Mr. Davis and others similarly inclined can give you not only their views, but the truth and realities about the ways of the NFL in practice.

My best personal regards to you and the other distinguished members of the Committee.

Sincerely,

Joseph L. Alioto

JLA/rc

ABA

AMERICAN BAR ASSOCIATION **SECTION OF INTELLECTUAL PROPERTY LAW**
750 N. Lake Shore Drive
Chicago, Illinois 60611
312/988-5598
FAX: 312/988-5628

February 15, 1996

The Honorable Henry Hyde
Chairman, Committee on the Judiciary
U.S. House of Representatives
Washington, D.C. 20515

Dear Mr. Chairman:

As Chair of the Section of Intellectual Property Law of the American Bar Association, I am writing to express the views of the Section on H.R. 2740, the "Fan Freedom and Community Protection Act of 1995." These views have not been approved by the House of Delegates or Board of Governors of the American Bar Association, and, accordingly, should not be construed as representing the position of the Association.

H.R. 2740, which concerns relocation of professional sports teams, contains both antitrust and trademark law provisions. The Section of Intellectual Property Law takes no position on the antitrust law provisions of the bill, but we oppose the provisions relating to trademark protection.

When a professional sports league approves the relocation of one of its teams, H.R. 2740 would statutorily transfer ownership of a registered mark that is used to identify the team from the owners of the team to the professional sports league involved. The league in turn would be required to "reserve" the mark for use by the losing community for an expansion team, which the league would be required to approve under certain conditions.

The Section of Intellectual Property Law opposes these provisions of H.R. 2740. We oppose them because they appear to not only reduce the protection available to trademark owners, but to affirmatively deprive mark owners of their assets.

The legislation would deprive mark owners of cognizable assets in contravention of well-established trademark law principles. To the extent that this deprivation of common law rights existing independently of federal legislation would be effected by the U.S. government, we believe that it may represent an unconstitutional taking in violation of the Fifth Amendment.

The Honorable Henry Hyde
February 15, 1996
Page 2

The philosophy behind this legislation might be equally applicable to efforts to stop relocations in other industries. For example, it might be argued that the Coca Cola mark is more closely associated with Atlanta than even the Atlanta Braves, or that the public's widespread association of the KODAK mark with Rochester, New York is as strong as the association of sports teams with particular cities. To the extent that the proposed legislation would apparently be limited to only one industry, it raises concerns regarding consistency with equal protection and due process requirements of the Constitution. Alternatively, the enactment of legislation such as H.R. 2740 might encourage the retaliatory use of trademark law for non-trademark purposes in disputes that go far beyond issues of sports team relocation, thus establishing a precedent for still further abusive use of trademark law.

Trademark law should not be used to achieve political ends which are unrelated to federal trademark policy. No legitimate trademark policy is promoted by the punitive denial of trademark protection to professional sports teams which relocate to new communities.

Thank you for the opportunity to present these views on behalf of the Section of Intellectual Property Law of the American Bar Association.

Sincerely,

Donald R. Dunner
Chair

DRD:lld

ONE HUNDRED FOURTH CONGRESS

Congress of the United States
House of Representatives
COMMITTEE ON THE JUDICIARY
2138 RAYBURN HOUSE OFFICE BUILDING
WASHINGTON, DC 20515-6216
(202) 225-3951

MAJORITY MEMBERS:
HENRY J. HYDE, ILLINOIS, CHAIRMAN
CARLOS J. MOORHEAD, CALIFORNIA
F. JAMES SENSENBRENNER, JR. WISCONSIN
BILL McCOLLUM, FLORIDA
GEORGE W. GEKAS, PENNSYLVANIA
HOWARD COBLE, NORTH CAROLINA
LAMAR S. SMITH, TEXAS
STEVEN SCHIFF, NEW MEXICO
ELTON GALLEGLY, CALIFORNIA
CHARLES T. CANADY, FLORIDA
BOB INGLIS, SOUTH CAROLINA
BOB GOODLATTE, VIRGINIA
STEVE BUYER, INDIANA
MARTIN R. HOKE, OHIO
SONNY BONO, CALIFORNIA
FRED HEINEMAN, NORTH CAROLINA
ED BRYANT, TENNESSEE
STEVE CHABOT, OHIO
MICHAEL PATRICK FLANAGAN, ILLINOIS
BOB BARR, GEORGIA

GENERAL COUNSEL
ALAN F. COFFEY, JR

MINORITY MEMBERS:
JOHN CONYERS, JR. MICHIGAN
PATRICIA SCHROEDER, COLORADO
BARNEY FRANK, MASSACHUSETTS
CHARLES E. SCHUMER, NEW YORK
HOWARD L. BERMAN, CALIFORNIA
RICK BOUCHER, VIRGINIA
JOHN BRYANT, TEXAS
JACK REED, RHODE ISLAND
JERROLD NADLER, NEW YORK
ROBERT C. "BOBBY" SCOTT, VIRGINIA
MELVIN L. WATT, NORTH CAROLINA
XAVIER BECERRA, CALIFORNIA
JOSE E. SERRANO, NEW YORK
ZOE LOFGREN, CALIFORNIA
SHEILA JACKSON LEE, TEXAS

MINORITY STAFF DIRECTOR
JULIAN EPSTEIN

March 15, 1996

The Honorable Bob Lanier
Office of the Mayor
City of Houston
900 Bagby Street
Houston, Texas 77002

Dear Mayor Lanier:

    Thank you for your testimony before the Committee on the Judiciary on Tuesday, February 6, 1996 at the hearing regarding sports franchise relocation.

    As noted during the hearing, due to time constraints, the Members of the Committee did not have an opportunity to ask all of their questions of the witnesses. I am therefore enclosing a list of questions for the record, which I am submitting on behalf of the members of the Committee. I would appreciate a response to these questions by Friday, April 5, 1996. If you have any questions regarding your responses, please contact Joseph Gibson, Committee counsel, at (202) 225-3951.

    Again, thank you for taking the time to appear before the Committee.

Sincerely,

HENRY J. HYDE
Chairman

HJH/jg:nr

Questions for the Record

Submitted by the Republican Members

Committee on the Judiciary

QUESTIONS FOR:

Hon. Bob Lanier, Mayor, City of Houston, Texas

1. You refer to the NFL as a statutorily unregulated monopoly. Is the NFL a monopoly because of federal policies, or is it a natural monopoly, or is there some other cause?

2. What are the public policy concerns in spending so many taxpayer dollars on a professional football team? How can a city, county or state justify this expenditure to taxpayers when scarce dollars are needed for schools, parks, police and fire departments, etc.

3. The argument has been made that there is a strong emotional benefit for a city in having a team. But, in Maryland, it appears that many taxpayers are actually opposed to spending so much money to bring the Browns to Baltimore. What are your thoughts on the psychological -- "community pride" -- benefits of having a team in town?

4. Cities are creating comprehensive financial deals to entice football teams to either relocate to a new area, or to remain where they are. This has been decried by some as an extortionist practice. Yet, cities compete with each other for industries and businesses, why shouldn't they compete for sports teams? How and why is this different?

5. What do you think of Mayor Daley's idea that teams that relocate must repay public subsidies they received from the city they're leaving? What types of public expenditures should be reimbursed?

CITY OF HOUSTON

Post Office Box 1562 Houston, Texas 77251 713/247-2200

OFFICE OF THE MAYOR

Bob Lanier, Mayor

RECEIVED
APR 9 1996
COMMITTEE OF THE JUDICIARY

April 4, 1996

The Honorable Henry J. Hyde
Chairman, U.S. House of Representatives
Committee on the Judiciary
2138 Rayburn House Office Building
Washington, DC 20515-6216

Dear Mr. Hyde:

Thank you for the opportunity to answer additional questions from your committee regarding sports franchise relocation. Attached are my responses.

I sincerely appreciate your assistance on this important issue. Please call me if I may provide any further information.

Regards,

Bob Lanier

Bob Lanier
Mayor

BL:sff

cc: Representative Martin Hoke

Questions for the Record

Submitted by the Republican Members

Committee on the Judiciary

QUESTIONS FOR AND RESPONSES FROM:

Hon. Bob Lanier, Mayor, City of Houston, Texas

1. You refer to the NFL as a statutorily unregulated monopoly. Is the NFL a monopoly because of federal policies, or is it a natural monopoly, or is there some other cause?

   RESPONSE: The NFL's monopoly is federal policy created by the existing anti-trust exemptions for pooling broadcast rights and the merger of two leagues.

   The Congress granted the NFL the two exemptions separately in the 1960's based on the NFL's testimony that the exemptions would allow the NFL to stabilize the league and ensure that teams competed on a more even basis. However, these exemptions created the monopoly because the league can still artificially control the supply, i.e., the number of franchises.

   The NFL now desires another anti-trust exemption to "help stabilize the league". Should Congress grant this additional exemption, the NFL will be further unconstrained in its actions as a monopoly unless protections are included as outlined in the bill by Rep. Martin Hoke. One specific protection from the unfettered exercise of monopoly power would be a requirement to grant an expansion franchise to a city losing a team that was profitable. This will address the League's ability to artificially control the supply.

2. What are the public policy concerns in spending so many taxpayer dollars on a professional football team? How can a city, county or state justify this expenditure to taxpayers when scarce dollars are needed for schools, parks, police and fire departments, etc.

   RESPONSE: Cities currently face many tough choices in determining the use of the limited tax dollars they receive. In Houston, we have chosen to use taxpayer money to add police to the streets, improve the infrastructure of our neighborhoods and parks, provide programs for our youth, and to fund many other basic programs. However, each community and its leaders must make their own decisions regarding the expenditure of public funds.

   For cities that believe that, for economic or other reasons, a sports facility is a high priority, then such expenditure of public funds should not be subject to abuse by owners who decide to leave even though taxpayer funds have contributed to their operations. The NFL currently has an unfair advantage over cities in this regard and federal legislation addressing part of the problem needs to correct it as well.

3. The argument has been made that there is a strong emotional benefit for a city in having a team. But, in Maryland, it appears that many taxpayers are actually opposed to spending so much money to bring the Browns to Baltimore. What are your thoughts on the psychological -- "community pride" -- benefits of having a team in town?

   RESPONSE: There is no question that sports teams bring a sense of pride and community spirit to the cities they serve. However, my experience with the Houston Oilers has shown me that citizens also take pride in being treated with respect; they do not appreciate blackmail.

   The working person is essentially asked to pay a higher or additional tax of some form to finance new facilities -- the major additions are luxury boxes to which the working person cannot afford seats. I don't believe that fans and taxpayers are satisfied with a "sense of pride" under these conditions.

4. Cities are creating comprehensive financial deals to entice football teams to either relocate to a new area, or to remain where they are. This has been decried by some as an extortionist practice. Yet, cities compete with each other for industries and businesses, why shouldn't they compete for sports teams? How and why is this different?

   RESPONSE: Cities are not the extortionist in this process. Oilers owner Bud Adams gave me less than two weeks to make a decision on the use of over $200 million in public funds to build a new stadium. He then shortly thereafter went on to negotiate with another city to relocate.

   In the 1980's he negotiated back and forth with another city until Houston gave in to over $65 million in renovations to the Astrodome.

   I strongly believe in free market competition and I do not fault cities for their efforts. However, the NFL is a monopoly and, therefore, the existing practice is not open market competition. No other business behaves in this fashion -- move even though profitable and then not allow a comparable competing business to replace you in the city you have left.

5. What do you think of Mayor Daley's idea that teams that relocate must repay public subsidies they received from the city they're leaving? What types of public expenditures should be reimbursed?

   RESPONSE: I fully support Mayor Daley's proposal. The types of public expenditures that should be reimbursed are bond proceeds, tax rebates, funds used for roads or other supporting infrastructure, the interest on those funds, and other similar items.

ONE HUNDRED FOURTH CONGRESS

Congress of the United States
House of Representatives
COMMITTEE ON THE JUDICIARY
2138 RAYBURN HOUSE OFFICE BUILDING
WASHINGTON, DC 20515-6216
(202) 225-3951

March 15, 1996

The Honorable Joe Chillura
County-Wide Commissioner
County Center
601 East Kennedy Boulevard
Tampa, Florida 33602

Dear Commissioner Chillura:

Thank you for your testimony before the Committee on the Judiciary on Tuesday, February 6, 1996 at the hearing regarding sports franchise relocation.

As noted during the hearing, due to time constraints, the Members of the Committee did not have an opportunity to ask all of their questions of the witnesses. I am therefore enclosing a list of questions for the record, which I am submitting on behalf of the members of the Committee. I would appreciate a response to these questions by Friday, April 5, 1996. If you have any questions regarding your responses, please contact Joseph Gibson, Committee counsel, at (202) 225-3951.

Again, thank you for taking the time to appear before the Committee.

Sincerely,

HENRY J. HYDE
Chairman

HJH/jg:nr

Questions for the Record

Submitted on behalf of the Republican Members

Committee on the Judiciary

QUESTIONS FOR:

Hon. Joe Chillura, Countywide Commissioner, Hillsborough County, FL

1. What are the public policy concerns in spending so many taxpayer dollars on a professional football team? How can a city, county, or state justify this expenditure to taxpayers when scarce dollars are needed for schools, parks, police and fire departments, etc?

2. The argument has been made that there is a strong emotional benefit for a city in having a team. But, in Maryland, it appears that many taxpayers are actually opposed to spending so much money to bring the Browns to Baltimore. What are your thoughts on the psychological -- "community pride" -- benefits of having a team in town?

3. Cities are creating comprehensive financial deals to entice football teams to either relocate to a new area, or to remain where they are. This has been decried by some as an extortionist practice. Yet, cities compete with each other for other industries and businesses, why shouldn't they compete for sports teams? How and why is this different?

4. What do you think of Mayor Daley's idea that teams that relocate must repay public subsidies they received from the city they're leaving? What types of public expenditures should be reimbursed?

Hillsborough County

Board of County Commissioners

JOE CHILLURA, JR
COUNTYWIDE
COMMISSIONER

COUNTY CENTER
601 E. KENNEDY BOULEVARD
TAMPA, FLORIDA 33602

PHONE (813) 272-5735
FAX (813) 272-7054

April 4, 1996

Representative Henry J. Hyde
Chairman, U.S. House of Representatives
Committee on the Judiciary
2138 Rayburn House Office Building
Washington, D. C. 20515-6216

Dear Representative Hyde:

It was an honor to testify before the Judiciary Committee and to have this further opportunity to share my views on the subject of professional sports franchises' facilities and their benefit to and burden on the communities that construct them. In response to your specific questions:

1. **What are the public policy concerns in spending so many taxpayer dollars on a professional football team? How can a city, county, or state justify this expenditure to taxpayers when scarce dollars are needed for schools, parks, police and fire departments, etc.**

There is always a strong competition for public dollars. However, as communities grow, there is a demand from the citizens and a responsibility of government to provide certain amenities: museums, parks, civic centers, and public stadiums. I consider a large public stadium an asset to a large community, beyond merely serving as a home field for professional sports teams. The current Tampa Stadium serves as the home for college and professional bowl games (The Florida Classic and the Outback Bowl), the Mutiny Professional Soccer team, and a variety of special events from equestrian to giant trucks. It is expected to serve as the home field for the University of South Florida, which expects to field its first football team in 1997. Such a stadium provides a variety of employment and recreational opportunities for the community, attracts tourists and is a symbol of civic pride, and a gathering place for the citizens. It was at Tampa Stadium that the community rallied to welcome home from the Persian Gulf War General Schwarzkopf and the contingent from MacDill Air Force Base.

Printed on Recycled Paper

The difficulty we are facing is the competition among communities to build bigger and more luxurious stadiums and provide bigger rent concessions and revenue streams in order to attract and retain professional sports teams. The communities have done this to themselves, but now the teams expect and demand these kinds of facilities. This competition among communities to attract
desirable businesses is not limited to sports teams, but sports teams, particularly the franchises of the NFL, are the most visible and currently making the most expensive demands.

The decision as to whether the cost is worth the prize is a hotly debated topic in the political arena and among the citizens. Therefore, in a democracy, it is the citizens who should make the choice to fund such a project. The Hillsborough County Board of County Commissioners voted unanimously to take any funding mechanism for a new stadium to the people in a referendum.

2. The argument has been made that there is a strong emotional benefit for a city in having a team. But, in Maryland, it appears that many taxpayers are actually opposed to spending so much money to bring the Browns to Baltimore. What are your thoughts on the psychological -- "community pride" -- benefits of having a team in town?

The tens of thousands of fans who show up for games, and the hundreds who show up for Board of County Commission meetings when the team's future seems in doubt, clearly indicates that many citizens love the Tampa Bay Buccaneers, perennial underdogs though they may be. Many residents have grown up with the team and closely followed its ups and downs. To them the team's leaving will be like losing a friend, plus eliminating ten holidays a year. I believe losing a team will be devastating for many; sports teams provide an identity to communities and a shared interest to its citizens.

However, just as in Baltimore, many Hillsborough County residents are opposed to spending so much to keep the Tampa Bay Buccaneers. That is the reason I feel it is imperative that it is the people who make that decision. To impose upon the citizens, without their consent, a financial burden to provide facilities to a team whose ultimate purpose is to make a profit would be unfair. Only a referendum can gauge if a local team is important enough to the community to make that sacrifice.

3. Cities are creating comprehensive financial deals to entice football teams to either relocate to a new area, or to remain where they are. This has been decried by some as an extortionist practice. Yet, cities compete with each other for other industries and businesses, why shouldn't they compete for sports teams? How and why is this different?

Recently Hillsborough County was in competition with other communities for the location of a regional U.S. Government Accounting Center. The County and its municipalities were prepared to provide significant incentives to lure such a major, stable employer, but lost out to a community prepared to offer more. Economic incentives to new and expanding businesses are available as joint efforts with the State through various statutory mechanisms and are becoming essential to attract major employers and businesses.

The difference with a sports team is the intangible nature of many of the benefits it provides. The economic impact can be estimated, but frequently communities are willing to pay more to attract or retain a professional sports franchise than they would a quiet employer that merely provided economic benefits. The intangible benefits provided by a professional sports team make it different; the elements of community pride and identification, the national attention and competition are different from the benefits provided by other industries. These intangible benefits are real and important. Putting a price tag on them is what's hard.

4. What do you think of Mayor Daley's idea that teams that relocate must repay public subsidies they received from the city they're leaving? What types of public expenditures should be reimbursed?

I favor substantial financial and other penalties for professional sports teams which break their leases with local governments, abandoning fans and supporters, when they have induced those governments to build expensive state-of-the-art facilities at public expense. Leases for major tenants of professional sports facilities don't require rents that reflect the cost to the community of providing the facility; and, there is not a large fluid pool of tenants for such facilities. Therefore, when such a tenant breaks its lease, the community has lost the "benefit of its bargain" beyond what could be compensated for by mere payments of sums that might be due under a lease.

I believe that all public tax money or general revenue (as opposed to facility or user fees) committed to a facility that was built to attract or retain a professional sports facility should be reimbursed to a community should a professional sports tenant break a lease. Further, I believe that the league has an obligation to replace any defaulting franchise.

Thank you for the opportunity to share my views with you and the committee. My colleagues and I follow your deliberations closely, the hardships wrought by these defaulting franchises have become a national problem which cannot be dealt with effectively at the local level. Your work is important.

Sincerely,

Joe Chillura, Jr.
Countywide Commissioner

cc: All Commissioners
    Daniel A. Kleman, County Administrator
    Dick Greco, Mayor, City of Tampa
    Steve Anderson, Chairman, Tampa Sports Authority
    Rick Nafe, Executive Director, Tampa Sports Authority
    Emeline C. Acton, County Attorney
    Helen Levine, Federal and State Liaison
hyde.resp.H:White

ONE HUNDRED FOURTH CONGRESS

Congress of the United States
House of Representatives
COMMITTEE ON THE JUDICIARY
2138 RAYBURN HOUSE OFFICE BUILDING
WASHINGTON, DC 20515-6216
(202) 225-3951

March 15, 1996

Mr. Paul Tagliabue
Commissioner
National Football League
410 Park Avenue
New York, New York 10022

Dear Commissioner Tagliabue:

    Thank you for your testimony before the Committee on the Judiciary on Tuesday, February 6, 1996 at the hearing regarding sports franchise relocation.

    As noted during the hearing, due to time constraints, the Members of the Committee did not have an opportunity to ask all of their questions of the witnesses. I am therefore enclosing a list of questions for the record, which I am submitting on behalf of the members of the Committee. I would appreciate a response to these questions by Friday, April 5, 1996. If you have any questions regarding your responses, please contact Joseph Gibson, Committee counsel, at (202) 225-3951.

    Again, thank you for taking the time to appear before the Committee.

Sincerely,

Henry J. Hyde
Chairman

HJH/jg:nr

Questions for the Record

Submitted on behalf of the Republican Members

Committee on the Judiciary

QUESTIONS FOR:

Paul Tagliabue, Esq., Commissioner, National Football League

1. What do you think of Mayor Daley's idea that relocating teams must repay public subsidies they received from the city they are leaving?

2. Some have argued that the NFL should not receive antitrust immunity so long as you are an unregulated monopoly. How do you answer this point?

3. You claim that the NFL is a joint venture -- a partnership. But the teams don't share profits; they don't share losses. They have separate sets of books and compete for the same players. Is this really a partnership?

4. You have stated that franchise moves are "hurting the NFL's credibility with the fans." As we face the prospect of as many as eight of the thirty NFL teams moving in just two seasons -- aside from federal legislation -- what is the answer?

5. Why is this a problem that justifies federal intervention? The owners of NFL franchises are successful, self-made men and women -- individuals who relied on the private sector marketplace for their financial success. Why do these people need to look to Washington for a solution of what is essentially an internal business problem? What is the compelling public interest here?

6. If the National Football League is a joint venture -- a genuine economic partnership -- isn't it the responsibility of the partners to influence and restrain the behavior of their other partners? For example, has the League or any of its owners ever claimed that an owner has breached his or her fiduciary duty to the joint venture in a franchise relocation case or in any other context? If so, what was the result? If not, why not?

7. Following the Oakland Raiders litigation, the National Football League established guidelines or criteria that would be applied in the case of proposed franchise relocations. Included among those factors is "adequacy of the stadium". What are the specific factors or criteria that are applied in terms of stadium adequacy? Isn't this a very subjective decision?

8. If the NFL were to receive an antitrust exemption, in your view

would it retain the three-fourths or seventy-five percent rule on franchise relocation? If so, that would mean that merely six owners could vote to block a move that the overwhelming majority of owners felt was warranted. Would you care to comment?

9. Last year, the Los Angeles Rams were permitted to move to St. Louis. In your view, did the Los Angeles Rams financial situation meet the criteria in the NFL guidelines justifying franchise relocation? If not, why were they permitted to move? Did some of the other NFL owners profit directly from the decision to allow the Rams to move to St. Louis? How?

10. Could you describe for the record the players salary cap as it operates in the National Football League. Some players argue that it is not a "real" cap -- could you explain?

11. It is my understanding that the National Football League teams all share equally in the receipts from the various television contracts (NBC, FOX, TNT, ABC, ESPN). What happens with respect to radio broadcasting rights and revenues? Do the teams share any of the radio broadcast revenues? In the aggregate, what were the revenues from radio in 1995?

12. Have you had any indication from the players how they might feel about an antitrust exemption for the NFL? Have you spoken with the player's union about this issue?

13. Do you feel that there are some valid reasons that would justify the relocation of a team? If so, what are those justifiable reasons or factors, in your estimation?

14. Your antitrust analysis is that pro sports leagues are not economic competitors -- and many think most courts would agree with that analysis. So, why not litigate the issue and get a final definitive decision? You are asking us to legislate because of the "threat of antitrust litigation" -- not because there has been a final, definitive federal court decision on this issue. Why shouldn't we require you to litigate this, rather than legislate now?

15. One of the main justifications you cite for giving the League an antitrust exemption is the uncertainty of litigation. Isn't litigation uncertainty a problem for all businesses? If we accept uncertainty as a valid justification for your antitrust exemption, how can we deny them to any number of other businesses?

Minority Question

1. As a follow up to Ms. Lofgren's question to Commissioner Tagliabue requesting that the League open up its books and records and to more properly assess the NFL's request for an antitrust exemption, please provide copies of: (i) pertinent

League, affiliate, and team financial records (on a cash and non-cash basis, if available), for the last five years, including stadium leases; and (ii) copies of materials relating to relocation decisions, including minutes, notes (of both League and ownership representatives), and voting records from all meetings at which relocation issues have been discussed (for all proposed relocations since the initial Raiders move to Los Angeles).

NATIONAL FOOTBALL LEAGUE

JUNE 11, 1996

**ANSWERS OF THE NATIONAL FOOTBALL LEAGUE
TO QUESTIONS FROM THE
HOUSE JUDICIARY COMMITTEE**

A. REPUBLICAN MAJORITY

1. We are not familiar with any precise delineation of the suggestion raised by this question, but we would oppose imposition on a departing sports franchise of penalties or sanctions of a kind that are not generally applicable to tenants of public facilities, or that would have the effect of locking a team into its current facility with the threat of potentially ruinous financial penalties. Such an approach would be patently unfair and wholly unwarranted.

    A governmentally-imposed penalty of that kind is unnecessary, since a stadium lessor can protect against a precipitous relocation in arm's-length negotiation of its lease terms. For example, if a certain number of years are required to retire bonded indebtedness incurred for stadium construction or renovation, a municipal lessor can require the team to commit to a tenancy of sufficient duration to enable recoupment of the public expenditures. (A lease that fails to do so presumably represents a considered judgment by the lessor that other, less direct benefits of the team's tenancy warrant assuming the risk that the indebtedness may not be fully retired when the lease terminates.)

*   *   *   *   *   *

Judiciary Committee
Answers Page 2

2, 3, 14 & 15. To characterize the NFL as a "monopoly" ignores the reality that the League competes in a broad sports and entertainment market with a variety of other producers. At the team-sport level alone, there is vigorous competition on a national basis between and among professional leagues and major college sports, whose seasons now substantially overlap, and in a large number of local and regional areas as well.

Following review of the record in the North American Soccer League's lawsuit against the NFL fourteen years ago, Chief Justice Rehnquist, in a highly unusual opinion dissenting from denial of certiorari, observed that the NFL "competes with other sports and other forms of entertainment.in the entertainment market," and that "the [NFL] competes as a unit against other forms of entertainment." National Football League v. North American Soccer League, 459 US. 1074, 1077 (1982).

At an earlier stage of that case, the plaintiff's own economist, in the District Court's words, recognized . . . "[t]he reality of league against league competition," and opined that "major professional team sports is a submarket of the general entertainment industry." North American Soccer League v. National Football League, 505 F.Supp. 659, 679 (S.D.N.Y. 1980). The trial court agreed, finding that "the sports leagues compete with each other as single entities, offering products which, but for the concerted action of the member clubs, simply would not exist." Ibid.

Thus, for example, when a sports fan "can easily predict the outcome of league contests, fan interest will decline in favor of alternative forms of entertainment, [including] television, at theaters, or in any number of places where Americans spend their leisure time and dollars . . . . [P]rofessional sports leagues may in fact face a glut of competition from alternative forms of

Judiciary Committee
Answers Page 3

entertainment." Rosenbaum, The Antitrust Implications of Professional Sports Leagues Revisited: Emerging Trends in the Modern Era, 41 U.Miami L. Rev. 729, 748 (1987). Just a few weeks ago, an economist active in sports matters wrote, in discussing a proposed new baseball stadium in Manhattan: "Nearly all spending at the stadium is simply shifted from other forms of entertainment like restaurants and movies." (R. Noll, "Wild Pitch," New York Times, April 11, 1996, at A25, col.2.)

Numerous other economists and legal commentators have recognized that a sports league essentially competes as a single unit against a variety of other entertainment alternatives. See, e.g., SCULLY, THE BUSINESS OF MAJOR LEAGUE BASEBALL 101 (1989) ("Of course, baseball competes with other spectator sports. . . . as well as other leisure activities"); WEILER & ROBERTS, SPORTS AND THE LAW: CASES, MATERIALS AND PROBLEMS 446 (1993) (sports leagues operate in a "strongly competitive environment when one takes account of the entire array of choices available to participants in the broader marketplace."); DEMMERT, THE ECONOMICS OF PROFESSIONAL TEAM SPORTS 10, 43 (1973); Grauer, Recognition of the National Football League as a Single Entity Under Section 1 of the Sherman Act: Implications of the Consumer Welfare Model, 82 Mich. L. Rev. 1 (1983); MARKHAM & TEPLITZ, BASEBALL ECONOMICS AND PUBLIC POLICY 19-21, 23-24 (1981); Morris, In the Wake of the Flood, 38 LAW & CONTEMP. PROB. 85, 90 (1973); Neale, the Peculiar Economics of Professional Sports, 78 Q.J. Econ. 1, 4-5, 14 (1964); Noll, "Attendance and Price Setting," GOVERNMENT AND THE SPORTS BUSINESS 115, 117, 128 (1974); Roberts, Sports Leagues and the Sherman Act: The Use and Abuse of Section 1 to Regulate Restraints on Intra-league Rivalry, 32 U.C.L.A. L. Rev. 219 (1984); Weistart, League Control of Market Opportunities: A Perspective on Competition and Cooperation in the Sports Industry, 1984 Duke L.J. 1013.

Likewise, business executives who run major professional sports franchises fully recognize that their franchises compete within the framework of a broad entertainment market, for a necessarily finite amount of consumer leisure time, interest, and discretionary income. President Larry Lucchino of the San Diego Padres recently observed that, "You're not just competing for the sports dollar but [also] the entertainment dollar." ("Baseball America," March 4, 1996).

Finally, within the professional sports industry alone, the number of franchises in each league has markedly increased. The various leagues' seasons increasingly and substantially overlap – to the point, for one example, where every week of the NFL's preseason, regular season, and post-season features head-to-head competition with major league baseball, basketball, and/or hockey. (College football, a major enterprise in itself, of course virtually parallels the NFL season).

This intense competition has contributed greatly to the business pressures that, by increasing franchise instability within leagues, have generated congressional interest in affording leagues the ability to make reasoned business decisions with respect to proposed franchise relocations.

The purpose of separately owned and managed teams is to enhance public confidence in the integrity of the athletic competition within the league. The reality – recognized by numerous courts and commentators – is that the NFL is a joint enterprise that produces a single product, NFL football, that could not be produced by any individual club.

The weight of serious scholarly opinion favors treating sports leagues as single entities, at least for purposes of internal governance decisions.

Judiciary Committee
Answers Page 5

In addition to the authorities cited above, several judicial decisions have turned on the courts' recognition that a sports league effectively functions as a single entity. See, e.g., San Francisco Seals, Ltd. v. NHL, 379 F.Supp. 966, 970 (C.D. Cal. 1974)(league's member clubs "are, in fact, all members of a single unit competing as such with other similar professional leagues"); NASL v. NFL, 505 F.Supp. 659, 684 (S.D.N.Y. 1980), aff'd in part, rev'd in part, 670 F.2d 1249 (2d Cir.), cert. denied, 459 U.S. 1074 (1982) (competition between plaintiff and defendant leagues "is . . . competition between two single economic entities"); see also Levin v. NBA, 385 F.Supp. 149, 152 (S.D.N.Y. 1974)("plaintiffs wanted to join with those unwilling to accept them, not to compete with them, but to be partners in the operation of a sports league . . . ").

While two appellate courts that have directly addressed the single-entity issue have held that leagues are collections of competitors for Section 1 purposes, key aspects of their opinions are markedly inconsistent with those holdings. For example, in reversing the District Court opinion in NASL v. NFL cited above, a Second Circuit panel, while declining to consider a league a single entity for purposes of limiting inter-league cross-ownership, recognized "the interdependence of professional sports league members and the unique nature of their business," and concurred in the trial court's finding that:

> "[T]he economic success of each franchise is dependent on the quality of sports competition throughout the league and the economic strength and stability of other league members. Damage to or losses by any league member can adversely affect the stability,

success and operations of other members."
670 F.2d at 1253.

Further, in affirming a Los Angeles jury's verdict that denying the Oakland Raiders permission to relocate to Los Angeles violated Section 1 of the Sherman Act, the Ninth Circuit panel majority acknowledged that "the NFL teams are not true competitors, nor can they be." Los Angeles Mem. Col'm Com'n v. NFL, 726 F.2d 1381, at 1391 (9th Cir.) ("Raiders"), cert. denied, 469 U.S. 990 (1984). Both decisions reflect, in our view, a not uncommon judicial inability to reach conclusions that are consistent with the courts' own premises concerning the interdependent and unitary nature of a sports league.

Not surprisingly, both of these appellate decisions spawned vigorous dissenting views. In Raiders, Judge Williams' lengthy dissent emphasized that, at least for the purpose of franchise-relocation decisions – the subject of these hearings – a league should be treated as a single entity. 726 F.2d at 1401-10. And, as previously noted, in a rare written dissent from a denial of certiorari, Chief Justice Rehnquist explained that:

> "The NFL owners are joint venturers who produce a product, professional football, which competes with other sports and other forms of entertainment in the entertainment marketplace. Although individual NFL teams compete on the playing field, they rarely compete in the marketplace . . . [Ordinarily,] the league competes as a unit against other forms of entertainment." NASL v. NFL, 459 U.S. at 1077 (1982).

Judiciary Committee
Answers Page 7

Importantly, both NASL and Raiders preceded Copperweld Corp. v. Independence Tube Corp., 467 U.S. 752 (1984), in which the Supreme Court held that agreements between a parent corporation and its subsidiary do not fall within Section 1 scrutiny because they do not "deprive[ ] the market place of . . . independent centers of decision making" or "represent a sudden joining of two independent sources of economic power previously pursuing separate interests." Id. at 769, 771. At least five appellate courts have since made clear that Copperweld's rationale extends well beyond the parent-subsidiary context, and that it applies despite the occasional existence of diverging interests between the enterprise and its members, or among the members themselves. Under these circumstances, there is every reason to question the prior appellate decisions denying the League single-entity status for its internal governance decisions. But in the absence of congressional action, the antitrust terrorism made possible by those decisions remains a powerful disincentive for a league to risk potentially ruinous treble-damage liability by determining collectively where its jointly-produced product is to be presented.

To a very limited extent, a league's members may occasionally be perceived as competing for fan patronage within the same geographic area. As a practical matter, this "competition" between two members of a single league is at most insignificant. As one commentator has aptly noted, each NFL team in a two-team area "will typically develop a cadre of loyal fans who identify with and follow that team, and seldom will such rabid followers attend the other team's games. The reality of the sports entertainment business is that in areas capable of supporting two teams, it is highly unlikely that one team will establish its ticket prices or make player personnel decisions with much if any regard for the other." Roberts, The Single Entity Status of Sports Leagues Under the Sherman Act:

Judiciary Committee
Answers Page 8

An Alternative View, 60 Tulane L. Rev. 562, 574, n. 31(1986); accord, Weistart, supra, 1984 Duke L. J. at 1027 n. 45 and 1030 n. 54.

With respect to player employment matters – a subject in no way affected by pending legislative proposals – various cases have treated the teams within a league as competitors. However, the players in all major American sports leagues are now unionized, and the Sherman Act has no application to the common terms and conditions of employment necessarily resulting from the collective bargaining relationships in such leagues.

A sports league's internal decisions thus in no way resemble the economic conduct at which Section 1 of the Sherman Act was meant to be directed: a group of independent horizontal business competitors acting collusively. While engaged in (and producing a product consisting of) football competition on the playing field, the teams are inherently interdependent and cooperative in a business sense – more so, for example, than are the members of a law firm, the "unitary" nature of which is never questioned. However, many courts that have recognized the inherent joint-enterprise nature of a sports league have failed to take account of that indisputable fact in applying the Sherman Act.

The NFL does not seek a blanket exemption from the antitrust laws of the kind available to major league baseball. A sports league's conduct may properly be subjected, in appropriate circumstances, to scrutiny under Section 2 of the Sherman Act, and certain agreements between a league and an outside party may appropriately be subjected to Section 1 scrutiny. For present purposes, it is enough to say that internal league governance decisions on fundamental matters, such as where and how the NFL's jointly-produced product is presented, must be made jointly, and they should not be subject to attack as antitrust "conspiracies".

Judiciary Committee
Answers Page 9

Further, if treated as an antitrust "conspiracy," a league may be exposed to unacceptable risks no matter how it decides franchise-relocation questions. For example, when the Raiders proposed to abandon Oakland for Los Angeles in 1980, they joined with the Los Angeles Memorial Coliseum Commission in suing the League for not approving the move. At the same time, Oakland representatives stated that they were prepared to sue the NFL had it approved the relocation.

We recently faced a suit filed in Baltimore by the State of Maryland and the Maryland Stadium Authority, claiming that the League had violated the antitrust laws by failing to approve the Browns' proposed relocation. At the same time, the mayor of Houston threatened an antitrust suit if the League approved the Oilers' proposed move. As the antitrust laws have been applied to sports leagues, we are thus "damned if we do and damned if we don't" with respect to franchise relocation issues.

The practical realty is that the proposed relocation of a major professional sports franchise excites local community passions to a greater extent that would be true of virtually any other type of business. Consequently, as matters now stand there is unlikely ever to be litigation that is not heavily influenced, if not determined, by deeply felt local pressures and interests, as well as by the history of antitrust cases that have improperly treated a league's member clubs as independent business competitors. This unusual combination of circumstances subjects to potentially devastating treble-damage liability conduct (a) of a type never contemplated by the antitrust laws (b) that is engaged in by an organization that does not fit well into the traditional antitrust frame of reference. It is not difficult to understand why this extraordinary risk may not be considered acceptable by a league, no matter how deeply it might wish to respect factors

Judiciary Committee
Answers Page 10

such as demonstrated fan and community support for a team that proposes to relocate.

*   *   *   *   *   *   *

4.   There is no question that the best – if not the only – "answer" to this problem is to affirm the right of <u>leagues</u> to decide where their respective jointly-produced products are to be presented. That affirmation may be expected to curb an individual club's instinct and ability to act unilaterally in its own self-interest, without due regard for factors such as demonstrated fan loyalty and community support.

*   *   *   *   *   *   *

5.   This situation warrants congressional intervention because the source of the problem is the irrational application by federal courts of a federal statute that was never intended by Congress to be applied in a manner that so obviously deserves the public interest. This is not an "internal business problem" that can be resolved within a league; the problem is the overhanging threat of punitive damage awards, rendered in self-interested forums, that prevents leagues from making rational business decisions and from taking full account of fan interests and community loyalty and support. The preambles to several bills already introduced in Congress articulate the various public-interest bases for affirming legislatively that the decision on franchise relocation rests with the league itself, which can take a broader and more responsible view of the issue than can the individual club.

*   *   *   *   *   *   *

Judiciary Committee
Answers Page 11

6. With respect to the first part of this question, see the answer to questions 2, 3, 14 & 15 above concerning the antitrust impediments to the ability "of the partners to influence and restrain the behavior of their other partners" in this context.

While fiduciary duty claims have been pleaded in some lawsuits, no decision in a franchise-relocation or related case has turned on that concept. With the overhang of treble-damage liability, it would be unwise for a league to rely on such an untested concept to block a move in the face of a litigation challenge. Moreover, the role of a fiduciary-duty concept in litigation brought by a third party (e.g., a would-be stadium landlord) is at best difficult to predict.

*   *   *   *   *   *

7. In determining the "adequacy of the stadium," attention would be focused on such factors as its seating capacity, its sight lines, the various amenities it affords to the fans (parking, concessions, rest rooms, access for the disabled, etc.), its age, structural condition, location, and accessibility, how it compares in attractiveness with other venues within the NFL and with those in the team's community that house other local sports teams, and its revenue-generating potential. This is less a "subjective" determination than a flexible and, over time, an evolving one.

*   *   *   *   *   *

8. The NFL is composed of clubs from a wide variety of communities that differ significantly in size, stadium arrangements, and other market factors. Accordingly, their managers may collectively approach a given subject from widely varying perspectives. A supermajority voting requirement compels

Judiciary Committee
Answers Page 12

substantial and continuing deliberation on matters at issue in order to achieve a high degree of consensus with respect to the ultimate decisions. Such voting requirements are not uncommon in sports-league, association and corporate governance, nor in Congress itself.

The NFL has operated for decades with a three-fourths voting requirement for virtually all significant decisions, from changing the playing rules to ratifying network television contracts and collective bargaining agreements to amending its operating documents and policies. Given the central importance of franchise location in League operations – and the fact that the location of any one franchise affects the interests of every other club – it is appropriate and reasonable to require approval of a relocation by the same margin as is required for other important League decisions. Accordingly, we do not plan a special exception for votes on franchise relocations.

The observation that a minority of owners "could vote to block a move that the overwhelming majority . . . felt was warranted" is not a realistic concern. Given the interdependence of all clubs' operations, it would make no practical sense to freeze any club in an untenable situation. The real problem is the reverse: the ability of an individual club to invoke antitrust terrorism to compel acquiescence in a relocation that the majority of clubs would deem unwarranted.

* * * * * *

9. The Rams had not, in Commissioner Tagliabue's view and in the view of most NFL club owners, met the League's relocation guidelines. While several other factors unique to St. Louis or to the Rams also came into play, the overhanging threat of protracted, divisive, and burdensome antitrust litigation – the outcome of which would not have been known for years, which would have

Judiciary Committee
Answers Page 13

drawn on prior case law improperly treating League members as independent business competitors, and which would have taken place in St. Louis – was the principal element in the League's ultimate decision to approve the Rams' relocation. The threat of a home-town verdict rendered in a distinctly self-interested forum, and the potential treble-damage exposure associated with such a verdict, was a prohibitive risk for NFL clubs that otherwise would have preferred to enforce their contractual rights to have the Rams remain in Southern California.

Other NFL clubs would "profit directly" by the Rams' relocation only to the extent that superior fan support in the new location engenders larger visiting-team shares from gate receipts for those clubs who play the Rams in St. Louis. However, such higher revenue levels create offsetting costs for all NFL clubs as they increase the player salary cap.

The Rams also agreed to pay a relocation fee, partly in recognition of the fact that their franchise value would be substantially enhanced largely as a result of the intense interest in and commitment to an NFL presence in St. Louis that the League, rather than the Rams themselves, had generated. As explained in Commissioner Tagliabue's December 8, 1995 letter to Senator DeWine (copy attached as Exhibit 1), the proceeds of that fee are earmarked for distribution to the League's lowest-revenue clubs, to ameliorate the effects on those clubs of the increases in operating costs that a stadium-induced relocation engenders for all NFL teams. A relocation fee itself is _not_ an inducement to approve an otherwise-unjustified franchise move.

*   *   *   *   *   *

10. In brief, the salary cap provisions of the NFL Collective Bargaining Agreement impose a range of revenues — expressed in terms of a percentage of League revenues calculated on an accrual basis — that must be devoted to player costs each year. There are club and League-wide maximums and minimums, which depend on the level of League revenues. The accrual accounting enables a club to pay large signing bonuses to star players and then, with certain limitations, to pro-rate such bonuses for cap purposes over the life of the players' multi-year contracts. In this way, higher-revenue clubs can gain an immediate advantage in signing outstanding players on what is, for cap accounting purposes, a "buy now, pay later" approach; however, the accrued up-front payments will limit those clubs' ability to make substantial cash payments in subsequent years.

* * * * * *

11. NFL clubs share in the CBS national radio package that currently pays a total of $6.5 million per year. Each participating team receives $40,000 per appearance in the 41-game regular-season package; post-season revenue, comprising approximately half of the annual CBS rights fee, is divided equally among the member clubs.

Most radio revenue is generated by individual club negotiations and retained by the respective clubs; such revenue totaled approximately $62 million league-wide in 1995.

Mutual Radio also broadcasts two games per week over the 17-week regular season, for which participating clubs receive $11,000 per appearance.

* * * * * *

Judiciary Committee
Answers Page 15

12. We have been advised that the NFL Players Association would not oppose legislation that would affirm the League's ability to enforce its rules with respect to franchise relocations.

*   *   *   *   *   *

13. In some cases, relocations of franchises are appropriate. For example, there was no serious dispute about the justification for the St. Louis Football Cardinals' relocation to Phoenix in 1988. Beyond that, it is impossible to enumerate every set of circumstances in which a relocation would be justified, but reference to the League's current relocation procedures (copy attached as Exhibit 2) will suggest such circumstances.

B. MINORITY QUESTION

1. As promised by Commissioner Tagliabue in response to Rep. Lofgren's question at the February 6 hearing (p.167 of the stenographic minutes), copies of the Commissioner's reports to the NFL membership on the proposed Rams' and Raiders' 1995 relocations are enclosed as Exhibits 3 and 4 to these answers.

The other items enumerated in the written "follow up" question, including the financial data, are maintained by the League Office subject to a confidentiality commitment to the member clubs. Stadium leases (to which the League is not a party) are private contracts which we could not properly release without the consent of the respective contracting parties. However, as to relocation matters themselves, in addition to the enclosed Commissioner's reports on the 1995 relocations, we will assemble and produce similar reports and League meeting minutes (including voting tabulations) with respect to proposed relocations since the initial Raiders move to Los Angeles.

EXHIBIT 1

NATIONAL FOOTBALL LEAGUE

Paul Tagliabue
Commissioner

December 8, 1995

The Honorable Mike DeWine
Senate Russell Office Building
Room 140
Washington, D.C. 20510

Dear Senator DeWine:

      I very much appreciated the opportunity to testify before the Judiciary Committee last week and to discuss with you the need for Congress to confirm that the antitrust laws do not apply to internal decisions of professional sports leagues, including decisions barring the relocation of League franchises.

      During the hearings, you asked about the use and distribution of relocation fees associated with team moves. For various reasons, relocation fees do not offer an incentive for the membership to endorse an otherwise unjustified move.

      For example, under a resolution adopted by the NFL's membership earlier this year, such fees are paid into a revenue sharing pool for distribution to low-revenue clubs, thereby ameliorating the inevitable impact of a lucrative stadium deal on the gap between the League's high-revenue and low-revenue teams.

      Because of the revenue sharing program, at least half of the NFL clubs do not receive any money from a relocation fee, even though each relocation will almost certainly increase the operating costs of every club in the League. These costs increase because, under the NFL's Collective Bargaining Agreement, any increased revenues realized by the moving club translate into increases in the Salary Cap and Minimum Team Salaries for all NFL clubs. That is true, of course, for clubs that receive distributions from the revenue sharing pool as well as those that do not. (The related issue that we discussed at the hearing -- the extent to which portions of the St. Louis Rams' relocation-related payments may be sharable with the players under our Collective Bargaining Agreement -- have not yet been finally resolved with the NFL Players Association.)

The Honorable Mike DeWine
December 8, 1995
Page 2

In short, for those clubs with below-average revenues, a relocation fee merely helps to offset the increased operating costs that the relocation entails; for the other clubs, such fees are essentially irrelevant.

Thank you again for your courtesy of last week. I look forward to seeing you again soon.

Sincerely,

Paul Tagliabue

EXHIBIT 2

Volume I, Administrative/Business Operations — General, Franchise Relocation Procedures   Page C89

PROCEDURES FOR PROPOSED FRANCHISE RELOCATIONS

Article 8.5 of the NFL Constitution and Bylaws vests in the Commissioner the authority to "interpret and from time to time establish policy and procedure in respect to the provisions of the Constitution and Bylaws and any enforcement thereof." Set forth below are procedures and policy to apply to League consideration, pursuant to Section 4.3 of the Constitution and Bylaws, of any proposed transfer of a home territory. These provisions were established in December of 1984 and remain in effect.

Section 4.3 requires prior approval by the affirmative vote of three-fourths of the member clubs of the League (the normal voting margin for League business) before a club may transfer its franchise or playing site to a different city either within or outside its home territory. While the following provisions apply by their terms to a proposed transfer to a different home territory, a transfer of a club's playing site to a different location within its home territory may also raise issues of League-wide significance. Accordingly, the pre-Annual Meeting notification date prescribed in section (A)(1) below also applies to a proposed intra-territory relocation, and the Commissioner may require that some or all of the following procedures be followed with respect to such a move.

A. Notice and Evaluation of the Proposed Transfer

Before any club may transfer its franchise or playing site outside its current home territory, the club must submit a proposal for such transfer to the League on the following basis:

1. A club proposing a transfer outside its home territory must give written notice of the proposed transfer to the Commissioner no later than 30 days prior to the opening date of the Annual Meeting in the year in which the club proposes to commence play in a new location. Such notice will be accompanied by a "statement of reasons" in support of the proposed transfer that will include the information outlined in Part B below.

2. The Commissioner will, with the assistance of appropriate League committees, evaluate the proposed transfer and report to the membership; if possible, he will do so within 20 days of his receipt of the club's notice and accompanying "statement of reasons." The Commissioner may also convene a special committee to perform factfinding or other functions with respect to any such proposed transfer.

3. Following the Commissioner's report on the proposed transfer, the transfer will be presented to the membership for action in accordance with the Constitution and Bylaws, either at a Special Meeting of the League held for that purpose or at the Annual Meeting.

B. "Statement of Reasons" for the Proposed Transfer

Any club proposing a transfer outside its home territory must, in its accompanying "statement of reasons," furnish information to the Commissioner essential to consideration of whether such a move is justified and whether it is in the League's interest.

In this connection, the club proposing to transfer must present in writing its views to why its recent financial experience would support a relocation of the club. Such information would include a comparison of the club's home revenues with League averages and medians; past and projected ticket sales and other stadium revenues at both the existing and proposed locations; and operating profits or losses during the most recent four seasons. The club should also comment on any other factors it regards as relevant to the League's consideration of the proposed transfer, including but not limited to operations of other professional or college sports in the existing and proposed home territories, and the effects of the proposed transfer on NFL scheduling patterns, travel requirements, current divisional alignments, traditional rivalries, League-wide television patterns and interests, the quality of stadium facilities, and fan and public perceptions of the NFL and its member clubs.

To permit such a review, at least the following information will accompany the "statement of reasons" for the proposed transfer:

1. A copy of the club's existing stadium lease and any other agreements relating to the club's use of its current stadium (e.g., concession agreements, box suite agreements, scoreboard advertising agreements) or to a stadium authority's or municipality's provision of related facilities (e.g., practice facilities).

2. Audited financial statements for the club for the fiscal years covering the preceding four seasons.

3. An assessment of the suitability of the club's existing stadium, costs of and prospects for making any desired improvements to the stadium, and the status of efforts to negotiate such improvements with the stadium authority.

4. A description and financial analysis of the projected lease and operating terms available to the club in its proposed new location.

5. A description and financial analysis of the stadium lease and operating terms available to the club in its existing home territory, on a basis that permits comparison with the projected arrangements in the proposed new location.

6. A budget projection, using accepted League charts of account, showing a projected profit and loss statement for the fiscal years covering the first three seasons in the proposed new location.

C. Factors to be Considered in Evaluating the Proposed Transfer

While the League has analyzed many factors in making expansion and team-move decisions in the past, the Commissioner will also give consideration to the factors listed below, among others, in reporting to the membership on any proposed transfer outside a home territory. Such factors were contained in a bill reported by a Senate committee in 1984; they essentially restate matters that the League has considered vital in connection with team location decisions in the past. Accordingly, any club proposing to transfer should, in its submission to the Commissioner's office, present the club's position as to the bearing of these factors on its proposed transfer, stating specifically why such a move is regarded as justified on these standards:

1. The adequacy of the stadium in which the team played its home games in the previous season, and the willingness of the stadium or arena authority to remedy any deficiencies in such facility;

2. The extent to which fan loyalty to and support for the team has been demonstrated during the team's tenure in the existing community;

3. The extent to which the team, directly or indirectly, received public financial support by means of any publicly financed playing facility, special tax treatment and any other form of public financial support;

4. The degree to which the ownership or management of the team has contributed to any circumstance which might otherwise demonstrate the need for such relocation;

5. Whether the team has incurred net operating losses, exclusive of depreciation and amortization, sufficient to threaten the continued financial viability of the team;

6. The degree to which the team has engaged in good faith negotiations with appropriate persons concerning terms and conditions under which the team would continue to play its games in such community or elsewhere within its current home territory;

7. Whether any other team in the League is located in the community in which the team is currently located;

8. Whether the team proposes to relocate to a community in which no other team in the League is located; and

9. Whether the stadium authority, if public, is not opposed to such relocation.

Any club proposing to transfer will have a full opportunity to state its position to the membership and to make its case for the proposed transfer. In order to fully assess a proposed transfer in light of the variety of League interests involved, and to fairly resolve the interests of all parties, it is essential that the membership be fully apprised of the relevant facts with respect to any proposed transfer. The procedures and policies outlined above are directed to that end.

EXHIBIT 3

REPORT TO THE
NFL EXECUTIVE COMMITTEE

Re: Request By the Los Angeles Rams To Transfer Their Home Playing Site To <u>St. Louis, Missouri</u>

February 16, 1995

TABLE OF CONTENTS

Page

I. The Los Angeles Rams -- 1980-1995: From Relocation to Proposed Relocation. 1

II. The League's Procedures For Evaluating Proposed Franchise Relocations. 5

III. The Los Angeles Rams' Proposal. 7

IV. Analysis Of The Club's Justifications For The Proposed Move to St. Louis 8

    A. Attendance and Local Revenues 9

    B. The Club's Profit Levels in Anaheim 12

    C. Alternatives in Anaheim 13

    D. Television and Related Considerations. . . . 16

    E. The Club's Profit Potential/Sale Potential . . 18

V. Conclusion 19

APPENDIX A -- Description of Rams-St. Louis Transactions

APPENDIX B -- Appendix to Statement of Reasons of Los Angeles Rams Supporting Transfer of Club to St. Louis, Missouri (Index)

APPENDIX C -- Chronology of the Rams in Anaheim

APPENDIX D -- Los Angeles Rams - Attendance versus 4-Year Trailing Winning Percentage

REPORT TO THE
NFL EXECUTIVE COMMITTEE

Re: Request By The Los Angeles Rams To
Transfer Their Home Playing Site To
St. Louis, Missouri

On February 1, 1995, the Los Angeles Rams formally advised the League of their desire to relocate from Anaheim to St. Louis beginning with the 1995 NFL season. In support, the Rams presented a 25-page Statement of Reasons and detailed related materials. In doing so, the Rams also "reserve[d] the right to challenge any . . . conclusion [disapproving the move] and any procedures, rules, or bylaws that might be invoked to bar relocation to St. Louis."

This report reflects my evaluation of the Rams' request and of their supporting Statement of Reasons in relation to the factors set forth in the League's Procedures for Proposed Franchise Relocations.

I. The Los Angeles Rams -- 1980-1995: From Relocation to Proposed Relocation

In 1980, with League approval, the Los Angeles Rams transferred their home location from the Los Angeles Coliseum to the "Big A" stadium in Anaheim/Orange County ("Anaheim").

At that time, Anaheim was regarded as a prime location for an NFL team. In the mid-1970s, the League's expansion process -- which led to teams in Seattle and Tampa Bay -- had identified Anaheim as a very strong expansion market. The area had a vibrant, broad-based economy with attractive demographics and strong consumer purchasing power. In addition, Orange County and nearby locations had increasingly become the suburban home of the Rams' season-ticket-holder base.

Anaheim Stadium was also regarded as one of the most attractive, modern suburban stadiums for NFL football, even though it was a dual-purpose stadium also used by Major League Baseball; the stadium, located near Disneyland, had excellent highway access, extensive parking, and other amenities. The stadium's capacity for NFL games was some 69,000; it was one of a limited number of NFL stadiums then to have a large number of attractive box suites; and the Rams' lease was one of the more rewarding of any in the entire League.

When the Rams transferred to Anaheim, the club's lease with the City covered a 35-year period, from 1980 to 2014. The lease was also tied to a land development agreement that authorized a Rams affiliate to engage in commercial development of valuable real estate adjacent to the stadium.

For the Rams' first decade in Anaheim, the club was very well supported. In the first two seasons (1980-1981), the club had annual season ticket sales averaging 63,000. For the first ten seasons (1980-1989), attendance remained at high levels, averaging 61,331.

By the mid-1980s, the Rams had become involved in protracted litigation with the California Angels and the City of Anaheim concerning development of the adjacent real estate. In June 1988, the Rams were effectively barred by a court injunction from participating in that commercial development.

In 1989-1990, the Rams' fortunes on the playing field and their relationship with the City of Anaheim both took sharp turns. In 1990, the club's won/loss record flipped to 5-11 from 11-5 in the prior season. In the fall of 1990, while an appeal of the injunction on commercial development was pending, the Rams and the City of Anaheim renegotiated their stadium lease for the fourth time, with the Rams receiving the right, effective April 1, 1994, to terminate the club's stadium lease upon 15 months' prior notice and payment of a forfeiture fee. In turn, the Rams gave up their rights to the development project.

In subsequent seasons, the sharp decline in the Rams' playing field fortunes continued. In the five seasons 1984-1989 (excluding the strike season of 1987), the Rams had made the NFL play-offs each season; had twice played (and lost) in the NFC Championship Game (in 1985 and 1989); and had a cumulative won/loss record of 52-28.

In contrast, in the five seasons from 1990-1994, the Rams had a combined won/loss record of 23-57, and the club did not win more than six games in any one season. Even so, in the first four of these seasons, through 1993, the Rams' attendance continued to average almost 56,000 per game.

By 1992 or 1993, the Rams' future in Anaheim began to be influenced as much by developments in the League's expansion process as by developments in Anaheim. In May 1992, five cities (Baltimore, Carolinas, Jacksonville, Memphis, and St. Louis) were identified as the final contenders for the two anticipated expansion franchises. In March 1993, after the Collective Bargaining Agreement cleared the way for League expansion, the League intensified and pursued the expansion process. During that process, St. Louis' plans for a soon to be completed domed stadium were presented to the League's Expansion Committee and outlined for the League's entire membership at a meeting in October 1993.

Soon after the League selected Jacksonville as the second expansion site in November 1993, the Rams publicly stated that they intended to pursue the possibility of moving to all three of the expansion finalists that were not selected, as well as other cities. Only weeks later, in January 1994, the Rams gave informal notice to the City of Anaheim that they intended to invoke the escape clause of their stadium lease. In May 1994, the Rams gave the City a letter of intent to terminate their stadium lease, formally exercising that escape clause.

In January 1995, having explored options in both St. Louis and Baltimore, the Rams announced an agreement by which they propose to "bring NFL football to St. Louis." In return, St. Louis interests would make substantial payments to the Rams, not unlike the payments made to the League's entire membership by the Carolinas and Jacksonville when those communities secured NFL expansion franchises.

II. The League's Procedures For Evaluating
Proposed Franchise Relocations

Under the League's Constitution and By-Laws, each member club holding an NFL franchise has "the exclusive right within its home territory to exhibit professional football games played by teams of the League. . . ." Whenever two franchises are located in the same city, such as in the Los Angeles area, each franchise has "equal rights within the home territory of such city." Under the Constitution and By-Laws, the approval by vote of three-fourths of the member clubs is required before a club may "transfer its franchise or playing site to a different city, either within or outside its home territory . . ."

To provide input to such a membership decision, the Procedures for Proposed Franchise Relocations, first promulgated in 1984, require the Commissioner to evaluate a proposed team transfer and to report to the membership on the club's request. Under these Procedures, the membership can consider a wide range of business factors bearing on a proposed relocation. In the first instance, a number of factors set forth in the Procedures need to be considered. These "were contained in a bill reported by a Senate Committee in 1984; they essentially restate matters that the League has considered vital in connection with team location decisions in the past."

These factors are stated in the League's Procedures as follows:

- The adequacy of the stadium in which the team played its home games in the previous season, and the willingness of the stadium or arena authority to remedy any deficiencies in such facility;

- The extent to which fan loyalty to and support for the team has been demonstrated during the team's tenure in the existing community;

- The extent to which the team, directly or indirectly, received public financial support by means of any publicly funded playing facility, special tax treatment, and any other form of public financial support;

- The degree to which the ownership or management of the team has contributed to any circumstance which might otherwise demonstrate the need for such relocation;

- Whether the team has incurred net operating losses, exclusive of depreciation and amortization, sufficient to threaten the continued viability of the team;

- The degree to which the team has engaged in good faith negotiations with appropriate persons concerning terms and conditions under which the team would continue to play its games in such community or elsewhere within its current home territory;

- Whether any other team in the League is located in the community in which the team is currently located;

- Whether the team proposes to relocate to a community in which no other team in the League is located; and

- Whether the stadium authority, if public, is not opposed to such relocation.

- 7 -

Based upon the Rams' submission and with the assistance of League Office staff, I have considered the Rams' proposal in relation to these factors. At this stage, I have not involved any League committees in this evaluation, although this may be done, as appropriate, prior to the League's Annual Meeting in March.

In my judgment, based on the information now available, the proposed Rams' relocation is not justified on the basis of these factors.

At the same time, given the importance of the issues raised by the Rams' proposal, I believe that the membership needs to evaluate a variety of other considerations, including the impact of the Rams' proposed relocation on the League's current two team representation in the Los Angeles market. These considerations also include questions of ownership policy; television circumstances; the relationship of the Rams' proposal to the League's recent expansion process and future expansion prospects; Collective Bargaining Agreement issues; and issues with respect to the relationship of member clubs to municipal and other landlords.

III. The Los Angeles Rams' Proposal

The Rams propose (a) to move, effective with the 1995 League season, to St. Louis, where in October they would begin play in a new stadium,[1] and (b) to sell to Stanley Kroenke, of Columbia, Missouri, for $60 million a 30 percent, non-controlling equity interest in the club, options to acquire an additional 10 percent, and a right of first refusal on the majority interest.

Appendix A to this Report summarizes the proposed arrangements, the details of which are reflected in two volumes of documents submitted to the League Office.

Appendix B lists the contracts and other documents contained in those two volumes.

Appendix C is a chronology of events leading up to the Rams' proposal.

IV. Analysis Of The Club's Justifications For The Proposed Move to St. Louis

The Rams' Statement of Reasons supporting transfer of the club to St. Louis offers a series of justifications for the club's proposal. The Rams' Statement is available to member clubs for review but, pursuant to the Rams' request, copies of the Statement will not be distributed to each club for general use.

In short, the Rams submit that because of allegedly inadequate attendance, inadequate local revenues, and an

---

[1] Initially, the Rams might play one or more 1995 games in Busch Stadium. By October, St. Louis will have in place a new domed facility with 65,000 seats, including over 6,300 club seats, 120 private suites, and room to expand the premium seat capacity.

inherently flawed stadium, which they claim the City is unwilling to improve, the club is not and cannot be profitable in Anaheim. They emphasize that the club would realize substantial profits in the new domed stadium in St. Louis, and that the League's television and other interests would be better served if the Rams were permitted to move there from the greater Los Angeles area.

Each of the Rams' proposed justifications is considered below.

A. <u>Attendance and Local Revenues</u>

The Rams moved to Anaheim in 1980. Throughout the 1980s, the greater Los Angeles area demonstrated substantial support for the club. Beginning in 1991, however, as the following chart demonstrates, that support began to wane.

NFL Season	Home Game Average Attendance
1980-88	61,824
1989	62,467
1990	63,745
1991	57,827
1992	51,813
1993	49,628
1994	44,772

For the last four years, the Rams' average home-game attendance, as a percentage of stadium capacity, has been among the lowest of all NFL clubs, despite a population in the greater Los Angeles area of over 15,000,000 persons. There has been a similar decline in the Rams' season ticket sales.

Particularly in 1994, the Rams' attendance and season ticket sales were undoubtedly affected by the club's public statements addressing possible relocation. Such public statements and their impact, in and of themselves, are not a material factor in my evaluation.

The attendance trends discussed above cannot be considered in isolation.

During the 1970's and 1980's, the Rams were among the League's most competitive teams on the field. During the 1970s, the Rams won nearly 70 percent of their regular season games, more than all but four other clubs, and they reached the playoffs eight consecutive seasons. From 1980 to 1988, the Rams won over 53 percent of their games, reaching the play-offs six seasons.

But following the 1989 season, the Rams' on-field fortunes began to change. It is thus not surprising or unusual that attendance and related club revenues have been under pressure.

During the four most recent seasons, the Rams won fewer than thirty percent of their games, a record worse than that of all but four NFL clubs; in the prior seven seasons, the Rams had had only one losing season: the 1987 strike season. The decline in the Rams' home game attendance was plainly caused by the decline in the Rams' on-field performance, as the graph in **Appendix D** confirms.

- 11 -

The Rams' Statement of Reasons asserts that "[g]iven the inherent problems of Anaheim Stadium, it is unreasonable to expect a reversal in the trend of declining attendance." I do not believe that this statement is supported or supportable. (I address the adequacy of Anaheim Stadium below.) The Rams' assertion cannot be reconciled with the levels of attendance achieved by the club in the same stadium during the period before 1991, when the club was fielding competitive teams; with the size and demographics of the potential NFL audience in greater Los Angeles; or with the experience of other NFL clubs.

The decline in Rams' home game attendance has, of course, resulted in a decline in the Rams' local revenues, which the Rams' Statement of Reasons discusses in detail. Nonetheless, until 1993, when their average attendance first fell below 50,000, the Rams' local revenues had been consistently above the League average. In fact, as recently as 1990, the Rams were among the top third of all NFL clubs in home gate receipts.[2/]

B. **The Club's Profit Levels in Anaheim**

Notwithstanding the recent decline in home game attendance, the Rams have been among the more profitable clubs

---

[2/] In contrast, when the Cardinals proposed to relocate from St. Louis to Phoenix, the club's local revenues were, and for a considerable period had been, among the lowest in the League. For nine of the ten years from 1977 until 1986, the Cardinals were among the lowest five clubs in home gate receipts.

in the League during each of the last four years for which data are available (1990-93). During that period, the net operating profit of the Rams and their football affiliates (before depreciation and amortization) ranged from $7.1 million to $10.9 million per year -- averaging $9.5 million per year -- a level consistently and substantially above the League average.[3/] This has been true despite general and administrative expenses, for which we do not have a detailed accounting, that have also been consistently in the top quartile of League clubs.

Moreover, during the last five years, the Rams' owner received from the club -- in dividends and other earnings -- substantial sums, which will be discussed in more detail at the League Meeting of February 16, 1995.[4/]

[3/] These and other financial data are based on the audited and conforming financial statements, which reflect revenues and expenses on a reasonably consistent basis for all NFL clubs. The Rams assert that their net income from operations for this period averaged about $1.9 million per year, but the Rams' numbers do not take into account operating income of the Rams' affiliate Business Properties, Inc., which leases the luxury suites at Anaheim. The Rams' numbers also reflect non-operating items, i.e., interest income and interest expense, which result in an understatement of the Rams' income. The conforming statement numbers represent the more complete and accurate picture of the Rams' financial performance and fully support the principal conclusions discussed in the text.

[4/] During the period in which substantial earnings were being paid out by the club, the Rams' player costs declined steadily from at or near the League average, where they had been since 1980, to near the bottom of all 28 clubs. Since 1991, the first full season after they secured the right to terminate their stadium lease (see Appendix C), the Rams have been among the teams spending the least on players; indeed,
(continued...)

In short, the financial data do not support the club's position that it is not and cannot be profitable in Anaheim.

C. **Alternatives in Anaheim**

For the last fourteen years, the Rams have played in Anaheim Stadium, one of ten dual-purpose (football/baseball) stadiums in the League; the Rams share the stadium with baseball's California Angels. With a current capacity of 67,821, Anaheim Stadium is the 14th largest facility in the NFL. While many of its seats have less than ideal sight lines and some have partially obstructed views, the stadium has an outstanding field, good locker room facilities, ample parking, and excellent transportation access. Like most NFL stadiums, Anaheim Stadium has virtually no club or "premium" seats, but the stadium has 108 suites.[5]

Though constructed principally for baseball, Anaheim Stadium is undoubtedly adequate for NFL football.[6]

---

[4] (...continued) in **each** of the three years prior to implementation of the salary cap, the Rams' player costs were, on average, $5.4 million less than the League average.

[5] The Rams' gross suite income of approximately $2.5 million per year ranks them among the top ten clubs in the League in that category.

[6] In contrast, when the Cardinals proposed to move from St. Louis to Phoenix, there was general agreement among all concerned that Busch Stadium was no longer adequate for NFL football. Busch Stadium, then the second smallest stadium in the League, had a capacity of only 51,517 seats; pending proposals to increase the stadium capacity would have resulted (continued...)

Nonetheless, Anaheim Stadium needs renovations to provide amenities (including improved suites, club seating areas, concessions, and restroom facilities) typical of the latest generation of state-of-the-art NFL stadia.

The Rams contend that the City of Anaheim is unwilling or unable to improve or replace the stadium or to improve the Rams' rental terms. It is difficult to assess this contention, but it is vigorously challenged by representatives of Anaheim/Orange County, including in recent discussions with League Office staff.

I understand that the City of Anaheim and other communities in Orange County, in conjunction with local civic and business leaders, have made various proposals to the Rams that offered significant improvements in Anaheim Stadium, improvements in the Rams' lease terms, a new training facility, guaranteed levels of ticket sales, and ultimately a new football-only stadium.[7]

At this stage, we are not able to evaluate the substance or merits of any of those proposals or to conclude that any would have led to an arrangement satisfactory to the

---

[6] (...continued)
in stadium capacity ranking only 22nd in the League, well below the League average.

[7] In addition, there have been reports of several substantial California businessmen who have offered -- or are prepared -- to purchase majority or minority interests in the Rams in order to maintain the franchise in the greater Los Angeles area.

Rams. Nor can we now determine whether the Rams engaged in serious negotiations or made a serious evaluation of any of these proposals.

The Rams' Statement essentially acknowledges, however, that the club's consideration has focused not on whether satisfactory alternative arrangements are available in Anaheim -- but instead on whether the club could significantly increase its profits by relocating to another city, including one of those that had aggressively pursued an NFL expansion franchise. According to the Rams' report,

> "Events, however, had overtaken the question of a new lease. The team's discussions with the other cities made it clear that <u>Anaheim</u> <u>could</u> <u>be</u> <u>economically</u> <u>competitive</u> <u>with</u> <u>the</u> <u>alternative</u> <u>cities</u> <u>only</u> <u>if</u> it helped to support the construction of a new stadium built for football.

As further explained below, the League's relocation criteria do not contemplate that a club may abandon its designated home territory simply because it is offered an "economically [more] competitive" arrangement elsewhere.

D. **Television and Related Considerations**

The Rams contend that a move from Los Angeles to St. Louis would permit the League to tap a promising marketplace (*e.g.*, for merchandise sales) and reverse a "disturbing trend" associated with television blackouts.

While St. Louis would be a strong venue for NFL football, and even though another NFL club would <u>presumably</u> remain in Los Angeles if the Rams were permitted to leave, the

Rams' proposed move would clearly weaken the NFC television package and, in the long-term, would not be likely to have a positive impact on the League's broadcast or other television interests.

Senior executives of the three principal broadcast networks (ABC, NBC and Fox) have advised us that, on a long-term basis, television considerations strongly suggest *two* NFL teams in the greater Los Angeles area. Los Angeles has the second largest population of any metropolitan area in the country; now over 15,000,000, the Los Angeles area population has historically experienced high growth, which is expected to continue. The St. Louis metropolitan area has barely *one sixth* that many people, a population level plainly sufficient to support an NFL franchise, but one dwarfed in size by that of the greater Los Angeles area.[8]

More importantly, the Los Angeles television market is crucial to the League's success. With 5 million television households, Los Angeles ranks as the country's second largest television market; in contrast, St. Louis, with 1.1 million television households, ranks 20th. If we expect to sustain and to increase our television revenues, a strong presence in Los Angeles will be necessary.

---

[8] In addition, the Orange County area's median household income (about $46,000) is about 25 percent greater than that of St. Louis (about $38,000).

In this light, Fox has informed us (by letter from its Chief Executive Officer, Chase Carey) that that network, whose flagship station is in Los Angeles, would consider a Rams departure to be a "material detraction from the rights [Fox] licensed" in its **current** television contract.[2]

Of course, the recent decline in Rams' home game attendance has affected the League's ability to take full advantage of the greater Los Angeles television market. During the four seasons from 1991 to 1994, all but four of the Rams' home games were blacked out, and only one Rams game was broadcast during prime time. Thus, a Rams' departure from Los Angeles might have a **short-term** positive effect on the NFL's Los Angeles area television ratings; but this would not enhance the revenues to be received by the League under the current television contracts and, as noted above, raises the possibility of a negotiated reduction in those revenues.

E. **The Club's Profit Potential/Sale Potential**

Given the guarantees and other inducements offered by St. Louis, there is little question (assuming no diminution in television rights fees) that the Rams would earn higher profits in St. Louis than in Anaheim. (Visiting team shares would also likely be higher in St. Louis than in Anaheim.) But these facts have to be considered in context.

---

[2] Executives from NBC and ABC have advised that they would **not** assert that a Rams move to St. Louis would be a material change in their broadcast contracts.

- 18 -

As the relocation criteria suggest, every club is entitled to a high level of confidence in its short-term and long-term financial viability. If that confidence is threatened by factors in the club's home territory that cannot be remedied, a move may well be justified.

On the other hand, a claim that a club is no longer viable in its designated home territory, and hence must be relocated, must at some point be compared with other alternatives, including current ownership's sale of the club at a reasonable price to new ownership that would be prepared to operate the team in its present territory. In current League circumstances, such a sale might well yield an extraordinary return on the current owner's investment.

The League must continue to encourage and maintain strong incentives (1) for clubs to "add value" to the League venture through the fielding of a competitive team that produces strong attendance and television ratings; and (2) for owners to invest in their clubs and club facilities, particularly stadiums. By providing windfalls to clubs and owners that fail to do both, the premature or poorly-grounded approval of team relocations would undermine rather than reinforce these essential League objectives.

In short, I do not believe that a club can reasonably expect to be assured of **extraordinary** returns -- such as those that the Rams claim could be realized in St. Louis -- that, **in the absence of conditions precluding a**

reasonable profit or sale price in its current location, can become the basis for abandoning its home territory. If that is a club's expectation, other alternatives, including a sale of the franchise, can fairly be considered.[10]

V. Conclusion

I assume that the proposed relocation would be good for the Rams, at least in the short term. In numerous respects, the new St. Louis stadium would have more modern amenities and a more desirable seating configuration than Anaheim Stadium. It also appears that, all other things being equal, in the short-term the Rams' profits, as well as visiting team shares, would be higher in St. Louis than in Anaheim.

Nonetheless, I am not now persuaded that allowing the Rams to abandon greater Los Angeles would be in the best interests of the League or its clubs in the **short or long term**. Based upon the information now available, the Rams' proposal is not supported by the factors set forth in the League's Relocation Procedures. Among other things:

---

[10] The Rams' proposed relocation to St. Louis would not have a material impact on inter-franchise rivalries and, under the current alignment scheme, would reduce travel time and expenses for three of their four NFC Western Division rivals; the travel time for the 49ers would be increased, but the increase in the 49ers' travel expenses would likely be more than offset by an increase in their Visiting Team Share. Such a move would, however, complicate television scheduling, requiring the League to retain absolute control over the start time for all Rams' Sunday afternoon home games. The effect of a Rams' move on possible realignment is uncertain.

- Anaheim was and is a prime location for an NFL team, with a broad-based economy and attractive demographics.

- Fan support for the team was proven for over a decade, before the club allowed its on-field performance to deteriorate, during which the Rams demonstrated the potential to be among the League's higher revenue (and profit) clubs.

- Rams' ownership and management have contributed to, if not caused, the circumstances upon which they rely in an effort to justify the move.

- The team has not had recurring net operating losses (exclusive of depreciation and amortization), and its continued viability is not in question. Indeed, with improved on-field performance, the Rams should be able to maintain a profitable, competitive franchise in Anaheim, even without regard to proposed improvements in their local circumstances.

- The Rams have not demonstrated that they engaged in a sustained effort to secure a satisfactory arrangement that would enable the club to remain in its home territory.

At the same time, as noted above, given the importance of the issues raised by the Rams' proposal, I believe that the membership needs to evaluate a variety of other considerations, including the impact of the Rams' proposed relocation on the League's current two team representation in the Los Angeles market. These considerations also include questions of ownership policy; television circumstances; the relationship of the Rams' proposal to the League's recent expansion process and future expansion prospects; Collective Bargaining Agreement issues; and issues with respect to the relationship of member clubs to municipal and other landlords.

                                         Paul Tagliabue

APPENDIX A

DESCRIPTION OF RAMS-ST. LOUIS TRANSACTIONS

The Rams' proposal consists of four component transactions involving the following parties:

- Los Angeles Rams Football Company, Inc.;
- the St. Louis Convention and Visitors Commission ("CVC"), a governmental entity that is the ultimate landlord of the St. Louis stadium;
- FANS, Inc., a Missouri nonprofit corporation chartered in 1993 to lead the effort to bring NFL football back to St. Louis, acting primarily as agent for the CVC; and
- E. Stanley Kroenke, a Columbia, Missouri, businessman who headed a St. Louis expansion ownership group in the fall of 1993.

1. **The Relocation Transaction**

Pursuant to a Relocation Agreement, the Rams would relocate their operations to St. Louis beginning in 1995, contingent upon League approval. The Rams would be paid $13,000,000 to defray moving and legal expenses and to defray their operating losses.

Pursuant to the Relocation Agreement and the new St. Louis stadium lease, CVC would arrange to defease certain provisions of the Rams' Anaheim Stadium lease relating to City of Anaheim bonds that funded stadium improvements. The

- 2 -

payments to Anaheim are to be made annually under the terms of the St. Louis lease. The principal amount of the Rams' obligations under the Anaheim lease is estimated to be about $30,000,000.

CVC would also be obligated to construct a training facility for the Rams and to make certain scheduled improvements to the new St. Louis domed stadium. Among other things, additional luxury suites are being built at the stadium.

Civic Progress (a coalition of St. Louis businesses) would guarantee the Rams certain minimum revenues following their relocation pursuant to an agreement that has not yet been provided to us. The Rams would also be indemnified for third-party claims related to previous NFL-related activities in St. Louis.

If the Rams' application to relocate is disapproved or if material conditions are imposed on a League approval, either the Rams or FANS, Inc. (as agent for all involved St. Louis parties) may terminate the Relocation Agreement within a specified period of time. If neither party terminates the agreement, both parties apparently are committed to challenge such disapproval or conditions pursuant to a litigation management agreement that has not been provided to us.

2. <u>Stadium Lease</u>

The lease would afford the Rams use of the stadium for a period of 30 years.

The lease gives the Rams certain reserved rights as to stadium club areas and luxury suites, which would be limited with respect to four specified events: the NCAA Final Four, either of the major political parties' national conventions, and the Super Bowl. The Rams would not generally participate financially in any such events. CVC, as the stadium lessor, would also be permitted to schedule other events at the stadium and would have scheduling priority outside the NFL season. The Rams would receive a portion of the proceeds (largely concessions, but excluding direct ticket proceeds) derived from the club and suite levels in connection with such other events.

Subject to CVC's scheduling priority, the Rams would also be permitted to arrange non-football events and football-related events other than the four events specified above, on days other than Rams' game days. The Rams would receive all gross income from those events, subject to the Rams' obligation to pay all incremental operating expenses related to such events.

The Rams would pay annual rent of $250,000 for 10 game dates and all post-season dates. The Rams would also pay half of game-day stadium operating expenses. The Rams would retain (1) all income from any remaining Personal Seat Licenses sold after September 1, 1995, (2) all annual club seat and luxury suite rental income, (3) two-thirds of the concession and non-Rams novelty income from the club and suite levels for non-Rams events, plus all of the income from Rams novelties on such levels at such events, (4) two-thirds of the payments from promoters related to ticket sales on the suite level from non-Rams events, (5) three-fourths of net advertising revenues from the stadium and convention center, up to $6 million (at which point the sharing rate changes), (6) all game-day concessions and novelty income, and (7) all ticket, concessions and novelty income from Rams events other than NFL games (with the Rams bearing incremental event-day stadium operating costs).

3. **Personal Seat License Sales**

FANS, Inc., as agent for the CVC, has the right to sell personal seat licenses for most of the seats in the stadium. The Rams would not be permitted to sell season tickets for a seat unless either they or FANS, Inc., have sold a personal seat license for that seat. All revenues derived from PSL sales and PSL transfer fees prior to September 1, 1995, would go to the CVC; all revenue derived from PSL sales and PSL transfer fees after that date would go to the Rams, who would be responsible for general and administrative expenses associated with such transfers.

If a PSL for a seat lapses after September 1, 1995 (including lapses due to the failure of the PSL holder to purchase new season tickets), the Rams may, but are not obligated to, issue a new PSL for the affected seat on whatever terms they choose. In such circumstances, the Rams may also sell season tickets for the seat to a new buyer without issuing a new PSL.

Unlike the Carolina PSLs, which can be repurchased and resold by the team if the original buyer attempts to transfer them within a certain period after they are issued, the St. Louis PSLs are "one-shot" rights. The team does not have a right to repurchase or reissue original-issue PSLs.

CVC is not obligated to use personal seat license revenues for any specified purpose. Rather, the revenues would become general funds of CVC that can be used to defray its expenses as it may see fit. We have been unable to ascertain the extent to which the Rams may benefit from these funds.

4. **The Kroenke Investment**

Mr. Kroenke would invest approximately $60,000,000 in exchange for a 30 percent, non-controlling equity interest in a new entity that would own the Rams. He would have an option to acquire an additional 10 percent of the team (in two 5 percent tranches) on the same economic terms. He would also have a right of first refusal on the current owner's interest in the team should she decide to sell.

Mr. Kroenke would have input into decisions to the extent that current Rams ownership permits it, but would not have voting or veto rights. His investment apparently would occur only if the Rams moved to St. Louis.

APPENDIX B

APPENDIX TO NOTICE AND STATEMENT OF REASONS OF LOS ANGELES RAMS
SUPPORTING TRANSFER OF CLUB TO ST. LOUIS, MISSOURI

VOLUME I

TAB	DOCUMENT
A	Diagram of Anaheim Stadium
B	Exhibition Agreement Between the City of Anaheim and the Los Angeles Rams Football Company
B1	First Amendment to the Exhibition Agreement Dated 3/13/79
B2	Second Amendment to the Exhibition Agreement Dated 6/14/83
B3	Third Amendment to the Exhibition Agreement Dated 2/21/89
B4	Fourth Amendment to the Exhibition Agreement Dated 9/18/90
B5	Fifth Amendment to the Exhibition Agreement Dated 9/15/92
C	City of Anaheim -- Los Angeles Rams Operations Agreement
C1	First Amendment to Operations Agreement Dated 6/14/83
C2	Second Amendment to Operations Agreement Dated 2/25/86
C3	Third Amendment to Operations Agreement Dated 12/15/87
C4	Fourth Amendment to Operations Agreement Dated 2/21/89
D	Los Angeles Rams Audited Financial Statements
	1. Fiscal Years 1992 and 1993
	2. Fiscal Years 1991 and 1992
	3. Fiscal Years 1990 and 1991

VOLUME II

TAB	DOCUMENT
E	Relocation Documents

1. Escrow Agreement
2. NFL Franchise Relocation Agreement
3. Amended and Restated St. Louis NFL Lease
4. Annex 1 -- Facilities, Status, Management, Maintenance and Repair
5. Annex 2 -- Advertising
6. Annex 3 -- Concessions
7. Annex 4 -- Parking
8. Assignment and Assumption Agreement (And Consents Thereto)
9. Master Parking Provider Agreement
10. Training Facility Program and Lease
11. Temporary Training Facility Term Sheet
12. Charter Personal Seat License Master Agreement
13. Non-Disturbance And Attornment Agreement
14. Indemnity and Hold Harmless Agreement
15. PSL Sale Requirements

F   St. Louis Projected Financial Proformas

G   Comparison of Anaheim and St. Louis Visitors Shares

H   Los Angeles Rams Attendance Figures 1991-93

APPENDIX C

CHRONOLOGY OF THE RAMS IN ANAHEIM

1937	The Cleveland Rams join the National Football League.
1946	The Rams move to Los Angeles, where they begin play at the Los Angeles Coliseum.
July 1978	The Rams sign a lease with the City of Anaheim to play their home games at Anaheim Stadium from 1980 to 2014. The lease is tied to an agreement that allows a Rams affiliate to engage in commercial development of the stadium parking lot area.
August 1980	The Rams begin play at Anaheim Stadium.
June 1988	A California court issues a permanent injunction effectively barring commercial development of the stadium parking lot.
September 1990	The City and the Rams renegotiate their stadium lease terms for the fourth time. The Rams receive the right, effective April 1, 1994, to terminate the lease upon 15 months' prior notice and payment of certain prescribed sums. The Rams give up their rights to the parking lot development.
1993	According to the Rams' Statement of Reasons, "alarm[caused] by the decline in attendance" caused them to "beg[i]n exploring options to improve the financial competitiveness of the franchise."
December 1993	Following selection of Jacksonville as the second expansion city, the Rams state publicly that they intend to pursue the possibility of moving to St. Louis or Baltimore.
January 1994	The Rams give informal notice to the City of Anaheim that they intend to invoke the escape clause of their stadium lease.
May 1994	The Rams give the City a letter of intent to terminate the stadium lease and a $2 million non-refundable check, exercising the 15-month escape clause.
January 1995	The Rams announce agreement with St. Louis interests to move to St. Louis for the 1995 season.
February 1, 1995	The Rams give formal notice to the League of their proposal to move to St. Louis.

APPENDIX D

Los Angeles Rams
Attendance versus 4-Year Trailing Winning Percentage

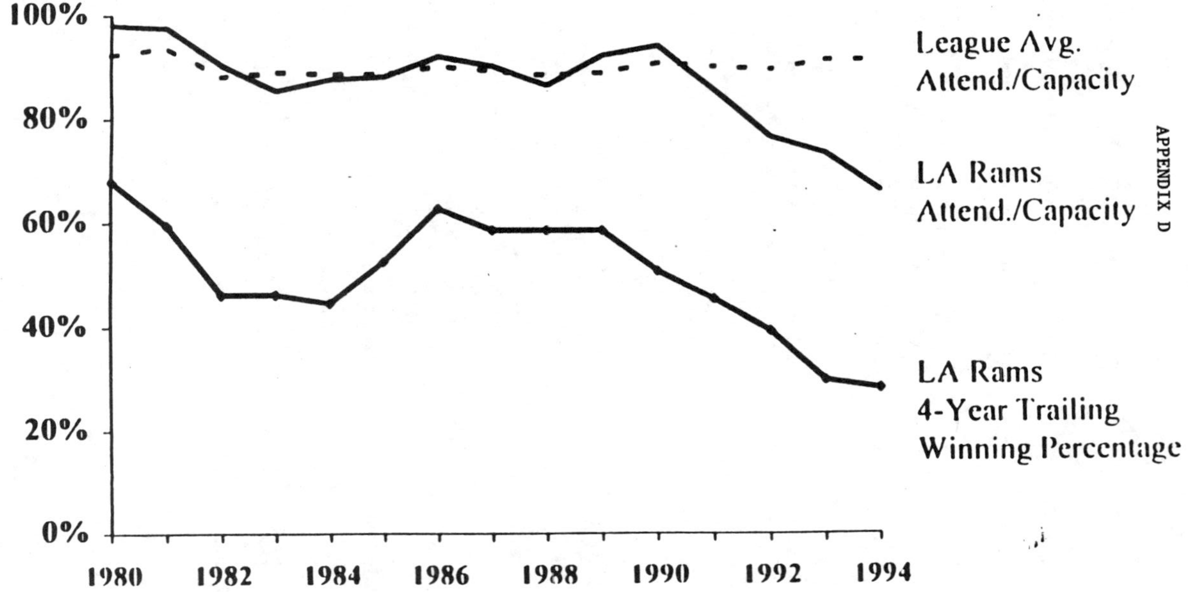

EXHIBIT 4

**REPORT TO THE
NFL EXECUTIVE COMMITTEE**

Re: <u>Request By The Los Angeles Raiders
To Transfer Their Home Playing Site
To Oakland, California</u>

July 21, 1995

TABLE OF CONTENTS

Page

I.	Overview	2
II.	The League's Procedures for Franchise Relocation	5
III.	The Oakland Offer	8
IV.	The Hollywood Park Alternative	12
	A. The Raiders' Lease at Hollywood Park	14
	B. The "Second-Team Option" at Hollywood Park	15
V.	The Raiders' Performance In Los Angeles	17
VI.	The Raiders' Negotiations to Secure Alternative Sites In Los Angeles	19
VII.	The Bay Area	20
VIII.	Television Issues	23
IX.	Conclusion	25

**REPORT TO THE
NFL EXECUTIVE COMMITTEE**

Re: Request By The Los Angeles Raiders
To Transfer Their Home Playing Site
To Oakland, California

On June 23, 1995, shortly before making a public announcement, Al Davis formally advised me of the Raiders' intention to sign a letter agreement committing the Raiders to relocate from Los Angeles to Oakland beginning with the 1995 NFL season, subject to certain approvals.

"Reserving [their] rights" on the issue of whether a membership vote is necessary for a franchise to relocate, the Raiders recently presented to the League Office a submission addressing the issues raised in the League's Relocation Procedures. That submission, and other materials submitted by the Raiders and the Oakland-Alameda County Commission at our request, supplement the extensive materials already available to the League Office as a result of (1) our consideration of Oakland as a potential expansion community; (2) our recent consideration of the Rams' proposed relocation from Los Angeles; and (3) our evaluation and negotiation of terms relating to the proposed Hollywood Park Stadium.

This report reflects my evaluation of the Raiders' request.

I. Overview

The Raiders propose to be the first major professional sports team in history to return to the community in which it was founded, in which it built its record and public appeal, and in which it prospered for many years, all under an ongoing ownership group with considerable continuity. Founded as the Oakland Raiders and having entered the League under the AFL-NFL "merger" agreement of 1966, the Raiders started regular NFL play as the Oakland Raiders in 1970. The Raiders shared the Bay Area territory with the San Francisco 49ers until 1982, when they moved to Los Angeles pursuant to a court order.

The Raiders' departure from Oakland was accomplished over the vigorous objections of the League's membership. As a result, the Raiders' current proposal raises a unique initial question: how should the League's franchise relocation criteria be applied to a club's proposed return to a territory that, from the League's standpoint, it never should have left?

There were numerous reasons for the membership's view that the Raiders' departure from Oakland was not justified. First, the Raiders were very successful in Oakland. Among the League's financially most successful clubs, the <u>Oakland</u> Raiders had (and seemingly still have) an intensely loyal following in the Bay Area. In its last season in Oakland, the club had the third highest ticket revenue in the

League, having sold out every home game, including pre-season games, for twelve consecutive seasons.

Second, notwithstanding promises to the Raiders of major improvements in the Los Angeles Coliseum (which were never delivered), the League believed that the Raiders would have difficulty succeeding in the Los Angeles Coliseum. Only four years before (in the fall of 1978), the League had approved the Rams' relocation to the "Big A" stadium in Anaheim, to take effect for the 1980 season, based in large part on the relative inadequacies of the Los Angeles Coliseum compared to the quality of the Anaheim stadium. The considerations underlying that decision were relatively fresh when the Raiders announced their intention to move into the Los Angeles Coliseum.

These concerns about the prospects for a successful Raiders' operation in the Coliseum were well founded. Despite fielding a competitive team and drawing substantial crowds on the road, every year since 1986 the Raiders' home game attendance in the Coliseum has been below the League average, both in absolute numbers and as a percentage of (adjusted) stadium capacity. See Attachments A and B. As a result, for years virtually every Raiders' home game has been blacked out in Los Angeles. See Attachment C.

Since 1978, when the Rams left for Anaheim Stadium, there have been changes in the configuration of the Los

Angeles Coliseum for NFL football, but there has been little material improvement in the quality of the Coliseum when assessed on the basis of current standards and needs. (The recent investment of $90 million was focused on repairing earthquake damage.) Today, located in a marginal area and lacking adequate parking, suites and other fan amenities, the Los Angeles Coliseum is not an attractive venue for NFL football.

Nor is a suitable alternative currently available in the greater Los Angeles area. Given the League's recent approval of the Rams' departure from Anaheim, it would be inappropriate to require the Raiders to play in Anaheim Stadium. There is also little reason to expect that the Raiders would receive greater community acceptance in Anaheim than they have received in Los Angeles. For a variety of other reasons, neither the Rose Bowl nor Dodger Stadium is now a suitable alternative.

If the Raiders remain in Los Angeles and the proposed Hollywood Park stadium is built, there would be a first-class, state-of-the-art facility in the Raiders' current home territory. But Hollywood Park is **not** currently available, and will not likely be available until 1998. (Even if the Raiders were to stay in Los Angeles, construction of that stadium is not yet a certainty given that only agreements in principle, and not final agreements or League approvals, have been reached with respect to that stadium.)

Giving due consideration to these and other factors addressed below, I have concluded that the League's interests would be best served by allowing the Raiders to return to Oakland, subject to conditions of the kind usually imposed on franchise relocations, with the understanding that the League collectively should move forward diligently to restore an NFL presence in the greater Los Angeles area.

II. **The League's Procedures for Franchise Relocation**

Under the Constitution and By-Laws, the approval by vote of three-fourths of the member clubs is required before a club may "transfer its franchise or playing site to a different city, either within or outside its home territory . . . ."

To provide input to such a membership decision, the Procedures for Proposed Franchise Relocations, first promulgated in 1984, require the Commissioner to evaluate a proposed team transfer and to report to the membership on the club's request. Under these Procedures, the membership can consider a wide range of business factors bearing on a proposed relocation. In the first instance, a number of factors set forth in the Procedures need to be considered. These "were contained in a bill reported by a Senate Committee in 1984; they essentially restate matters that the League has considered vital in connection with team location decisions in the past."

These factors are stated in the League's Procedures as follows:

- The adequacy of the stadium in which the team played its home games in the previous season, and the willingness of the stadium or arena authority to remedy any deficiencies in such facility;

- The extent to which fan loyalty to and support for the team has been demonstrated during the team's tenure in the existing community;

- The extent to which the team, directly or indirectly, received public financial support by means of any publicly funded playing facility, special tax treatment, and any other form of public financial support;

- The degree to which the ownership or management of the team has contributed to any circumstance which might otherwise demonstrate the need for such relocation;

- Whether the team has incurred net operating losses, exclusive of depreciation and amortization, sufficient to threaten the continued viability of the team;

- The degree to which the team has engaged in good faith negotiations with appropriate persons concerning terms and conditions under which the team would continue to play its games in such community or elsewhere within its current home territory;

- Whether any other team in the League is located in the community in which the team is currently located;

- Whether the team proposes to relocate to a community in which no other team in the League is located; and

- Whether the stadium authority, if public, is not opposed to such relocation.

- 7 -

The Raiders' formal "notice" of their intention to relocate to Oakland (June 23, 1995) was submitted to the League Office long after the mid-February date prescribed by the League's relocation procedures. The Raiders appear to take the position (1) that the mid-February notice date is invalid, or (2) that the League had actual notice on a timely basis of the possibility that the Raiders might relocate for the 1995 season, or (3) that the absence of compliance with the mid-February date will not cause any problems or disadvantage the League or the membership in any event.

While each of these points involves a variety of factual and other issues, most of which need not be addressed here, it is my recommendation that the membership consider the Raiders' proposed relocation on its merits, rather than decline to consider the matter because of the absence of a formal submission by mid-February.[1]

---

[1] For one thing, because the Raiders advised the League Office in February or March of the possibility of a proposed relocation to Oakland, the 1995 playing schedule was constructed in a manner that minimizes potential television conflicts regardless of whether the Raiders play in Oakland or in Los Angeles.

However, the Raiders' statements about the possibility of relocating to Oakland -- whether made to the League Office or in League meetings -- were made at the same time that the Raiders' clearly preferred alternative was said to be the Hollywood Park stadium. As a result of the absence of formal notice by mid-February, a variety of issues are raised with respect to the operations of NFL Properties and Properties' licensees. These issues, which concern potential costs and liabilities involving Los Angeles Raiders merchandise, should
(continued...)

III. **The Oakland Offer**

The City of Oakland, Alameda County, and the Oakland-Alameda Coliseum Commission have negotiated a number of agreements with the Raiders governing the proposed relocation. The agreements apparently were to have been signed last week and held in escrow pending the expiration of a "referendum risk period" on August 12, 1995; we have been told that none of the agreements has yet been executed.

The basic framework of the Oakland arrangements is as follows:

- The City, County, and Coliseum Commission will form Joint Authority, a Financing Corporation, and a Marketing Association.

 - The Joint Authority will sell approximately $190 million in lease-obligation revenue bonds.

 - The Marketing Association will (i) sell approximately $90 million in 10-year PSLs for Raiders games, and (ii) sell approximately $12 million in suites for Raiders games. All sales will be for the account of the Joint Authority.

 - The Marketing Association will also sell approximately $75 million in five-year PSLs for Raiders games for the seasons following the expiration of the Raiders' initial PSLs. All sales will be for the account of the Joint Authority.

 - All funds from the sales described above will be deposited in a Revenue Trust Account maintained by the Joint Authority, as will (i) "loge maintenance fees" charged on an annual basis to PSL purchasers, and (ii) "location

---

[1]/(...continued)
be considered in any League decision with respect to the Raiders' relocation.

premiums" charged to Raiders season ticket purchasers who did not also buy PSLs.

- The Financing Corporation will loan the Raiders money from the funding sources described above (i) to pay for approximately $120 million in stadium renovations to be owned by the Raiders (this number reflects both hard and soft costs), (ii) to construct a $10 million training facility to be owned by the Raiders, and (iii) to fund Raiders operations (including construction of a "Raiders Hall of Fame"). The "operations" loans would total approximately $54 million.

    - $22 million of the operations loans (specifically designated as being made in lieu of the Raiders' receiving concessions, advertising and parking revenue streams that the Joint Authority and/or the Oakland Athletics are retaining) will come from PSL funds. It is likely that the balance of the loans will come from bond revenues, although a "subaccount" of PSL funds will be established as a backup for the balance of the loans.

    - The Joint Authority will pay the Raiders approximately $5.7 million per year for the right to license others to use of the stadium improvements owned by the Raiders. This income stream will secure the Raiders' obligation to repay the Financing Corporation's loans to them.

    - The loans will bear interest at 10% per year and will mature in 40 years. Accrued but unpaid interest will be added to loan principal and will itself bear interest. Maturity of the loans will be accelerated if the Raiders cease to play in the Coliseum.

    - The Raiders will pay the Financing Corporation approximately $6.2 million per year in respect of these loans. The Financing Corporation will also apply the Joint Authority's 50% share of net concessions and parking income streams to the loans.

    - Title to the improvements will revert to the Joint Authority at the end of the Raiders' stadium lease. Upon reversion, the Raiders

will receive a credit towards the loans equal
to the lesser of the outstanding loan balances
or the fair market value of the reverting
improvements (the stadium improvements, the
training facility, and the Raiders Hall of
Fame).

- The loans will be non-recourse against the
  Raiders and their partners at maturity and at
  all other times, unless (i) the Raiders become
  insolvent, (ii) the Raiders fail to play home
  games at the Coliseum in the absence of a court
  order preventing them from doing so, or
  (iii) the Raiders breach their agreements with
  the Joint Authority in a way that will
  materially impair its or the Marketing
  Association's ability to earn the revenues
  expected to be earned under their marketing
  strategy. In the three listed circumstances,
  the Raiders would be liable for any deficiency
  remaining after application of all specified
  revenue streams and reversion credits towards
  repayment of the loans; otherwise, the
  Financing Corporation's only recourse would be
  against the specified revenue streams and
  reverting assets.

- The Coliseum Commission will manage the construction
  of certain stadium improvements at Oakland-Alameda
  Coliseum. The improvements include (i) an additional 118 luxury suites (bringing the total to 175
  from the current 57), and (ii) an increase in
  regular admission seating and (iii) addition of
  approximately 9,000 new club seats on the second
  tier of the Coliseum, bringing stadium capacity from
  the current 50,000-52,000 to 65,000. Construction
  is to be "substantially completed" (as defined in
  the construction agreement) by August 15, 1996; if
  it is not, the Raiders will be entitled to receive
  up to $5,000,000 in damages or to terminate their
  agreements with the Oakland-Alameda parties (and
  presumably to relocate).

- The Coliseum Commission will license the Raiders to
  use the Oakland-Alameda Coliseum for Raiders games
  for a total of 16 years. The first year, the
  Raiders will be licensed to use the existing 52,000-
  seat, 57-suite stadium. Thereafter, the license
  will cover the improved stadium.

- If the stadium improvements are not timely completed, or if the arrangements are rejected by the voters in a referendum, we have been told that the Raiders would have the right to play in the Coliseum for no charge in 1995 and to relocate in 1996.

- The Marketing Authority will sell all Raider game tickets, and will bear all marketing costs (to be paid from funds on deposit in the Revenue Trust Account). The Coliseum Commission will bear all day-of-game costs (including ticket takers, ushers, and the like), which can also be paid out of the Revenue Trust Account.

- The Raiders will receive (i) 100% of suite revenues from the Coliseum, (ii) 100% of 1995 club seat revenues, 50% of 1996-2005 club seat revenues and, provided that the bonds are fully amortized, 100% of club seat revenues thereafter, (iii) 100% of football ticket revenues, (iv) 50% of net concession revenues, (v) 50% of net parking revenues; and (vi) 100% of net novelty revenues. In addition, the Raiders will receive 100% of the revenues from advertising within the new "club areas" to be constructed at the Coliseum; $500,000 annually from non-club area advertising as long as the A's play at the Coliseum, and 50% of such advertising revenues thereafter; and 100% of in-game television net advertising revenues.

- The Raiders and the Joint Authority will share equally in net proceeds remaining from the "second round" of PSL sales, after stadium construction bonds and refundable suite deposits are paid in full and a $15 million "stadium modernization fund" is established and funded.

- In addition to the "loge maintenance fees" and "location premiums" that the Joint Authority will charge in respect of Raiders tickets, the Joint Authority will impose a $1 per ticket surcharge, with all funds earmarked for "public benefit" programs such as public schools or social welfare programs.

The Coliseum Commission has separate arrangements with the A's, which we have been told will remain largely unchanged despite the move. The Raiders will not receive any revenues in respect of A's events at the Coliseum, and the A's will have no obligation to help pay down stadium renovation debt.

The relocation and stadium renovation arrangements have received all necessary approvals of the Oakland City and Alameda County Commissions. They are subject, under California and local law, to a "referendum risk period" of 30 days. If, in that time, sufficient signatures of registered voters are gathered on petitions, the agreements will be placed on the November ballot for ratification. A drive to place the issue on the November ballot is currently ongoing.

The Raiders and the Oakland parties are committed to litigate with the League, if necessary, as to the propriety of the relocation. Once they sign the agreements, the Raiders may not terminate them in the absence of an injunction or legislation precluding their performance.

IV. **The Hollywood Park Alternative**

Before deciding to move to Oakland, the Raiders engaged in protracted discussions with Hollywood Park, Inc. ("HPI") concerning the construction of a new, 68,000-seat, state-of-the-art, football-only stadium at Hollywood Park Racetrack in Inglewood, California. The stadium would have had 10,000 club seats and 200 suites, and could have been expanded to 82,000 seats for Super Bowls.

The Raiders would have been the "anchor tenant" in the stadium, and would have been required to sign a 20-year lease for the facility. This long-term, non-terminable Raiders lease was the key to HPI's efforts to obtain stadium financing.

HPI has not yet obtained financing for, or environmental approvals with respect to, its proposed stadium. Nevertheless, HPI believes that the stadium could be completed in time for the 1997 League season, and has expressed its willingness to pay the Raiders $3 million if they were to sign a lease and construction were not begun by December of this year (which HPI believes would permit completion by 1997).

On several occasions dating back to January of this year, the Raiders asked the League to commit cash, Super Bowls and Super Bowl ticket concessions to help the club successfully conclude negotiations for the Hollywood Park stadium project. In response to the Raiders' requests, the League adopted 1995 Resolution FC-7 at the May meeting in Jacksonville.

Under FC-7, the League committed, subject to completion of the stadium arrangements and other conditions, to play one Super Bowl at Hollywood Park and to afford up to 10,000 purchasers of Raider "club seat" season tickets the opportunity to purchase tickets to that Super Bowl. (This ticket allotment was in addition to the Raiders' basic "host team"

Super Bowl ticket allotment.) FC-7 also set forth a League commitment to play a second Super Bowl at the Hollywood Park stadium if the League and HPI, as stadium landlord, reached agreement on a satisfactory option for a second NFL team to play at the stadium.

    A.   **The Raiders' Lease at Hollywood Park**

We understand that the lease between the Raiders and HPI would have had the following terms:

- HPI would have funded most stadium construction expenses. The Raiders would have been required to commit approximately $20 million in PSL funds towards construction.

- The lease would have had a 20-year term, automatically extended by five years if Al Davis were no longer in control of the team.

- The Raiders would not have been required to pay any rent, and would have borne approximately half of day-of-game expenses. They would have: received 100% of ticket revenues; divided suite and club seat revenues with HPI, as stadium landlord, on what is ultimately a 50/50 basis; received 10% of net parking revenues; received 25% of net concessions revenues; received 50% of advertising and stadium naming revenues; and received 100% of net of novelty revenues. The Raiders' net stadium income would have been approximately $20 million per year.

Of course, the Raiders and HPI never reached final agreement on a stadium lease, so these terms may not accurately reflect what would have been the parties' final deal. Nevertheless, it was clear that HPI was willing to grant the Raiders a lease that would have kept the team in Los Angeles on terms that would have placed the Raiders among the top six League clubs in terms of revenues.

B. **The "Second-Team Option" at Hollywood Park**

As noted above, 1995 Resolution FC-7 also embodied a League commitment to play a second Super Bowl at the Hollywood Park stadium, on terms identical to those applicable to the first such Super Bowl, if HPI granted the League a satisfactory option to put a second NFL team into the stadium as a tenant. Pursuant to FC-7, a Special Committee, consisting of Neil Austrian, Pat Bowlen, Carmen Policy, and Jerry Richardson negotiated such an option with HPI's CEO, R.D. Hubbard, in meetings and conference calls between June 1 and June 8. That option had the following terms:

- The League had the option to place a second team in the new stadium, exercisable up to the March 1 following the first regular season NFL game played at the stadium.

- Once the League exercised the option, it would have been obligated to place a second team in the stadium no later than two years after the first regular season NFL game at the stadium.

- The second NFL tenant at the stadium would have had a right to terminate its lease without penalty after either five or ten seasons at Hollywood Park. (The Raiders would have remained bound to their 20-year lease term.)

- The second team would have paid 10% of its gross gate to HPI as rent, and would have received annual stadium revenues, net of (1) rent, (2) visiting team share payable on club seat premiums, and (3) monies paid

- 16 -

to HPI for HPI's share of parking and concession revenue, of $14 million over and above its ticket receipts.[2/]

- If the second team were to have sold PSLs (it was not anticipated that it would do so), it would have been required to share the "tenant portion" of Hollywood Park stadium construction costs with the Raiders by paying PSL proceeds to the Raiders, in an amount of up to 50% of the Raiders' investment in stadium construction, not to exceed $15 million.

- The second team would not have been a "host team" for the purpose of either designated Super Bowl at the stadium, but rather would have received a standard non-participant, non-host share of Super Bowl tickets.

During their direct negotiations, the League and HPI also agreed that Hollywood Park would not have had the right to use the NFL or Super Bowl logos to cross-promote any of HPI's racetrack or casino activities. The card club located at HPI's Inglewood property would have been required to be closed for 12 hours on Super Bowl game days, and for three hours prior to kickoff and two hours after the game's end on the dates of all other postseason games played at the stadium. It would not have been required to close on regular-season game days.

[2/] These revenue projections assumed that the second team would have sold suits at a net annual price of $60,000 (compared to the Raiders' $90,000) and club seats at an annual premium of $820 (compared to the Raiders $1,220). They also assumed that the second team would not sell PSLs, as it was believed unrealistic to anticipate that two NFL teams could successfully sell PSLs in the greater Los Angeles area.

The Special Committee strongly believed that it had fulfilled its mandate to secure for the second team an option to enter into a lease on "satisfactory lease terms (including suite sale, concession, parking, and other rights [other than naming rights], and income related thereto) that [were] no less favorable to the second club than the terms of the Raiders' lease [were] to the Raiders . . . . ." The Finance Committee concurred in the Special Committee's judgment, and on June 15 voted unanimously to recommend that the membership approve two resolutions (FC-8 and FC-9) that would have ratified the Special Committee's second-team-option and authorized the League to enter into definitive agreements with the Raiders and HPI to finish implementing the FC-7 arrangements. Those resolutions were never submitted to the membership, however, as shortly after the Finance Committee's vote, the Raiders announced their proposed relocation to Oakland.

V. **The Raiders' Performance In Los Angeles**

Over the last four years, the Raiders' net operating profit has consistently ranked in the bottom quartile of the League's clubs. In 1993, the last full year for which we have data, the Raiders had an operating loss of over $1 million before interest, taxes, depreciation and non-operating League cash flow.

- 18 -

A comparison of the Raiders' operating profit performance with that of the Rams will help to put these facts in perspective:

Operating Profits

	1990	1991	1992	1993	Four-Year Average
Raiders	24th	23d	23d	23d	$1,100,000
Rams	6th	9th	8th	10th	$8,400,000
League Average					$5,500,000

The Raiders' unsatisfactory financial performance in Los Angeles must be considered in the context of the club's consistent and generally successful efforts to build a winning club and to provide an attractive product on the field. As illustrated by the graph attached as Attachment D, for over a decade the Raiders' expenditures on players have been above the League average and substantially above those of the Rams. Nonetheless, as illustrated in Attachment A, since at least 1986 the Raiders' home game attendance has been consistently below the League average, reflecting the unattractiveness of the Los Angeles Coliseum and unsatisfactory fan loyalty and support in the Los Angeles area.[3]

---

[3] Even if Los Angeles-area fans had demonstrated greater loyalty to the Raiders, the balance of equities might warrant placing reduced emphasis on that factor. Those fans were, of course, the beneficiaries of the Raiders' departure from Oakland, a relocation that adversely affected loyal Oakland fans who will benefit from the return of Raiders football to Oakland.

VI. The Raiders' Negotiations To Secure Alternative Sites In Los Angeles

The Raiders have made substantial efforts, over an extended period of time, to secure a first-class venue for their games in Los Angeles. The Hollywood Park arrangement, discussed above, was pursued after protracted efforts by the Raiders and the League Office to identify other suitable venues in the greater Los Angeles area[1]/, and was ultimately endorsed by the League notwithstanding serious reservations expressed by numerous members.

Hollywood Park was not the Raiders' first effort of that kind. At the time they moved to Los Angeles, the Raiders secured from the Los Angeles Coliseum Commission promises, reflected in a Memorandum of Understanding, to implement major improvements in the Coliseum. Those promised improvements were never delivered.

As another example, in 1990, the Raiders agreed to continue playing at the Los Angeles Coliseum on the condition that the Coliseum be modernized. The Coliseum Commission and Spectacor, the private management firm that ran the Coliseum, pledged that a $175-200 million renovation, including construction of luxury suites and club seats, would be

---

[1]/ Among the alternatives explored by the Raiders in Southern California were sites in Irvine, Long Beach (Convention Center Area), San Pedro (Worldport), El Segundo (Aerospace Industrial site), Playa Vista, Cornfield, Pasadena (the Rose Bowl), and Van Nuys (General Motors Plant site).

undertaken. For two years, there was no meaningful progress on that front, in part because of Spectacor's inability to market the proposed premium seats. In 1992, Spectacor cancelled the contract.

These and similar efforts by the Raiders, in my judgment, satisfy this element of the relocation criteria.

VII. The Bay Area

Operating in the Oakland Coliseum, the Raiders are almost certain to be well-supported by a very strong East Bay fan base. Since the earlier decades of Raiders' operations in Oakland, the population of the East Bay has grown considerably, extending to the east into Contra Costa County and northward towards Sacramento. Even apart from these developments, the Raiders operated very successfully in the East Bay before their departure to Los Angeles in 1982, as noted above.

Excerpts from the expansion briefing book on the Oakland market, which contains detailed demographic data, are attached as Attachment E. That volume confirms that in 1991, the Northern California Bay Area had a population of over 6 million, with over 2 million in the East Bay area itself, and was increasing at a substantial rate. Per capita income in the area was and is among the highest in the country. At the time of our expansion evaluation, the total effective buying income for Oakland, considered independent of San Francisco, was greater than that of every other expansion community under consideration at the time. In addition, the Northern California Bay Area is now the fifth largest television market in the country; during the expansion process, the number of television households in the Oakland area was more than twice that of every other expansion candidate. The briefing book also reports on the results of a 1990 season ticket campaign, and notes the sellout -- in less than two hours -- of the Raiders-Oilers pre-season game in 1988.

While the Expansion Committee determined that Oakland, one of the initial eleven expansion applicants, should not be one of the five expansion "finalists" for the franchises awarded in late 1993, that decision did not rest on the demographics or population base of the East Bay. Instead, the judgment was based upon a comparative evaluation of the Oakland application in relation to the other very strong applications before the League at that time, including those of the eventually selected expansion communities -- the Carolinas and Jacksonville -- and of St. Louis.

If specific factors relative to Oakland's exclusion from the final expansion derby need to be identified, two might be regarded as having been significant: (1) the Oakland community's inability or unwillingness in 1993 to commit to a state-of-the-art facility and (2) the fact that there was not an ownership group in place for the proposed expansion franchise.

Those factors are plainly not present in the context of the Raiders' proposed return to Oakland. Indeed, if any community has ever earned "special" consideration in the context of a team relocation, it is the City of Oakland and the East Bay community in relation to the Raiders. The area's past support for the club made "Oakland" and "the Raiders" synonymous in the national mind in the 1960s and 1970s; the community engaged in extraordinary efforts in an attempt to prevent the Raiders from leaving in the 1980s; and the community has not only continued to identify intensely with the club during its tenure in Los Angeles, but also engaged in a long-standing effort "to bring the Raiders back." Indeed, it is reasonable to conclude that only the Raiders -- and no other current NFL club or expansion franchise -- could generate in Oakland the level of public excitement and support that has emerged with the prospect of the Raiders' return. Moreover, as far as I know, no NFL club other than the Raiders has evidenced a serious interest in the Oakland opportunity.

In short, it appears that Oakland's interest has been directed primarily at the Raiders, rather than at NFL teams generally, and that the opportunity now available for the Raiders in Oakland exists primarily because of that community's historic, special relationship with the club.

VIII. Television Issues

The League has a long-term interest in maintaining a significant presence in Los Angeles, the nation's second largest television market. However, the short-run television impact of the Raiders' proposed relocation would be positive in Los Angeles, and neutral to positive in San Francisco/Oakland.

Our ratings in Los Angeles have been depressed in recent years because neither the Rams nor the Raiders sold out their home games. As a result of blackouts, Los Angeles only received 36 televised games in 1994. If the Raiders move, substantially more games will be telecast in the market this year -- 51 as compared to last year's 36. This 42% increase will more than offset any per-game ratings decline, even though ratings for neutral games will most likely be lower than for home-team games. (If "national" quality games are telecast in Los Angeles, this may not turn out to be the case.) The end result will almost certainly be an increase in ratings for each network on a national basis.

In the Bay Area, if the Raiders move, fewer games will be telecast than last year (37 as compared to 46). However, if the Raiders sell out their games in Oakland, most games televised in the Bay Area (23 of 37) will be "home club" games that historically draw higher ratings than out-of-market games. (Indeed, even after 13 years away from the Bay Area,

Raiders' games telecast in the San Francisco market substantially outdrew all AFC games telecast there last year, except for the games of the Joe Montana-led Chiefs. The average NBC Raiders rating in San Francisco was 16.8, while non-Raiders, non-Chiefs games drew an average 9.4 rating.) Thus, it seems likely that overall, our network partners will be able to equal or exceed their 1994 gross ratings points from San Francisco.

As a result, NBC (the network with primary AFC rights) is satisfied that its current contract position will be protected with the Raiders in Oakland -- still in the Pacific time zone and back in the city where tremendous fan support originally made "the Raiders" synonymous with "Oakland." However, we will be giving up a "home team" ratings premium in Los Angeles, which amounted to five ratings points over non-Raiders games in 1994. Our long-term television interests -- and our other interests as a *national* league -- therefore will best be served if we reestablish strong home team representation in the greater Los Angeles market.[5]

---

[5] There is no reason for me to discuss in detail several of the relocation criteria that are plainly met by the Raiders' proposal. For example, there are no significant local funding considerations, special tax treatments, or lease obligations that require the club to stay in Los Angeles.

IX. Conclusion

I recommend that the Raiders' proposed relocation to Oakland be approved on the terms reflected in 1995 Resolution G-7, which will be distributed at our July 21 meeting. Of course, the resolution will not detract from the Raiders' obligation to comply with all applicable provisions of the League's Constitution and Bylaws, resolutions, and policies, and of their agreements with League companies such as Properties and Films.

Paul Tagliabue

Attendance per Game
Raiders vs. League Average

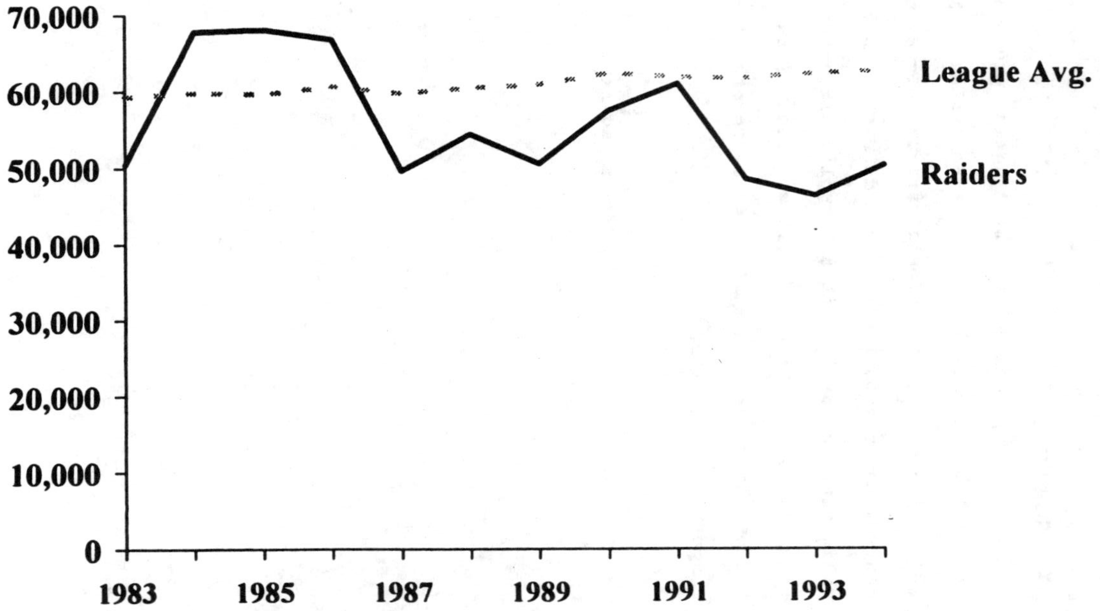

A

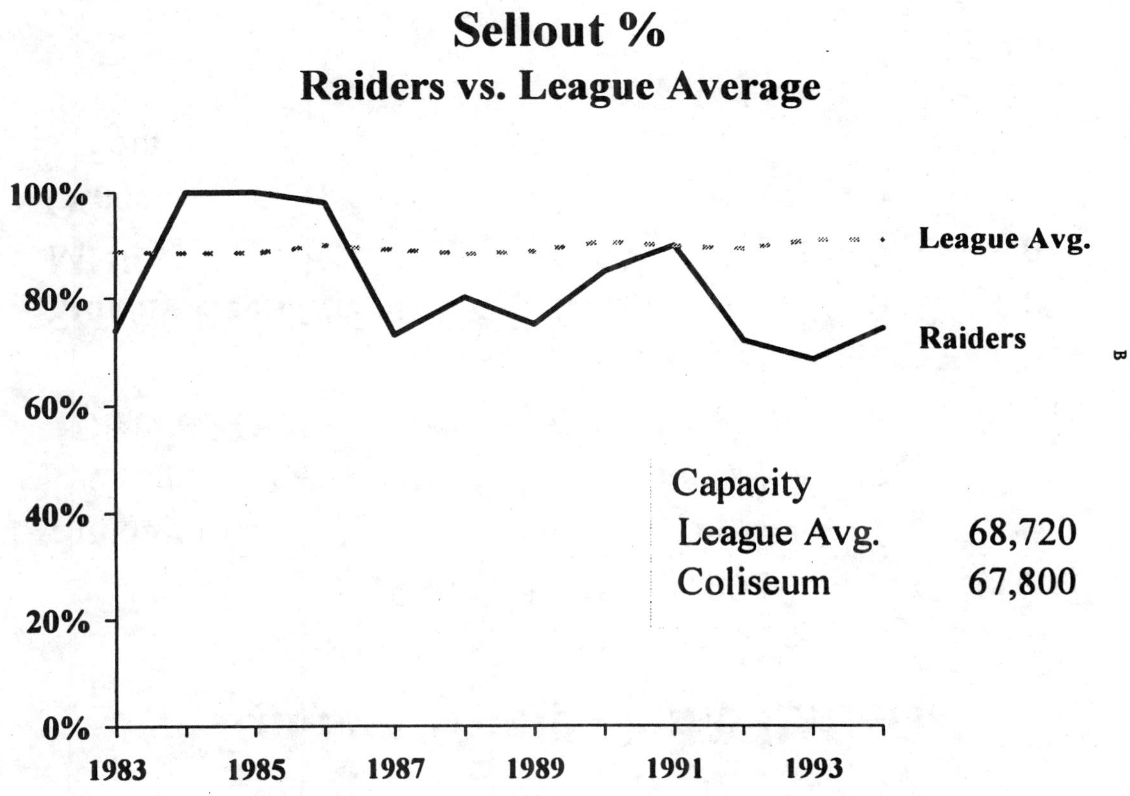

Sellout %
Raiders vs. League Average

B

Capacity	
League Avg.	68,720
Coliseum	67,800

Raiders Home Game Pattern

	1990	1991	1992	1993	1994
Sunday PM					
Aired	0	1	0	2	1
Blacked Out	8	7	8	6	7
Sunday Evening	0	0	0	0	0
MNF	0	0	0	0	0
Other	0	0	0	0	0
Total	8	8	8	8	8

Player Costs
Raiders vs. League Average

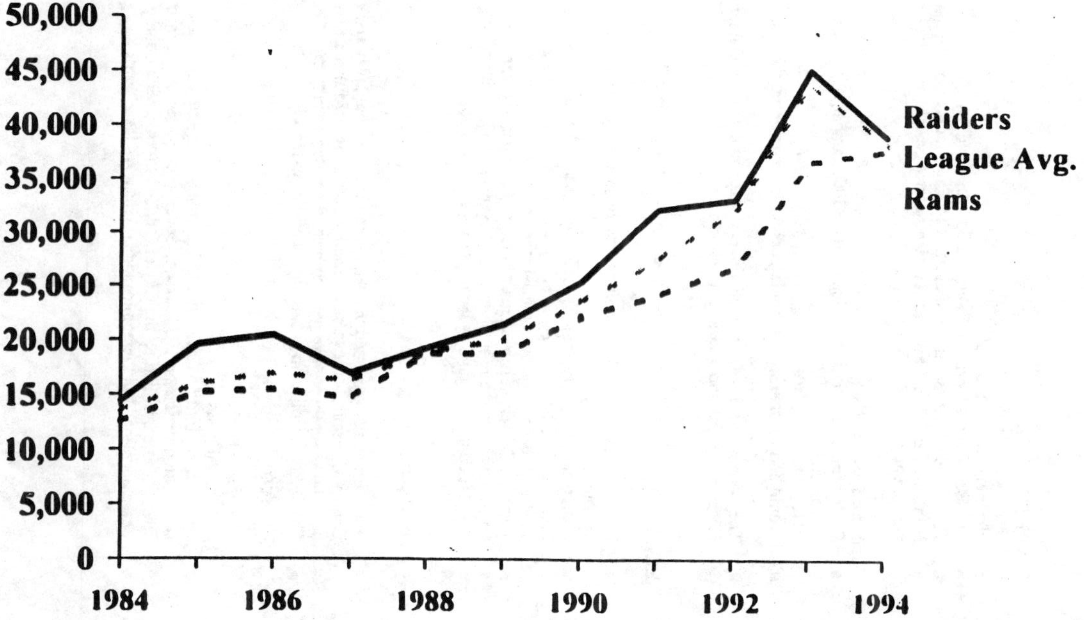

OAKLAND

MARKET AREA

Self-defined market area
- East Bay and the Northern California Bay Area (NCBA)
- The East Bay represents approximately a 25 mile radius from the stadium.
- Northern California Bay Area represents approximately an 80 mile radius and includes nine counties.

Basis and evaluation
- Raider ticket deposit distribution from the 1990 campaign:
  East Bay   60%
  NCBA   40% (including 6% Sacramento)
- Would end up sharing the 5th largest ADI television market with the San Francisco 49ers
- The 49ers sell 9,946 season tickets to people in the Oakland/East Bay area, representing just under 20% of sales

ECONOMY

- Major industries include computers, financial services, telecommunications and agribusiness.
- Manufacturing employment is declining with a shift to a service economy.
- From 1965 to 1976, area unemployment was higher than the national average, since then it has been lower than the average.
- Northern California is headquarters for 36 Fortune 500 companies.
- 66 companies in the region with sales/revenues of $150 million or greater
- There is concern regarding the increasing traffic congestion.

STADIUM

- It was originally proposed that the expansion team would play at the Oakland-Alameda County Coliseum. It has subsequently been suggested that a new stadium would be built, however there have been no specifics presented regarding financing or design.
- The Oakland Coliseum is currently configured as:
  - 55,000 seats
  - 53 luxury boxes
  - open air
  - natural grass
- Proposal to build an additional 15 boxes and designate a 5,000-seat area for premium seating in time for the 1994 season. Seven more boxes are planned for a later time.
- Owned and controlled by the City of Oakland and Alameda County
- Lease undefined but the application presented A's lease terms as a guide

KPMG Peat Marwick
Management Consultants

OAKLAND

OWNERSHIP

- Seattle Seahawks' 40% owner, Ken Hofmann, was suggested in the application as the principal partner in an Oakland ownership group which may include:

Joseph Cotchett, Jr.	Attorney
Edwin O. DeSilva	Real Estate
Dr. Bonnie Guiton	Government Official
Edwin Heafy	Attorney
Stephen Schott	Real Estate Development
Barry L. Williams	Venture Capital

- Hofmann has stated that the ownership structure and his partners' financial statements will be released when the NFL announces the franchise fee.

PUBLIC & PRIVATE SUPPORT

- Raiders were sold out for 12 consecutive seasons.
- In 1990, $5 million in deposits were collected for rights to purchase Raider tickets in the event that they returned. This represented 40,000 season tickets and 81 private suites ($5,000 per suite).
- The only survey performed was directed at the Raiders, and the application does not discuss methodology or sample selection and therefore is not considered relevant.

PRESENTATION RECAP

Attendees:

Dr. Bonnie Guiton	Government Official
Ken Hofmann	Seattle Seahawks (minority owner)
Steve Schott	Real Estate developer
Barry Williams	Venture Capital
George Vukasin	Oakland/Alameda County Stadium Authority

- Presentation included a video addressing the suitability and proven track record of Oakland
- Ken Hoffman
    - his involvement is focused on giving back to Oakland
    - he will not be involved if price is too high and economically infeasible
    - No definitive indication that he will be part of the ownership group
- Now talking about playing in the current facility for a short period of time and then building a new football-only stadium
- Discussed new stadium financing with Morgan Stanley last month and the investment bankers said it could be financed via the public markets. Very non-commital response by these advisors.
- Nothing substantive in place regarding the lease.
- The Authority claims that it "will build a new Warriors facility" which is different from the recent observations of the Warriors

KPMG Peat Marwick
Management Consultants

OAKLAND

PRESENTATION RECAP (cont'd)

- A percentage of the profits from the Coliseum Authority go to educational programs
- Chairpersons of the Contra Costa and Alameda County Supervisors and Mayor Elihu Harris appeared on the video in support of the expansion application.
- 70-mile radius claimed as the market area, extending beyond Sacramento, is based on Raider ticket drives and preseason games
- Oakland Coliseum opened in '66 and started sellouts in '70 after four years of losing teams
- The SF/Oakland market has proven that it can support two franchises, especially if they are successful on the field.
- The Authority provided a preseason game guarantee of $500K per team for earlier games and state that they are providing the 49ers a guarantee of $800,000 for a preseason game in '92

OAKLAND

MARKET AREA

- Among the candidate cities:
  - Largest population within 25 miles of the stadium
  - Largest weighted population
  - Highest household income after adjusting for cost of living
  - 3rd highest Buying Power Index
  - Highest household effective buying income
  - 3rd highest household income growth from 1980 to 1991
- 5th largest TV market in the US shared with San Francisco

STADIUM

- New facility proposed but not financed
- Class B facility in place
- Mid-level visiting team revenue share (tied for 3rd highest with three other cities at approximately $900,000 per game)

OWNERSHIP

- Partnership not clearly defined
- Includes minority representation

PUBLIC & PRIVATE SUPPORT

- Hoffman appeared during the presentation to represent the support of the business community rather than representing a committed ownership group.
- Elected government officials have participated only as part of the video, not as part of the application effort which has been guided by the Coliseum Authority

STRENGTHS

- Available stadium; however, no lease terms were provided.
- Historic support of Raiders
- High income of the population
- Large population and TV market

KPMG Peat Marwick
Management Consultants

OAKLAND

WEAKNESSES

- Proximity to San Francisco; close to 10,000 49er season tickets are sold to Oakland/East Bay residents.
- Reliance on San Jose/San Francisco/Oakland market demographics with no discussion of the impact of dilution of the 49ers market
- No indication of public sector support for the application outside of the Coliseum Authority's involvement

OUTSTANDING ISSUES

- A clear definition of the level of support from the private and public sectors.
- A more accurate estimate of possible lease terms between the team and the facility is still needed; however, they stated that the Stadium Authority's philosophy is to provide flexibility in both good and bad times.
- How advanced are the contingent renovation plans? Is there anything specific that can be said about the plan to build a new facility?

AVERAGE HOUSEHOLD EFFECTIVE BUYING INCOME
Geography: Primary Metropolitan Area

City	1990 Average Household EBI	1995 Average Household EBI	2000 Average Household EBI (1)	1990 Rank	1995 Rank	2000 Rank	Expansion City Rank 2000
Washington	53,429	68,633	88,164	1	1	1	
San Francisco	52,420	67,832	87,775	2	2	2	
Los Angeles	52,247	66,302	84,138	3	3	3	
Los Angeles - Anaheim	52,247	66,302	84,138	3	3	3	
Seattle	44,936	60,192	80,627	8	7	4	
New England	48,246	62,133	79,708	6	6	5	
Oakland	48,502	62,177	77,450	5	5	6	1
Chicago	44,019	58,389	77,309	9	8	7	
Dallas	41,015	56,310	76,561	14	11	8	
Denver	40,340	55,574	76,166	17	13	9	
Philadelphia	43,638	57,652	73,464	10	9	10	
San Diego	45,163	57,601	73,298	7	10	11	
Minnesota	42,292	55,677	71,956	11	12	12	
Cincinnati	38,191	52,422	67,449	23	16	13	
Sacramento	41,969	53,205	67,346	12	14	14	2
Indianapolis	36,452	49,547	67,256	25	22	15	
New York	41,947	53,115	67,124	13	15	16	
Atlanta	40,912	52,404	67,095	15	17	17	
St. Louis	39,676	51,595	66,762	19	18	18	
Detroit	39,530	51,372	66,417	20	19	19	3
New Orleans	33,417	47,111	66,109	34	26	20	
Cleveland	38,296	50,316	65,962	22	21	21	
Kansas City	39,978	51,352	63,257	18	20	22	
Phoenix	36,535	48,074	61,150	24	25	23	
Baltimore	40,715	49,897	61,040	16	23	24	4
Houston	38,789	48,659	60,659	21	24	25	
Jacksonville	36,066	46,773	60,054	28	27	26	5
Carolinas	35,313	46,051	59,962	30	29	27	6
Miami	36,382	46,707	59,191	27	28	28	
Memphis	33,601	44,597	56,615	32	30	29	7
Tampa Bay	33,463	43,526	54,299	33	32	30	
Green Bay	35,112	43,664	51,175	31	31	31	
Pittsburgh	35,437	42,585	48,473	29	33	32	
Buffalo	36,421	42,017		26	34	33	

Note 1: Projected based on extrapolation of the data provided by Sales and Marketing Management.

Source: Sales and Marketing Management, 1991.

BUYING POWER SUMMARY
Geography: MSA

	Baltimore	Carolinas	Jacksonville	Memphis	Oakland	Sacramento	St. Louis
Household Effective Buying Income							
1989	39,448	33,431	33,561	31,152	44,471	37,811	37,745
1994	54,414	47,656	47,239	45,630	61,515	52,248	53,395
Total Effective Buying Income ($000s)							
1989	32,442,578	13,155,397	10,906,457	10,322,038	32,855,273	19,428,745	32,474,159
1994	50,376,565	22,651,072	19,169,474	17,471,724	52,865,660	33,302,805	51,168,784
Buying Power Index							
1989	1.0102	0.4560	0.3781	0.3648	0.9676	0.6271	1.0262
1994	0.9760	0.4650	0.3935	0.3644	0.9697	0.6577	0.9971

Notes: Effective Buying Income (EBI) is defined as all personal income less personal tax and non-tax payments (i.e. disposable or "after tax" income). Buying Power Index (BPI) is a weighted index which converts population, EBI, and retail sales into a measure of the market's "ability to buy" as a percentage of the national total.

	Baltimore	Carolinas	Jacksonville	Memphis	Oakland	Sacramento	St. Louis
Household EBI Rating	1	3	3	3	1	2	2
Total EBI Rating	1	2	3	3	1	1	1
Buying Power Index Rating	1	2	3	3	1	2	1
Overall Rating	1	2	3	3	1	2	1

Key for HH EBI Rating
1 = HH EBI > $38 K
2 = HH EBI $35 K to $38 K
3 = HH EBI < $35 K

Key for Total EBI Rating
1 = Total EBI > $15 B
2 = Total EBI $11 B to $15 B
3 = Total EBI < $11 B

Key for BPI Rating
1 = BPI > .9
2 = BPI .45 to .9
3 = BPI < .45

BUYING POWER INDEX RANKING
Geography: MSA

City	1989 BPI	Rank	Candidate City Rank
Los Angeles	3.8702	1	
New York	3.5355	2	
Chicago	2.7031	3	
Philadelphia	2.1421	4	
Washington	1.9717	5	
New England	1.8768	6	
Detroit	1.8386	7	
Houston	1.3021	8	
Atlanta	1.2562	9	
Los Angeles - Anaheim	1.1500	10	
Dallas	1.1368	11	
Minnesota	1.1099	12	
San Diego	1.1084	13	
St. Louis	1.0262	14	1
Baltimore	1.0102	15	2
Oakland	0.9676	16	3
Seattle	0.9135	17	
San Francisco	0.8742	18	
Phoenix	0.8736	19	
Tampa Bay	0.8686	20	
Pittsburgh	0.8108	21	
Miami	0.7637	22	
Cleveland	0.7464	23	
Denver	0.7234	24	
Kansas City	0.6800	25	
Sacramento	0.6271	26	4
Cincinnati	0.5962	27	
Indianapolis	0.5299	28	
New Orleans	0.4827	29	
Carolinas	0.4560	30	5
Jacksonville	0.3781	31	6
Buffalo	0.3774	32	
Memphis	0.3648	33	7
Green Bay	0.0795	34	

Source: Sales and Marketing Management, 1990.

BUYING POWER INDEX RANKING
Geography: Primary Metropolitan Area

City	1990 BPI	1995 BPI	2000 BPI (1)	1990 Rank	1995 Rank	2000 Rank	Candidate City Rank - 2000
Los Angeles	3.8050	3.8208	3.8367	1	1	1	
New York	3.4639	3.3445	3.2292	2	2	2	
Chicago	2.6730	2.7028	2.7329	3	3	3	
Philadelphia	2.1031	2.0752	2.0477	4	4	4	
Washington	1.9964	1.9820	1.9677	5	5	5	
Detroit	1.8192	1.7717	1.7254	6	6	6	
New England	1.8165	1.6916	1.5753	7	7	7	
Dallas	1.1648	1.3019	1.4551	11	10	8	
Atlanta	1.2695	1.3072	1.3460	9	9	9	
Houston	1.3305	1.3147	1.2991	8	8	10	
Minnesota	1.1126	1.1868	1.2659	12	12	11	
San Diego	1.1115	1.1772	1.2468	13	13	12	
Los Angeles - Anaheim	1.1915	1.1911	1.1907	10	11	13	
Seattle	0.9681	1.0619	1.1648	17	14	14	
Phoenix	0.8806	0.9541	1.0337	18	17	15	1
Oakland	0.9854	0.9975	1.0097	16	16	16	2
St. Louis	1.0241	1.0136	1.0032	14	15	17	
Tampa Bay	0.8733	0.9046	0.9370	19	19	18	3
Baltimore	0.9991	0.9344	0.8739	15	18	19	
San Francisco	0.8654	0.8517	0.8382	20	20	20	
Denver	0.7225	0.7683	0.8170	24	21	21	
Miami	0.7723	0.7638	0.7554	22	22	22	
Sacramento	0.6556	0.6929	0.7333	26	26	23	4
Kansas City	0.6817	0.6941	0.7067	25	25	24	
Cleveland	0.7509	0.7098	0.6709	23	24	25	
Pittsburgh	0.8118	0.7203	0.6391	21	23	26	
Cincinnati	0.5971	0.6046	0.6122	27	27	27	
New Orleans	0.4778	0.5329	0.5944	29	28	28	
Indianapolis	0.5239	0.5310	0.5382	28	29	29	
Carolinas	0.4657	0.4687	0.4717	30	30	30	5
Jacksonville	0.3768	0.3987	0.4219	32	31	31	6
Memphis	0.3692	0.3603	0.3516	33	32	32	7
Buffalo	0.3854	0.3363	0.2915	31	33	33	
Green Bay	0.0812	0.0851	0.0892	34	34	34	

Note 1: Projected based on extrapolation of the data provided by Sales and Marketing Management.

Source: Sales and Marketing Management, 1991.

SPENDING SUMMARY
Geography: 25-mile Radius

	Baltimore	Carolinas	Jacksonville	Memphis	Oakland	Sacramento	St. Louis
Median Income Per Household							
1991	41,106	35,172	30,682	28,664	41,194	32,696	34,302
1996	53,154	45,091	38,417	34,984	52,317	40,182	41,842
HH Income Growth 1991-1996	29.3%	28.2%	25.2%	22.0%	27.0%	22.9%	22.0%
1980-1991	111.3%	106.4%	98.8%	87.2%	107.2%	88.7%	85.5%
Cost of Living Index (1)							
1991	110.3	101.3	96.3	94.3	106.3	106.3	97.8
Adjusted Income Per Household							
1991	37,267	34,721	31,861	30,397	38,753	30,758	35,074
Sports Spending Per Household (2)							
1991	48	45	41	39	48	42	43
1996	55	51	47	45	54	48	49
Entertainment Spending Per Household (3)							
1991	499	446	406	389	500	422	432
1996	597	542	491	461	588	501	511
Ranking							
Median Income Per Capita	2	3	6	7	1	5	4
Cost of Living Index	7	4	2	1	5	5	3
Adjusted Income Per Capita	2	4	5	7	1	6	3
Sports Spending Per Capita	1	3	6	7	1	5	4
Entertainment Spending Per Capita	2	3	6	7	1	5	4

Notes: (1) Cost of Living estimates are from the American Chamber of Commerce Researchers Association figures in the respective expansion applications.
(2) Sports Spending includes admission to sporting events.
(3) Entertainment Spending includes admissions to sporting events, movies, concerts, plays, club memberships, recreational lessons or instructions, rental of movies, and recreational expenses on trips.

	Baltimore	Carolinas	Jacksonville	Memphis	Oakland	Sacramento	St. Louis
Rating							
Income	1	2	3	3	1	3	2
Spending	1	2	3	3	1	2	2
Overall	1	2	3	3	1	2	2

Key for Adjusted Income Rating	Key for Spending Rating
1 = Adjusted Inc > $37 K	1 = Sports > $47 : Entertainment > $450
2 = Adjusted Inc $34 K to $37K	2 = Sports $44 - $47 : Entertainment $400-$450
3 = Adjusted Inc < $34 K	3 = Sports < $44 : Entertainment < $400

Source: National Planning Data Corp

DISTRIBUTION OF WORKFORCE
Geography: MSA

	U.S.	Baltimore	Carolinas	Jacksonville	Memphis	Sacramento	St. Louis
0-25 Mile Radius Population	N/A	2,409,146	984,296	821,214	963,454	1,314,548	2,088,979
Number of Companies with:							
1 - 500 employees	8,149,413	66,462	26,174	28,517	25,842	41,661	59,310
501 - 1,000 employees	10,766	111	38	38	41	41	96
> 1,000 employees	13,986	74	40	28	27	43	88
TOTAL	8,174,165	66,647	26,252	28,583	25,910	41,745	59,494
Number of Service & FIRE (1) companies with 1-500 employees	N/A	30,043	10,729	11,368	11,895	18,373	30,812

	Baltimore	Carolinas	Jacksonville	Memphis	Sacramento	St. Louis
Rating						
Large Companies	1	2	3	3	2	—
Local Companies	—	3	3	3	2	—
Local Service & FIRE Companies	—	3	3	3	2	—
Overall	1	3	3	3	2	—

Notes: Workforce data for Oakland was not available.
(1) Finance, insurance and real estate

Key for Large Company Rating
1 = >70 companies with >1,000
2 = 35-70 companies with >1,000
3 = <35 companies with >1,000

Key for Local Company Rating
1 = >50,000 companies with 1-500
2 = 30-50K companies with 1-500
3 = <30K companies with 1-500

Source: Dun & Bradstreet
National Planning Data Corp.

KPMG Peat Marwick Management Consulting

INDUSTRY D... ..RSIFICATION VS. U.S.
Geography: MSA

	United States (1)	Baltimore	Carolinas	Jacksonville	Memphis	Sacramento	St. Louis
Employee Diversification							
Agriculture, Forestry & Fishing	1.31%	0.72%	0.77%	1.42%	0.86%	1.41%	0.62%
Mining	0.66%	0.11%	0.10%	0.05%	0.04%	0.11%	0.38%
Construction	5.03%	6.72%	0.67%	7.91%	5.66%	5.93%	5.58%
Manufacturing	18.86%	15.69%	24.64%	10.93%	14.46%	8.73%	20.09%
Transportation & Public Utilities	5.44%	5.28%	8.52%	9.77%	10.17%	4.72%	5.64%
Wholesale Trade	5.76%	5.77%	9.24%	6.57%	8.31%	2.70%	7.22%
Retail Trade	15.96%	14.42%	13.10%	17.57%	16.86%	15.97%	14.84%
Finance, Insurance & Real Estate	7.42%	8.22%	9.34%	13.26%	7.19%	7.22%	8.31%
Services	34.29%	34.86%	30.20%	26.12%	32.96%	33.82%	33.59%
Public Administration	5.26%	8.22%	3.42%	6.40%	3.49%	19.40%	3.72%
Relative Distribution (2)							
Agriculture, Forestry & Fishing		0.55	0.58	1.08	0.65	1.08	0.47
Mining		0.16	0.15	0.08	0.06	0.17	0.58
Construction		1.33	0.13	1.57	1.12	1.18	1.11
Manufacturing		0.83	1.31	0.58	0.77	0.46	1.06
Transportation & Public Utilities		0.97	1.57	1.80	1.87	0.87	1.04
Wholesale Trade		1.00	1.60	1.14	1.44	0.47	1.25
Retail Trade		0.90	0.82	1.10	1.06	1.00	0.93
Finance, Insurance & Real Estate		1.11	1.26	1.79	0.97	0.97	1.12
Services		1.02	0.88	0.76	0.96	0.99	0.98
Public Administration		1.56	0.65	1.22	0.66	3.69	0.71

Notes:
(1) The percentage distribution of employees in the U.S.
(2) The industry distribution of employees and companies for each city, relative to the U.S. distribution. The 0.55 for Baltimore in Agriculture indicates that the percentage of employees in that industry in Baltimore is 55% of the U.S. percentage.

	Baltimore	Carolinas	Jacksonville	Memphis	Sacramento	St. Louis
Rating						
Employee Diversification	3	3	3	3	3	1

Note: Industry diversification data for Oakland was not available.

Source: Dun & Bradstreet

Key for Ratings
1 = 1-2 Industries > 1.3 or < .70
2 = 3 Industries > 1.3 or < .70
3 = 4-5 Industries > 1.3 or < .70

TELEVISION SUMMARY
Geography: Designated Market Area

	Baltimore	Carolinas	Jacksonville	Memphis	Oakland	Sacramento	St. Louis
NFL Audience Ratings (1)	10.7	6.8	12.5	10.8	18.4	15.2	10.8
Television Households	938,520	734,210	470,950	604,090	2,231,040	1,033,780	1,088,550
National Ranking of Television HH	22	31	55	39	5	21	18
Cable TV Households	467,990	417,200	312,300	319,620	1,387,550	560,050	490,180
Cable Penetration Percentage	49.86%	56.82%	66.31%	52.91%	62.19%	54.17%	45.03%

Notes: (1) Audience rating is a measure of the percentage of total television households in the market that are watching a specific program. Figures presented are averages of 1990 Sunday afternoon broadcasts.

	Baltimore	Carolinas	Jacksonville	Memphis	Oakland	Sacramento	St. Louis
Television Households	1	2	3	3	1	1	1

Key for TV HH Rankings
1 = HH > 900K
2 = HH of 650K to 900K
3 = HH < 650K

Source: Nielsen Media Research

ONE HUNDRED FOURTH CONGRESS

Congress of the United States
House of Representatives
COMMITTEE ON THE JUDICIARY
2138 RAYBURN HOUSE OFFICE BUILDING
WASHINGTON, DC 20515-6216
(202) 225-3951

March 15, 1996

Professor Gary R. Roberts
Tulane Law Street
6329 Freret Street
New Orleans, Louisiana 70118

Dear Professor Roberts:

Thank you for your testimony before the Committee on the Judiciary on Tuesday, February 6, 1996 at the hearing regarding sports franchise relocation.

As noted during the hearing, due to time constraints, the Members of the Committee did not have an opportunity to ask all of their questions of the witnesses. I am therefore enclosing a list of questions for the record, which I am submitting on behalf of the members of the Committee. I would appreciate a response to these questions by Friday, April 5, 1996. If you have any questions regarding your responses, please contact Joseph Gibson, Committee counsel, at (202) 225-3951.

Again, thank you for taking the time to appear before the Committee.

Sincerely,

HENRY J. HYDE
Chairman

HJH/jg:nr

Questions for the Record

Submitted on behalf of the Republican Members

Committee on the Judiciary

QUESTIONS FOR:

Professor Gary Roberts, Tulane Law School

1. Should there be a federal law to protect sports fans against team relocation? If so, how should it be accomplished and what form should it take? Aren't sports fans essentially consumers of an entertainment product? That is, why should federal law protect sports fans any more than it does music lovers or moviegoers?

2. In your view, professional sports leagues are natural monopolies. Do you believe that only one professional football league can succeed financially on a national basis?

3. Could you describe the terms of the Sports Broadcasting Act and explain its antitrust significance for the members of the Committee?

4. In your view, is the National Football League franchise relocation rule "reasonable" -- that is, would it pass antitrust muster? If so, can there be any real justification for federal legislation in this area? Do you have any explanation as to why the League has not been more diligent in seeking judicial resolution of this issue?

5. Doesn't the fact that the NFL owners are suing the league, and consequently each other, undermine the argument that they act, and should be treated, as a partnership?

Tulane

Tulane Law School
6329 Freret Street
Tulane University
New Orleans, Louisiana 70118-5670
(504) 862-8826
Fax (504) 862-8855
groberts@law.tulane.edu

GARY R. ROBERTS
Professor of Law
Director, Sports Law Program

April 1, 1996

Hon. Henry J. Hyde, Chairman
Committee on the Judiciary
2138 Rayburn House Office Bldg
United States House of Representatives
Washington, DC 20515-6216

Re: Responses to Questions on Sports Franchise Relocations

Dear Chairman Hyde:

The following are my responses to your questions submitted in writing in your letter of March 15.

Question 1: Should there be a federal law to protect sports fans against team relocation? If so, how should it be accomplished and what form should it take? Aren't sports fans essentially consumers of an entertainment product? That is, why should federal law protect sports fans any more than it does music lovers or moviegoers?

Answer to Question 1: I agree with the basic premise of the question -- that consumers of sports entertainment are entitled to no greater rights than consumers of any other type of entertainment product. But consumers of all products have historically been thought to have the right to be as free as possible from the effects of excessive market power. That is the very premise underlying the Sherman and Clayton Acts. In those markets that professional sports leagues exert enormous market power, consumer welfare is undoubtedly injured and Congress can legitimately intervene, and should do so if the benefits are predictably greater than the harmful side effects. Such intervention is appropriate, not because sports consumers are special, but because the producers in those cases possess undersired power over the market. Thus, it is appropriate for Congress to try to find ways to mitigate the effects of substantial market power on consumers. It is for this very reason that I have suggested that Congress consider ways to regulate sports league conduct in markets over which they possess such substantial power. Such regulation can be limited and specific, which is what some of the bills currently pending dealing specifically with franchise relocation try to do, or it can be general with the authority to adopt and to enforce specific regulations delegated to an administrative or executive body. But whatever approach is attempted, it should be targeted at mitigating the leagues' market power, not at some specific business decision that someone's constituents happen not to like. The fact is that when a team moves from one city to another, the fans in one community are furious while the fans in the other are thrilled. Unless there is an underlying general consumer or public welfare harm from such activity, Congress and the courts should not impose their policy preferences as to which city more deserves a team. To the extent there is such general harm, mitigating it should be the focus of Congress' attention, not merely playing to the emotions of voters back home.

If Congress cannot find a way reasonably to regulate sports franchise relocation, it is also appropriate for it to grant leagues an antitrust exemption from decisions by the league relating to the location or relocation of member franchises. In most instances, leagues do exert substantial market power in the market in which frachises are sold, a phenominon that is characterized by there being far fewer franchises in each league than there are viable cities who want a franchise. This allows existing franchises to create a bidding process between cities that drives up public subsidies to teams and enhances their value generally. However, if direct regulation of this market is not politically or practically feasible, it is far better to allow the league's market power to be exercised by the league, which has a much broader and longer term perspective, than by individual franchise owners who often act primarily for short term profits in a manner detrimental to both the public and the league. The fact is that league decisions relating to franchise location or ownership do not raise legitimate section 1 conspiracy issues, but local federal courts whose communities have an interest in where a team locates will almost invariably distort antitrust doctrine and manipulate the legal process to achieve the desired political result, which often involves finding a violation of section 1. This is a perversion of antitrust law and the legal system, and Congress would be acting responsibly to curb such frivolous lawsuits by granting an exemption for leagues in such cases. This would not really be creating an exemption, but merely recognizing that these types of cases do not properly raise section 1 issues in the first place.

Question 2: In your view, professional sports leagues are natural monopolies. Do you believe that only one professional football league can succeed financially on a national basis?

Answer to Question 2: Yes, I do believe that only one professional football league generally recognized as "major league" can succeed for for any substantial period of time. If two football leagues tried to compete against one another at the major league level, the unique nature of the athletic competition product they produce and the low marginal cost/high fixed cost nature of the industry would quickly combine to cause one to go broke and out of business within a period of a few years. (This phenominon and the reasons for it are described in more detail in my written testimony to the Committee.) The experience of professional sports in this country (the Federal League in baseball, the ABA and the CBA in basketball, the All American Conference, the AFL, the WFL, and the USFL in football, and the WHA in hockey) confirms this conclusion, although one could argue that in every such case either predatory conduct by the dominant league or the enormity of barriers to entry for brand new leagues made the upstart league's survival impossible, which might not be the case if two leagues started out on equal footing after a court or congressionally ordered breakup of an existing league. I strongly believe, however, that under no circumstances can two major leagues compete against one another and both survive for more than a few years.

Question 3: Could you describe the terms of the Sports Broadcasting Act and explain its antitrust significance for the members of the Committee?

Answer to Question 3: With all due respect, I truly do not clearly understand what this question asks. Obviously, the terms of the 1961 Sports Broadcasting Act, 15 U.S.C. §§1501-05, are what they are. I could write a treatise on the legislative history, ambiguities, enforcement history, and overall implications of the SBA, but I doubt that is what you want here. I can say that generally the effect of the SBA on the franchise relocation issue is indirect, and I found references during the hearing to the SBA being a problem in causing such relocations to be puzling at best. There is, however, some connection between franchise relocation pressures and the SBA which I will try to describe briefly here.

First, by giving leagues a mechanism free from antitrust risk for sharing network television revenues equally among the member teams of a league, and thereby reducing the revenue disparities that would exist absent such mechanism, the pressures on smaller market teams to increase stadium revenues in order to compete in the free agent market for players are less than they would be without the SBA. In this respect, the SBA probably reduces market forces causing some smaller revenue franchises to seek better stadium deals in new markets.

On the other hand, by reducing (or in the case of the NFL, eliminating) revenue disparities from television among member teams, the SBA greatly diminishes the effect of franchise relocations on the relocating team's television revenues. Thus, from the Oilers' standpoint, it might be economically smart to move from the nation's fourth largest TV market in Houston to a much smaller market in Nashville because the decline in TV ratings and thus revenues caused by that move will be borne only 1/30th by the Oilers. In this sense, the SBA makes a community's ability to offer a heavily subsidized stadium with lucrative luxury boxes and seat licenses a much greater factor in a team's analysis than it would be if television factors also were fully considered. (This is one of the reasons why the league, which feels the full impact of the relocation on television ratings and shared television revenues, has a legitimate interest in the move -- a natural result of the inherent partnership nature of the league.) Thus, in this respect one could argue that the SBA may in some cases increase the likelihood of relocations from larger market cities to smaller market cities (although for the same reasons it might reduce the chance of relocation from a smaller market to a larger market).

Because the two identifiable influences of the SBA on franchise relocations generally cut in opposite directions, the best guess is that on balance the SBA has no significant effect on the number or frequency of relocations.

Question 4: In your view, is the National Football League franchise relocation rule "reasonable" -- that is, would it pass antitrust muster? If so, can there be any real justification for federal legislation in this area? Do you have any explanation as to why the League has not been more diligent in seeking judicial resolution of this issue?

Answer to Question 4: I gather that this question asks whether I believe the NFL's rule is "reasonable" in the antitrust sense of that term, not whether I think that it is reasonable in some generic or visceral sense. If so, the answer is that my opinion is irrelevant and thus I decline to give one. Since I believe that a league is a single firm whose internal governance decisions are inherently not conspiracies subject to section 1, I suppose I would thus automatically conclude that such league rules would be reasonable under the rule of reason. But the fact is that reasonableness is a fact issue for judges or juries (depending on the legal context in which the issue arises), and the extremely ambiguous and indeterminate nature of the legal definition of reasonableness (i.e., whether the rule is more procompetitive or anticompetitive -- with a definition of "competitive" being quite elusive) makes predicting how a judge or jury will answer the question in any given case almost impossible. In fact, the only realistic basis for predicting the outcome of such a case is not on how the ambiguous legal standard appears most sensibly to apply to the facts of the case, but rather on the political climate in the courtroom in which the case is being heard. I have very little doubt that had the NFL blocked the Cleveland Browns' move to Baltimore, that action would have been found reasonable in a Cleveland court but unreasonable in a Baltimore court.

The fact that it is impossible to define the legal parameters or standards of a section 1 rule of reason case involving franchise location or ownership issues probably explains why leagues have not been willing to block franchise moves and litigate the reasonableness of the action. The chances of the case ending up in a forum sympathetic to the team and community supporting the move and having the case be manipulated by the court into finding a violation (as happened in the infamous *Raiders* case in the early 1980s) are too great, especially with mandatory treble damages and attorneys fees, for leagues to risk. This is undoubtedly the explanation for, as the question phrases it, league unwillingness to be "more diligent in seeking judicial resolution of this issue."

Question 5: Doesn't the fact that the NFL owners are suing the league, and consequently each other, undermine the argument that they act, and should be treated, as a partnership?

Answer to Question 5: I hope that by asking this question, nobody having anything to do with the Judiciary Committee seriously thinks the answer might be "yes." Partners in all kinds of partnerships often have disputes over governance of the partnership's business, the allocation of governance power among themselves, the distribution of income or assets, or the sharing of losses. These disputes often end up in litigation, but that fact in no way diminishes the status of the partnership as a partnership. It is nonsense to think that a business whose equity investors at any time end up in litigation over some issue relating to the business cannot be a partnership, or that the fact of such litigation is in any way relevant to whether the business is a partnership. This is especially true when then the product of the partnership is athletic competition entertainment that inherently requires a highly decentralized form of decision-making within the larger wholly integrated framework.

I hope that I have adequately responded to all of the Committee's questions. If not, or if you have any further inquiries, please don't hesitate to get back in touch with me. And thank you for giving me the opportunity to participate in this important work of the Committee.

Best wishes.

Respectfully Submitted,

Gary R. Roberts
Professor of Law

ONE HUNDRED FOURTH CONGRESS

Congress of the United States
House of Representatives
COMMITTEE ON THE JUDICIARY
2138 RAYBURN HOUSE OFFICE BUILDING
WASHINGTON, DC 20515-6216
(202) 225-3951

March 15, 1996

Dr. Andrew Zimbalist
Department of Economics
Smith College
Northampton, Massachusetts 01063

Dear Dr. Zimbalist:

Thank you for your testimony before the Committee on the Judiciary on Tuesday, February 6, 1996 at the hearing regarding sports franchise relocation.

As noted during the hearing, due to time constraints, the Members of the Committee did not have an opportunity to ask all of their questions of the witnesses. I am therefore enclosing a list of questions for the record, which I am submitting on behalf of the members of the Committee. I would appreciate a response to these questions by Friday, April 5, 1996. If you have any questions regarding your responses, please contact Joseph Gibson, Committee counsel, at (202) 225-3951.

Again, thank you for taking the time to appear before the Committee.

Sincerely,

HENRY J. HYDE
Chairman

HJH/jg:nr

Questions for the Record

Submitted on behalf of the Republican Members

Committee on the Judiciary

QUESTIONS FOR:

Professor Andy Zimbalist

1. In your view, have the owners of professional sports leagues kept a number of franchises artificially scarce? Should Congress get involved at all in the issue of expansion for professional sports leagues?

2. Based on your knowledge of major league baseball, what, in your opinion, has been the impact on baseball of having an antitrust exemption? Do you feel that it has helped stabilize the league? What conclusions do you draw from the fact that baseball has not had many franchise relocations in recent years?

**Responses to Questions to Andrew Zimbalist
from the Republican Members
of the House Judiciary Committee
March 1996**

I have addressed these two questions in several of my writings; in particular, my article "Baseball Economics and Antitrust Immunity" from the Seton Hall Journal of Sport Law, vol. 4, no. 1 (1994). I enclose a copy of this article which I would like to submit for the record. Accordingly, I will be brief in my answers below.

1. There is no question in my mind that each of the monopoly sports leagues has maintained an artificial scarcity of franchises. The demand for franchises from economically viable cities exceeds the supply of franchises from the leagues, and this is the root cause of frequent franchise relocation and exploitation of the cities. As I argued in my written testimony, I believe it is appropriate for Congress to reshape its involvement and its legislative policies toward these leagues. Since Congress is clearly already involved, the question is not whether Congress "should get involved" but what are the best policies to pursue. Extending baseball's presumed exemption either in part or in whole to the other leagues, without putting other controls in place, would not be in the public's best interest. I have elaborated on this question in my written testimony.

2. MLB's exemption has insulated the sport from competitive leagues; unlike the NHL, the NFL and the NBA baseball has not had competition since 1914-15. The result is predictable. Baseball's unchallenged monopoly has led to arrogance, complacency and mismanagement. Further, because ownership has been protected from collusive labor practices and the players' union has been unable to protect itself through the court system in response to such practices, baseball has been characterized by more turbulent labor relations. While MLB's exemption has deterred franchise relocations since 1972, it has not prevented teams from threatening to move and extorting new publicly-funded stadiums with sweetheart leases from its host cities. And while the exemption has curtailed litigation relative to the circus-like atmosphere surrounding the NFL today, it has certainly not eliminated it. Finally, I do not believe that there are compelling arguments that the exemption is necessary for the preservation of minor league baseball. The principle effect here has been to allow the major league

clubs to sign amateur players and retain the better players under indentured servitude contracts for seven years in the minor leagues. This has been an important deterrent to the formation of rival leagues. I elaborate on this point in the Seton Hall Journal of Sport Law article.

[signature]
March 24, 1996

ONE HUNDRED FOURTH CONGRESS

Congress of the United States
House of Representatives
COMMITTEE ON THE JUDICIARY
2138 RAYBURN HOUSE OFFICE BUILDING
WASHINGTON, DC 20515-6216
(202) 225-3951

March 15, 1996

Mr. Bruce Keller, Esq.
Debevoise & Plimpton
875 3rd Avenue
New York, New York 10022

Dear Mr. Keller:

Thank you for your testimony before the Committee on the Judiciary on Tuesday, February 6, 1996 at the hearing regarding sports franchise relocation.

As noted during the hearing, due to time constraints, the Members of the Committee did not have an opportunity to ask all of their questions of the witnesses. I am therefore enclosing a list of questions for the record, which I am submitting on behalf of the members of the Committee. I would appreciate a response to these questions by Friday, April 5, 1996. If you have any questions regarding your responses, please contact Joseph Gibson, Committee counsel, at (202) 225-3951.

Again, thank you for taking the time to appear before the Committee.

Sincerely,

HENRY J. HYDE
Chairman

HJH/jg:nr

Questions for the Record

Submitted on behalf of the Republican Members

Committee on the Judiciary

QUESTIONS FOR:

Bruce Keller, Esq., International Trademark Association

1. Can you discuss ways to strengthen the trademark provisions of the bill, to bring this section more in line with constitutional principles? Would compensation for the owners satisfy these concerns? If so, how do you suggest fair and equitable compensation be awarded?

2. The NFL already has a joint Marketing Agreement ("NFL Properties") where the 30 teams share equally in the revenues from hats, T-shirts, jerseys, etc. carrying team names and logos. In essence, isn't this a contractual waiver of their trademark rights? Why couldn't the League require, as a condition of membership or entry into the League, that the name stays with the city or region?

International Trademark Association
1133 Avenue of the Americas, New York, NY 10036-6710 USA
Telephone: 212-768-9887   Fax: 212-768-7796

April 4, 1996

The Hon. Henry J. Hyde
Chairman
Committee on the Judiciary
2138 Rayburn House Office Building
Washington, DC 20515-6216

H.R. 2740

Dear Mr. Chairman:

On behalf of the International Trademark Association ("INTA") let me thank you again for the opportunity to have testified before the Committee on February 6, 1996 in connection with the hearings on Professional Sports Franchise Relocation: Antitrust Implications. This letter (i) responds to the Questions for the Record Submitted on behalf of the Republican Members and (ii) offers some additional views on issues that were raised at the hearing.

I. **Committee Questions**.

1. Can you discuss ways to strengthen the trademark provisions of the bill, to bring this section more in line with constitutional principles? Would compensation for the owners satisfy these concerns? If so, how do you suggest fair and equitable compensation be awarded?

Because the Fifth Amendment prohibits the taking of "private property . . . for public use, without just compensation," it is clear, under a long line of cases cited in INTA's written testimony, that the trademark provisions of the bill could not pass constitutional muster unless additional provisions were added to compensate a club owner for the taking of its trademark. See, e.g., Williams & Humbert Ltd. v. W. & H. Trade Marks (Jersey) Ltd., 840 F.2d 72, 75 (D.C. Cir. 1988) (United States recognized Spain's

---
Founded in 1878 as The United States Trademark Association

The Hon. Henry J. Hyde   2   April 4, 1996

expropriation of plaintiff's trademark because Spain offered plaintiff compensation for mark).

A fair and equitable system for seeking such award compensation would be the first element necessary to address this constitutional problem; adequate compensation for the relocating owner would be the second. See Williamson Planning Comm'n v. Hamilton Bank, 473 U.S. 172, 194-95 (1985) ("if the government has provided an adequate process for obtaining compensation, and if resort to that process 'yield[s] just compensation,' then the property owner 'has no claim against the Government' for a taking." (quoting Ruckelshaus v. Monsanto Co., 467 U.S. 986, 1013 (1984)(negotiation or arbitration a means of yielding just compensation))).[1]

Such compensation from the federal government could be very substantial. Recent valuations of famous trademarks have been in the hundreds of millions of dollars and beyond. K. Badenhausen, "Brands: The Management Factor," Financial World (Aug. 1, 1995) 51. Financial World magazine uses a complicated formula to value brands, based on the brand's operating and net incomes. Robert L. Meschi, "Value Added: Refinements in Our Brand Valuation Methodology," Financial World (Aug. 1, 1995) 52. If a similar calculation were done to determine a fair and equitable value of a team name, taking into account media revenue and sales from tickets, as well as sales from sports souvenirs memorabilia, that value also is likely to be placed in the many millions of dollars.

2. The NFL already has a joint Marketing Agreement ("NFL Properties") where the 30 teams share equally in the revenues from hats, t-shirts, jerseys, etc. carrying team names and logos. In essence, isn't this a contractual waiver of their trademark rights? Why couldn't the League require, as a condition of membership or entry into the League, that the name stays with the city or region?

---

1. INTA notes, however, that even such a system could not address the other serious problems with the bill, identified in its prior written and oral testimony, that still leave H.R. 2740 in conflict with the Lanham Act and common law principles.

The Hon. Henry J. Hyde   3   April 4, 1996

INTA is not familiar with the details of internal NFL policies and procedures, although it understands that the clubs have granted to NFL Properties their intellectual property rights for certain marketing purposes, in return for which they share equally the net revenues generated from the marketing effort. This is fundamentally different from a contractual waiver of trademark rights or a contractual condition that completely would strip a relocating team of its trademark assets.

Additionally, in light of recent events, we question whether a "trademark stripping" condition of the kind suggested by question two, is necessary or desirable. As you know, the City of Cleveland recently negotiated with the National Football League and the Browns® organization an agreement under which the trademark rights belonging to the Cleveland Browns® "stay with the city or region"; those rights will be transferred to a successor franchise that will begin to play in Cleveland not later than 1999. Leonard Shapiro, <u>Browns' Path to Baltimore is Cleared; NFL, Cleveland Agree to Move Team, Leave Name</u>, The Washington Post, Feb. 9, 1996, at A1. Similarly, when the Seattle Seahawks® announced their intention to move, they publicly stated their intention to leave in Seattle the Seahawks name and logo. T. J. Simers, <u>Seahawks Announce They Will Leave Seattle</u>, Los Angeles Times, Feb. 3, 1996, A1. In both cases, therefore, the result that would be imposed by H.R. 2740 was achieved without the need for legislation. Moreover, from the standpoint of the public fisc, that result was achieved *without government compensation* to the owner.

It is significant that public officials such as Mayor Bob Lanier of Houston, King County Executive Gary Locke and Hillsborough County Commissioner Joe Chillura all testified that, as far as their communities were concerned, retaining the names and logos of a relocating sports team were of no consequence. Mayor Lanier said that if he gave up the Houston Oilers® mark, he "wouldn't be giving up a fortune." Mr. Locke confessed to not ever having "reviewed that portion of the legislation" and Mr. Chillura said he wouldn't "get heartburn" over the Tampa Bay Buccaneers "taking the name and the logo with them."

The Hon. Henry J. Hyde   4   April 4, 1996

Given the testimony[2] from the witnesses most directly affected by recent team relocations that the trademark provisions are superfluous, given recent evidence that those provisions are unnecessary, and given that the trademark provisions are in irreconcilable conflict with fundamental principles of trademark law, INTA urges the Committee not to adopt those provisions.

II. Additional Issues Raised at the Hearing.

Having had an opportunity to hear the other witnesses, and more recently, to review the transcript, INTA also would like to supplement the record with two more points. Once again, its concerns are limited to those portions of H.R. 2740 that would require a relocating sports team owner to relinquish its trademark rights without any compensation.

A. The Rationale of H.R. 2740 Cannot Be Limited To Trademarks of Sports Teams.

In its written and oral testimony, INTA observed that the rationale underlying the findings in Section 2 of H.R. 2740 (which justify the bill on the basis of the important and symbiotic relationship between sports business and certain cities), apply with equal force, if not more, to the relationship between certain cities and non-sports businesses. In other words, the logic of H.R. 2740 could be applied to strip any relocating business of its trademark. The implications of such an interpretation of Section 2 are significant and certainly were not lost on the others who testified at the hearing.

When discussing the economic impact of the relocation of the Seattle Seahawks®, Mr. Locke said it was clear that if either Boeing or Microsoft "left town," "it would devastate our communities." He specifically contrasted that with the situation that would result if "our football or baseball team left town." In the latter case, he emphasized, "the economy of the Pacific Northwest would not fall apart." Mayor Lanier echoed those sentiments. Simply put, the logic of Section 2 of H.R. 2740 applies with

---

2. INTA's co-panelists, from Tulane Law School and Smith College, also agreed that H.R. 2740 appeared to work well without the trademark provisions.

The Hon. Henry J. Hyde   5   April 4, 1996

greater force in many non-sports areas, and represents a dangerous precedent that should be rejected.

Rep. Hoke suggested that names like *Cleveland Browns*®, *Houston Oilers*® may be "connected inextricably" to names of cities "every time they are used," and that thus the "mark becomes part of the city name." With all due respect, that suggestion is wrong as a matter of trademark law. See Indianapolis Colts, Inc. v. Metropolitan Baltimore Football Club, 34 F.3d 410, 413 (7th Cir. 1994)(Colt's switch from "Baltimore" to "Indianapolis" failed to break "the continuity of the team in its different locations -- it was the same team, merely having a different home base and therefore a different geographical component in its name").

The suggestion also is wrong as a matter of fact; sports teams often register and use their names and logos alone -- without any geographic identifier. See, e.g., National Football League Properties, Inc. v. New Jersey Giants, Inc., 637 F. Supp. 507, 511 (D.N.J. 1986) (describing how Giants®, used alone, has acquired secondary meaning). Furthermore, as members of the Committee may well know from their own experience, sports souvenirs often are sold with either the logo alone or just the team name, with no indication of the team's location. Thus, it simply is not true that sports team names always and inexorably are linked with the name of the city in which the team resides.

  B.   Any Power to Legislate Trademark Law is Based Solely on The Commerce Clause.

When INTA raised in its testimony constitutional concerns about H.R. 2740, Rep. Hoke responded by quoting the Copyright Clause of the U.S. Constitution. It is important to emphasize that Congressional authority to promulgate trademark legislation does not derive from that Constitutional provision. The Copyright Clause gives Congress the power to legislate only with regard to patents and copyrights, pursuant to its mandate "to promote the progress of science and useful arts . . . ." U.S. Const., art. I, § 8, cl. 8. Trademarks are not included within the scope of that mandate. Trade-Mark Cases, 100 U.S. 82, 94 (1879). Instead, the power to legislate over trademarks stems from Congress' authority to regulate interstate commerce. Id. ("The other clause of the Constitution . . . to confer the requisite authority is [the Commerce Clause].") The legal significance of the distinction between the sources of Congressional authority is twofold.

The Hon. Henry J. Hyde   6   April 4, 1996

First, unlike copyrights or patents, trademark rights do not depend on federal law for their existence -- they are created through actual use of a mark in commerce.[3] Id. (Trademark rights are "not created by the act of Congress, and [do] not now depend upon it for its enforcement.") In short, the property rights in trademarks are not dependent on federal legislation, but are created and can be maintained quite apart from any federal scheme.

Second, because Congressional authority over trademark legislation is based on the Commerce Clause, it must be exercised in connection with actual uses of trademarks in or affecting interstate commerce. It is, at best, inconsistent with that limitation to enact legislation that would preclude all uses of certain marks in commerce, as does H.R. 2740. Although Congress' authority under the Commerce Clause is broad, it is not limitless. Legislation which does not permit trademarks to be used at all, let alone in interstate commerce, seems beyond its scope.

Conclusion

INTA will not repeat here the other flaws it sees with the trademark provisions of H.R. 2740; these are set forth in detail in its prior testimony. It wishes to underscore, however, that those problems were entirely avoided -- without the need for governmental compensation -- when the NFL and the Cleveland Browns® were left free to work out the settlement that resulted in the Browns® mark remaining in Cleveland. INTA urges that Congress not enact unfortunate trademark legislation that would preclude such privately-negotiated, amicable resolutions, and would impose additional unnecessary costs on the government.

Respectfully yours,

Bruce P. Keller
INTA Counsel

---

3. Even federal trademark rights are created only through use of the mark in interstate commerce. S. Rep. No. 100-515, 100th Cong., 2d Sess. 2 (1988), reprinted in 1988 U.S.C.C.A.N. 5577, 5585.

ISBN 0-16-052708-2